Advancement in Business Analytics Tools for Higher Financial Performance

Reza Gharoie Ahangar
Lewis University, USA

Mark Napier
Lewis University, USA

A volume in the Advances in Business Information Systems and Analytics (ABISA) Book Series

IGI Global
PUBLISHER of TIMELY KNOWLEDGE

Published in the United States of America by
IGI Global
Business Science Reference (an imprint of IGI Global)
701 E. Chocolate Avenue
Hershey PA, USA 17033
Tel: 717-533-8845
Fax: 717-533-8661
E-mail: cust@igi-global.com
Web site: http://www.igi-global.com

Library of Congress Cataloging-in-Publication Data

Names: Ahangar, Reza Gharoie, editor. | Napier, Mark, editor.
Title: Advancement in business analytics tools for higher financial performance / edited by Reza Gharoie Ahangar, Mark Napier.
Description: Hershey, PA : Business Science Reference, [2023] | Includes bibliographical references and index. | Summary: "This book seeks to demonstrate the financial applications of business analytics tools (e.g., machine learning) that can help financial managers and investors to better understand financial theory and improve institutional investment practices. Further, this book targets the value extraction process through the use of more accurate financial data via business analytical tools to help investors and portfolio managers to develop more modern financial planning processes"-- Provided by publisher.
Identifiers: LCCN 2023012712 (print) | LCCN 2023012713 (ebook) | ISBN 9781668483862 (hardcover) | ISBN 9781668483879 (paperback) | ISBN 9781668483886 (ebook)
Subjects: LCSH: Corporations--Finance--Technological innovations. | Business enterprises--Finance--Technological innovations. | Machine learning--Economic aspects.
Classification: LCC HG4026 .A338 2023 (print) | LCC HG4026 (ebook) | DDC 658.15--dc23/eng/20230331
LC record available at https://lccn.loc.gov/2023012712
LC ebook record available at https://lccn.loc.gov/2023012713

This book is published in the IGI Global book series Advances in Business Information Systems and Analytics (ABISA) (ISSN: 2327-3275; eISSN: 2327-3283)

British Cataloguing in Publication Data
A Cataloguing in Publication record for this book is available from the British Library.

For electronic access to this publication, please contact: eresources@igi-global.com.

Advances in Business Information Systems and Analytics (ABISA) Book Series

Madjid Tavana
La Salle University, USA

ISSN:2327-3275
EISSN:2327-3283

Mission

The successful development and management of information systems and business analytics is crucial to the success of an organization. New technological developments and methods for data analysis have allowed organizations to not only improve their processes and allow for greater productivity, but have also provided businesses with a venue through which to cut costs, plan for the future, and maintain competitive advantage in the information age.

The **Advances in Business Information Systems and Analytics (ABISA) Book Series** aims to present diverse and timely research in the development, deployment, and management of business information systems and business analytics for continued organizational development and improved business value.

Coverage

- Business Intelligence
- Information Logistics
- Business Information Security
- Data Management
- Data Strategy
- Geo-BIS
- Business Decision Making
- Algorithms
- Decision Support Systems
- Business Systems Engineering

IGI Global is currently accepting manuscripts for publication within this series. To submit a proposal for a volume in this series, please contact our Acquisition Editors at Acquisitions@igi-global.com or visit: http://www.igi-global.com/publish/.

The Advances in Business Information Systems and Analytics (ABISA) Book Series (ISSN 2327-3275) is published by IGI Global, 701 E. Chocolate Avenue, Hershey, PA 17033-1240, USA, www.igi-global.com. This series is composed of titles available for purchase individually; each title is edited to be contextually exclusive from any other title within the series. For pricing and ordering information please visit http://www.igi-global.com/book-series/advances-business-information-systems-analytics/37155. Postmaster: Send all address changes to above address.

Titles in this Series

For a list of additional titles in this series, please visit: www.igi-global.com/book-series

Cases on Enhancing Business Sustainability Through Knowledge Management Systems
Meir Russ (University of Wisconsin-Green Bay, USA & Stellenbosch University, South Arica)
Business Science Reference • © 2023 • 366pp • H/C (ISBN: 9781668458594) • US $240.00

Streamlining Organizational Processes Through AI, IoT, Blockchain, and Virtual Environments
Marisol Hernández Hernández (Universidad Autónoma del Estado de México, Mxico)
Business Science Reference • © 2023 • 253pp • H/C (ISBN: 9781668486399) • US $250.00

Data-Driven Approaches for Effective Managerial Decision Making
Anubha (Jaipuria Institute of Management, Ghaziabad, India) and Himanshu Sharma (IILM Institute for Higher Education, New Delhi, India)
Business Science Reference • © 2023 • 336pp • H/C (ISBN: 9781668475683) • US $255.00

Handbook of Research on AI and Machine Learning Applications in Customer Support and Analytics
Md Shamim Hossain (Hajee Mohammad Danesh Science and Technology University, Bangladesh) Ree Chan Ho (Taylor's University, Malaysia) and Goran Trajkovski (Western Governors University, USA)
Business Science Reference • © 2023 • 423pp • H/C (ISBN: 9781668471050) • US $325.00

Building Secure Business Models Through Blockchain Technology Tactics, Methods, Limitations, and Performance
Shweta Dewangan (ICFAI University, Raipur, India) Sapna Singh Kshatri (Shri Shankaracharya Institute of Professional Management and Technology, India) Astha Bhanot (Princess Nourah Bint Abdulrahman University, Saudi Arabia) and Mushtaq Ahmed Shah (Lovely Professional University, India)
Business Science Reference • © 2023 • 283pp • H/C (ISBN: 9781668478080) • US $250.00

Enhancing Business Communications and Collaboration Through Data Science Applications
Nuno Geada (ISCTE - University Institute of Lisbon, Portugal) and George Leal Jamil (Informações em Rede Consultoria e Treinamento, Brazil)
Business Science Reference • © 2023 • 262pp • H/C (ISBN: 9781668467862) • US $270.00

Revolutionizing Business Practices Through Artificial Intelligence and Data-Rich Environments
Manisha Gupta (Sharda University, India) Deergha Sharma (The NorthCap University, India) and Himani Gupta (Jagannath International Management School, India)
Business Science Reference • © 2022 • 300pp • H/C (ISBN: 9781668449509) • US $250.00

IGI Global
PUBLISHER of TIMELY KNOWLEDGE

701 East Chocolate Avenue, Hershey, PA 17033, USA
Tel: 717-533-8845 x100 • Fax: 717-533-8661
E-Mail: cust@igi-global.com • www.igi-global.com

Table of Contents

Detailed Table of Contents

The field of machine learning (ML) has grown to be a prominent subject within developed businesses while aiming to implement data-driven techniques to better day-to-day business activities. The reader is introduced to the most popular learning models in this chapter. Although unsupervised learning, reinforcement learning, and semi-supervised learning are incredibly important, the authors won't go into further detail about them here. This section will go into great length about supervised learning environments. The authors propose the following as a summary of the contributions to this chapter: Emphasizing some of the earlier works of literature that tackled these problems and discussing their limitations. In order to do so, the authors propose to review the regression family (i.e., simple regression and multiple linear regression) and decision tree family (i.e., CART, ID3, C4.5, chi-squared automatic interaction detection (CHAID), bagging and boosting). Examining the function and promise of ML techniques to resolve dilemmas and present potential implementation strategies.

Information technology has profoundly disrupted the world as we know it. Advances in technology have enabled management accountants to gain access to an unprecedented amount of information, through the use of business analytics and machine learning tools. This research delves deeper into the above described context, in an attempt to collect empirical data on how business analytics tools have reshaped the modern day accounting profession and how they will continue to shape the future, according to management accountants themselves. In an effort to investigate the topic, several semi-structured interviews were conducted with management accounting professionals. Through the qualitative analysis of their contributions, the authors draw conclusions on how business analytics tools have affected their professional career, how they expect their future to be shaped, and to what extent they believe technology has allowed them to become more efficient.

Non-convex optimization problems belong to a class of classical nonlinear optimization problems, which are often difficult to solve. An optimization problem becomes non-convex due to the presence of non-convex functions in the objective function or constraints. A function is a convex function if its Hessian matrix is positive and semi-definite for all values; otherwise, it is a non-convex function. A Hessian matrix is called positive semi-definite when the eigenvalues of the matrix are non-negative. A non-convex function can be either a concave function or a function that is neither a concave nor a convex function. A concave function is always negative semi-definite, indicating that the eigenvalues of the matrix are non-positive. This chapter starts with a short introduction to non-convex problems, followed by a discussion on different non-convex problems arising in supply chain and finance. Thereafter, the authors discuss different algorithms used for solving non-convex problems. Finally, the chapter conclude with the limitations of different algorithms.

Improving quality of care is one of the priorities of policymakers in the U.S. While the spending on quality of care in the U.S. is the highest among all the developed nations, the desired health outcomes achieved have been below many of them. The largest portion of personal health care spending in 2019 went toward hospital care (37.2%), which was followed by physician and clinical services (24.1%). In this chapter, the authors focus on these direct care services, specifically explaining how hospitals and clinics can improve health and financial outcomes using data analytics. Specifically, building on CRISP-DM, a data mining process model, the authors explain the healthcare data analytics processes for hospitals and clinics to improve quality and financial performance.

This chapter investigates the potential role of OpenAI's ChatGPT in investments to assess its proposed solutions' accuracy, potential benefits and drawbacks, and implications for financial decisions. The study utilizes empirical examples to evaluate ChatGPT's performance in providing financial advice. The results indicate that while ChatGPT can define financial terms and explain them in detail, it cannot provide investment suggestions. Moreover, the analysis suggests that the ChatGPT can provide more accurate information when users break down their questions into more specific topics. The study also highlights the need for more comprehensive training data to allow ChatGPT to provide more accurate advice. In addition, the research advises investors to be aware of ChatGPT's limitations and recommends breaking down financial questions into more specific topics to maximize the benefits of this technology. It is concluded that ChatGPT can be a helpful resource for financial experts but not for those with limited financial expertise and knowledge.

Financial performance assesses how well a company can manage resources from its primary line of business and create income. Financial performance is critical for the healthcare sector, especially pharmaceutical supply chains. Medicine shortage is the main problem in healthcare management. Medicine shortages negatively affect patient care and financial performance. This chapter explains how blockchain technology and machine learning framework can contribute to pharmaceutical supply chains regarding financial performance. The proposed framework contributes to business analytics tools by presenting a hybrid machine learning method to improve financial performance.

This study focuses on the future development of an insurance company during difficult circumstances, which can be described by a stochastic process that must be effectively managed to achieve the best goals for the company. Effective risk or loss management models can bring in more revenue for the insurer and result in less conditional pay-out of claims to the insured. While insurance losses, risks, and premium calculation are important topics in the field, existing literature has not always stood the test of time due to the dynamic nature of insurance principles and practices. There is a need for a suitable loss model that can adjust loss rating to a particular experience and provide an appropriate and equitable premium. The aim of this research is to find sufficient conditions for the convergence of an algorithm towards a fixed point under typical insurance loss and actuarial circumstances, resulting in a uniquely determined solution. The study presents a unique fixed point, which the algorithm converges towards through straightforward and simplified generalised formulae and functions.

The purpose of this chapter is to study the behaviour and measure the performance of different UCITS over a period of time. For this purpose, an analysis was carried out using several measures taking into account systematic, specific, and total risk. This led to a modelling of the behaviour of these UCITS, in addition to a description of the relationships linking these behaviours and that of the market index. The aim of this work is to better orient Moroccan investors in their choice of collective investment funds.

In today's business landscape, predicting the financial health of a company is essential for informed decision-making by investors, creditors, and other stakeholders. Using historical financial data and machine learning techniques, it is now possible to predict the likelihood of a company going bankrupt. This chapter provides a step-by-step guide on how to predict company bankruptcy using the "company bankruptcy prediction" dataset available on UCI machine learning repository. The chapter covers data analysis, pre-processing, applying various machine learning algorithms, evaluating model performance, and applying models to new datasets. The aim is to equip readers with the necessary skills to analyze and predict the financial health of companies, making it a valuable resource for investors, creditors, and financial analysts.

This study presents a comparative analysis of various machine learning algorithms for credit risk assessment. The algorithms were tested on two credit datasets: German Credit Dataset and Australian Credit Dataset. The performance of the algorithms was evaluated based on several metrics, including sensitivity, specificity, accuracy, F-score, and Kappa. The results showed that the FCPFS-QDNN algorithm outperformed other algorithms in both datasets, achieving high accuracy, sensitivity, specificity, and F-score. On the other hand, the ACO Algorithm and Multilayer Perceptron algorithms were found to perform poorly in both datasets. The findings of this study have significant implications for credit risk assessment in banking and financial institutions. The study recommends the use of the FCPFS-QDNN algorithm for credit risk assessment due to its superior performance compared to other algorithms.

This chapter is a comparison between one of the most stable, and one of the most precariously managed retirement systems in the world. Both systems grew through the private sector, but their non-parallel trajectories over time offer hints about possible future developments. The system of governing in Greece has garnered little wisdom from financial bankruptcy. The partly unregulated retirement industry of the United States leaves room for en masse asset liquidation. In both systems the transfer of responsibility for pension performance is enabled by non-market-capitalizing mechanisms. The wave of central bank intervention that underpins excessive tail risk-taking combined with lack of fiduciary responsibility, may entice the ultimate liquidation of assets held by retirees, leading to another financial crisis.

Lightweight deep learning is a subfield of artificial intelligence and machine learning that prioritises efficiency and compactness while developing deep learning models. It is ideal for low-powered mobile phones, embedded systems, and internet-of-things devices due to their speed and low latency. To make lightweight deep learning models, pruning and quantization are used to remove unnecessary parameters and reduce model weight accuracy. Transfer learning is used to fine-tune a pre-trained deep learning model on a smaller dataset. This chapter introduces the fundamentals of lightweight deep learning, including various lightweight models and their applications across different industries.

There could be huge effects from incorporating data analytic techniques into economics teaching. Students can get the practical skills necessary in today's data-driven economy and improve their comprehension of economic theory by integrating these tools into the curriculum. The use of data analysis tools can help increase student interest in the subject and motivation. Students with data analysis skills have chances outside of the classroom in a variety of industries, encouraging the use of evidence in decision-making and promoting economic growth. Overall, incorporating data analytic techniques into economics education helps to advance the economy and society while preparing students for success in the modern workplace.

Investment analysis is a systematic process of evaluating various investment opportunities and choosing the best solutions. It involves the analysis of financial metrics such as past performance, earnings, cash flows, and market trends to make informed decisions. Analytical tools such as financial ratios, time value of money calculations, capital budgeting techniques, and portfolio analysis are used to simplify complex financial data, identify trends, and make informed investment decisions. Financial ratios offer a straightforward and uncomplicated approach to analyzing the financial performance of various investments. Investors can estimate the future value of an investment and its prospective return using time value of money formulas. Long-term investments are assessed for viability using capital budgeting. Portfolio analysis helps investors to diversify their investments and manage risk by analyzing the relationships between different investments. This chapter proposal aims to provide an overview of investment analysis and the various analytical tools used in this process.

Preface

THE IMPORTANCE OF THIS BOOK TO ACADEMICIANS, RESEARCHERS, INVESTORS, GOVERNMENT AGENCIES, AND COLLEGE STUDENTS

The relentless growth of data in financial markets has boosted the demand for more advanced analytical tools to facilitate and improve financial planning. The ability to constructively use this data is limited for managers and investors without the proper theoretical support. Within this context, there is an unmet demand for combining analytical finance methods with business analytics topics to inform better investment decisions. Advancements in business analytics, including machine learning tools and derivative techniques, are uniquely positioned to transform this arena of finance through improved portfolio construction and enhanced investment strategy. As novel concepts, they need to be captured as a financial resource to be used by future generations of scholars, investors and educational programs that can armor investors with sufficient knowledge to distinguish themselves in this ever-changing financial landscape. This can open a new range of possibilities for professional investment managers, enabling them to analyze data more rapidly and accurately to make increasingly informed decisions. With the amount of data that is out there now, combined with the power of modern computing, this could lead to further profitability and market stability for investors and traders. Furthermore, combining financial analytical methods with business analytics will provide a much-needed interdisciplinary approach in the finance laboratory that can bridge the gap between data science and financial theory. This could allow for more efficient and intelligent data-driven decision making, creating new opportunities for interested market participants.

This book seeks to demonstrate the financial applications of business analytics tools (e.g., machine learning) that can help financial managers and investors to better understand financial theory and improve institutional investment practices. Further, this book targets the value extraction process using more accurate financial data via business analytical tools to help investors and portfolio managers to develop more modern financial planning processes. Theoretically this book examines the principles of finance in comparison to the practical applications of business analytics with respect to investing and managing financial risk. It presents the idea that numerous challenges can be resolved or at least better managed using these techniques. The book also delves into the importance and value of analytics in understanding debt and equity investments, portfolio construction, risk management, as well as optimal asset allocation techniques. Ultimately, this book provides financial theory and business analytical tools to make financial decision making more successful.

The initial target audiences are scholars in business and engineering schools. In addition, this book is a guide and a source for investors of different companies in the world. The book also provides an analysis of current challenges, and insights on how modern businesses have evolved using analytical advancements.

Consideration is also given to the future of analytical technology, and its impact on human resources, marketing, and operations of businesses. Furthermore, the book provides forward looking strategies for various companies to stay ahead in the game and to best utilize the available analytical resources.

ORGANIZATION OF THE BOOK

This book is organized into 15 chapters, and a brief description of each chapter is as follows:

Chapter 1 presents the process of machine learning methods. In this chapter, the author discusses the most popular analytical models with an overview of machine learning (ML) methods and their usage in the development of data-driven techniques for businesses. The chapter focuses primarily on supervised learning, examining the popular models including the regression family (simple regression and multiple linear regression) and decision tree family (CART, ID3, C4.5, Chi-squared Automatic Interaction Detection (CHAID), Bagging and Boosting). The author discusses the earlier works of literature that have tackled these problems and their limitations. Additionally, this chapter focuses on the capabilities of ML techniques to resolve dilemmas and present potential implementation strategies.

Chapter 2 discusses management accountants' skills and competencies: how business analytics tools reshape the future. In this chapter, the authors provide an in-depth overview into the complexities of how business analytics and data science tools are reshaping the management accounting profession by examining the changes that technology has brought to the profession today and its implications for management accountants' future careers. Through data obtained from interviews with experienced management accounting professionals, this chapter seeks to illustrate how management accounting practices are transitioning towards data-driven techniques to improve effectiveness and efficiency and explains how accounting professionals' skills and competencies must evolve to keep up with technological advancements.

Chapter 3 discusses non-convex optimization problems arising in supply chain design and finance: non-convex problems in supply chain and finance. The author describes the non-convex optimization problems, which are a type of classical nonlinear optimization problems. This chapter discusses the various types of non-convex functions and explains how these functions arise within supply chain design and finance. The chapter analyzes the different algorithms employed to solve non-convex optimization problems, in addition to the limitations of these algorithms. Finally, provides a concise summary of the challenges associated with non-convex optimization problems.

Chapter 4 focuses on quality improvement of healthcare services through data analytics process. This chapter of the book explores the use of data analytics to improve the quality of healthcare services. While healthcare spending in the United States is the highest amongst developed countries, the health outcomes it achieves have fallen behind many other nations. Most of the personal healthcare spending in 2019 was towards hospital care (37.2%) and physician and clinical services (24.1%). To address this challenge and meet the demands of modern healthcare services, this chapter explores the use of data analytics processes within hospitals and clinics to improve both health and financial performance. Drawing on the CRISP-DM data mining model, this chapter outlines the key steps and insights along the healthcare data analytics journey, to help hospitals and clinics achieve greater efficiency and quality.

Chapter 5 explores the potential of ChatGPT in financial decision making. Through a case study on stock market, the authors investigate the role of OpenAI's ChatGPT in investments to assess its proposed solutions' accuracy, potential benefits and drawbacks, and implications for financial decisions. Using empirical examples, this chapter evaluates ChatGPT's performance in providing financial advice. This chapter's findings reveal the need for more comprehensive training data to provide more accurate advice. Ultimately, the chapter shows that ChatGPT may be beneficial for financial experts but not for those with limited financial expertise and knowledge.

Chapter 6 presents a review of blockchain and machine learning framework for financial performance in pharmaceutical supply chains to improve the performance. The authors discuss how financial performance is a critical element for the healthcare sector, especially regarding the prevalence of medicine shortage. The chapter further explains how blockchain technology and machine learning framework can contribute to pharmaceutical supply chains when it comes to financial performance. The proposed framework introduces a hybrid machine learning method to improve financial performance in this sector through business analytics tools.

Chapter 7 presents fixed point theory and insurance loss modeling, an unlikely pairing. Through this chapter, the author explores the development of insurance companies amidst difficult circumstances. The aim is to find a suitable loss model which is able to adjust loss rating to a particular experience and provide an accurate and equitable premium. With the help of straightforward and simplified generalized formulae and functions, the author describes sufficient conditions for the convergence of an algorithm towards a fixed point under typical insurance loss and actuarial circumstances. By doing this, the chapter aims to present a reliable and efficient way of risk or loss management which can benefit insurers and insureds alike.

Chapter 8 focuses on measuring performance and profitability of mutual and profitability funds collective investment funds in securities. By using several measures related to systematic, specific, and total risk, the authors analyze the behavior and measure the performance of different UCITS over a given period. The results are then modeled to evaluate and describe the relation between the UCITS and the market index, providing investors with useful insights into their investment decision and choice of collective investment funds. The goal of this chapter is to provide better guidance to Moroccan investors when making their mutual fund choices.

Chapter 9 discusses predicting company bankruptcy using machine learning techniques: A step-by-step guide. In this chapter, the author examines the use of machine learning techniques to predict company bankruptcy. In today's business world, it is essential to be able to accurately assess the financial status of any company to make informed decisions. Utilizing historical financial data along with machine learning algorithms, it is now possible to predict the likelihood of a company becoming bankrupt. This chapter provides a comprehensive and step-by-step guide on how to predict company bankruptcy using the "Company Bankruptcy Prediction" dataset available on UCI Machine Learning Repository. The aim is to equip readers with the necessary knowledge and skills for analyzing and predicting the financial conditions of companies, making it an indispensable reference for investors, creditors, and financial analysts.

Chapter 10 focuses on prediction and analyzing financial crises by using Machine Learning. This chapter presents a comparative analysis of various machine learning algorithms used for credit risk assessment based on two datasets: the German Credit Dataset and the Australian Credit Dataset. The chapter evaluates the performance of the algorithms in terms of several metrics such as sensitivity, specificity, accuracy, F-score, and Kappa. The findings have significant implications for banking and financial institutions, and the author recommends the use of the proposed algorithm in this chapter for credit risk assessment due to its superior performance compared to other algorithms.

Chapter 11 presents an En-route to Greece - A market-capitalized versus a government-run retirement system: comparison and chronological development. This chapter provides a comparison and chronological development of two of the most contrasting retirement systems in the world: the market-capitalized system of the United States versus the government-run system of Greece. The chapter explores the growth of these two systems, compares their different trajectories over time, and tries to identify possible paths towards financial stability for both systems. In addition, author examines the effect of various factors that have played different roles in the development and current formulation of the Greek and US retirement systems, and discusses how central bank intervention, lack of fiduciary responsibility, and excessive tail risk-taking can lead to further financial crises and asset liquidations among retirees. In the end, the chapter attempts to identify how the identified challenges can be addressed in order to create a secure and sustainable retirement system.

Chapter 12 presents lightweight deep learning: introduction, advancements, and applications. This chapter introduces the fundamentals of lightweight deep learning and the advancements in this field, with a focus on pruning, quantization, and transfer learning. Additionally, discusses the applications, advantages, and implications of lightweight deep learning. Throughout the chapter, the authors provide real-world examples to illustrate its utility across various industries. In this chapter, the readers gain a comprehensive understanding of the key concepts and advancements of lightweight deep learning, enabling them to effectively implement models in real-world scenarios, and identify trends and opportunities for applying it in future.

Chapter 13 investigates the impact of business analytics tools in statistical arbitrage models in trading. The chapter explores how business analytics tools can be leveraged to enhance the performance of statistical arbitrage models in trading. The authors discuss how incorporating data analysis into economic education can have a far-reaching and positive impact on students, allowing them to develop crucial practical skills associated with working in today's data-driven economy. The use of data analysis tools can help to develop student engagement and interest in the subject and empower them to pursue rewarding careers in a diverse range of industries from finance to marketing. The chapter looks at how data analytic techniques not only benefit students, but also strengthen the economy by data-driven evidence in decision-making, providing tangible growth for society overall.

Chapter 14 provides an overview of maximizing returns through investment analysis: An overview of analytical tools. This chapter covers the use of analytical tools to help investors make informed decisions. Topics discussed include financial ratios, time value of money calculations, capital budgeting techniques, and portfolio analysis. These analytical tools are designed to simplify complex financial data, identify trends, and assess various investment opportunities. This chapter offers a comprehensive look at how these analytical tools can be used to make sound investments.

In conclusion, the field of business analytics and finance are ever-changing and responding to new and available technology and data. This book demonstrates how business analytics tools, such as machine learning, can be used in tandem with financial methods to inform better investment strategies and decisions. This combination can help open the possibilities of more efficient and intelligent data-driven decision-making to the benefit of investors and traders. Financial analysts, portfolio managers, and scholars of business and engineering schools, as well as investors, can all use this book as a reliable source to help make informed decisions based on the most current market data. The book serves as a tool to bridge the gap between data science and financial theory, ultimately helping to create more stable financial markets and increase profitability for everyone involved in the financial industry.

Chapter 1
Process of Machine Learning Methods

Hulya Kocyigit
Karamanoglu Mehmetbey University, Turkey

ABSTRACT

The field of machine learning (ML) has grown to be a prominent subject within developed businesses while aiming to implement data-driven techniques to better day-to-day business activities. The reader is introduced to the most popular learning models in this chapter. Although unsupervised learning, reinforcement learning, and semi-supervised learning are incredibly important, the authors won't go into further detail about them here. This section will go into great length about supervised learning environments. The authors propose the following as a summary of the contributions to this chapter: Emphasizing some of the earlier works of literature that tackled these problems and discussing their limitations. In order to do so, the authors propose to review the regression family (i.e., simple regression and multiple linear regression) and decision tree family (i.e., CART, ID3, C4.5, chi-squared automatic interaction detection (CHAID), bagging and boosting). Examining the function and promise of ML techniques to resolve dilemmas and present potential implementation strategies.

1. INTRODUCTION

Automated analysis strategies have been facing a unique difficulty because of developments in data gathering, storage, and processing technologies. Enormous volumes of data constantly are gathered from various sources, including stock trading, medical healthcare systems, electronic sales records, and significant scientific research. Additionally, more researchers and professionals than ever before have been striving to use automated approaches to examine their data. There has been a corresponding demand for reliable, effective, and adaptable data exploration methods as the amount and variety of data that may be accessed by these approaches expand. The ability to foresee events is an illustration of one's ability to judge others based on what they have learned. Prediction analysis has grown in popularity in a variety of fields, including spatial inference, regression analysis, and causal inference, as communities and technology have advanced.

DOI: 10.4018/978-1-6684-8386-2.ch001

Regression is the main line of research in the disciplines of machine learning and statistics. The primary goal of a regression problem is to train a learner using the available data and mapping the input to the matched output result to achieve the prediction goal. In its simplest form, regression analysis assists an organization in making more informed choices by enabling them to comprehend what their data points signify and make use of them appropriately. Given the growing importance of the business sector and the popularity of regression analysis, it is crucial for business analysts to comprehend these possibilities and be equipped to use them. Such as, if we've ever worried about how fluctuations in joblessness or inflation affect Gross Domestic Product, we need to analyze estimates relying on the relationship between covariates, and then at this point, regression analysis might be worthwhile. Note that a regression mode doesn't mean that the factors are related in a cause-and-effect manner. It is possible for two or more variables to have a strong empirical relationship, but this is not proof that the regressor variables and the answer are causally associated. The association between the regression variables and the response needs to have a foundation outside of the sample data to prove causality. The regression models will examine in the subsections of this chapter are applicable to both randomized control trial design and observational study. Regression models must have criteria that are acceptable for the data at hand, whether the data are experimental or observational, for the model to be usable.

Regression model construction is an iterative procedure. Figure 1 provides an illustration of the model-building procedure.

Figure 2 illustrate types of regression methods, and the use of each method depends on the number of variables. The significance of each type varies depending on the circumstances, but fundamentally, all regression techniques examine the impact of the explanatory variables on the response variable.

Figure 1. The process of regression model

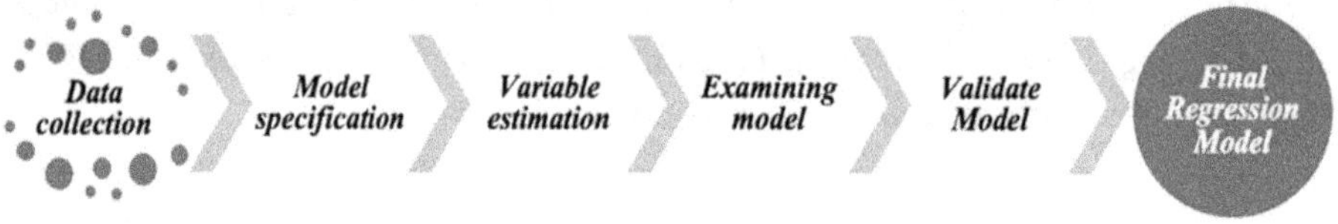

Figure 2. The process of regression model

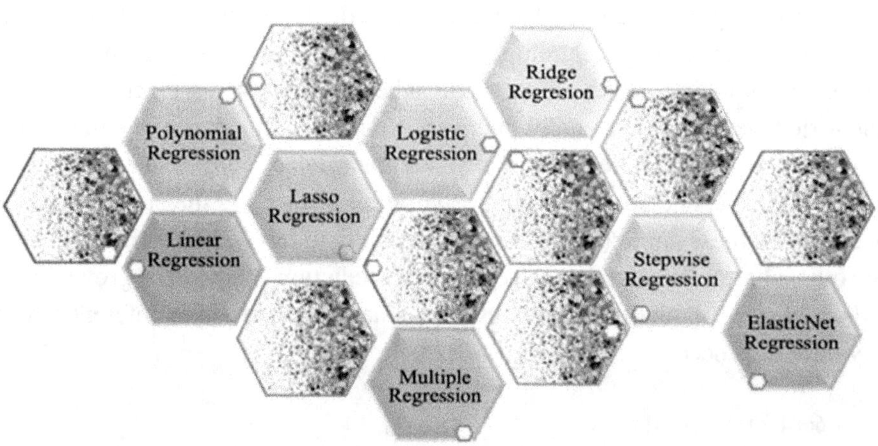

The use of machine learning (ML) methods in regression challenges has grown as an important area of research in the discipline of ML with the advancement of ML technologies and the increasing use of Artificial intelligence. Arthur Samuel (1959) first presented machine learning in a seminal paper. Since then, it has developed into a multi-disciplinary technique for artificial intelligence with the goal of giving machines the ability to learn. In other terms, the goal of machine learning is to create methods, approaches, processes, and algorithms that enable computers to become more proficient and effective at carrying out activities, either independently or with the assistance of a consultant. In other words, Machine learning has developed into a crucial area of computational engineering, with a focus on plug-and-play methods provided accessible by open-source machine learning software packages, owing to the trend toward greater computer resources and larger datasets. The main users of this technology have been in areas of finance that are algorithm-focused, including online trading. But much of the field is still a mystery outside of engineering. As a result, the study of machine learning (ML) seeks to understand how a computer can "learn" specific tasks including character recognition, assisting in the detection of patients with serious illnesses, investing money in banks, or estimating the cause of cancer disease.

The following causes led to this striking advancement at the beginning of the 2000s (Kubat and Kubat, 2017):

- Enormous datasets of photos/videos/graphics are readily available because of the Internet.
- The accessibility of a lot of computing power is backed by lots of ram and storage capacity.
- Effective techniques that are geared at handling massive datasets.
- Collinearity is less of a problem with machine learning techniques than it is with classical regression since the algorithms do not indicate the statistical significance of variables that collinearity can compress.
- Machine learning techniques, in contrast, choose the parameters that best their function automatically.

Machine learning is typically categorized into four learning techniques: supervised, unsupervised, semi-supervised, and reinforcement learning, as illustrated in Figure 3. These four categories of ML can be distinguished based on the method's output and whether the training data contains labels. Also, each type of ML has been involved in many ML methods based on its aim.

The goal of *supervised learning* is to identify the optimal classifier $f: X \rightarrow Y$ for a specified task. The classification method, which derives a model from each input sample $x \in X$ and its associated class $y \in Y$, is responsible for determining this mapping. To effectively anticipate the dependent variable for the forthcoming observations or to gain a deeper knowledge of the relationship between the dependent and the independents, we want to construct a model that relates the response to the predictor. To effectively anticipate the dependent variable for the forthcoming observations or to gain a deeper knowledge of the relationship between the dependent and the independents, it is wanted to construct a model that relates the response to the predictor. Note that even though unsupervised learning, reinforcement learning, and semi-supervised learning are remarkably crucial, we won't go into more detail about them here. So, the supervised learning settings will be covered in detail throughout this chapter.

This chapter presents a text for supervised learning under the fundamental machine learning course. It includes many of the more recent themes as well as the usual ones for such courses. It presents theory and application in such a way that the reader will comprehend the essential concepts required to use supervised learning approaches in plenty of application scenarios.

Figure 3. The types of machine learning

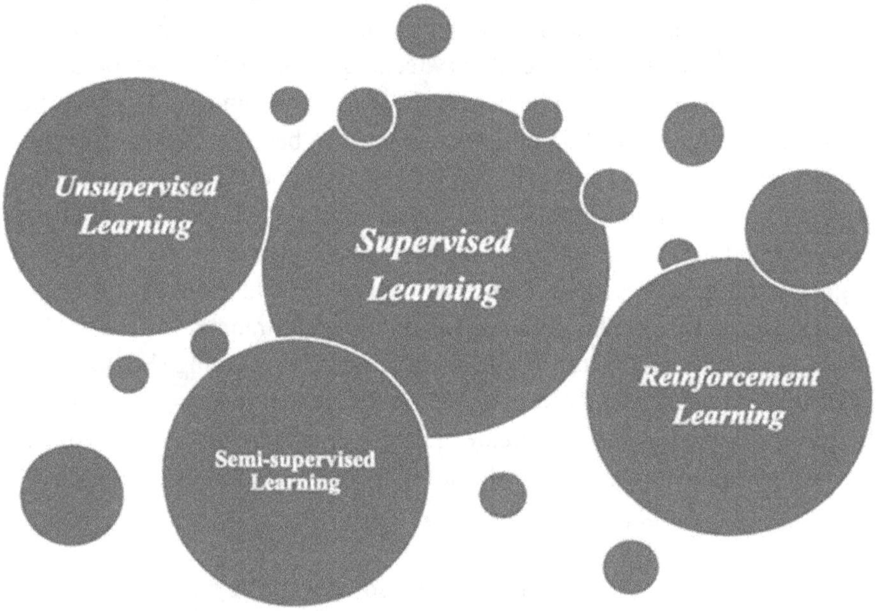

2. DATA COLLECTION PROCESSES

Collecting data is a crucial component of regression analysis. The accuracy of any analysis depends entirely on the data used to generate it. There are some basic methods for collecting data as follows:

- Retrospective study
- Observational study
- Designed experiment

Retrospective studies are ones in which researchers draw conclusions about a present study subject from information gathered in the past. Data can be gathered through insurance claims, medical records, or results of national surveys. There are some main goals for retrospective studies, which can be either cohort or case-control studies: (1) as a check tool for comparing historical data with future procedures, (2) to evaluate a hypothesis about presumed risk variables regarding an outcome, (3) to inquire into uncommon or uncommon cases, where prospective research would be too big and take too long to complete. Retrospective studies ' main drawbacks are often as follows: (i) having some pertinent data gaps, (ii) the data's dependability and quality are seriously in doubt, and (iii) the analyst trying to utilize the data in ways that weren't originally anticipated. In contrast, attendees in prospective studies have been kept up throughout time to ascertain the presence of outcomes even though the outcome (and maybe even the exposure or intervention) is yet to happen when the study begins.

When the investigators are unable to manipulate the course of treatment, or independent variable, that is connected to the main research question, an *observational study* employs sample data to identify correlations. An observational study is one in which individuals are not assigned to the control or treatment groups; rather, the individuals are just observed.

The method of conducting research in a systematic, controlled procedure—known as the *experimental design*—ensures that accuracy can be optimized and that specific inferences about a hypothesis statement can be made. Typically, the goal is to determine the impact a factor, independent variable, or dependent variable has on another. In other words, experimental design is the process that conducts research in a controlled, objective manner to ensure that accuracy can be optimized and specific inferences about a hypothesis statement.

3. REGRESSION

This chapter will discuss machine learning techniques, however, what exactly do researchers mean by those terms? Firstly, we will focus on regression analysis, which is a type of statistical and machine-learning method that enables you to examine functional correlations between variables and generate predictions.

3.1. Simple Regression

$(x_1, y_1), (x_2, y_2)\ldots (x_n, y_n)$ pairs are observed and it aims that x and y have a linear relationship. Specifically, the data are close to the line, and then, the simple regression model (called the bivariate regression model) is:

$$y= \alpha_0 + \alpha_1 x + \varepsilon \tag{3.1}$$

where the independent variable, x is sometimes called the explanatory variable, treatment variable, or regressor variable. The dependent variable, y is also called the response or the outcome variable. Besides, α_0 and α_1 coefficients are unknown regression parameters. ε represents a random error term.

Assume that Figure 4 depicts the data plotted for a sample of n values of response variable y representing n distinct settings of the explanatory variable x. The graph makes it abundantly evident that while the expected value of y may decrease as a linear function of x, a model is unable to adequately capture reality. Repeating trials at x=3 would result in varying values of y. As a result, we can infer that the model does not accurately capture the relationship between two variables. Furthermore, there would be an unknown amount of inaccuracy in the prediction if the model were used to forecast y at x=3.

Example 3.1: As an illustration of a subject where regression analysis may be useful, the Longley dataset includes the percentage of people who were employed during a specific year based on some economic variables. There are six main covariates that explain and provide the percentage of employed people in the "Employed" column. So, one may predict how many people will be employed in the future based on economic covariates for a given year. Besides, the "Longley" dataset is available in RStudio programming. These six covariates with the 16 observations represent by Gross National Product (GNP) implicit price deflator ("GNP.def"), Gross National Product ("GNP"), number of unemployed ("Unemployed"), number of people in the armed forces ("Armed"), 'noninstitutionalized' population 14 years of age ("Population"), the year ("Year"). The 16 observations are plotted between the "Employed" variable as a response variable and the "GNP.def" variable as an explanatory variable in Figures 5a and 5b. A scatter plot can be employed to illustrate the relationship between the "Employed" on the y-axis and the "GNP.def" on the x-axis variables in the Longley dataset. It appears the data points approximately, but not quite, follow a straight line.

Figure 4. The plot of data for the simple regression model

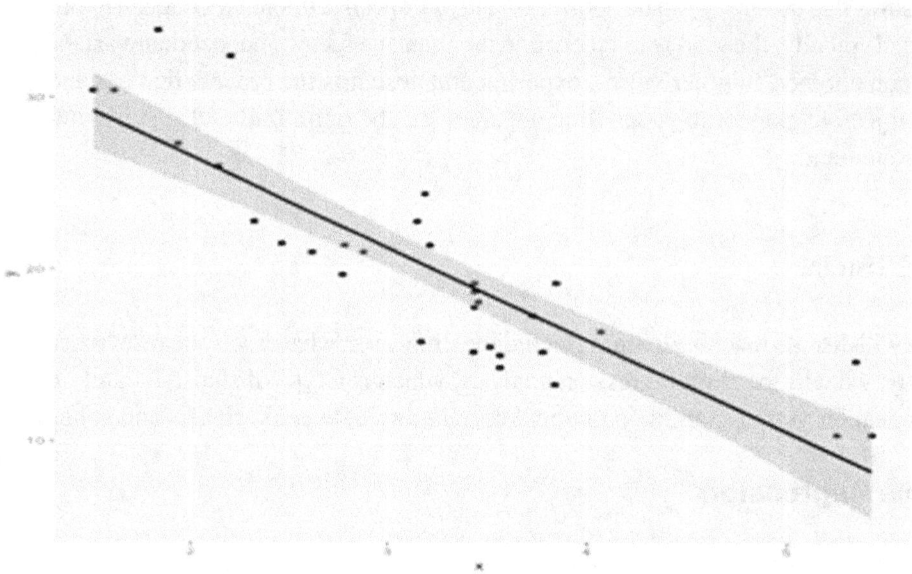

Figure 5. Scatter plot between the "Employed" and the "GNP.def" covariates (a). Scatter plot defining a straight-line relationship between the "Employed" and the "GNP.def" covariates (b).

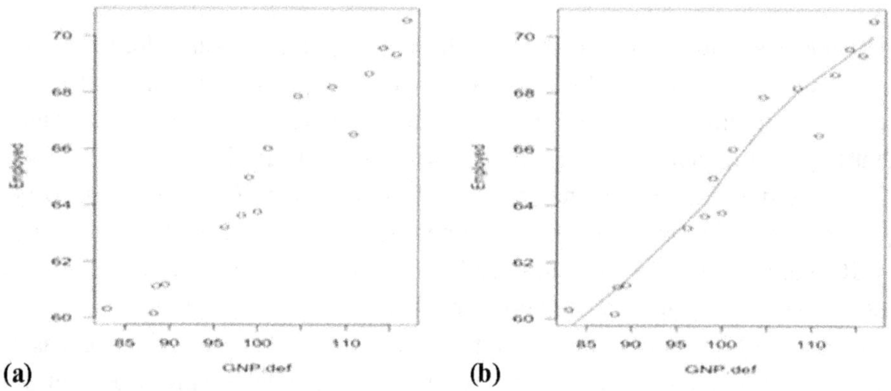

3.1.1 Parameter Estimation Using Least Square

It is necessary to predict the unknown parameters and utilize sample data. Accordingly, α_0 and α_1 are estimated using the least squares method. The goal of ordinary least squares estimates in simple linear regression is to provide a line of best fit that describes the possible relationship between x and y variables. The ordinary least-square (OLS) estimates are minimized:

$$Q\left(\alpha_0, \alpha_1\right) = \sum_{i=1}^{n}\left(y_i - \alpha_0 - \alpha_1 x_1\right)^2 \tag{3.2}$$

when taking partial derivatives of (3.2) with respect to α_0 and α_1 are

$$\frac{\partial Q}{\partial \alpha_0} = -2\sum_{i=1}^{n}\left(y_i - \alpha_0 - \alpha_1 x_i\right) \tag{3.3}$$

and

$$\frac{\partial Q}{\partial \alpha_1} = -2\sum_{i=1}^{n}\left(y_i - \alpha_0 - \alpha_1 x_i\right)x_i \tag{3.4}$$

Let α_0 and α_1 denote as $\hat{\alpha}_0$ and $\hat{\alpha}_1$ rely on the least square estimation. After Eq. (3.3) is set up to zero, the following equations are produced:

$$\frac{\partial Q}{\partial \alpha_0} = -2\sum_{i=1}^{n}\left(y_i - \hat{\alpha}_0 - \hat{\alpha}_1 x_i\right) = 0 \tag{3.5}$$

The solution to the normal equations is:

$$\sum_{i=1}^{n} y_i - n\hat{\alpha}_0 - \hat{\alpha}_1 \sum_{i=1}^{n} x_i = 0$$

$$n\overline{y} - n\hat{\alpha}_0 - n\hat{\alpha}_1\overline{x} = 0$$

$$\hat{\alpha}_0 = \overline{y} - \hat{\alpha}_1\overline{x} \tag{3.6}$$

It is formulated from Eq. (3.4) to obtain the least square estimator of $\pm_1$:

$$-2\sum_{i=1}^{n}\left(y_i - \hat{\alpha}_0 - \hat{\alpha}_1 x_i\right)x_i = 0$$

$$\sum_{i=1}^{n} x_i y_i - \hat{\alpha}_0 \sum_{i=1}^{n} x_i - \hat{\alpha}_1 \sum_{i=1}^{n} x_i^2 = 0$$

$$= n\overline{y} - n\hat{\alpha}_0 - n\hat{\alpha}_1\overline{x}$$

$$\sum_{i=1}^{n} x_i y_i - \left(\overline{y} - \hat{\alpha}_1\overline{x}\right)\sum_{i=1}^{n} x_i - \hat{\alpha}_1 \sum_{i=1}^{n} x_i^2 = 0$$

$$\sum_{i=1}^{n} x_i y_i - n\overline{x}\overline{y} + \hat{\alpha}_1 \left[\frac{1}{n} \left(\sum_{i=1}^{n} x_i \right)^2 - \sum_{i=1}^{n} x_i^2 \right] = 0$$

$$\hat{\alpha}_1 = \frac{\sum_{i=1}^{n} x_i y_i - \frac{\left(\sum_{i=1}^{n} y_i\right)\left(\sum_{i=1}^{n} x_i\right)}{n}}{\sum_{i=1}^{n} x_i^2 - \frac{\left(\sum_{i=1}^{n} x_i\right)^2}{n}}$$

or

$$\hat{\alpha}_1 = \frac{\sum_{i=1}^{n} \left(x_i - \overline{x}\right)\left(y_i - \overline{y}\right)}{\sum_{i=1}^{n} \left(x_i - \overline{x}\right)^2} \tag{3.7}$$

Let $\hat{\alpha}_0$ and $\hat{\alpha}_1$ from Eqs. (3.6) and (3.7) denoted the least-squares estimators of the intercept and slope. The regression equation is produced by this process:

$$\hat{y} = \hat{\alpha}_0 + \hat{\alpha}_1 x \tag{3.8}$$

Example 3.2 *(Continue) Longley dataset*

Sixteen observations on "employed" and the "GNF.def" have been collected and illustrated in Table 1. The scatter plot presents in Figure 5, appears that "employed" as an outcome variable and "GNP.def" as an explanatory variable have a significant statistical association.

First, we provide to estimate of the model parameters from Eqs. (3.7) and (3.8) and they are computed in the following for the Longley dataset:

$$\hat{\alpha}_1 = \frac{\sum_{i=1}^{n} x_i y_i - \frac{\left(\sum_{i=1}^{n} y_i\right)\left(\sum_{i=1}^{n} x_i\right)}{n}}{\sum_{i=1}^{n} x_i^2 - \frac{\left(\sum_{i=1}^{n} x_i\right)^2}{n}} = \frac{106816.2 - \frac{1045.1 * 1626.9}{16}}{167172.1 - \frac{\left(1626.9\right)^2}{16}} = \frac{549.12}{1746.87} = 0.3143$$

$$\hat{\alpha}_0 = \overline{y} - \hat{\alpha}_1 \overline{x} = 65.317 - 0.314 * 101.681 = 33.353$$

where

$$\bar{y} = \frac{\sum_{i=1}^{n} y_i}{n} = \frac{1045.1}{16} = 65.318 \text{ and } \bar{x} = \frac{\sum_{i=1}^{n} x_i}{n} = 101.681$$

The least-square fit is written as:

$$\hat{y} = \hat{\alpha}_0 + \hat{\alpha}_1 x = 33.35 + 0.31x$$

We interpret that the intercept and slope are founded 33.78 and 0.31, respectively. It can be commentated as the predicted employed unit for a zero Gross National Product implicit price deflator. Table 3.2 presents the observed values, the fitted values, and the residuals.

Residuals are simply the error between the measured value and the value estimated from the model. They are crucial in determining the suitability of a model. Therefore, we must determine whether the residuals resemble a random sample from a distribution with these characteristics in order to validate the constant variance and uncorrelated error assumptions.

Table 1. Longley data set and its computations

Individual, i	**Employed, y_i**	**GNP.deflator, x_i**	y_i*x_i	x_i^2
1	60.32	83.0	5006.80	6889.00
2	61.12	88.5	5409.29	7832.25
3	60.17	88.2	5307.08	7779.24
4	61.18	89.5	5476.23	8010.25
5	63.22	96.2	6081.86	9254.44
6	63.64	98.1	6242.98	9623.61
7	64.99	99.0	6433.91	9801.00
8	63.76	100.0	6376.10	10000.00
9	66.02	101.0	6681.12	10241.44
10	67.85	104.6	7097.84	10941.16
11	68.17	108.4	7389.52	11750.56
12	66.51	110.8	7369.64	12276.64
13	68.65	112.6	7730.55	12678.76
14	69.56	114.2	7944.20	13041.64
15	69.33	115.7	8021.59	13386.49
16	70.55	116.9	8247.41	13665.61
	$\sum_{i=1}^{n} y_i = 1045.1$	$\sum_{i=1}^{n} x_i = 1626.9$	$\sum_{i=1}^{n} x_i y_i = 106816.2$	$\sum_{i=1}^{n} x_i^2 = 167172.1$

Table 2. Response value, fitted value, and residual for Longley data in example 3.1

Individual, i	Employed, y_i	Fitted value, $\hat{y}_i$	Residual, e_i
1	60.32	52.05	8.272
2	61.12	52.29	8.824
3	60.17	52.00	8.167
4	61.18	52.31	8.869
5	63.22	52.94	10.272
6	63.64	53.07	10.560
7	64.99	53.49	11.492
8	63.76	53.11	10.645
9	66.02	53.81	12.203
10	67.85	54.38	13.471
11	68.17	54.48	13.686
12	66.51	53.96	12.543
13	68.65	54.63	14.021
14	69.56	54.91	14.649
15	69.33	54.84	14.488
16	70.55	55.22	15.330
	$\sum_{i=1}^{n} y_i = 1045.1$	$\sum_{i=1}^{n} \hat{y}_i = 857.57$	$\sum_{i=1}^{n} e_i = 187.49$

Figure 6. Scatter diagram between observed value (y_i) and fitted value ($\hat{y}_i$) in the first plot, and between residual value (e_i) versus fitted value ($\hat{y}_i$) in the second plot.

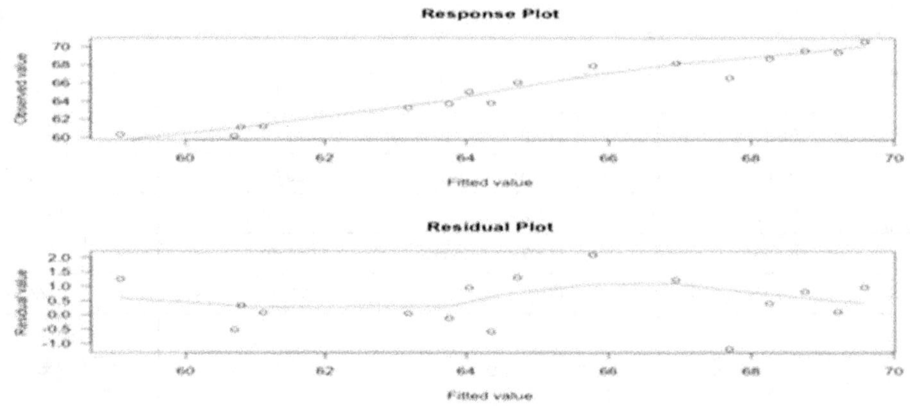

3.1.2 Properties of the Least-Squares Estimators for Simple Linear Regression

We must first understand OLS's statistical properties to employ least-squares estimators for making statistical inferences. We will yield some properties of the least squares estimators $\hat{\alpha}_0$ and $\hat{\alpha}_1$ in this section. The form of simple linear regression from Eq (3.1):

$$y = \alpha_0 + \alpha_1 x + \varepsilon$$

From section 3.1.1, we stated that:

$$\hat{\alpha}_1 = \frac{\sum_{i=1}^{n} x_i y_i - \frac{\left(\sum_{i=1}^{n} y_i\right)\left(\sum_{i=1}^{n} x_i\right)}{n}}{\sum_{i=1}^{n} x_i^2 - \frac{\left(\sum_{i=1}^{n} x_i\right)^2}{n}} = \frac{\sum_{i=1}^{n}\left(x_i - \overline{x}\right)\left(y_i - \overline{y}\right)}{\sum_{i=1}^{n}\left(x_i - \overline{x}\right)^2} = \frac{S_{xy}}{S_{xx}}$$

where it can be written as

$$\hat{\alpha}_1 = \frac{\sum_{i=1}^{n}\left(x_i - \overline{x}\right) y_i - \overline{y}\sum_{i=1}^{n}\left(x_i - \overline{x}\right)}{S_{xx}}$$

which $\sum_{i=1}^{n}\left(x_i - \overline{x}\right)=0$, we offer hold the least squares estimators of $\hat{\alpha}_1$ in following that:

$$\hat{\alpha}_1 = \frac{\sum_{i=1}^{n}\left(x_i - \overline{x}\right) y_i}{S_{xx}} \quad \text{for } i=1,2,\ldots,n$$

To illustrate the expected and variance values of $\hat{\alpha}_1$:

$$E\left(\hat{\alpha}_1\right) = E\left[\frac{\sum_{i=1}^{n}\left(x_i - \overline{x}\right) y_i}{S_{xx}}\right] = \frac{\sum_{i=1}^{n}\left(x_i - \overline{x}\right) E\left(y_i\right)}{S_{xx}} = \frac{\sum_{i=1}^{n}\left(x_i - \overline{x}\right)\left(\alpha_0 + \alpha_1 x_i\right)}{S_{xx}}$$

$$= \alpha_0 \frac{\sum_{i=1}^{n}\left(x_i - \overline{x}\right)}{S_{xx}} + \alpha_1 \frac{\sum_{i=1}^{n}\left(x_i - \overline{x}\right) x_i}{S_{xx}}$$

$$= \alpha_0 \frac{\sum_{i=1}^{n}(x_i - \overline{x})}{\sum_{i=1}^{n}(x_i - \overline{x})x_i} + \alpha_1 \frac{\sum_{i=1}^{n}(x_i - \overline{x})x_i}{\sum_{i=1}^{n}(x_i - \overline{x})x_i}$$

Note that $\sum_{i=1}^{n}(x_i - \overline{x})$=0 and $\sum_{i=1}^{n}(x_i - \overline{x})x_i = \sum_{i=1}^{n}(x_i - \overline{x})^2$, then it can be written as

$$E(\hat{\alpha}_1) = 0 + \alpha_1 = \alpha_1$$

The least-square estimator of $\hat{\alpha}_0$ is provided in Eq (3.6) as

$$\hat{\alpha}_0 = \overline{y} - \hat{\alpha}_1\overline{x}$$

Furthermore, the expectation of the least square estimator $\hat{\alpha}_0$ is:

$$E(\hat{\alpha}_0) = E(\overline{y} - \hat{\alpha}_1\overline{x})$$

$$= E(\overline{y}) - \overline{x}\ E(\hat{\alpha}_1)$$

$$= \alpha_0 + \alpha_1\overline{x} - \alpha_1\overline{x} = \alpha_0$$

So, $\hat{\alpha}_0$ and $\hat{\alpha}_1$ are unbiased estimators of $\alpha 0$ and $\alpha 1$, respectively. To find the variance of $\hat{\alpha}_1$ as

$$Var(\hat{\alpha}_1) = Var\left[\frac{\sum_{i=1}^{n}(x_i - \overline{x})y_i}{S_{xx}}\right]$$

$$= \left(\frac{1}{S_{xx}}\right)^2 \sum_{i=1}^{n}(x_i - \overline{x})^2\ Var(y_i)$$

where

$Var(y_i)=\sigma^2$, for $i=1,\ldots,n$

$$= \left(\frac{1}{\sum_{i=1}^{n}(x_i - \overline{x})^2}\right)^2 \sum_{i=1}^{n}(x_i - \overline{x})^2\sigma^2$$

$$Var\left(\hat{\alpha}_1\right) = \frac{\sigma^2}{S_{xx}}$$

Besides, the variance of $\hat{\alpha}_0$ is illustrated as

$$Var\left(\hat{\alpha}_0\right) = Var\left(\overline{y} - \hat{\alpha}_1\overline{x}\right)$$

$$Var\left(\hat{\alpha}_0\right) = Var\left(\overline{y}\right) + \overline{x}^2 Var\left(\hat{\alpha}_1\right) - 2\overline{x}Cov\left(\overline{y}, \hat{\alpha}_1\right) \tag{3.9}$$

Accordingly, we need to compute $Var\left(\overline{y}\right)$ and $Cov\left(\overline{y}, \hat{\alpha}_1\right)$ in terms of having *y*= $\alpha_0+\alpha_1 x_i+\varepsilon$, it can be computed as

$$Var\left(\overline{y}\right) = Var\left(\frac{1}{n}\sum_{i=1}^{n} y_i\right) = \frac{1}{n}\sigma^2 \tag{3.10}$$

and

$$Cov\left(\overline{y}, \hat{\alpha}_1\right) = Cov\left(\frac{1}{n}\sum_{i=1}^{n} y_i, \sum_{i=1}^{n}\frac{\left(x_i - \overline{x}\right)y_i}{S_{xx}}\right) = \frac{\sigma^2}{n}\Sigma\left(\frac{x_i - \overline{x}}{\sum_{i=1}^{n}\left(x_i - \overline{x}\right)^2}\right) = 0 \tag{3.11}$$

Using Eq.s (3.10) and (3.11) to implement into Eq. (3.9)

$$Var\left(\hat{\alpha}_0\right) = \frac{1}{n}\sigma^2 + \overline{x}^2\frac{\sigma^2}{S_{xx}} - 0 = \frac{\sigma^2 \sum x_i^2}{nS_{xx}}$$

A reminder that covariance between $\hat{\alpha}_0$ and $\hat{\alpha}_1$ might be performed as $Cov\left(\hat{\alpha}_0, \hat{\alpha}_1\right) = \frac{-\overline{x}\sigma^2}{S_{xx}}$. If $\overline{x}$ =0 is satisfied, there is no correlation between $\hat{\alpha}_0$ and $\hat{\alpha}_1$. From Eq. (3.2), we define the expectation of SSE by

$$E\left(SSE\right) = E\left[\Sigma\left(y_i - \hat{y}_i\right)^2\right] = E\left[\Sigma\left(y_i - \hat{\alpha}_0 - \hat{\alpha}_1 x_i\right)^2\right]$$

$$= E\left[\Sigma\left(y_i - \overline{y} + \hat{\alpha}_1\overline{x} - \hat{\alpha}_1 x_i\right)^2\right]$$

$$= E\left[\sum\left[\left(y_i - \overline{y}\right) - \hat{\alpha}_1\left(x_i - \overline{x}\right)\right]^2\right]$$

$$= E\left[\sum\left(y_i - \overline{y}\right)^2 + \hat{\alpha}_1^{\,2}\sum\left(x_i - \overline{x}\right)^2 - 2\hat{\alpha}_1\sum\left(x_i - \overline{x}\right)\left(y_i - \overline{y}\right)\right]$$

Note that $\sum\left(x_i - \overline{x}\right)\left(y_i - \overline{y}\right) = \hat{\alpha}_1\sum\left(x_i - \overline{x}\right)^2$ and so, the expectation of SSE performs as

$$= E\left[\sum y_i^2 - n\overline{y}^2 - \hat{\alpha}_1^{\,2}\sum\left(x_i - \overline{x}\right)^2\right]$$

$$= \sum E\left(y_i^2\right) - nE\left(\overline{y}^2\right) - \sum\left(x_i - \overline{x}\right)^2 E\left(\hat{\alpha}_1^{\,2}\right)$$

$$= \sum\left(Var\left(y_i\right) + \left[E\left(y_i\right)\right]^2\right) - n\left(Var\left(\overline{y}\right) + \left[E\left(\overline{y}\right)\right]^2\right) - \sum\left(x_i - \overline{x}\right)^2\left(\frac{\sigma^2}{\sum\left(x_i - \overline{x}\right)^2} + \alpha_1^{\,2}\right)$$

This definition might be facilitated to $(n-2)\sigma^2$. The unbiased estimator of σ^2 is given as

$$S^2 = \left(\frac{1}{n-2}\right)\sum\left(y_i - \hat{y}_i\right)^2 = \left(\frac{1}{n-2}\right)SSE$$

According to being illustrated the properties of least square estimators in simple linear regression in this section, we might summarize them in the following that:

i. $E\left(\hat{\alpha}_1\right) = \alpha_1$ and $E\left(\hat{\alpha}_0\right) = \alpha_0$. Thus, the $\hat{\alpha}_1$ and $\hat{\alpha}_0$ estimators are unbiased.

ii. $Var\left(\hat{\alpha}_1\right) = \dfrac{\sigma^2}{S_{xx}}$ and $Var\left(\hat{\alpha}_0\right) = \dfrac{\sigma^2\sum x_i^{\,2}}{nS_{xx}}$ for i=1,…,n

iii. σ2 estimator is $S^2 = \left(\dfrac{1}{n-2}\right)\sum\left(y_i - \hat{y}_i\right)^2$

iv. $Cov\left(\hat{\alpha}_0, \hat{\alpha}_1\right) = \dfrac{-\overline{x}\sigma^2}{S_{xx}}$

Moreover, the sample correlation coefficient ρ is given by

$$\rho = \frac{\sum_{i=1}^{n}\left(x_i - \overline{x}\right)\left(y_i - \overline{y}\right)}{\sqrt{\sum_{i=1}^{n}\left(x_i - \overline{x}\right)^2\sum_{i=1}^{n}\left(y_i - \overline{y}\right)^2}} = \frac{S_{xy}}{\sqrt{S_{xx}S_{xy}}} = \hat{\alpha}_1\sqrt{\frac{S_{xx}}{S_{yy}}}$$

Lastly, we can employ the $(100-\alpha)$ percent confidence intervals ($C.I.$) for the $\hat{\alpha}_0$ and $\hat{\alpha}_0$ in following that:

$$\hat{\alpha}_1 - t_{(n/2,n-2)} se(\hat{\alpha}_1) \le \alpha_1 \le \hat{\alpha}_1 + t_{(n/2,n-2)} se(\hat{\alpha}_1) \tag{3.12}$$

and

$$\hat{\alpha}_0 - t_{(n/2,n-2)} se(\hat{\alpha}_0) \le \alpha_0 \le \hat{\alpha}_0 + t_{(n/2,n-2)} se(\hat{\alpha}_0) \tag{3.13}$$

where the sampling distribution of both Eq.'s (3.12) and (3.13) is t with n-2 degrees of freedom (df) when we assume that errors are independently and normally distributed. In addition, a $(100-\alpha)$ percent confidence intervals ($C.I.$) for the estimated point of σ^2 is given by

$$\frac{(n-2)MS_{Res}}{\chi^2_{\alpha/2,n-2}} \le \sigma^2 \le \frac{(n-2)MS_{Res}}{\chi^2_{1-\alpha/2,n-2}}$$

where the sampling distribution of both $\left.(n-2)MS_{res}\right/\sigma^2$ is chi-square with n-2 df.

Example 3. Below table presents nine observations (n=9) to employ the least square method.

Table 3.

Observation, i	Explanatory variable, x_i	Response variable, y_i	$y_i * x_i$	x_i^2
1	-8	0	0	64
2	-4	0	0	16
3	-2	-1	2	4
4	-1	1	-1	1
5	0	1	0	0
6	1	1	1	1
7	2	2	4	4
8	4	6	24	16
9	8	12	96	64
	$\sum_{i=1}^{n=9} x_i = 0$	$\sum_{i=1}^{n=9} y_i = 22$	$\sum_{i=1}^{n=9} x_i * y_i = 126$	$\sum_{i=1}^{n=9} x_i^2 = 170$
	$\overline{x} = 0$	$\overline{y} = 2.44$		

$$\hat{\alpha}_1 = \frac{\sum_{i=1}^{n} x_i y_I - \frac{\left(\sum_{i=1}^{n} y_i\right)\left(\sum_{i=1}^{n} x_i\right)}{n}}{\sum_{i=1}^{n} x_i^2 - \frac{\left(\sum_{i=1}^{n} x_i\right)^2}{n}} = \frac{126 - \frac{1}{9} * 0 * 22}{170 - \frac{(0)^2}{9}} = 0.741$$

$$\hat{\alpha}_0 = \overline{y} - \hat{\alpha}_1 * \overline{x} = 2.44 - 0.741 * 0 = 2.44$$

The least-square fit is presented as:

$$\hat{y} = \hat{\alpha}_0 + \hat{\alpha}_1 x = 2.44 + 0.741 * x$$

Table 4.

Individual, i	Employed, y_i	Fitted value, $\hat{y}_i$	Residual, e_i
1	0	-3.48	3.48
2	0	-0.52	0.52
3	-1	0.95	-1.95
4	1	1.69	-0.69
5	1	2.44	-1.44
6	1	3.18	-2.18
7	2	3.92	-1.92
8	6	5.40	0.60
9	12	8.36	3.64
	$\sum_{i=1}^{n} y_i = 22$	$\sum_{i=1}^{n} \hat{y}_i = 21.96$	$\sum_{i=1}^{n} e_i = 0.06$

Thus, we provided that $\sum_{i=1}^{n=9} x_i = 0,\ \sum_{i=1}^{n} y_i = 22,\ \overline{x} = 0,\ \overline{y} = 2.44,\ S_{xx} = \sum_{i=1}^{9} \left(x_i - \overline{x}\right)^2 = 170.$

It follows that $\overline{x} = 0$,

$$Var\left(\hat{\alpha}_0\right) = \frac{\sigma^2 \sum_{i=1}^{9} x_i^2}{n S_{xx}} = \frac{\sigma^2 * 170}{9 * 170} = \frac{1}{9} * \sigma^2$$

$$Var\left(\hat{\alpha}_1\right) = \frac{\sigma^2}{S_{xx}} = \left(\frac{1}{170}\right) * \sigma^2$$

Note that $Cov\left(\hat{\alpha}_0, \hat{\alpha}_1\right) = 0$ in this case since $\sum_{i=1}^{n=9} x_i = 0$.

Moreover, we can perform that computing the formulas of SSE and S^2 are followed by

$$SSE = \sum_{i=1}^{n} \left(y_i - \overline{y}\right)^2 - \hat{\alpha}_1 \sum_{i=1}^{n} \left(x_i - \overline{x}\right)\left(y_i - \overline{y}\right)$$

where

$$S_{yy} = \sum_{i=1}^{n} \left(y_i - \overline{y}\right)^2 \text{ and } S_{xy} = \sum_{i=1}^{n} \left(x_i - \overline{x}\right)\left(y_i - \overline{y}\right)$$

S_{yy}=134.22 and S_{xy}=126

SSE= 134.22 – 0.741 * 126 = 40.85

and

$$S^2 = \frac{SSE}{n-2} = \frac{40.85}{9-2} = 5.84$$

3.2 Multiple Linear Regression

Multiple linear regression seeks to identify a linear relationship between a dependent variable and several independent factors. Multiple regression enables researchers to simultaneously assess the impact of multiple independent factors on the response. In other words, multiple regression is utilized to analyze the impact of the dependent variable while considering several potential influencing factors. Assume that at least one explanatory variable (x_i) and the dependent variable (y) are measurable. Following that, the multiple linear regression model is written as

$$y = \alpha_0 + \alpha_1 x_1 + \alpha_2 x_2 + \alpha_3 x_3 + \ldots + \alpha_k x_k + \varepsilon \tag{3.14}$$

Eq. (3.14) is called the multiple regression model with k regressor variables. Moreover, Eq. (3.14) has linear terms and unknown parameters, α_1, …, α_k in the k-dimensional space of the regressor variables. Even though the Longley dataset has presented six dependent variables as indicated in section 3.1, we only present two explanatory variables (i.e., Gross National Product implicit price deflator and the number of people in the armed force) and a response variable (i.e., Employed) in Table 4 to employ multiple linear regression for this section. It may be illustrated by relying on some variables of the Longley dataset as the following:

$$y_i = \alpha_0 + \alpha_1 x_{i1} + \alpha_2 x_{i2} + \varepsilon_i \quad (3.15)$$

where the eq. (3.15) involves the employed variable (i.e., y_i), Gross National Product implicit price deflator (i.e., x_{i1}), and the number of people in the armed forces (i.e., x_{i2}).

Table 5. Longley data in multiple linear regression

Individual, i	Employed, y_i	GNP.deflator, x_1	Armed.Force, x_2
1	60.32	83.0	159.0
2	61.12	88.5	145.6
3	60.17	88.2	161.0
4	61.18	89.5	165.0
5	63.22	96.2	309.9
6	63.64	98.1	359.4
7	64.99	99.0	354.7
8	63.76	100.0	335.0
9	66.02	101.0	304.8
10	67.85	104.6	285.7
11	68.17	108.4	279.8
12	66.51	110.8	263.7
13	68.65	112.6	255.2
14	69.56	114.2	251.4
15	69.33	115.7	257.2
16	70.55	116.9	282.7

3.2.1 The Properties of Least Squares Estimation in Multiple Regression Model

The multiple regression model has the following form:

$$y_i = \alpha_0 + \alpha_1 x_{i1} + \alpha_2 x_{i2} + \ldots + \alpha_j x_{ij} + \varepsilon_i \quad i=1,2,\ldots,n \text{ and } j=1,2,\ldots,k \quad (3.16)$$

where suppose that y calls the dependent variable, α's define the observation of regressors, and ε denotes the error term of observation. We employ the methods of matrix algebra to build an ideal least squares solution that enables one to estimate all $k+1$ parameters. As was mentioned in section 3.1, the derivation may theoretically be performed without the use of matrix algebra. The ordinary least-square function is written for a multiple linear regression model:

Figure 7. Scatterplot matrix for the Longley dataset

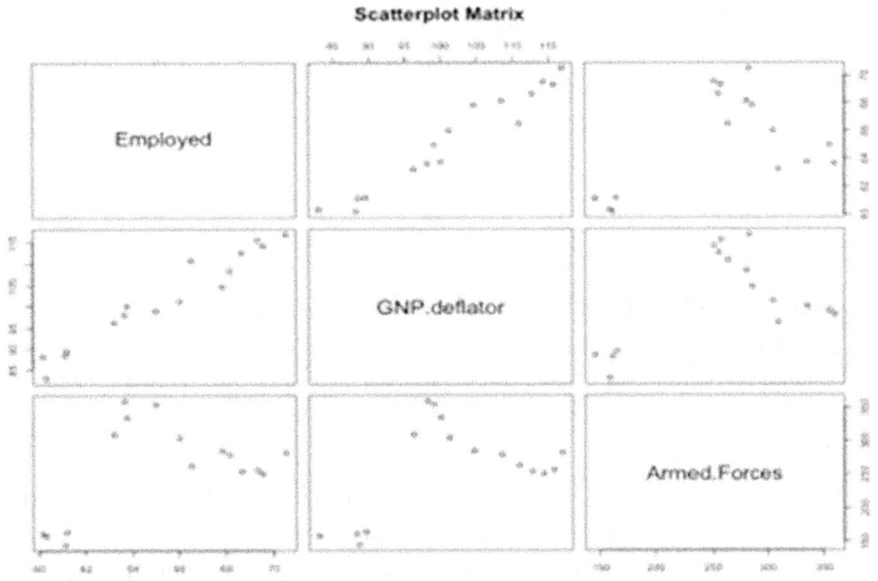

$$Q\left(\alpha_0, \alpha_1, \ldots, \alpha_k\right) = \sum_{i=1}^{n}\left(y_i - \left(\alpha_0 + \sum_{j=1}^{k}\alpha_j x_{ij}\right)\right)^2$$

We compute all partial derivates of Q regarding each α-coefficient and then, establish all partial derivates of Q to zero. Thus,

$$\frac{\partial Q}{\partial \alpha_0} = -2\sum_{i=1}^{n}\left(y_i - \hat{\alpha}_0 - \sum_{j=1}^{k}\hat{\alpha}_j x_{ij}\right) = 0 \quad (3.17)$$

and

$$\frac{\partial Q}{\partial \alpha_j} = -2\sum_{i=1}^{n}\left(y_i - \hat{\alpha}_0 - \sum_{j=1}^{k}\hat{\alpha}_j x_{ij}\right)x_{ij} = 0 \quad (3.18)$$

Let's continue with Eq. (3.17). Multiplication produces the result:

$$\sum_{i=1}^{n} y_i = n\hat{\alpha}_0 + \hat{\alpha}_1\sum_{i=1}^{n} x_{i1} + \hat{\alpha}_2\sum_{i=1}^{n} x_{i2} + \hat{\alpha}_3\sum_{i=1}^{n} x_{i3} + \ldots + \hat{\alpha}_k\sum_{i=1}^{n} x_{ik} \quad (3.19)$$

After extending Eq. (3.18), the OLS equations are provided:

$$\begin{aligned}
\sum_{i=1}^{n} y_i x_{i1} &= \hat{\alpha}_0 \sum_{i=1}^{n} x_{i1} + \hat{\alpha}_1 \sum_{i=1}^{n} x_{i1}^{\ 2} + \hat{\alpha}_2 \sum_{i=1}^{n} x_{i1} x_{i2} + \hat{\alpha}_3 \sum_{i=1}^{n} x_{i1} x_{i3} + \ldots + \hat{\alpha}_k \sum_{i=1}^{n} x_{i1} x_{ik} \\
\sum_{i=1}^{n} y_i x_{i2} &= \hat{\alpha}_0 \sum_{i=1}^{n} x_{i2} + \hat{\alpha}_1 \sum_{i=1}^{n} x_{i2} x_{i1} + \hat{\alpha}_2 \sum_{i=1}^{n} x_{i2}^{\ 2} + \hat{\alpha}_3 \sum_{i=1}^{n} x_{i2} x_{i3} + \ldots + \hat{\alpha}_k \sum_{i=1}^{n} x_{i2} x_{ik} \\
&\vdots \\
\sum_{i=1}^{n} y_i x_{ik} &= \hat{\alpha}_0 \sum_{i=1}^{n} x_{ik} + \hat{\alpha}_1 \sum_{i=1}^{n} x_{ik} x_{i1} + \hat{\alpha}_2 \sum_{i=1}^{n} x_{ik} x_{i2} + \hat{\alpha}_3 \sum_{i=1}^{n} x_{ik} x_{i3} + \ldots + \hat{\alpha}_k \sum_{i=1}^{n} x_{ik}^{\ 2}
\end{aligned} \tag{3.20}$$

Therefore, Eq.'s (3.19) and (3.20) will produce the OLS estimators $\hat{\alpha}_0, \ldots, \hat{\alpha}_k$. The model presented in (3.16) can be expressed in matrix form:

$$y = \alpha X + \varepsilon \tag{3.21}$$

where y is the vector of the dependent variable, X is the matrix of the independent variables, α is the vector of coefficients, and is the vector of error. In addition, X is $n\times(k+1)$ matrix, α is a $(k+1)\times 1$ vector, y and ε are $(n\times 1)$ vectors. The matrix and vectors are listed below in the appropriate terms. Thus, it is simplified written:

$$y = \alpha X + \varepsilon$$

$$\begin{bmatrix} y_1 \\ \vdots \\ y_n \end{bmatrix} = \begin{bmatrix} 1\, x_{11}\ x_{21} \cdots x_{1k} \\ \vdots\ \ \vdots \quad \vdots \ \ \cdots \ \ \vdots \\ 1\, x_{n1}\ x_{n2} \cdots x_{nk} \end{bmatrix} \begin{bmatrix} \alpha_0 \\ \vdots \\ \alpha_k \end{bmatrix} + \begin{bmatrix} \varepsilon_1 \\ \vdots \\ \varepsilon_N \end{bmatrix}$$

The total squared errors could be considered to minimize the best estimate of α.

$$Q(\alpha) = \sum_{i=1}^{n} \left(y_i - \alpha_0 + \alpha_1 x_{i1} + \alpha_2 x_{i2} + \ldots + \alpha_k x_{ik}\right)^2 = \left(y - X\alpha\right)^T \left(y - X\alpha\right) \tag{3.22}$$

Expanding the Eq. (3.22) equation, it is rewritten as

$$Q(\alpha) = y^T y - \alpha^T X^T y - y^T X\alpha + \alpha^T X^T\ X\alpha \tag{3.23}$$

$$Q(\alpha) = y^T y - 2\alpha^T \left(X^T y\right) + \alpha^T \left(X^T X\right)\alpha$$

Note that $y^T X\alpha$ equals $\alpha^T(X^T y)$, and it is a scalar. We might differentiate it regarding α and then set the derivative to zero would allow us to minimize Eq. (3.23).

$$\frac{\partial Q}{\partial \alpha} = -2X^T y + 2X^T X\alpha = 0 \tag{3.24}$$

Eq. (3.24) was derived based on the geometric approach and then, replaced α by $\hat{\alpha}$ .When X^TX is non-singular, the least squares estimate of α:

$$(X^TX)\alpha = X^Ty$$

$$\hat{\alpha} = \left(X^T X\right)^{-1} X^T y \tag{3.25}$$

The residuals can be written as the difference between the measured value and the corresponding fitted value following:

$$e = y - \hat{y} \tag{3.26}$$

where

$$e = \begin{bmatrix} e_1 \\ \vdots \\ e_2 \end{bmatrix},\ \hat{y} = \begin{bmatrix} \hat{y}_1 \\ \vdots \\ \hat{y}_n \end{bmatrix} = X\hat{\alpha} = X\left(X^T X\right)^{-1} X^T y = Hy \tag{3.27}$$

and $H= X(X^TX)^{-1}X^T$ is denoted the "hat-matrix". Also, the residuals $\left(\hat{\varepsilon}\right)$, the predicted values $\left(\hat{\varepsilon}\right)$, and the residual sum of squares $\left(\hat{\varepsilon}^T\hat{\varepsilon}\right)$ might be illustrated based on the hat matrix as shown:

- Predicted values: $\hat{y} = Hy = X\hat{\alpha}$
- Residuals: $\hat{\varepsilon} = y - X\hat{\alpha} = y - \hat{y} = \left(I - H\right)y$
- Residual sum of squares: $\hat{\varepsilon}^T\hat{\varepsilon} = y^T\left(I - H\right)\left(I - H\right)y = y^T\left(I - H\right)y$

If some presumptions do not hold, the least squares criterion won't always produce results that make sense. The following supplementary assumption applies to Eq. (3.16):

i. $E(\varepsilon_i)=0$ for all

The estimation of α will be challenging if this assumption is broken. More significantly, this shows that the model lacks a crucial systematic component that should have been included but was instead incorporated into the error terms.

ii. $Var(\varepsilon_i)=\sigma^2$ for all i

Homoscedasticity is the term for the assumption of constant variance, and heteroscedasticity is the term for its violation. Circumstances, where that presumption has been violated, imply that the true parameters can be estimated more accurately using other methods than least squares estimation.

iii. $Cov(\varepsilon_i,\varepsilon_j)=0$ for all $i\neq j$

There is no relationship between the errors. It cannot be true that understanding that the model under-predicts y for one specific observation indicates anything at all about what it does for any other observation. This violation most frequently happens when data are arranged in time because errors that occur close together in time frequently resemble one another. Inaccurate judgments of the regression's strength can result from the violation of this premise.

iv. ε_i is normally distributed for all individual i

This is necessary if we intend to perform the typical hypothesis tests that we conduct as well as any confidence or prediction interval building. Hypothesis tests and C.I. can all be exceedingly deceptive if this presumption is broken.

A crucial component of any regression study is to verify the above three assumptions employing different graphs, tests, and diagnostics because their violation could potentially result in utterly deceptive results. We wrote the matrix form of the model in Eq. (3.21) and the least squared estimator of α in Eq (3.25) as:

$$y = \alpha X + \varepsilon$$

and

$$\hat{\alpha} = \left(X^T X\right)^{-1} X^T y$$

Thus, it is simple to show the statistical features of the OLS estimator of $\hat{\alpha}$, which is called an unbiased estimator of α:

$$E\left(\hat{\alpha}\right) = E\left[\left(X^T X\right)^{-1} X^T y\right] = E\left[\left(X^T X\right)^{-1} X^T \left(\alpha X + \varepsilon\right)\right]$$

$$= E\left[\left(X^T X\right)^{-1} X^T X\alpha + \left(X^T X\right)^{-1} X^T \varepsilon\right]$$

$$= E\left[\left(X^T X\right)^{-1} X^T X\alpha\right] + E\left[\left(X^T X\right)^{-1} X^T \varepsilon\right] = \alpha \qquad (3.28)$$

where $(X^TX)^{-1}X^TX=I$ and $E(\varepsilon)=0$.

Similarly, the statistical properties of the least squares for the variance of $\hat{\alpha}$ might be illustrated:

$$Var\left(\hat{\alpha}\right) = Var\left[\left(X^T X\right)^{-1} X^T y\right] = \left(X^T X\right)^{-1} X^T Var\left(y\right)\left[\left(X^T X\right)^{-1} X^T\right]^T$$

$$= \sigma^2 \left(X^T X\right)^{-1} X^T X \left(X^T X\right)^{-1} = \sigma^2 \left(X^T X\right)^{-1} \tag{3.29}$$

Recall that the estimator of σ^2 can be presented based on the SSE by

$$\text{SSE} = \sum_{i=1}^{n} \left(y_i - \hat{y}_i\right)^2 = \sum_{i=1}^{n} e_i^2 = e^T e \tag{3.30}$$

From Eq. (3.22), we can re-write it as

$$\text{SSE} = e^T e = \left(y - X\hat{\alpha}\right)^T \left(y - X\hat{\alpha}\right) \tag{3.31}$$

where

$$\hat{\varepsilon} = y - X\hat{\alpha} = y - \hat{y}$$

Expanding Eq. (3.31), we have

$$\text{SSE} = y^T y - \hat{\alpha}^T X^T y - y^T X\hat{\alpha} + \hat{\alpha}^T X^T X\hat{\alpha}$$

where

$$X^T X\hat{\alpha} = X^T y$$

$$\text{SSE} = y^T y - \hat{\alpha}^T X^T y \tag{3.32}$$

Thus, we can find the expectation of SSE as

$$E\left(\text{SSE}\right) = E\left[\left(y - X\hat{\alpha}\right)^T \left(y - X\hat{\alpha}\right)\right] = E\left[\left(y - X\left(X^T X\right)^{-1} X^T y\right)^T \left(y - X\left(X^T X\right)^{-1} X^T y\right)\right]$$

$$= E\left[y^T \left(I - X\left(X^T X\right)^{-1} X^T\right) y\right]$$

$$= trace\left(\left(I - X\left(X^T X\right)^{-1} X^T\right)\sigma^2 I\right) + E\left[y^T \left(I - X\left(X^T X\right)^{-1} X^T\right) y\right]$$

$$= trace\left(\left(I - X\left(X^T X\right)^{-1} X^T\right)\sigma^2 I\right) + E\left(y\right)^T\left[I - X\left(X^T X\right)^{-1} X^T\right]E\left(y\right)$$

E(*SSE*) = (*n* – *k*)σ2

Note that the SSE has *(n-k)* degrees of freedom when k represents the numbers of coefficients in multiple regression models.

The MSE can be presented by

$$MSE = \frac{SSE}{n - k}$$

The expectation of MSE is

$$E\left(MSE\right) = E\left(\frac{SSE}{n - k}\right) = \frac{\left(n - k\right)\sigma^2}{\left(n - k\right)} = \sigma^2$$

As we compute the least-squares estimators in this section, we summarized them in the following that:

i. $E\left(\hat{\alpha}\right) = \alpha$ and thus, the estimator of $\hat{\alpha}$ is unbiased α.
ii. $Var\left(\hat{\alpha}\right) = \sigma^2\left(X^T X\right)^{-1}$ where $(X^T X)^{-1}$ represents the elements in row and column *i*.
iii. $Cov\left(\hat{\alpha}_i, \hat{\alpha}_j\right) = \left(X^T X\right)^{-1}$ σ^2 where $(X^T X)^{-1}$ represents the element in row i and the element in column *j*.
iv. The unbiased estimator of σ^2 is $S^2 = \dfrac{y^T y - \hat{\alpha}^T x^T y}{\left(n - k - 1\right)}$, where $(k+1)$ denote the number of unknown αi values in the multiple regression model.

Example 3.2: Continue Longley dataset in Multiple Linear Regression Model

$$X = \begin{bmatrix} 1 & 83.0 & 159.0 \\ 1 & 88.5 & 145.6 \\ 1 & 88.2 & 161.0 \\ 1 & 89.5 & 165.0 \\ 1 & 96.2 & 309.0 \\ 1 & 98.1 & 359.4 \\ 1 & 99.0 & 354.7 \\ 1 & 100.0 & 335.0 \\ 1 & 101.0 & 304.8 \\ 1 & 104.6 & 285.7 \\ 1 & 108.4 & 279.8 \\ 1 & 110.8 & 263.7 \\ 1 & 112.6 & 255.2 \\ 1 & 114.2 & 251.4 \\ 1 & 115.7 & 257.2 \\ 1 & 116.9 & 282.7 \end{bmatrix} \ldots y = \begin{bmatrix} 60.32 \\ 61.12 \\ 60.17 \\ 61.18 \\ 63.22 \\ 63.64 \\ 64.99 \\ 63.76 \\ 66.02 \\ 67.85 \\ 68.17 \\ 66.51 \\ 68.65 \\ 69.56 \\ 69.33 \\ 70.55 \end{bmatrix}$$

$$\mathrm{X^T X} = \begin{bmatrix} 1 & 1 & 1 & \ldots & 1 \\ 83.0 & 88.5 & 88.2 & \ldots & 116.9 \\ 159.0 & 145.6 & 161.0 & \ldots & 282.7 \end{bmatrix} \begin{bmatrix} 1 & 83.0 & 159.0 \\ 1 & 88.5 & 145.6 \\ 1 & 88.2 & 161.0 \\ \vdots & \vdots & \vdots \\ 1 & 116.5 & 282.7 \end{bmatrix} = \begin{bmatrix} 16.0 & 1626.9 & 4170.7 \\ 1626.9 & 167172.1 & 429317.4 \\ 4170.7 & 429317.4 & 1159816.8 \end{bmatrix}$$

$$\mathrm{X^T y} = \begin{bmatrix} 1 & 1 & 1 & \ldots & 1 \\ 83.0 & 88.5 & 88.2 & \ldots & 116.9 \\ 159.0 & 145.6 & 161.0 & \ldots & 282.7 \end{bmatrix} \begin{bmatrix} 60.32 \\ 61.12 \\ 60.17 \\ \vdots \\ 70.55 \end{bmatrix} = \begin{bmatrix} 1045.07 \\ 106816.17 \\ 274094.13 \end{bmatrix}$$

$$\hat{\alpha} = \left(X^T X\right)^{-1} X^T y$$

$$\begin{bmatrix} \pm_0 \\ \pm_1 \\ \pm_2 \end{bmatrix} = \begin{bmatrix} 16.0 & 1626.9 & 4170.7 \\ 1626.9 & 167172.1 & 429317.4 \\ 4170.7 & 429317.4 & 1159816.8 \end{bmatrix}^{-1} \begin{bmatrix} 1045.07 \\ 106816.17 \\ 274094.13 \end{bmatrix}$$

$$= \begin{bmatrix} 6.015 & -0.06053 & 0.00077 \\ -0.06053 & 0.00073 & -0.00005 \\ 0.00077 & -0.00005 & 0.00002 \end{bmatrix} \begin{bmatrix} 1045.07 \\ 106816.17 \\ 274094.13 \end{bmatrix} = \begin{bmatrix} 31.838 \\ 1.012 \\ 0.945 \end{bmatrix}$$

$\hat{y} = 31.838 + 1.012 *$ GNP.deflator+ 0.945 * Employed

Table 6.

Individual, i	*Employed, y_i*	*Fitted value, $\hat{y}_i$*	*Residual, e_i*
1	60.32	59.39	0.92
2	61.12	61.12	0.00
3	60.17	61.03	-0.86
4	61.18	61.44	-0.25
5	63.22	63.61	-0.38
6	63.64	64.22	-0.58
7	64.99	64.50	0.48
8	63.76	64.81	-1.05
9	66.02	65.18	0.83
10	67.85	66.24	1.61
11	68.17	67.43	0.73
12	66.51	68.18	-1.67
13	68.65	68.75	-0.09
14	69.56	69.25	0.31
15	69.33	69.72	-0.39
16	70.55	70.11	0.43
	$\sum_{i=1}^{n} y_{i=} 1045.1$	$\sum_{i=1}^{n} \hat{y}_i = 1044.98$	$\sum_{i=1}^{n} e_i = 0.04$

Note that the variance of $\hat{\alpha}$ is given by

$$Var\left(\hat{\alpha}\right) = \sigma^2 \left(X^T X\right)^{-1} = \sigma^2 \begin{bmatrix} 16.0 & 1626.9 & 4170.7 \\ 1626.9 & 167172.1 & 429317.4 \\ 4170.7 & 429317.4 & 1159816.8 \end{bmatrix}^{-1}$$

$$-\upsilon^2\begin{bmatrix}6.015 & -0.061 & 0.001\\ -0.061 & 0.001 & 0.000\\ 0.001 & 0.000 & 0.000\end{bmatrix}$$

4. DECISION TREE

A hierarchical construction known as a decision tree presents the categorization of a dataset into several categories. Building a model that predicts the values of a variable given the values of other variables is the objective here, as it is in any classification problem. Decision trees involve supervised learning, training a model using a sample of recorded data as input and established answers as outputs. A decision tree, which is a non-parametric method, assumes neither a fixed data probability distribution nor a set of interacting variables (Zacharis,2018). A simple decision tree comprises the main three nodes, which are the decision node, the root node, and the test node. After running a divided test in the test nodes, the last decisions for the target class are found on the decision nodes. A probability vector for the setpoint of a certain scenario is present in complicated issues at the decision node. A variety of methods, including ID3, C4.5, C5.0, Classification and regression trees (CART or CRT), chi-squared automatic interaction detector (CHAID), Quick, unbiased, efficient, and statistical trees (QUEST), and many others, are actively used depending on the features.

A goal of no companies experiencing financial distress and going bankrupt is unattainable, as history has shown. However, we can strengthen our capacity to recognize companies that could face future financial difficulties. This forewarning may help some companies (i.e., especially small businesses) take the necessary action to prevent financial difficulties and perhaps bankruptcy in the future. Small business challenges are frequently varied and complex, thus any attempt to solve them must be founded on research on its demographic traits. As a result, establishing an efficient small business support program necessitates considering several crucial organizational and management elements that have a significant impact on the performance of small businesses. So, researchers collect covariates that influence the kinds of help required for the company. Using a decision tree method, the gathered data is analyzed, and a model is created that could be utilized to find the answers to the study questions. This approach uses systematic data analysis to identify significant connections between the input (independent) variables and the objective (dependent) variable and displays them in a tree structure. The nodes, branches, and leaves make up the tree. A subset of values for each branch of the tree, which corresponds to the relevant target variable, is associated with each node, which represents one of the input variables. The tree is referred to as a classification tree and each leaf reflects one value of the goal if the objective variable is discontinuous. The Decision tree method also produces the frequency ratio for each leaf or the probability that a leaf will belong to the class it represents. Recursively splitting up the first collection of data into smaller sets is the procedure of induction of the tree. Each iteration aims to produce the best division, or the purest set, in regard to the ascertained value of the target variable. The DT algorithm may affect how the division is done. It specifies the variable that will be associated with each node in the tree and splits a collection of data into subsets based on the values of the variable, maximizing the purity of the subsets that result. The set of obtained subsets is each represented by a branch of the tree that leaves that node. In this instance, we illustrate a customer's preferences for buying a car by using the decision tree technique. When buying a car, we take a person's preferences into account. If the brand of the vehicle is A, you might consider additional restrictions and requirements, such as the engine's power and the cargo space it offers. If not, then maintaining its mileage as the priority is preserved. The car won't be purchased if any of these requirements are not met as illustrated in Figure 8.

Figure 8. Customer's preferences for buying a car by using the decision tree technique

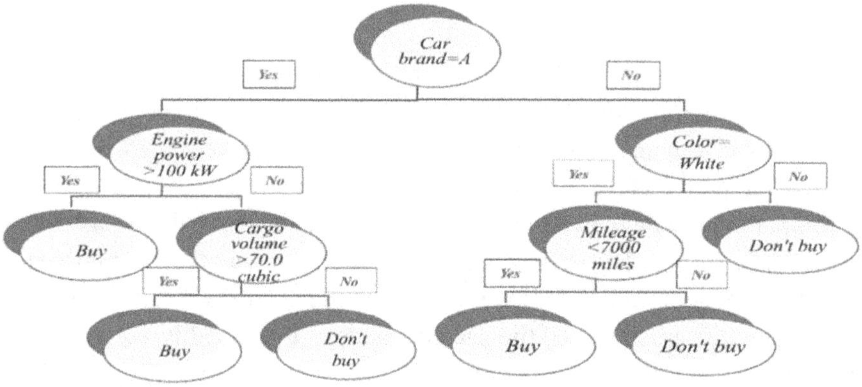

There are a few advantages to using of decision tree relying on the classification:

- The restriction of learning from a specific subject is avoided by learning from pre-classified samples.
- It is non-parametric as well and; thus, tree approaches are exploratory rather than inferential. Trees can represent a wide variety of data distributions since just a few presumptions are made about the model and the data distribution.
- A more efficient utilization of the given information and increased computational speed are implied by hierarchical decomposition.
- Unlike some statistical techniques, tree classifiers can handle both uni-modal and multi-modal data equally.
- Trees are simple to use in deterministic and incomplete contexts.
- Trees classify data using a series of straightforward tests whose semantics are intuitively evident to subject-matter experts.

The key challenge is to identify the most crucial variable or set of variables at each node in creating a decision tree when many variables are involved. This variable selection, also known as attribute selection, is typically carried out using the Gini impurity criteria or information gain. When the variables are categorical, that is, when they have values placed into classes or categories but no logical order, information gain is utilized. When a variable's values are continuous, or numerical, as in the case of an individual's age, the Gini impurity is utilized. Entropy is a crucial metric in information theory. Entropy measures how much uncertainty there is in a random variable's value. Entropy is expressed as

$$H = -\sum_{i=1}^{n}\left(p_i log p_i\right) \tag{4.1}$$

where H is called the measured entropy, p_i is defined as the probability of the event of *ith* value and n is the total value.

4.1 Classification and Regression Trees (CART)

Breiman et al. (1984) introduced CART as a nonparametric technique to analyze classification cases either categorical or continuous dependent parameters. While CART has produced a regression tree when we use continuous parameters for analysis, it has produced a classification tree when considering categorical parameters as dependent variables. Furthermore, CART models are sometimes called regression-type models that estimate the value of continuous parameters from the number of continuous and/or categorical predictor parameters. A binary decision tree is identified and built as part of CART utilizing a sample of training data for which the correct classification is available. The number of subjects in the two sub-groups created at each binary split, which relates to the two branches arising from each intermediate node, decreases over time, necessitating a big training sample in order to achieve satisfactory results (Bittencourt and Clarke,2003). To sum up, a CART analysis typically has three phases. An overgrown tree is constructed in the first stage, which is a good representation of the training dataset. This tree, known as the maximum tree, is constructed utilizing the binary split procedure. The overgrown tree that exhibits overfitting is pruned in the following stage. This process involves deriving several simpler trees from the maximal tree. Using a cross-validation (CV) technique, the tree with the ideal tree size is chosen in the last stage (Deconinck et al., 2005).

The CART algorithm is quite straightforward and operates quickly:

i.) Start with the decision node.
ii.) Finds the split s* that reduces impurity to the purest degree within the available candidates.
iii.) Divide the decision node into two nodes, which are called the interior nodes employing the split s* as illustrated in Figure 9.
iv.) Until the tree growing requirements are satisfied, repeat the divided search process (i.e., interior node) as shown in the previous three steps.

Figure 9. The simple CART process

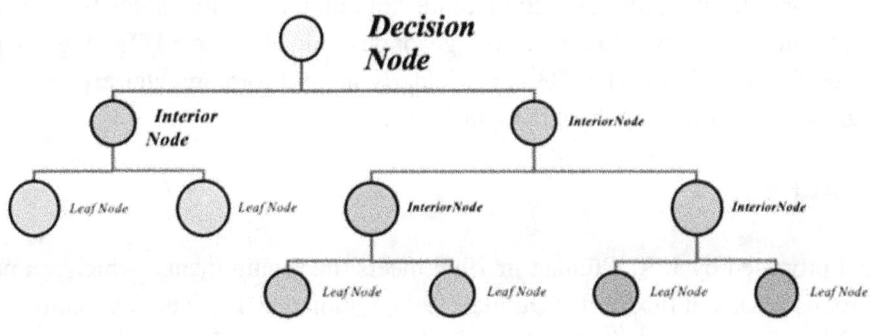

CART is progressively the most popular form of decision tree available owing to broadly utilized statistical programming such as R, SAS, Python, and MATLAB software. Why should we employ CART should be a key question that is addressed in this section. Before using CART in a real sector, it's critical to evaluate CART in comparison to other statistical classification techniques and pinpoint its benefits and potential drawbacks. CART is notably appropriate for analyzing complicated decision-making processes because it offers several key advantages as follows:

- The hierarchical structure of CART models is frequently more comprehensible than conventional regression models because it imitates decision-making heuristics.
- CART may predict outcomes better than conventional regression models even in the existence of nonlinear linkages.
- The datasets have more flexibility to interpret for themselves with CART.
- Variable selection in CART is not necessarily beforehand.
- Outliers are easily handled with CART.
- CART is quick to compute and requires no assumptions.
- CART is adaptable and has the capacity to make changes quickly.

The most important drawback the CART algorithm has a high sample variance. As a result, the branch structure, and the estimations it produces are not always robust in new data. As we've seen, pruning is one strategy that might help with this problem. An alternative approach is to use bootstrap techniques, which generate fresh data sets periodically by sampling from recorded data with replacement, applying the CART model to each bootstrap sample, and averaging the findings to identify the most durable tree properties. The utilization of CART has been substantially replaced by "ensemble" approaches, which consider CART's potential unstable by averaging the outcomes of numerous trees. It is assumed that these methods have small variances and excellent predicted accuracy (Hayes et al.,2015).

4.2 ID3 (Iterative Dichotomizer 3)

The ID3 was created by Quinlan (1993) and is straightforward decision tree learning system. The ID3 technique, which forms the basis of Quinlan's immensely popular C4.5 decision tree algorithm, constructs decision trees by a top-down, greedy search process. A top-down, greedy search across the supplied sets is used to build the decision tree in the ID3 algorithm, testing each feature at each tree node. We present a measure of knowledge gain to choose the attribute that is most helpful for categorizing a given set. The ID3 method can deal with continuous attributes by discretizing them or by examining the values to identify the appropriate split point by setting a threshold on the feature values.ID3 does not support pruning. ID3 algorithm is employed to get knowledge for designing tolerances. The logistic performance is calculated using this algorithm. The ID3 is particularly helpful for computer criminal forensics and predicting/ diagnosing diseases (Singh and Gupta,2014).

4.3 C4.5 Algorithm

The C4.5 model proposed by J. R. Quinlan in 1993 meets the requirements, which are predictive accuracy, speed, robustness, and flexibility (Quinlan,1996; Quinlan,2014). The foundation of C4.5 is the well-known ID3 tree learning technique, which can be used to learn discrete classes in advance from instances that have been tagged. The information gain ratio is the standard criterion for selecting dividing features in C4.5 as an extension of ID3. The information gain ratio prevents the bias of choosing features with multiple values in place of information gain instead of using ID3. There are a few enhancements for the C4.5 technique over ID3. Firstly, the model with the C4.5 method utilizes the information gain ratio as a feature selection criterion while the model with the ID3 method employs the information gain of the subset-tree. Second, pruning can be used during the decision tree construction process to prevent overfitting. Third, C4.5 Decision Tree is capable of handling both discrete and incomplete data (Wang et al.,2019). The C4.5 algorithm's primary drawback is that as the number of samples rises, more memory and central processing unit time are needed to run it (Mu,2017).

The C4.5 algorithm's decision tree creation procedure involves these four steps:

i. Selecting features as roots depending on present features with the largest value gain.
ii. Constitute a branch based on the number of the variable values that gain the most, one for each value.
iii. Given the calculation of the greatest gain value, split every scenario in the branch. The computation is completed after the initial highest gain value calculation and is then repeated without taking the primary gain variable value into account.
iv. Repeating every step to determine the biggest gain for each branch scenario until no longer possible, ensuring that all scenarios in each branch have the same class.

We must first identify the attributes or variables that make up its root to create a decision tree. Entropy, gain, split information, and gain ratio can be used to identify the rooted parameter. Entropy is a measure used to assess the variability of a data set. Entropy can be calculated using the following formula:

$$Entropy\left(S\right)\sum_{i=1}^{n}\left(-p_i * log_2 p_i\right)$$

where S, n, and p_i notations denote the dataset, the number of classification classes, and the sample proportions at each classification class *i*, respectively.

Gain is a metric used to assess how well a variable classifies data. The formula for computing gain is the following formula:

$$Gain\left(S,A\right) = Entropy\left(S\right)\sum_{i-1}^{n}\frac{|S_i|}{|S|} * Entropy\left(Si\right)$$

where A denoted as variables, S_i is represented for the number of samples for *ith* case and S is expressed by the number of samples for all datasets. The information gain ratio, which is the ratio of information gain to its split information, is computed:

$$gain\,ratio = \frac{Gain\left(S,A\right)}{Split\,information\left(S,A\right)}$$

where $split\,information = -\sum_{i=1}^{n} \frac{S_i}{S} log_2 \frac{S_i}{S}$.

4.4 CHAID (Chi-Squared Automatic Interaction Detector)

CHAID is a decision tree technique that is based on a modified test of association. CHAID tree is created by continually dividing subgroups of the space into two or more subtrees, starting with the complete set of data. That acceptable pairing of predictor parameter classes is combined until there is no longer a statistically significant difference between them regarding the target parameter in order to identify the optimal split at any node. This process is done to discover the appropriate split at any node. Interactions between the independent parameters that are clearly discernible from a tree analysis are dealt with naturally by this CHAID approach. Subsets formed by various sets of independent parameters are identified by the final nodes. Nominal or ordinal categorical variables are considered by the CHAID algorithms. The preceding procedure is applied when continuous variables are converted into ordinal variables. CHAID is frequently used in direct marketing to choose consumer segments and forecast how their answers to some parameters influence other parameters (Ture et al.,2009; Bhatt et al., 2015).

4.5 Bagging

Leo Breiman(1996a) developed the bagging technique, which got its name from the term "Bootstrap aggregating". The bagging approach can be combined with a variety of classification and regression techniques to lower the variation in predictions and hence enhance them. Several bootstrap samples are taken from the existing data, and various prediction methods are used for each bootstrap sample. The results are then aggregated, using simple voting for classification and regression, to provide the overall prediction, with the variance being decreased by virtue of the averaging. The bagging method has the advantage of reducing the variance of the foundation techniques and precisely tuning the estimation to the reliability and credibility for increasing the model accuracy. Because it is sensitive to even small changes in the test dataset, bagging has been demonstrated to be a successful strategy in susceptibility models and may therefore be able to improve prediction accuracy. Bagging works well for issues where the training datasets are scarce and tiny.

The phases of the bagging method, which is developed by Breiman (1996), are as described in the following:

1. Let $\mathcal{D}$ and $\mathcal{D}_t$ denote the original data set and training data set, respectively.
2. Attract $\mathcal{B}$ bootstrap samples from the training data, $\mathcal{D}_t$.
3. Add up all the bootstrap samples: $\sum_i^b \left(\mathcal{B}_i\right)$
4. By generating numerous trees without pruning and then accounting for the number of times across trees that each instance is classified in each category, one can train predictors employing these bootstrapped and aggregated data.
5. Cases are assigned in accordance with the combined predictors, which are combined using majority voting or averaging throughout the grouping of trees (Barboza,2017).

Figure 10. The process of bagging (bootstrap and aggregation)

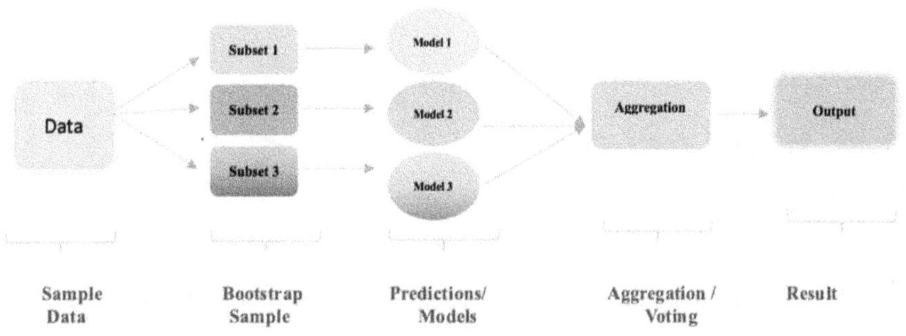

4.6 Boosting

This research builds on an intriguing technique known as "boosting," which combines the effectiveness of numerous "weak" classifiers to create a potent "committee." Boosting is a concept that was first introduced in the literature in computational learning theory (Schapire,1990; Freund,1995). By comparing the boosting algorithm to widely recognized statistical techniques, Friedman et al. (2000) were the initial researchers to shed light on the algorithm's inner workings. Boosting, like other regression algorithms, is improper for data where the important response variable is latent. An ensemble of weak models or learners, frequently decision trees, is created via boosting to create a prediction model. It is a type of stage-wise additive modeling where the model is built with each stage focusing on fixing the flaws of the preceding stage's model, with model flaws being measured by a loss function.

Classifiers and training sets are created in a purely deterministic manner in boosting. In the procedure, training data sets and classifiers are acquired repeatedly, as opposed to bagging, where training data sets and classifiers are acquired arbitrarily and independently (parallelly) from the prior stage of the process. In order to give objects that were mistakenly identified in the training set a larger weight, training data are reweighed at each stage of the boosting process. The two classes are labeled for dependent variables $y=\{-1,1\}$. Denote X is a vector of independent variables. $C(X)$ and $C_m(x)$ define classifiers and sequence classifiers for $m=1,2,\ldots,M$.

The steps of Boosting process are as follows:

1. Each sample in the first set of training should be given starting same weights: $w_i=1/N$ for $i=1,2,\ldots,N$
2. For m=1 to M:
    i. Employ weighted resampling to choose a dataset of N samples at random from the first training set. The weight of a sample affects the probability that it will be chosen. A sample that is more heavily weighted is more likely to be chosen. So, weights w_i are used to be fitted a classifier $C_m(x)$ to the training data.
    ii. Figure out the error's probability estimates.

$$error_m = \frac{1}{n}\sum_{i=1}^{n} w_i \xi_i^m$$

where

$$\xi_i^m = \begin{cases} 0, & if\ X_i\ is\ classified\ correctly \\ 1, & otherwise \end{cases}$$

Each $C_m(x)$ is given a weight by the α's, which favors more proper classifiers and devalues less accurate ones.

$$\alpha_m = log\left(\frac{1 - error_m}{error_m}\right)$$

iii. Set $w_i^{m+1} = w_i^m exp\left(\alpha_m \xi_i^m\right)$ for i=1,2,…,N

3. Result $C\left(x\right) = sign\left[\sum_{m=1}^{M} \alpha_m C_m\left(x\right)\right]$

Figure 11. The processes of the Boosting algorithm

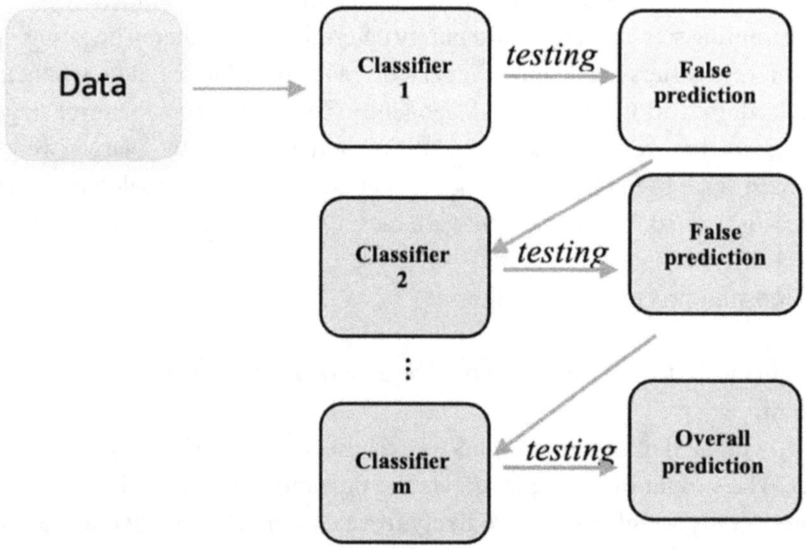

We must compare how well various approaches perform on standardized criteria, which we refer to as evaluation metrics for supervised learning. Firstly, a table that can be created for a classifier on a binary data set and used to express the efficiency of the classification is known as a confusion matrix. A confusion matrix, sometimes referred to as a contingency table or an error matrix, is a table structure that makes it possible to see how well a supervised learning method is working.

Table 7. Confusion matrix

		Actual Value	
Predicted Value	Positives	Positives	Negatives
		True Positive	*False Positive*
	Negatives	*False Negative*	*True Negative*

True positives (TPs), false positives (FPs), false negatives (FNs), and true negatives (TNs), all of which are collated as seen in Table 5, are used to compute classification metrics.

Thus, the confusion matrix is defined relying on the terms:

True Positives (TP): prediction and actual both positives
True Negatives (TN): prediction and actual both negatives
False Positives (FP): actual is negative and prediction is positive.
False Negatives (FN): actual is positive and prediction is negative.

There are four classification metrics from the confusion matrix in a way that:

i. *Accuracy:* Accuracy is the simplest and most direct classification metric. The proportion of the total diagonal items to the total components of the confusion matrix is used to assess the overall accuracy of a classifier, which is also true for attributes with multiple classes. The formula is:

$$Accuracy = \frac{TP + TN}{TP + TN + FP + FN}$$

ii. *Precision and Recall:* The proportion of affirmative cases that are genuinely positive is known as precision. The mathematical formula for the precision is defined as

$$Precision = \frac{TP}{TP + FP}$$

Recall (also called sensitivity or the true positive rate), which is the percentage of verified positives that are accurately predicted, is an important metric for comprehending FNs.

$$Recall = \frac{TP}{TP + FN}$$

iii. *F score:* The most widely used score is the F_α score, which employs the parameter α to determine and balance recall precision and is expressed as

$$F_\alpha = \left(1 + \alpha^2\right) \frac{Precision x Recall}{Precision + Recall}$$

The weighted average of recall and precision is the F_1 score when α is 1. Precision and recall must both be strong for the classifier to have a high F-score.

iv. *ROC and AUC:* A ROC curve (receiver operating characteristic curve) is a widely recognized tool for visualizing classification results. The graphic displays the classification accuracy for various threshold levels. A ROC differentiates the "signal" from the "noise" by plotting the true positive rate against the false positive rate at different threshold values.

Computing the true positive rate and the false positive rate, which is formulated in the following, is necessary to plot the ROC curve.

$$True\, positive\, rate\left(TPR\right) = \frac{TP}{TP + FN}$$

$$False\, positive\, rate\left(FPR\right) = \frac{FP}{FP + TN}$$

A classifier's capacity to differentiate between classes is measured by the area under the curve (AUC). The model performs better at various threshold points between positive and negative classifications the higher the AUC. The classifier can properly discriminate between all Positive and Negative class points when AUC is equal to 1. AUC equals 0 means that the classifier will predict all negatives as positive and vice versa. The classifier is unable to discriminate between the Positive and Negative classes when AUC equals 0.5.

5. REFERENCES

Barboza, F., Kimura, H., & Altman, E. (2017). Machine learning models and bankruptcy prediction. *Expert Systems with Applications*, *83*, 405–417. doi:10.1016/j.eswa.2017.04.006

Bhatt, H., Mehta, S., & D'mello, L. R. (2015). Use of ID3 decision tree algorithm for placement prediction. *International Journal of Computer Science and Information Technologies*, *6*(5), 4785–4789.

Bittencourt, H. R., & Clarke, R. T. (2003, July). Use of classification and regression trees (CART) to classify remotely-sensed digital images. In *IGARSS 2003. 2003 IEEE International Geoscience and Remote Sensing Symposium. Proceedings (IEEE Cat. No. 03CH37477)* (*Vol. 6*, pp. 3751-3753). IEEE. 10.1109/IGARSS.2003.1295258

Breiman, L. (1996). Bagging predictors. *Machine Learning*, *24*(2), 123–140. doi:10.1007/BF00058655

Breiman, L., Friedman, J., Olshen, R., & Stone, C. (1984). *Cart.* Classification and regression trees. . doi:10.1201/9781315139470

Deconinck, E., Hancock, T., Coomans, D., Massart, D. L., & Vander Heyden, Y. (2005). Classification of drugs in absorption classes using the classification and regression trees (CART) methodology. *Journal of Pharmaceutical and Biomedical Analysis*, *39*(1-2), 91–103. doi:10.1016/j.jpba.2005.03.008 PMID:15946819

Freund, Y. (1995). Boosting a weak learning algorithm by majority. *Information and Computation*, *121*(2), 256–285. doi:10.1006/inco.1995.1136

Friedman, J., Hastie, T., & Tibshirani, R. (2000). Additive logistic regression: A statistical view of boosting (with discussion and a rejoinder by the authors). *Annals of Statistics*, *28*(2), 337–407. doi:10.1214/aos/1016218223

Hayes, T., Usami, S., Jacobucci, R., & McArdle, J. J. (2015). Using Classification and Regression Trees (CART) and random forests to analyze attrition: Results from two simulations. *Psychology and Aging*, *30*(4), 911–929. doi:10.1037/pag0000046 PMID:26389526

Kubat, M., & Kubat, J. A. (2017). *An introduction to machine learning* (Vol. 2). Springer International Publishing. doi:10.1007/978-3-319-63913-0

Mu, Y., Liu, X., Yang, Z., & Liu, X. (2017). A parallel C4. 5 decision tree algorithms based on MapReduce. *Concurrency and Computation*, *29*(8), e4015. doi:10.1002/cpe.4015

Quinlan, J. R. (1996). Improved use of continuous attributes in C4. 5. *Journal of Artificial Intelligence Research*, *4*, 77–90. doi:10.1613/jair.279

Quinlan, J. R. (2014). *C4. 5: programs for machine learning*. Elsevier. doi:10.1016/j.procs.2016.04.224

Samuel, A. L. (1959). Some studies in machine learning using the game of checkers. *IBM Journal of Research and Development*, *3*(3), 210–229. doi:10.1147/rd.33.0210

Schapire, R. E. (1990). The strength of weak learnability. *Machine Learning*, *5*(2), 197–227. doi:10.1007/BF00116037

Singh, S., & Gupta, P. (2014). Comparative study ID3, cart, and C4. 5 decision tree algorithm: A survey. [IJAIST]. *International Journal of Advanced Information Science and Technology*, *27*(27), 97–103.

Ture, M., Tokatli, F., & Kurt, I. (2009). Using Kaplan–Meier analysis together with decision tree methods (C&RT, CHAID, QUEST, C4. 5 and ID3) in determining recurrence-free survival of breast cancer patients. *Expert Systems with Applications*, *36*(2), 2017–2026. doi:10.1016/j.eswa.2007.12.002

Wang, X., Zhou, C., & Xu, X. (2019). Application of C4. 5 decision tree for scholarship evaluations. *Procedia Computer Science*, *151*, 179–184. doi:10.1016/j.procs.2019.04.027

Zacharis, N. Z. (2018). Classification and regression trees (CART) for predictive modeling in blended learning. *International Journal of Intelligent Systems and Applications*, *3*(3), 1–9. doi:10.5815/ijisa.2018.03.01

Chapter 2
Management Accountants' Skills and Competencies:
How Business Analytics Tools Reshape the Future

Giorgio Cinciripini
Asso Controller, Italy

Edoardo Crocco
University of Turin, Italy

Daniele Giordino
https://orcid.org/0000-0001-5507-6270
Università degli Studi di Torino, Italy

Maurizio Grillini
Asso Controller, Italy

ABSTRACT

Information technology has profoundly disrupted the world as we know it. Advances in technology have enabled management accountants to gain access to an unprecedented amount of information, through the use of business analytics and machine learning tools. This research delves deeper into the above described context, in an attempt to collect empirical data on how business analytics tools have reshaped the modern day accounting profession and how they will continue to shape the future, according to management accountants themselves. In an effort to investigate the topic, several semi-structured interviews were conducted with management accounting professionals. Through the qualitative analysis of their contributions, the authors draw conclusions on how business analytics tools have affected their professional career, how they expect their future to be shaped, and to what extent they believe technology has allowed them to become more efficient.

DOI: 10.4018/978-1-6684-8386-2.ch002

1. INTRODUCTION

Management accountants (or controllers) are often described as critical partners and employees of businesses due to their beneficial role in supporting various managerial decisions (Goretzki, 2013). However, the abovementioned role demands higher skills outside the scope of traditional management accounting competencies (Karlsson et al., 2019). Therefore, management accountants must continuously evolve and improve to support the management decision system with prosperous and forward-looking skills and information from an array of new topics such as sustainability and digitalization (Ascani et al., 2021; Baldvinsdottir et al., 2009; Giacosa et al., 2022). There is literature that highlights the importance of the aspects mentioned earlier, and it empathizes that employers hire management accountants that possess, besides the traditional accounting skills, the necessary competencies to address today's new challenges and promote the company's long-term resilience and survivability (Budding et al., 2022; Lepisto & Ihantola, 2018).

Additionally, the literature discusses the importance of management accountants' aptitude for business partnering (Karlsson et al., 2019) since they must conform to their company's cultural norms and attitudes (Endenich, 2014). Controllers operate in social networks within various dimensions of a business; thus, their soft skills became central to their role alongside their technical knowledge (Weber, 2011). Furthermore, this is particularly relevant given today's business structure and decentralization (Giacosa et al., 2023; Hyvonen et al., 2015). The business mentioned above requires skills that aid the management accountant, such as solid communication skills but, most importantly, the capability to understand the various operations that might be present within the different units and dimensions of the organization in which they operate (Dolce et al., 2020). Moreover, management accountants must possess the necessary skills to properly utilize business intelligence tools and technologies to support decision-making and performance evaluation (Rikhardsson & Yigitbasioglu, 2018). Therefore, it becomes necessary to address the fluidity and encompassing role under which modern management accountants must operate since they must be able to diagnose and adapt their skills and competencies to every situation in which they might operate, as well as diagnose it properly to provide upper management with the necessary information to make a meaningful decision which benefits both short and long term of firms, as well as other dimensions such as its corporate social responsibility (Nnorom & Olagbaju, 2020).

Consequently, the literature tailors the management accountant position as one that goes beyond scorekeeping and reporting professional, which focuses on the financial information of one's business (Oesterreich & Teuteberg, 2019). Part of the literature describes the controller as a business partner engaging in management-oriented decisions and as an internal consultant (Nnorom & Olagbaju, 2020; Karlsson et al., 2019). Therefore, if the management controller is defined as a business partner, it becomes an operational actor of sorts by strengthening the bond between financial and operational information and the decision-making process by enhancing the interactions with other components of the business, such as operational managers (Oesterreich & Teuteberg, 2019). Moreover, empirical evidence further suggests that presenting the figure of the controller as a business partner it helps improve workers' ability to resolve conflict resolution and engage in activities such as team building, motivation enhancements, and negotiation with both internal and external stakeholders and actors (Dolce et al., 2020).

Even with the abovementioned empirical findings, the complete set of skills and capabilities requested from managerial accountants remains to be seen (Karlsson et al., 2019). Moreover, as far as the authors are concerned, there needs to be more research concerning how management accountants assess and evaluate their competencies to remain attractive to businesses as professionals (Karlsson et al., 2019).

Therefore, additional empirical research should be directed toward investigating the hybrid role of management accountants in today's business world and firms' structure (Graham et al., 2012). Especially when considering how said changes affect the traditional hierarchical structure and role (Byrne & Pierce, 2007; Karlsson et al., 2019). Therefore, the chapter's authors seek to gather empirical evidence from professionals operating under the management accountant umbrella to expand our current understanding of their skills, competencies, and assessment techniques of one's business, as well as their employability and strength as professionals. Hence, the following research questions are proposed:

RQ1: How has the management accountant role changed their required skills and competencies over the last years due to analytics tools?
RQ2: How do analytics tools shape the future of management accounting as a profession?

Since our research seeks to explore the above-mentioned research gap and questions deeply, the authors have deemed relevant the use of a qualitative approach to it. Therefore, data were gathered through interviews and online surveys (Bell et al., 2022). The utilization of the foregoing techniques of research allows the authors of the book chapter to understand a complex phenomenon at hand better and answer in depth the previously discussed research questions. The management accountants selected for our sample are operating within Italian companies. They must be part of the ASSO Controller group and society so to further highlight their commitment and active participation within the management accounting community and profession. Therefore, ASSO Controller was deemed the most appropriate community to draw our sample since it is considered one of the most important organizations of management accountants within the Italian territory, making it particularly relevant to our study.

The present book chapter hopes to contribute to the present literature by providing both theoretical and practical implications. First, the obtained results should help management accountants better understand what are considered to be their necessary skills and competencies, as well as role's boundaries or lack of. Second, the obtained results should support institutions and organizations which have degrees and modules focused for management accountants' formation so as to emphasize what the professional deem necessary. Third, the obtained results further contribute to the theory concerning the hybrid role that management accountants have in today's businesses.

2. LITERATURE REVIEW

2.1 The Evolution of the Management Accountants' Role

Traditionally speaking, the management accountant role is often associated with tasks and responsibilities aimed at utilizing numerical data of firms' various control systems to evaluate performance of various dimensions of a business in reference to the goals and strategies of said entity (Karlsson et al, 2019; Tuomela, 2005). Examples of the various dimensions that fall within the scope of the management accountant are: individuals, business units, corporate etc. The foregoing view management accountant underlines the importance of methodological rigor, meticulousness and technical accounting skills for the professional figure of management accountants (Byrne and Pierce, 2007). This is because the traditional view of the management accountant role highlights the role's technical skills since the scope and aim of this figure is limited to the evaluation of performance of various dimensions of a business (as previously discussed) (Byrne and Pierce, 2007; ten Rouwelaar et al., 2020). Consequently, there is less emphasis on other sets of skills and competencies such as interpersonal and communication capabilities (Coad, 1996). This is because they are often deemed less necessary in a well structured and rigorous view of the management accounting profession (Karlsson et al, 2019). Nonetheless, today's dynamic business environment and the necessity for firms to maintain dynamic structures and processes might not be the environment in which the traditional view of management accountants is the most adequate (Burns and Baldvinsdottir, 2005). Hence, there is a string of the literature which argues that the role of management accountants must evolve in order to continuously add value to businesses (Karlsson et al, 2019).

Many academics and professionals believe that the management accountant role should evolve and become more of a business partner in order to support firms in their contemporary issues (Jönsson, 2009; Karlsson et al, 2019; Linsley and Linsley, 2014). This is because the management accountant figure has evolved into a less structured and mechanical approach to its work thanks to instruments and tools such as the balanced scorecard (Chenhall and Moers, 2015). Management accountants are now required to develop and understand a multitude of factors which are outside of the traditional and technical view of the management accounting subject matter (Weber, 2011). Therefore, the introduction of the idea of the management accountant as a business partner extends the tasks and responsibilities of the management accountant beyond the historical and numerical analysis (Yazdifar and Tsamenyi, 2005; Weber, 2011). Therefore, strategic and long term information should be provided by management accountants in an attempt to support and closely contribute to organizations management and decision making processes (Hyvönen et al, 2015; Karlsson et al, 2019). In fact, the literature underlines the importance that business partners have on timely and relevant handling of financial information to address strategies and initiatives for companies; thus, if management accountants are to be viewed as business partners, they must be able to proactively contribute to the foregoing dimensions (Goretzi et al, 2018). Therefore, a future and historical view of organizations' information and scenarios seems necessary for management accounts if they should be viewed as business partners rather than "bean counters" (Dolce et al, 2020; Karlsson et al, 2019; Lepisto and Ihantola, 2018).

Nonetheless, the business partner literature exists alongside the hybrid accountant literature (Karlsson et al, 2019). The hybrid accountant literature argues that the traditional tasks remain an essential part of the management accountant daily work hours (Karlsson et al, 2019). Consequently, the stream of literature which focuses on the hybrid idea of a management accountants, argues that management accountants should not merely shift into a business partner figure but rather merge the traditional view (and tasks, skills competencies) of management accountant with today's new business orientation (Burns and Baldvinsdottir, 2005; Graham et al, 2012; Karlsson et al, 2019). First, hybrid management accountants actively partake into team processes and customize numerical information (financial and operational information) to satisfy demands from various dimensions of an organizational group (Byrne and Pierce, 2007). Hybrid management accountants tasks fall within various levels of analysis (internal and external), performance evaluation and risk management (De Loo et al, 2011; Karlsson et al, 2019; Windeck et al, 2015). Therefore, the hybrid management accountant should possess skills and competencies concerning business processes, market conditions and evolution, markets and be somewhat aware of various dimensions and evolution of the business and the environment in which it operates in (Karlsson et al, 2019; Windeck et al, 2015).

Nonetheless, there are studies and publications which argue that the hybrid figure of a management accountant depicts a balancing act between traditional views and today's dynamic needs; thus, it does not necessarily constitute an evolution of the role, skills, competencies and tasks of management accountants (Lambert and Sponem, 2012). Consequently, this stream of literature further highlights the need for additional empirical findings to better understand today's required skills and competencies, as well as better comprehend how the management accountant role has changed from its traditional view (Karlsson et al, 2019). Additionally, further research should investigate the evolution of the hierarchical stewardship role of management accountants (Byrne and Pierce, 2007).

2.2 Factors Influencing Changes Within the Management Accountants' Profession

The role that management accountants assume is often associated with the environment and business in which they operate since they must develop competencies and skills which are appropriate to their role and context (Karlsson et al, 2019; Lepisto and Ihantola, 2018).

First, there are studies which have gathered empirical findings that underline the importance of environmental concerns within the management accountant role (Halbouni and Nour, 2013). This is because a greater focus has been put on by companies seeking to comply with environmental concerns (Karlsson et al, 2019; Huff, 2014; Lepisto and Ihantola, 2018). Additionally, firms seeking to decentralize force management accountants to further expand their understanding of the business, as well as the environment in which the firms operate in; hence, they must consider their sustainability performance and impact on the consumption of natural resources which are central to their business core activities (Halbouni and Nour, 2013).

Second, previous publications underline the necessity for management accountants to possess communication skills, as well as have the necessary capabilities to operate in group settings when they are employed within decentralized firms and entities (Endenich, 2014). The need for strong communication capabilities is further emphasized by the rise of modern information technology (Karlsson et al, 2019). Moreover, management accountants must interact with various professional figures from within the business in a cooperative manner (Karlsson et al, 2019). Communicational capabilities have also further increased the need for management accountants to better comprehend the firm in which they operate in; thus, management accountants are now expected to understand and fully grasps various dimensions of the organization that they work in (Dolce et al, 2020; Karlsson et al, 2019).

Third, there are articles that underline the necessity for management accountants to possess capabilities which are viewed positively within society such as cultural norms, especially when the management accountant falls within the business partner category (Hiller et al, 2014). This is because cultural organizational norms further support the development of firms through smooth implementation of management practices aimed at promoting change or by fostering cooperative activities, as well as ease the problem-solving processes (Endenich, 2014; Oesterreich and Teuteberg, 2019). When considering the management accountant as a business partner, there are studies which highlight the additional emphasis that top managers put onto the competencies and skills aimed at developing management accountants focus on the empowerment of leadership roles (Weber, 2011).

Finally, the increasingly higher relevancy of business analytics (BA) tools and technologies have further emphasized the need for management accountants to develop the necessary skills and competencies to take advantage of the above mentioned tools and technologies so to aid the decision making and evaluation process of various dimensions of a business or corporate (Rikhardsson and Yigitbasioglu, 2018). The skills and competencies normally associated with BA is considered to be central to the role of management accountants because of its impact on organizations strategy and long term plan (Maisel and Cokins, 2014). Through the analysis of data obtained from BA tools, management accountants create value for their employees; hence the BA tools are perceived as necessary to firms' management (Rikhardsson and Yigitbasioglu, 2018). Consequently, management accountants must continuously develop their competencies and skills in order to remain up to date with new technologies and tools aimed at BA (Rikhardsson and Yigitbasioglu, 2018).

Nonetheless, there are publications which suggest that management accountant skills and competencies are often restrained or limited by different factors such as the limitations imposed by accounting regulatory bodies and norms (De Loo et al, 2011). In fact, regularized systems and legislations regarding the control systems often act as constraints to the full evolution of the management accountant profession thus promoting the more hybrid role of management accountants previously described (Karlsson et al, 2019; Lepisto and Ihantola, 2018). Professional legislation and norms do not support the required capabilities of management accountants which can be considered firms' cultural norms (Dolce et al, 2020; Karlsson et al, 2019). Therefore, managers that are forced by legislation to remain merely "bean counters" might not be able to develop the necessary skills and capabilities to fully support and foster firms' growth and long term survival in today's dynamic business world (Karlsson et al, 2019; Lepisto and Ihantola). Consequently, studies which focus on today's skills and competencies and the evolution of the management accountant role are extremely relevant and necessary (Dolce et al, 2020; Karlsson et al, 2019).

3. METHODOLOGY

Researchers deem qualitative approaches appropriate when delving into topics that have yet to be fully explored. Additionally, they can be useful in understanding complex phenomena that cannot be synthesized in quantitative data. Since our contribution explores the ever changing role of management accountants and seeks to deeply explore the research gap tied to their nature, our choice of a qualitative approach suits the research design. However, the above described nature of the study is not the only reason as to why a qualitative approach was chosen. In fact, when it comes to the identification and interpretation of processes that are embedded within organizations, several authors have suggested that qualitative research would be the most appropriate choice in terms of research design (Bluhm et al., 2011; Eisenhardt & Graebner, 2007; Graebner et al., 2012).

In terms of sampling, we used management accountants operating within the Italian context and active members of the ASSO Controller group and society. ASSO Controller is the prominent organization that operates within Italy, and they feature a vast sample of management accountants actively operating in companies. Our sampling was purposeful, as we specifically looked into a sample that could provide an in-depth understanding of the phenomenon, as opposed to a random sample that might have not had the answers we looked for.

A survey was then conducted and sent out to ASSO Controller members and 45 answers were collected. Drawing upon recent qualitative research (Bots et al., 2009; Talwar et al., 2021), we chose open-ended essays to inquire about the evolution of the management accountant role and how newly introduced BA tools imply challenges, obstacles and opportunities for the professional accountant. The survey was structured in two distinct, yet consecutive portions. The first half featured descriptive information, inquiring about the background of the respondents, along with their sector of operation. The second half featured the open-ended essays, with questions focused on the evolution of their role and how BA tools have impacted their profession. Below we present a few descriptive statistics of the sample. Figure 1 features the age of the respondents.

Age wise, the sample is rather diverse and representative of different age groups, with varying degrees of seniority and experience. This characteristic has allowed us to explore different perspectives and points of view concerning the topics of our investigation. Furthermore, Figure 2 illustrates the sectors to which the company of each respondent operates in.

Figure 1. Age of the sample

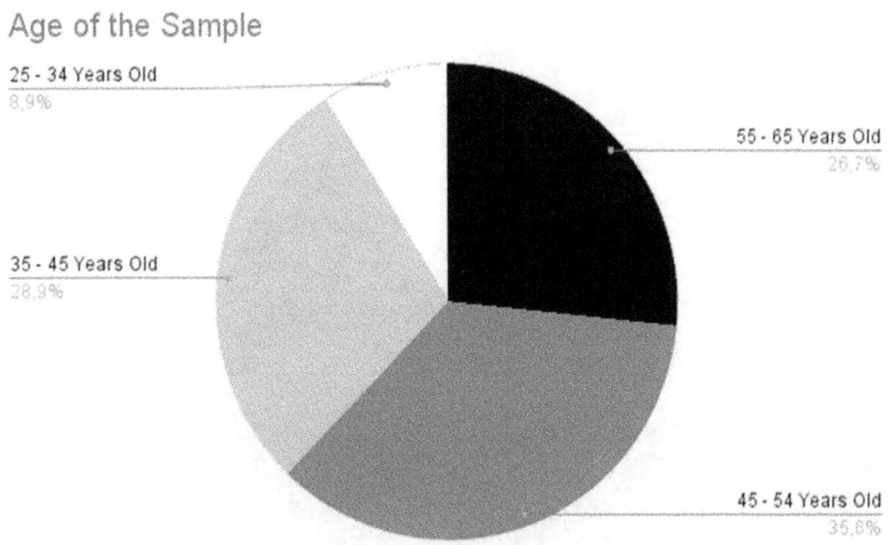

Figure 2. Sector to which the management accountants belong

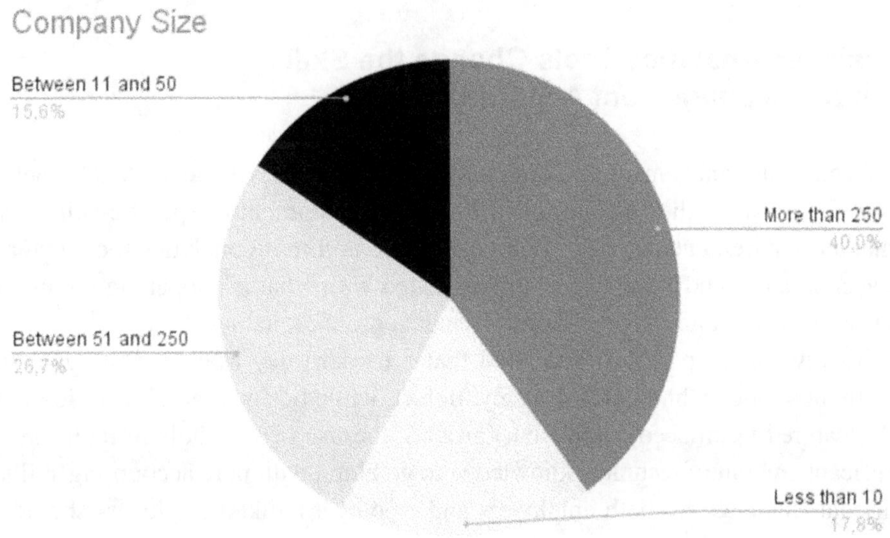

As illustrated above, the sample is rather varied in terms of sectors as well, featuring contributions from commerce, manufacturing, retail and services companies. Given how volatile the current competitive landscape is and the need for management accountants to tailor their work to the context they operate in, a varied sample was vital to investigate different competitive contexts and gather as much information as possible. Finally, Figure 3 summarizes the size of the companies featured in the investigation.

Once again, Figure 3 testifies the varied nature of our sample, as respondents are almost equally distributed between small, medium and large companies.

Figure 3. Sector to which the management accountants belong

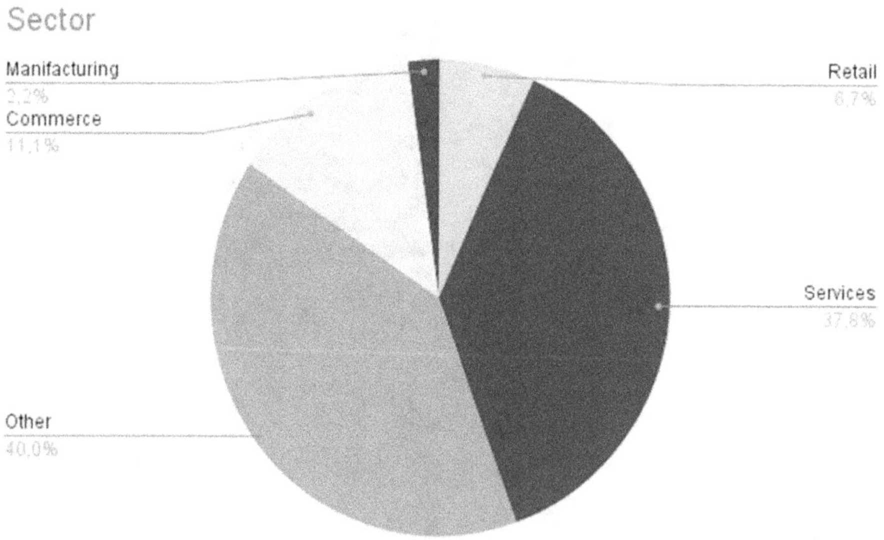

4. RESULTS

4.1 How Business Analytics Tools Change the Skill Requirements of Management Accountants

Our results indicate that management accountants are nowadays heavily dependent on new technology and analytics tools. As such, they need to prioritize the development of specific skill sets that match the current market requirements. In other words, as more and more analytics tools enter the market, management accountants need to stay constantly updated with what is happening around them and be willing to constantly adapt, and reinvent themselves on a professional level.

More specifically, our respondents indicated that a modern day Management accountant can no longer exist without strong technological literacy. In fact, while business administration literacy is still predominantly featured in an accountant's background, the use of BA tools in their daily operations require a significant amount of technical knowledge to go along with pure accounting skills. The above poses a significant challenge for both employers and employees alike. Employers should, in fact, not only consider the level of technical literacy when screening potential candidates, but also evaluate the possible implementation of specific training programs for employees, in order to keep them updated with the ever changing landscape of technology. Employees, on the other hand, are tasked with the difficult challenge of developing a varied set of skills, ranging from pure IT competencies to more specific business administration skills.

Table 1. Relevant quotes

Relevant Quotes
"The skills necessary to work in management control are complex and include knowledge of analytical and general accounting, the ability to plan and monitor the company's economic performance through accounting, budgeting and forecasting, to follow the drafting and analysis activities balance sheet and internal auditing, knowledge of forecasting/controlling/reporting techniques and strategic surveillance tools such as balanced scorecards (BSC)."
"Information technology literacy occupies an important part in the training of a management accountant, who must be able to use not only the main Office applications (especially Excel for financial reporting: Vlookups, pivot, etc.), but also specific programs for accounting and management software such as ERP and SAP systems."
"In addition to traditional business economics, planning and control technical skills, he must have strong relational skills. Must have the ability to narrate performance to a variety of business users. Additionally, the ability to use internal company data as well as external data (competitors, markets, etc.)"
"In addition to strong training in the economic field and experience gained preferably in auditing firms, he should have the following soft skills: lateral thinking, curiosity, skepticism, collaboration with all company functions and ability to relate at all levels."
"A management accountant must be smart, flexible and open to novelty, brilliant with rationality, attentive observer, only in the second instance computer skills at the level of system implementation, DB management, data visualization and accounting"
"It depends on the company reality in which it operates: mainly financial and accounting skills, but also data analysis and IT"

4.2 How Business Analytics Tools Change the Role Played by Management Accountants

Technological advancements have profoundly changed the way management accountants operate, thus enabling them to perform a multitude of tasks powered by BA tools. Said tools have played a pivotal role in th progressive shift of the management accountant position, which has moved from being historically considered a "bean counter", to a more recent iteration of "business partner". In other words, through the use of BA tools, management accountants are no longer limited to the mere tracking of costs, instead moving towards a more strategic iteration of the role. The above described cultural shift underpins a progressively diffuse trend that sees management accountants actively gathering and monitoring data through the use of BA tools, to then interpret them and provide strategic advice to their company.

4.3 How Business Analytics Tools Change the Tasks Required From Management Accountants

Our respondents have highlighted the cultural shift of management accountants, who have progressively moved from a pure accountancy based role, often referred to as "bean counter" in scientific research, to a more modern, strategic role of "business partners" and consultants. In this regard, BA tools play a pivotal role, as they enable management accountants to not only keep track of data, numbers and information, but to also draw conclusions of strategic value based on what the data seems to suggest. What has resulted from this cultural shift, is management accountants moving from a more centralized role amid their companies.

4.4 How Business Analytics Tools Will Shape the Future of Management Accountants as a Profession

When asked about how they see the future evolution of the management accounting profession and how BA tools are going to shape it, our findings highlight the importance of digital technologies and the need for a greater understanding of what is digital. Granted that management accountants will progressively move towards a more strategic role, almost blurring the lines between consultants and pure accountants, our respondents stress how this evolution will necessarily pass through digital transformation and BA tools. The general perception is that management accountants will need to keep a keen eye on the market trends and how digital advancements will shape the competitive landscape as time progresses. In turn, they will need to update their skillset and situational awareness to respond to the newest trends and the progressively more liquid nature of digital competition.

Table 2. Relevant quotes

Relevant Quotes
"The role of the Management Accountant is that of the company's metronome, the one who measures what the company does, in technical terms, in economic-financial terms, finally in process analysis. He is the one who suggests the company's operational strategies, and evaluates any strategic decision that the board intends to address.
"The management accountant or head of management control is the professional who is responsible for ensuring that the corporate accounting, reporting and financial management of the company function correctly and effectively, thus allowing the company to achieve the objectives (patrimonial, economic, management) set."
"The role of the management accountant is precisely that of controlling the pursuit of corporate objectives, verifying and calculating any deviations from the objectives and proposing suitable corrective actions aimed at obtaining the established objectives."
"The person or organization that designs, manages and improves the corporate management control system, with numerous major implications on decision-making processes and people's behavior. The implications sometimes have a strategic dimension, they concern choices that have an impact in the long term. In a hyper-competitive scenario, it stimulates and directs learning of human resources and company adaptation to tend towards sustainability."
"I think the role of the Controller is a strategic one. In fact, in addition to supporting the main Finance processes (for example: annual balance and quarterly closings, Budgeting and Forecasting process, definition of cost centers, definition of reporting guidelines, etc...) it has a strategic role for the whole company. In fact, the Controller should participate in the strategic meetings of the Management Team not only to present analyzes and reports, but to be able to participate with an active role in supporting the company's strategic decisions."
"I would define him as the person who has a global view of the business from a financial and accounting point of view (personally I am a financial controller with a past as an accounting manager) Budget, cash flow, monthly closures are his tools, his knowledge of accounting allow him to move in depth if necessary."
"The management accountant is a business partner in support of the entrepreneur / top management (I am a controller consultant and my company is the consultancy firm with which I collaborate: the answer is therefore out of phase in the current position); in my previous experience as a controller, the figure was already on staff at the general management."

Table 3. Relevant quotes

Relevant Quotes
"We have moved from the analysis of basic analytical accounting participation in the development of an integrated management control system"
"I have noticed a reduction of operational assignments and a higher focus on value-added activities. More proactive behavior to identify improvements in organizational processes"
"I went from very operational and widespread corporate tasks (accounting, financial statements, treasury, management control) to more specific tasks with responsibility for management control and information systems, up to coordinating a team of three people."
"Compared to an initial activity related to the analysis of results and short-term planning, I started collaborating in medium-long term and strategic planning."
"I have moved towards a more central role within the company, holder of the numbers but also the one who sees the future and who tries to guide the company in order to be proactive to the changes and needs of the client's company and to market trends."
"In my company, the controller coordinates and controls the work of the AF team, prepares the reports for the management, works on the automation of Erp systems, and creates procedures to streamline the activity. Cash Flow to ensure the right finances and ultimately ensures compliance with tax deadlines Interfaces with auditors, external consultants and banks. Monthly adjustment writings. Indication of active billing."
"I now must provide adequate information on company performance (actual/preventive), try to anticipate events, facilitate communication within the company and highlight any inadequacies at the organizational structure level (people/roles/processes) to be removed. Additionally, I take care of the construction of the ideal path for planning and control activities, verification of the training of the internal figures assigned to the various processes from a planning and control perspective, and verification of the presence of adequate tools for analysis. Finally, I support top management in achieving corporate objectives, through the control and monitoring of resources"

Table 4. Relevant quotes

Relevant Quotes
"The evolution is towards the increasingly automated management of accounting documents, also with the help of Artificial Intelligence for the preparation of specific studies and evaluations."
"He will be more involved in digitization processes by actively participating in the definition of new tools that will automate part of the tasks currently performed manually in Excel. Greater focus on analysis activities and less on data construction."
"Given the continuous change in market conditions that shift the model for using the contents we sell more and more towards the "Liquid/Digital", compared to the traditional Retail or GDO market, I expect that the strategic study activities of the new markets will change significantly and new channels compared to those we are currently applying for the study of the profitability obtained by current customers operating on the physical market."
"We will have to rely more on our relational skills as we will be more in demand as "readers" and "interpreters" of the data that comes from management control and accounting, the latter activities which will certainly go against greater and in some cases definitive automation."
"With the advent of Business Intelligence, the Controller can move from "information provider" to a more active role in corporate strategy as well. The evolution is towards the increasingly automated management of accounting documents, also with the help of Artificial Intelligence for the preparation of specific studies and evaluations."
"At the moment the ongoing evolution is connected with the rapid development of IT possibilities, which in some contexts can be a threat and which requires quick acculturation and planning ability to design the digitization of processes; the second point is the development of the role as a result of the changes that companies will have to plan to achieve sustainability: the controller can be a promoter of the assessment analysis (the current state), coordinator of the definition of changes, planner of economic results and of financial requirements, designer of non-financial information"
"BA tools will allow for greater technical knowledge, specifically in the ICT field."

5. DISCUSSION OF THE FINDINGS

When comparing the results of our empirical investigation to what has been already said in scientific literature, a few interesting conclusions can be drawn. First, our results strengthen the cultural shift of management accountants from "bean counters" to "business partners", at least partially due to the introduction of BA tools (Jönsson, 2009; Karlsson et al, 2019; Linsley and Linsley, 2014). The available literature depicts the role of management accountants as being more than just a scorekeeper and financial information reporter for their organization, as highlighted by Oesterreich and Teuteberg (2019). In fact, some literature refers to controllers as business partners who participate in management-oriented decisions and serve as internal consultants, as described by Nnorom and Olagbaju (2020) and Karlsson et al. (2019). In this regard, we see how the tools and instruments now available to management accountants have dramatically increased their potential and productivity (Chenhall and Moers, 2015), albeit at the expense of an increased need for constant learning and education to keep up with recent trends (Weber, 2011). Our findings stress the importance of data and information, and their related availability to management accountants. In this regard, BA tools allow for a much for effective, streamlined and enhanced access to critical information (Hyvönen et al, 2015; Karlsson et al, 2019), thus improving the productivity and efficiency of management accountants (Dolce et al, 2020; Karlsson et al, 2019; Lepisto and Ihantola, 2018).

Additionally, our research has substantiated the notion that BA and associated technologies have become increasingly significant for management accountants. Our survey participants frequently emphasized how the implementation of BA tools has transformed their daily tasks and routines, as evidenced by research conducted by Rikhardsson and Yigitbasioglu (2018). The use of BA tools has enabled management accountants to work more efficiently and with greater precision, as highlighted by Maisel and Cokins (2014). However, the aforementioned shift towards BA tools necessitates active participation from management accountants themselves (De Loo et al, 2011; Karlsson et al, 2019; Windeck et al, 2015). They must continually adapt and reinvent their skill sets (Dolce et al., 2020), adopt an open-minded approach, and remain receptive to learning about BA tools, as indicated by research conducted by Franke and Hiebl (2022) and Rikhardsson and Yigitbasioglu (2018). Our study shows how the competencies and skills typically associated with BA are deemed crucial to the role of management accountants, given their impact on an organization's long-term strategy and plan, as noted by Maisel and Cokins (2014). By analyzing data derived from BA tools, management accountants generate value for their employees, underscoring the importance of such tools to organizational management, as observed by Rikhardsson and Yigitbasioglu (2018). Consequently, management accountants must persistently enhance their competencies and skills to keep up with the constantly evolving BA technologies and tools, as highlighted by Rikhardsson and Yigitbasioglu (2018).

6. CONCLUSION, LIMITATIONS, AND FUTURE RESEARCH

The world as we know it has been significantly disrupted by information technology. The advancements in this field have enabled management accountants to gain access to an unprecedented amount of data, thanks to the use of business analytics and machine learning tools. As the profession continues to evolve and adapt to these disruptive changes, the role of management accountants has been reshaped by the tools and technologies available to them. To gain a deeper understanding of how business analytics tools have influenced the modern accounting profession and their potential impact on the future, we conducted empirical research by interviewing management accounting professionals. Using a semi-structured approach, we gathered qualitative data on how these tools have affected their professional careers, their expectations for the future, and to what extent they believe technology has increased their efficiency. Through our analysis of their contributions, we have drawn conclusions on the significant impact of business analytics tools on the accounting profession. We also explore the ways in which these tools will continue to shape the future of management accounting, as perceived by the professionals themselves.

The present study comes with a few caveats that need to be considered. From a methodological perspective, our sample lacks generalizability as it is focused on a specific country. While we attempted to gather as many responses as possible, future research could build upon our empirical findings and replicate the study in different contexts to determine whether or not the results are similar. Future research could, for instance, investigate cultural differences that might arise when interviewing management accountants belonging to different countries. Additionally, still on the topic of replicability, future research could determine whether or not significant differences exist when comparing small and large sized companies, and the expectations put on management accountants on their daily work life. A further limitation is connected to the methods used to analyze the findings. Qualitative research leaves data to be interpreted by authors, thus making their conclusions subjective and open to critique. While we addressed this limitation by making use of an iterative process of coding, triangulated with frequent comparisons with the theoretical framework discussed earlier in the work, the risk of subjectivity cannot be completely eliminated, thus making our conclusions open for discussion and debate.

Several future trajectories can be identified from this study. First, future studies could collect empirical data from different contexts, possibly through a cross-cultural approach aimed at highlighting differences between various geographical scenarios. Additionally, cross-sector analysis could potentially unveil differences between companies belonging to different competitive markets. From a methodological perspective, our qualitative approach could be complemented by a follow up, quantitative study focused, for instance, on topics such as acceptance of digital technologies, their moderating effect on overall performance and the impact of training in digital literacy.

REFERENCES

Ascani, I., Ciccola, R., & Chiucchi, M. S. (2021). A Structured Literature Review about the Role of Management Accountants in Sustainability Accounting and Reporting. In Sustainability, 13(4). MDPI AG. doi:10.3390u13042357

Baldvinsdottir, G., Burns, J., Nørreklit, H., & Scapens, R. W. (2009). The image of accountants: From bean counters to extreme accountants. *Accounting, Auditing & Accountability Journal*, *22*(6), 858–882. doi:10.1108/09513570910980445

Bell, E., Harley, B., & Bryman, A. (2022). *Business Research Methods* (6th ed.). Oxford University Press.

Bluhm, D. J., Harman, W., Lee, T. W., & Mitchell, T. R. (2010). Qualitative Research in Management: A Decade of Progress. In Journal of Management Studies, 48 (8), 1866–1891. Wiley. doi:10.1111/j.1467-6486.2010.00972.x

Bots, J. M., Groenland, E., & Swagerman, D. M. (2009). An empirical test of Birkett's competency model for management accountants: Survey evidence from Dutch practitioners. In Journal of Accounting Education, 27 (1). Elsevier BV. doi:10.1016/j.jaccedu.2009.06.001

Budding, T., de Jong, G., & Smit, M. (2022). New development: Bridging the gap—analysis of required competencies for management accountants in the public sector. In Public Money & Management, 42 (7), 565–568). Informa UK Limited. doi:10.1080/09540962.2022.2068862

Burns, J., & Baldvinsdottir, G. (2005). An institutional perspective of accountants' new roles—The interplay of contradictions and praxis. *European Accounting Review*, *14*(4), 725–757. doi:10.1080/0963818050019417 1

Byrne, S., & Pierce, B. (2007). Towards a more comprehensive understanding of the roles of management accountants. *European Accounting Review*, *16*(3), 469–498. doi:10.1080/09638180701507114

Chenhall, R. H., & Moers, F. (2015). The role of innovation in the evolution of management accounting and its integration into management control. *Accounting, Organizations and Society*, *47*, 1–13. doi:10.1016/j.aos.2015.10.002

Coad, A. (1996). Smart work and hard work: Explicating a learning orientation in strategic management accounting. *Management Accounting Research*, *7*(4), 387–408. doi:10.1006/mare.1996.0022

Dolce, V., Emanuel, F., Cisi, M., & Ghislieri, C. (2020). The soft skills of accounting graduates: Perceptions versus expectations. *Accounting Education*, *29*(1), 57–76. doi:10.1080/09639284.2019.1697937

Eisenhardt, K. M., & Graebner, M. E. (2007). Theory Building From Cases: Opportunities And Challenges. In Academy of Management Journal, 50(1). doi:10.5465/amj.2007.24160888

Endenich, C. (2014). Economic crisis as a driver of management accounting change: Comparative evidence from Germany and Spain. *Journal of Applied Accounting Research*, *15*(1), 123–149. doi:10.1108/JAAR-11-2012-0075

Franke, F., & Hiebl, M. R. W. (2022). Big data and decision quality: the role of management accountants' data analytics skills. In International Journal of Accounting & Information Management, 31(1), 93–127. Emerald. doi:10.1108/IJAIM-12-2021-0246

Giacosa, E., Alam, G. M., Culasso, F., & Crocco, E. (2023). Stress-inducing or performance-enhancing? Safety measure or cause of mistrust? The paradox of digital surveillance in the workplace. In Journal of Innovation & Knowledge, 8(2) 100357. Elsevier BV. doi:10.1016/j.jik.2023.100357

Giacosa, E., Culasso, F., & Crocco, E. (2022). Customer agility in the modern automotive sector: how lead management shapes agile digital companies. In *Technological Forecasting and Social Change* (Vol. 175, p. 121362). Elsevier BV. doi:10.1016/j.techfore.2021.121362

Goretzki, L., Lukka, K., & Messner, M. (2018). Controllers' use of informational tactics. *Accounting and Business Research*, *48*(6), 700–726. doi:10.1080/00014788.2017.1407627

Goretzki, L., Strauss, E., & Weber, J. (2013). An institutional perspective on the changes in management accountants' professional role. *Management Accounting Research*, *24*(1), 41–63. doi:10.1016/j.mar.2012.11.002

Graebner, M. E., Martin, J. A., & Roundy, P. T. (2012). Qualitative data: Cooking without a recipe. In Strategic Organization, 10(3). SAGE Publications. doi:10.1177/1476127012452821

Graham, A., Davey-Evans, S., & Toon, I. (2012). The developing role of the financial controller: Evidence from the UK. *Journal of Applied Accounting Research*, *13*(1), 71–88. doi:10.1108/09675421211231934

Halbouni, S. S., & Nour, M. A. (2013). An empirical investigation of the impact of globalisation and information technology on the role of the management accountant: Evidence from the United Arab Emirates. International Journal of Accounting. *Auditing and Performance Evaluation*, *9*(3), 286–306. doi:10.1504/IJAAPE.2013.055898

Hiller, K., Mahlendorf, M. D., & Weber, J. (2014). Management accountants' occupational prestige within the company: A social identity theory perspective. *European Accounting Review*, *23*(4), 671–691. doi:10.1080/09638180.2013.849204

Huff, P. L. (2014). The GoalProject: A Group Assignment to Encourage Creative Thinking, Leadership Abilities and Communication Skills. In Accounting Education, 23(6). Informa UK Limited. doi:10.1080/09639284.2014.974198

Hyvönen, T., Jarvinen, J., & Pellinen, J. (2015). Dynamics of creating a new role for business controllers. *Finnish Journal of Business Economics*, *64*(1), 21–39.

Jönsson, S. (2009). The study of controller agency. In Accounting, organizations and institutions: Essay in honour of Anthony Hopwood. doi:10.1093/acprof:oso/9780199546350.003.0011

Karlsson, B., Hersinger, A., & Kurkkio, M. (2019). Hybrid accountants in the age of the business partner: Exploring institutional drivers in a mining company. *Journal of Management Control*, *30*(2), 185–211. doi:10.100700187-019-00280-1

Lambert, C., & Sponem, S. (2012). Roles, authority and involvement of the management accounting function: A multiple case-study perspective. *European Accounting Review*, *21*(3), 565–589.

Lepistö, L., & Ihantola, E. M. (2018). Understanding the recruitment and selection processes of management accountants: An explorative study. *Qualitative Research in Accounting & Management*, *15*(1), 104–123. doi:10.1108/QRAM-11-2016-0080

Linsley, P., & Linsley, A. (2014). Cultural theory of risk and the notion of "management accountants as strategists". In *Management control and uncertainty* (pp. 224–238). Palgrave Macmillan. doi:10.1057/9781137392121_15

Maisel, L., & Cokins, G. (2013). *Predictive business analytics: Forward looking capabilities to improve business performance*. John Wiley & Sons.

Nnorom, S. U., & Olagbaju, O. O. (2020). Principals' quality management skills as determinants of goal attainment in secondary schools in Ahiazu Mbaise local government area, Imo state. *International Journal on Integrated Education*, *3*(10), 87–91. doi:10.31149/ijie.v3i10.692

Oesterreich, T. D., & Teuteberg, F. (2019). The role of business analytics in the controllers and management accountants' competence profiles: An exploratory study on individual-level data. *Journal of Accounting & Organizational Change*.

Paulsson, G. (2012). The Role of Management Accountants in New Public Management. In Financial Accountability & Management, 28 (4), 378–394. Wiley. doi:10.1111/j.1468-0408.2012.00552.x

Rikhardsson, P., & Yigitbasioglu, O. (2018). Business intelligence & analytics in management accounting research: Status and future focus. *International Journal of Accounting Information Systems*, *29*, 37–58. doi:10.1016/j.accinf.2018.03.001

ten Rouwelaar, H., Schaepkens, F., & Widener, S. K. (2020). Skills, Influence, and Effectiveness of Management Accountants. In Journal of Management Accounting Research, 33(2) 211–235. American Accounting Association. doi:10.2308/jmar-18-048

Tuomela, T. S. (2005). The interplay of different levers of control: A case study of introducing a new performance measurement system. *Management Accounting Research*, *16*(3), 293–320. doi:10.1016/j.mar.2005.06.003

Weber, J. (2011). The development of controller tasks: Explaining the nature of controllership and its changes. *Journal of Management Control*, *22*(1), 25–46. doi:10.100700187-011-0123-x

Windeck, D., Weber, J., & Strauss, E. (2015). Enrolling managers to accept the business partner: The role of boundary objects. *The Journal of Management and Governance*, *19*(3), 617–653. doi:10.100710997-013-9277-2

Yazdifar, H., & Tsamenyi, M. (2005). Management accounting change and the changing roles of management accountants: A comparative analysis between dependent and independent organizations. *Journal of Accounting & Organizational Change*, *1*(2), 180–198. doi:10.1108/18325910510635353

ADDITIONAL READING

Bhimani, A., & Willcocks, L. (2014). Digitisation, 'Big Data' and the transformation of accounting information. In Accounting and Business Research, 44(4) 469–490) Informa UK Limited. doi:10.1080/00014788.2014.910051

Heinzelmann, R. (2018). Occupational identities of management accountants: the role of the IT system. In Journal of Applied Accounting Research, 19(4), 465–482. Emerald. doi:10.1108/JAAR-05-2017-0059

Nespeca, A., & Chiucchi, M. S. (2018). The Impact of Business Intelligence Systems on Management Accounting Systems: The Consultant's Perspective. In Lecture Notes in Information Systems and Organisation (pp. 283–297). Springer International Publishing. doi:10.1007/978-3-319-62636-9_1

Nielsen, S. (2018). Reflections on the applicability of business analytics for management accounting – and future perspectives for the accountant. In Journal of Accounting & Organizational Change, 14(2), 167–187. Emerald. doi:10.1108/JAOC-11-2014-0056

Nielsen, S. (2022). Business analytics: an example of integration of TD-ABC and the balanced scorecard. In *International Journal of Productivity and Performance Management*. Emerald. doi:10.1108/IJPPM-05-2020-0244

Oesterreich, T. D., & Teuteberg, F. (2019). The role of business analytics in the controllers and management accountants' competence profiles. In Journal of Accounting & Organizational Change, 15(2). doi:10.1108/JAOC-10-2018-0097

Pervan, I., & Dropulić, I. (2019). The impact of integrated information systems on management accounting. In Management, 24(1). doi:10.30924/mjcmi.24.1.2

Seifian, A., Bahrami, M., Shokouhyar, S., & Shokoohyar, S. (2023). Data-based drivers of big data analytics utilization: moderating role of IT proactive climate. In *Benchmarking: An International Journal*. Emerald., doi:10.1108/BIJ-11-2021-0670

Uyar, M. (2021). The Role of Business Analytics in Transforming Management Accounting Information into Cost Performance. In Ege Akademik Bakis (Ege Academic Review) (pp. 373–389). Ege Akademik Bakis (Ege Academic Review). doi:10.21121/eab.1015665

KEY TERMS AND DEFINITIONS

Accounting: Accounting involves the systematic measurement, processing, and dissemination of financial and other pertinent data concerning businesses and corporations.

Business Analytics: Business analytics refers to the practice of utilizing statistical techniques and technological tools to examine past data with the objective of obtaining fresh insights and enhancing the effectiveness of strategic decision-making within a company.

Business Strategy: A business strategy encompasses all the decisions and actions taken by a company to accomplish its overarching goals. Having a comprehensive understanding of business strategy and executing it effectively can aid businesses in establishing themselves as market leaders within their industry. Essentially, a business strategy serves as the foundation of any enterprise, and any deficiencies in its execution can result in the abandonment of business objectives.

Digital Technology: Digital technology encompasses electronic devices, software systems, and resources that facilitate the creation, storage, and management of data. One significant component of digital technology is information technology (IT), which involves the use of computers for processing information and data. Nowadays, the majority of businesses employ digital technology to streamline operations, optimize processes, and enhance the overall customer experience.

Digital Transformation: Digital transformation involves the incorporation of digital technology across all aspects of a business, leading to a fundamental shift in how the organization operates and delivers value to its customers. Additionally, it represents a cultural shift that necessitates companies to regularly challenge established practices, experiment, and become accustomed to setbacks.

Management Accounting: The act of providing a company with financial information and guidance for the purpose of improving and expanding its operations.

Qualitative Research: Qualitative research entails the gathering and examination of non-numeric information, such as text, video, or audio, to comprehend concepts, opinions, or experiences. It can serve the purpose of acquiring comprehensive insights into a problem or developing fresh research ideas. In contrast to quantitative research, which involves the collection and analysis of numerical data for statistical analysis, qualitative research deals with non-numerical information.

Chapter 3
A Discussion on Non-Convex Optimization Problems Arising in Supply Chain Design and Finance

Arka Das
Micron Technology, Inc., India

ABSTRACT

Non-convex optimization problems belong to a class of classical nonlinear optimization problems, which are often difficult to solve. An optimization problem becomes non-convex due to the presence of non-convex functions in the objective function or constraints. A function is a convex function if its Hessian matrix is positive and semi-definite for all values; otherwise, it is a non-convex function. A Hessian matrix is called positive semi-definite when the eigenvalues of the matrix are non-negative. A non-convex function can be either a concave function or a function that is neither a concave nor a convex function. A concave function is always negative semi-definite, indicating that the eigenvalues of the matrix are non-positive. This chapter starts with a short introduction to non-convex problems, followed by a discussion on different non-convex problems arising in supply chain and finance. Thereafter, the authors discuss different algorithms used for solving non-convex problems. Finally, the chapter conclude with the limitations of different algorithms.

INTRODUCTION

Non-convex optimization problems belong to a class of classical nonlinear optimization problems, which are often difficult to solve. Non-convex problems have been of interest for the last eighty years. An optimization problem becomes non-convex due to the presence of non-convex functions in the objective function or constraints. A non-convex function can be either a concave function or a function that is neither concave nor convex. Let's consider a non-convex optimization problem of the following kind:

DOI: 10.4018/978-1-6684-8386-2.ch003

$$\min_x f\left(x\right)+\phi\left(x\right) \quad (1.1)$$

Subject to $g_i(x)\leq 0, \forall i=1,2,\ldots,I$ (1.2)

$$x_k^l \leq x_k \leq x_k^u \forall k = 1,\ldots,n\,. \quad (1.3)$$

where $g_i(x)$ and $f(x)$ are convex functions, $\phi(x)$ is either a non-convex function. Constraints (1.3) set the bounds for the variable xk which may be continuous or discrete. Next, we will briefly discuss the properties of non-convex functions.

NON-CONVEX FUNCTION

A function is non-convex when the function does not act as a convex function. A function is a convex function if and only if its Hessian matrix is positive semi-definite for all values; otherwise, it is a non-convex function. A hessian matrix is called positive semi-definite if and only if all eigenvalues of the matrix are non-negative. For example, consider a function of n variables $f(x)$ defined on a convex set D. $f(x)$ is said to be a convex function when the following conditions hold.

- For any two points x^1 and x^2 and $0 \leq \lambda \leq 1, f\left[x^1\lambda + x^2\left(1-\lambda\right)\right] \leq f\left(x^1\right)\lambda + f\left(x^2\right)\left(1-\lambda\right)$.
- The hessian matrix of $f(x)$ is positive semi-definite for all values of $x_1,\ldots,x_n$.

Figure 1a shows an example of convex functions. A non-convex function can be either a concave function or a function that is neither a concave nor a convex function. A function is a concave function if its hessian matrix is negative semi-definite, which happens only when all eigenvalues of the matrix are non-positive. For example, consider a concave function of n variables ϕ(x) defined on a convex set D. ϕ(x) is said to be concave when the following conditions hold.

- Foranytwopointsx*1*andx*2*and0≤λ≤1, $0 \leq \lambda \leq 1, f\left[x^1\lambda + x^2\left(1-\lambda\right)\right] \geq f\left(x^1\right)\lambda + f\left(x^2\right)\left(1-\lambda\right)$.
- The hessian matrix of $f(x)$ is negative semi-definite for all values of $x_1,\ldots,x_n$.

An example of a non-convex function, which is neither concave nor convex, includes an inverse S-shaped function. An inverse S-shaped function is concave in nature initially up to a certain point above which the function changes its shape to convex. The point is often referred as a deflection point or economic point. In Figure 1.1b, we show an inverse S-shaped function. Historically, non-convex optimization problems have been of interest due to several real-world applications. Next, we briefly describe some of the non-convex application problems.

Figure 1. Different non-linear functions

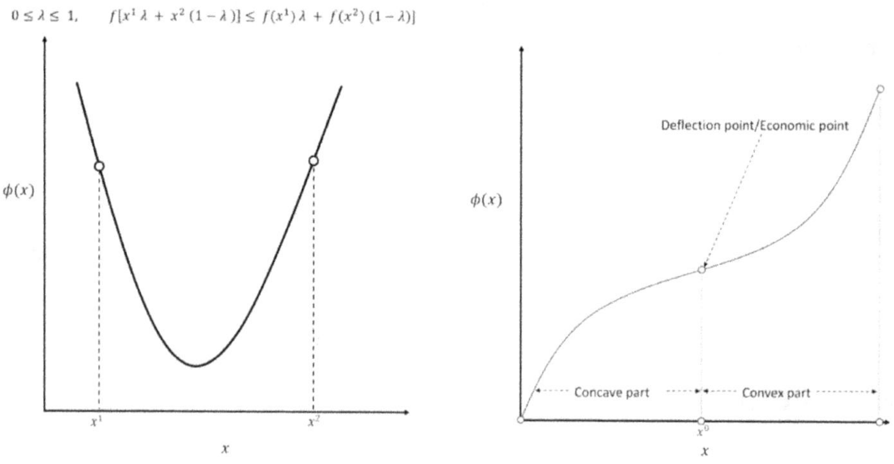

(a) Convex function, *f(x)* (b) Inverse S-shaped function, *ϕ(x)*

NON-CONVEX APPLICATION PROBLEMS

Non-convexity appears in several application problems including facility locations problems (Soland 1974, Ni et al. 2021), hub locations O'Kelly and Bryan (1998), location-inventory network design problem (Li et al. 2021, Farahani et al. 2015, Shen and Qi 2007, Jeet et al. 2009), production transportation problems (Holmberg and Tuy 1999, Kuno and Utsunomiya 2000, Saif 2016), concave minimum cost network flow problems (Guisewite and Pardalos 1990, Fontes and Gonçalves 2007), etc. In Figure 2, we classify non- convex problems into various categories depending on application areas, and then we briefly describe each category.

Figure 2. Application of non-convex problems

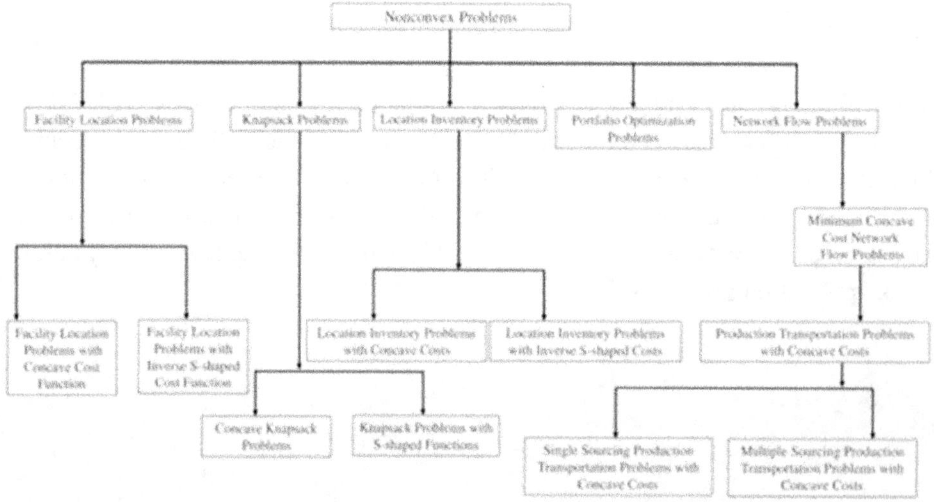

Facility Location Problems

The facility location problem (FLP) is a classic network design problem, which involves finding the locations of facilities and assigning customers to them at a minimum total cost. The total cost consists of fixed facility opening costs, facility operating costs, and transportation costs between the facilities and their assigned customers. To the best of our knowledge, Feldman et al. (1966) was the first to consider facility fixed cost and facility operating cost to be a concave function due to economies of scale. Later Soland (1974) and Hajiaghayi et al. (2003) assumed that variable cost acts as a concave function. To the best of our knowledge, Lu et al. (2014) was the first to assert that the production cost function of the facility acts as an inverted S-shaped function. Lu et al. (2014) concluded that in a large production spectrum, the production cost function initially acts as a concave function up to a certain point, beyond which it turns convex. The point is often referred as a deflection or economic point. Initially, the production cost acts as concave in nature due to economies of scale, but after the economic point, the system begins over-utilizing resources, leading to convex behavior due to dis-economies of scale. Lu et al. (2014) was the first to model the facility location problem with an inverse S-shaped function. Here, we briefly discuss facility location problem with economies and dis-economies of scale.

To formally define a facility location problem, let U be a set of m potential locations of facilities, and V denotes a set of n customer locations. F_j is the fixed cost for opening facility $j \in U$ and $\phi_j(z_j)$ is an inverse S-shaped production cost function of l_j production units at facility $j \in U$. Let, K_j be the production capacity of facility $j \in U$ and each customer $i \in V$ faces a demand d_i. c_{ij} denotes the transportation cost between customer $i \in V$ and facility $j \in U$. l_j^0 is the deflection point. Lets, x_{ij} be the quantity transported from facility $j \in U$ to customer $i \in V$. If we define y_{j0} as the binary variable indicating the facility $j \in U$ produces at or under economic point and y_{j1} as the binary variable indicating the facility produces over economic point, then a facility location problem with economies and dis-economies of scale can be mathematically stated as follows:

$$min_{\lambda,x,y,z} \sum_{j \in U} F_j \left(y_{j0} + y_{j1}\right) + \sum_{i \in V} \sum_{j \in U} c_{ij} x_{ij} + \sum_{j \in U} \phi_j \left(l_j\right) \tag{1.4}$$

$$\text{Subject to } \sum_{j \in U} x_{ij} \geq d_i, \forall i \in V \tag{1.5}$$

$$y_{j0} + y_{j1} \leq 1, \forall j \in U \tag{1.6}$$

$$l_j^0 y_{j1} \leq l_j \leq K_j y_{j1} + l_j^0, \forall j \in U \tag{1.7}$$

$$l_j \geq \sum_{i \in V} x_{ij}, \forall j \in U \tag{1.8}$$

$$y_{j0}, y_{j1} \in \{0,1\}, \forall j \in U \tag{1.9}$$

$$x_{ij} \geq 0, \forall j \in U \tag{1.10}$$

Constraints (1.5) and (1.7) are demand and capacity constraints, respectively. Constraints (1.6) indicate that any facility can either be operating below economic point l_j^0 or above it. $\phi_j(l_j)$ is a continuous inverse S-shaped function but not necessarily differentiable.

Lu et al. (2014) decomposed the non-convex capacitated facility location problem into separate concave and convex subproblems using Lagrangian relaxation. The subproblems were solved using heuristics before solving using different column generation techniques to arrive at the best feasible solution. The method was able to perform satisfactorily, terminating with some gaps for most of the data instances.

Knapsack Problems

The integer/binary knapsack problem involves finding the items to be selected from a given collection of items with certain weights and values by maximizing the total value after maintaining a pre-specified weight limit. The non-convex knapsack problem appears when the value function becomes non-convex. Broadly, non-convex knapsack problems can be classified into: (i) Concave knapsack problems; and (ii) Knapsack problems with S-shaped functions. The concave knapsack problem arises when the value function acts as a concave function. Concave knapsack problems appear in several application areas including communication satellite selection (Witzgall 1975), weighted maximum b-clique problems (Park et al. 1996, Dijkhuizen and Faigle 1993, Pisinger 2007, Caprara et al. 1999), pluviometer selection in hydrological studies (Gallo et al. 1980, Caprara et al. 1999), compiler design (Johnson et al. 1993, Pisinger 2007). Recently, Wang (2019) reported an exact method that combines the *contour cut* (Li et al. 2006) with a special cut to solve a multidimensional concave separable integer knapsack problem (CSINK), which is a concave knapsack problem with multiple knapsack constraints. The problem is mathematically stated as follows:

$$min_x \phi(x) = \sum_{i=1}^{n} \phi_i(x_i) \tag{1.11}$$

Subject to: $Ax \leq b$ (1.12)

$$x \in X = \{x \in \mathbb{Z}^n \mid l_i \leq x_i \leq u_i\} \tag{1.13}$$

Even though Wang (2019) was able to solve the problem exactly across several dimensions, the reported average CPU time was commensurately very high across higher dimensions of the test data-sets. Recently, Sinha et al. (2023) reported an inner-approximation-based exact general algorithm for solving mixed- integer concave minimization problems. They showed that the reported algorithm was able to outperform against Wang (2019)'s method by an order of magnitude. Research into knapsack problems with S-shaped functions has been very limited. Ag˘ralı and Geunes (2009) assumed the return from investment in an activity as an S-curve and formulated a knapsack problem with S-curve return functions. They reported a pseudo-polynomial time algorithm for the integer variable version of the problem and developed efficient solution methods for special cases of the problem.

Location Inventory Problems

A location inventory problem entails integrating the design decisions of a strategic supply chain along with tactical and operational inventory management decisions so as to minimize the total cost, which includes distribution costs in the supply chain, location costs, and inventory costs at the distribution centers. Location inventory models can be classified into: (i) Location Inventory Problems with Concave Costs; and (ii) Location Inventory Problems with Inverse S-shaped Costs. Concave costs typically arise in Lo- cation Inventory models (Daskin et al. 2002, Shen et al. 2003, Shu et al. 2005) due to pooling, which is the effect of inventory-cost savings achieved by grouping retailers. Recently, Li et al. (2021) studied a warehouse–retailer network design problem by assuming the warehouse operating cost to be an inverse S-shaped function of the volume of demand assigned to the warehouse. After formulating this problem as a set-covering model, they solved its linear relaxation using a column generation based approach. The pricing problem of the column generation process was solved efficiently by a branch-and-bound method using its structural properties.

Portfolio Optimization Problems

Historically, portfolio optimization problems have been quite popular among investors who want to sell or purchase a property. This problem involves the selection of different assets to invest so as to maximize the total return by minimizing the overall risk. The modern portfolio theory proposed by Markovitz (1952) made a breakthrough in solving the problem of portfolio selection for investors so as to form a portfolio by achieving the highest expected return at an expected level of risk tolerance. The model is also called mean-variance (MV) model, which investigates an optimal trade-off between risk and return leading to a convex optimization problem. Next, we briefly discuss the MV portfolio optimization model. Let's assume that n assets are available and the expected return of asset i is denoted by μ_i. ρ_{ij} is the covariance of returns for asset i and asset j when $i,j \in 1,2,\ldots,n$. If we assume σ to be the required level of return for the portfolio, the problem can be mathematically stated as follows:

$$\min_{x} \sum_{i=1}^{n}\sum_{j=1}^{n} \rho_{ij} x_i x_j \tag{1.14}$$

$$\text{Subject to } \sum_{i=1}^{n} \mu_i x_i = \sigma \tag{1.15}$$

$$\sum_{i=1}^{n} x_i = 1 \tag{1.16}$$

$$x_i \geq 0, \forall i=1,\ldots,n \tag{1.17}$$

This model is the convex quadratic programming model, which can be solved by any standard con- vex solving algorithm. However, this model has many drawbacks, which attracted many researchers to study many variants of the model to make it more practical. Cesarone and Tardella (2009) proposed a

Limited Asset Markowitz (LAM) model to capture real-world restrictions on actual investments with the introduction of quantity and cardinality constraints. However, the cardinality constraint significantly makes the problem more difficult to solve due to the introduction of binary decision variables, leading to the formulation of non-convex problem. Kim et al. (2019) proposed a three-step heuristic algorithm for solving the non-convex portfolio optimization problem. Researchers have come up with different kinds of non-convex portfolio optimization problems to make the model more realistic. Anagnostopoulos and Mamanis (2011) formulated portfolio optimization problem as a bi-objective optimization problem by ensuring that the rewards should be maximized and the risk should be minimized. Khan et al. (2022) reported an optimization-based tax-aware portfolio problem, which aims to maximize the profit at a minimal risk and tax liabilities by fulfilling other constraints. They proposed a non-deterministic meta-heuristic algorithm for solving the non-convex tax-aware portfolio optimization problem. The conventional portfolio problems are asset-based, whereas the tax-aware optimization problem depends on tax lots.

Network Flow Problems

In combinatorial optimization, one of the important classes of problems in optimization is the network flow problem, which belongs to a class of optimization problems where the input is a flow network (a graph with its edges), and the objective is to construct a flow such that the incoming flow is equal to outgoing flow at all vertices except for certain designated terminals. One of the categories of network flow problems is the minimum concave cost network (MCNF) flow problem (Guisewite and Pardalos 1990, 1993, Tuy et al. 1993), in which flow cost within each edge is assumed to be concave in nature. The production transportation problem (Kuno and Utsunomiya 2000, Saif 2016) can be viewed as a real-life application of MCNF. The production transportation problem (PTP) involves finding the production quantity at each source and the transportation quantities from the supply sources to demand centers so as to meet the demands of the demand centers at the minimum total cost. The total cost consists of production cost at the source or production centers and the transportation cost from production centers to demand centers or destinations. Researchers have assumed the production cost to be concave (Kuno and Utsunomiya 2000, Saif 2016) in nature due to economies of scale leading to a concave minimization problem, which is very difficult to solve. The production transportation problem (PTP) can be further sub-divided into two categories: PTP with single sourcing (Saif 2016) and PTP with multiple sourcing (Kuno and Utsunomiya 2000). In the case of PTP with single sourcing, demand centers can accept supply from a single source, whereas for PTP with multiple sourcing, demand centers can fulfill their demand from multiple sources. Due to the complexity of the problems, the researchers have not been able to solve these problems very efficiently. Next, The mathematical model for PTP with multiple sourcing is stated below.

Let's consider $G=(M,N,E)$ to be a bipartite graph, where M and N denote the sets of m sources and n destinations, respectively, and E denotes the set of transportation arcs $(m \times n)$ between the sources and the destinations. The non-negative transportation cost per unit product across arc $(i,j) \in E$ is denoted by c_{ij}. We assume $\phi_i(z_i)$ to be the production cost of zi units at source $i \in M$. Further, we define y_{ij} as the quantity transported on the arc $(i,j) \in E$, and z_i as the production quantity at source i. If we define d_j and k_i as the demand at destination $j \in N$ and the production capacity at source $i \in M$, respectively, then the production transportation problem can be mathematically formulated as below:

$$\min_{y,z} \sum_{(i,i)\in E} c_{ij} y_{ij} + \sum_{i\in M} \phi_i\left(z_i\right) \tag{1.18}$$

Subject to $\sum_{j\in N} y_{ij} \le z_i, \forall i \in M$ (1.19)

$z_i \le k_i, \forall i \in M$ (1.20)

$$\sum_{i\in M} y_{ij} \ge d_j \forall j \in N \tag{1.21}$$

$y_{ij} \ge 0, \forall (i,j) \in E$ (1.22)

$z_i \ge 0, \forall i \in M$ (1.23)

Constraint (1.19) is a supply capacity constraint. Constraints (1.19)- (1.20) essentially indicate that a source $i \in M$ can supply up to its maximum production capacity k_i. Constraint (1.21) is demand constraint for the demand center $j \in N$. The single-sourcing variant of the problem requires any destination $j \in N$ to receive its shipment from only one supply source $i \in M$. This can be modeled by putting a binary restriction on the z variables in the model. The model for single sourcing is shown below:

$$\min_{y,z} \sum_{(i,j)\in E} c_{ij} y_{ij} d_j + \sum_{i\in M} \phi_i\left(z_i\right) \tag{1.24}$$

Subject to $\sum_{j\in N} y_{ij} d_j \le z_i, \forall i \in M$ (1.25)

$z_i \le k_i, \forall i \in M$ (1.26)

$$\sum_{i\in M} y_{ij} \ge 1 \forall j \in N \tag{1.27}$$

$y_{ij} \in \{0,1\}, \forall (i,j) \in E$ (1.28)

$z_i \ge 0, \forall i \in M$ (1.29)

Next, we briefly describe some of the important algorithms and heuristics reported to solve the non-convex problems.

ALGORITHMS FOR SOLVING NON-CONVEX PROBLEMS

The non-convex problems are very difficult to solve due to the presence of multiple local optima. A local optimum is a solution that is optimal within a neighboring set of candidate solutions as shown in Figure 3. A global optimum is an optimal solution among all feasible solutions. Conventional convex solving algorithms often fail to solve non-convex problems globally as these algorithms converge to local optima. The exact algorithms for solving convex minimization problems tend to converge to local optima while solving the non-convex problems. Hence, they are not suitable for solving non-convex problems. Re- searchers have come up with several algorithms and heuristics which are suited to solve different classes of non-convex problems. These algorithms can be broadly classified into the following categories: (i) Branch and bound techniques; (ii) Branch and reduce techniques; (iii) Spatial Branch and bound techniques; (iv) Cutting plane techniques; (v) Second-order conic programming; and (vi) Lagrangian approaches. They are briefly described below.

Spatial Branch and Bound Algorithm

The spatial branch and bound (SBB) algorithm consists of a process to partition the entire feasible region along the coordinate direction of the variables. In each iteration, tightening of bounds is carried out by scrapping a region whenever the lower bound for a region exceeds the upper bound, or the problem becomes infeasible. The method uses a feasible solution to find the upper bound. It solves the convex relaxation of the main problem to find the lower bound. The algorithm was first reported by McCormick (1976). Later several researchers (Smith & Pantelides 1997, Quesada & Grossmann 1995, Lee & Grossmann 2001) used this algorithm to solve various application problems. Later Belotti et al. (2009) studied two crucial parts of SBB, such as branching strategies and bound tightening. The drawback of SBB is its limited applicability in solving non-convex problems and its inefficiency in solving high dimensional problems.

Branch and Bound Algorithm

The Branch and bound (B&B) algorithm is often used to solve a general class of concave minimization problems. The method approximates the concave function using convex envelopes through an iterative procedure. The algorithm involves creating refined compact partitions in each iteration through branching and solving the subproblems by minimizing the convex envelopes within each partition. For the SBB algorithm, it is important to select a variable to successively partition the feasible region along with the direction of the selected variable whereas B&B algorithm does not require selection of any variable to make partitions. The B&B algorithm converges to global optima in a finite number of iterations. Since the method involves refining the partitions in each iteration through branching, the number of subproblems grows rapidly after certain iterations. This causes B&B to be less efficient while solving the high dimensional problems. Several researchers reported several varieties of B&B techniques by changing branching strategies and partitioning techniques. To the best of our knowledge, Falk and Soland (1969) was the first to report a branch and bound algorithm for minimizing separable non-convex function over convex sets, and this algorithm was modified by Soland (1971) for minimizing separable non-convex function over the closed set. Later Shectman and Sahinidis (1998) reported another version of branch and bound algorithm using domain reduction techniques for minimizing separable concave programs.

Horst (1976) proposed a branch and bound algorithm for globally minimizing continuous the non-convex function by carrying out refinements through general compact partitions. Benson (1985) modified the B&B algorithm reported by Horst (1976) such that the linear subproblems solved in each iteration can have the same feasible space, but its applicability is limited to solve non-separable concave function over a polyhedron. Falk and Hoff- man (1986), Thakur (1991), Tuy (1992), Bretthauer et al. (1994), Androulakis et al. (1995),Shectman and Sahinidis (1998) and Locatelli and Thoai (2000) reported several varieties of branch and bound algorithms for solving concave problems exactly. Benson and Erenguc (1990) and Horst and Thoai (1998) established different versions of the branch and bound algorithm for solving the integer concave minimization problem. Though many authors reported several improvements over B&B algorithm for solving non-convex problems efficiently, the algorithm doesn't scale up well while solving the high dimensional data-sets.

Figure 3. An illustration of local optima and global optimum in non-convex function, $\phi(x)$

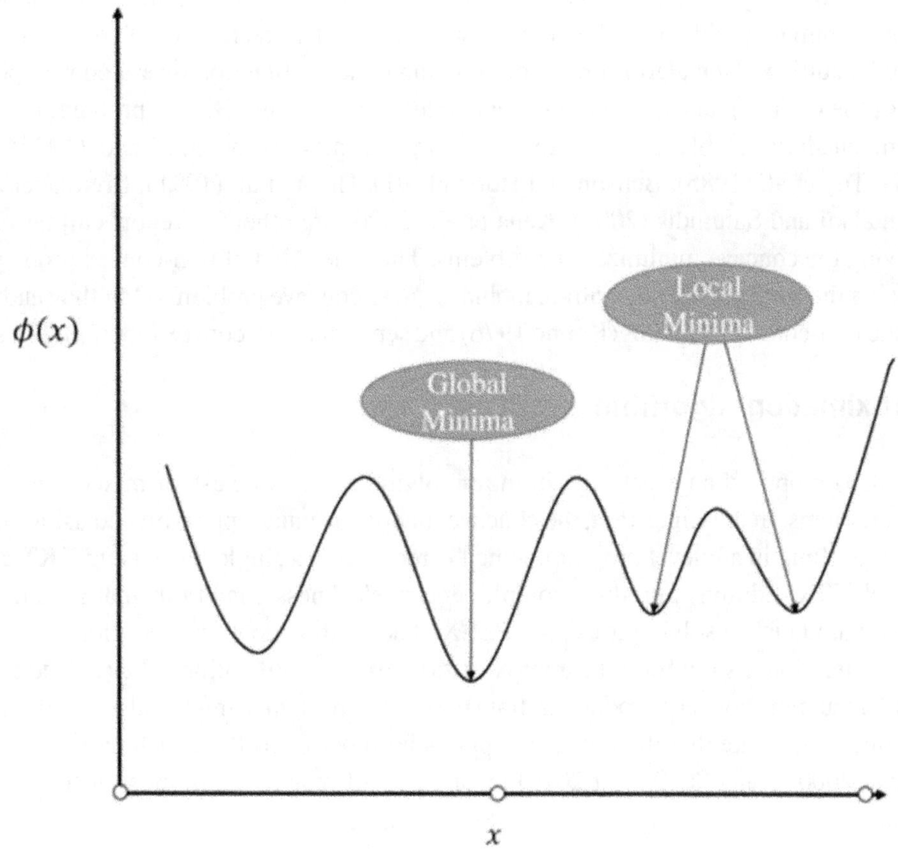

Branch and Reduce Algorithm

A breakthrough in the development of B&B for solving non-convex problems was the branch and reduce (B&R) technique reported by Ryoo and Sahinidis (1995) and Ryoo and Sahinidis (1996). Attempts were made to reduce the domain further than branching. The following two operations were carried out consecutively to achieve the goal; (i) Reduction of the domain of any variable without losing the feasible solution before solving subproblems; and (ii) To check the possibility of further domain reduction without losing an optimal solution using the sensitivity information after solving the subproblems. These operations result in a drastic reduction in the problem size. Tawarmalani and Sahinidis (2004) and Belotti et al. (2009) were others to add some further refinements.

Cutting Plane Algorithm

This approach is very similar to the B&R approach, except for the fact that this algorithm explicitly adds cuts to find tighter polyhedrons in each iteration, thereby reducing the CPU solve time. There have been several investigations on this approach to find a computationally efficient algorithm. To the best of our best knowledge, Tuy (1964) was the first person to report a cutting plane algorithm for solving non-convex programming problems with linear constraints, which attracted lots of attention. Later Taha (1973) reported a cutting plane algorithm for minimizing concave function over a convex polyhedron. Applications of the cutting plane algorithm to separable concave minimization problem include, fixed charge problem, quadratic problem, and the mixed 0-1 mixed-integer problem. Cabot (1974), Gallo and Ülkücü (1977), Tuy et al. (1985), Benson and Horst (1991), Horst et al. (1991), Bretthauer and Cabot (1994),Tawarmalani and Sahinidis (2005), Keha et al. (2006) are others to report cutting plane algorithms for solving the concave minimization problems. The other kind of non-convex problems, which were solved using the cutting plane algorithm, includes quasi-concave problems (Majthay and Whinston 1974), quadratic non-convex problems (Konno 1976) and separable non-convex function (Benson 1990).

Inner-Approximation Algorithm

Sinha et al. (2023) proposed an exact algorithm for solving a general class of mixed-integer concave minimization problems. In this algorithm, the concave function is inner-approximated using an auxiliary linear program resulting in a bilevel program, which is reduced to a single level using KKT conditions. How- ever, the KKT conditions introduce complimentary slackness conditions that are linearized using the BigM method before solving it using CPLEX. The method converges to global optima over a finite number of iterations as it refines the approximation over every iteration. They solved the concave knapsack problem and the concave production transportation problem using the algorithm. The computational experiments indicate that the proposed approach outperforms the benchmark methods (Kuno and Utsunomiya 2000, Wang 2019, Saif 2016) by an order of magnitude in most of the test cases for both problems.

Second Order Conic Programming

Second order conic programming (SOCP) is a popular technique to be used for solving convex minimization problems. Historically several researchers used the SOCP technique (Kian and Kargar 2016, Wu and Zhang 2014, Dhyani Bhatt et al. 2021) to solve the convex minimization problem efficiently. The use of the SOCP method for solving non-convex optimization problems has been limited. Atamtürk et al. (2012) reformulated the concave joint facility location and inventory management problems with stochastic retailer demand as conic quadratic mixed-integer programs and solved directly using standard software CPLEX. Valid inequalities, extended polymatriod cuts, and cover cuts were used to improve the computational efficiency of the SOCP approach. Later Elhedhli et al. (2018) modeled a concave cost system design problem as a network of M/M/1 queues. They reformulated the problem using second-order conic programming after decomposing the problem using Lagrangian relaxation before solving it using CPLEX.

Lagrangian Relaxation Approach

Historically, researchers used the Lagrangian approach embedded with heuristics to find good solutions while solving non-convex problems, and they have been quite successful in reporting a very close gap in some cases. Balakrishnan and Graves (1989) reported a composite Lagrangian algorithm for solving the problem of routing multiple commodities between source and destination where the cost function is concave. The Lagrangian formulation used dual ascent combined with sub-gradient optimization to generate a lower bound and a local improvement method to generate an upper bound. The algorithm was able to find good solutions with a minimal gap while solving high dimensional data-sets. Later Adams and Sherali (1993),Tawarmalani and Sahinidis (2004),, Ruan and Sun (2006), Shen and Qi (2007),Ozsen et al. (2008),Lu et al. (2014), Saif and Elhedhli (2016b) and Saif and Elhedhli (2016a) studied the Lagrangian relaxation approach for solving non-convex problems. Though most of them were able to find a good solution in a reasonably low computation time, they have not been able to close the optimality gap.

Other Exact Approaches

Here, we discuss a few other exact approaches to solve non-convex optimization problems. Falk and Hoffman (1976) reported a new exact method that produces a sequence of subproblems and carries out pivoting operations while solving concave problems. Hence it is not mandatory to cut the feasible region in each iteration while solving using the algorithm, nor to keep track of the subproblems. Following this approach, Hoffman (1981) reported an algorithm for globally minimizing the concave functions over con- vex sets using pivoting operations and univariate search operations. Later Kesavan et al. (2004) presented a rigorous decomposition technique for solving non-convex problems globally. Next, we discuss different non-convex application problems reported in the literature.

CONCLUSION

In this chapter, we discussed different non-convex application problems arising in supply chain design and finance. We also discussed different reported algorithms to solve those classes of problems. We found that the availability of exact algorithms for solving non-convex problems is scarce. Though some heuristics can find a good solution within a short time, they do not guarantee optimality. Most reported algorithms also have a limitation of solving only some specified class of problems. Recently, Sinha et al. (2023) reported an efficient general algorithm to solve a general class of concave problems, thereby addressing the needs. They proved that the reported algorithm is efficient and scalable. However, the availability of an efficient algorithm to solve the general class of non-convex problems is at scarce.

REFERENCES

Adams, W. P., & Sherali, H. D. (1993). Mixed-integer bilinear programming problems. *Mathematical Programming*, *59*(1-3), 279–305. doi:10.1007/BF01581249

Agˇralı, S., & Geunes, J. (2009). Solving knapsack problems with s-curve return functions. *European Journal of Operational Research*, *193*(2), 605–615. doi:10.1016/j.ejor.2007.10.060

Anagnostopoulos, K. P., & Mamanis, G. (2011). Multiobjective evolutionary algorithms for complex portfolio optimization problems. *Computational Management Science*, *8*(3), 259–279. doi:10.100710287-009-0113-8

Androulakis, I. P., Maranas, C. D., & Floudas, C. A. (1995). *α*bb: A global optimization method for general constrained nonconvex problems. *Journal of Global Optimization*, *7*(4), 337–363. doi:10.1007/BF01099647

Atamtürk, A., Berenguer, G., & Shen, Z.-J. (2012). A conic integer programming approach to stochastic joint location-inventory problems. *Operations Research*, *60*(2), 366–381. doi:10.1287/opre.1110.1037

Balakrishnan, A., & Graves, S. C. (1989). A composite algorithm for a concave-cost network flow problem. *Networks*, *19*(2), 175–202. doi:10.1002/net.3230190202

Belotti, P., Lee, J., Liberti, L., Margot, F., & Wächter, A. (2009). Branching and bounds tighteningtechniques for non-convex minlp. *Optimization Methods & Software*, *24*(4-5), 597–634. doi:10.1080/10556780903087124

Benson, H. P. (1985). A finite algorithm for concave minimization over a polyhedron. *Naval Research Logistics Quarterly*, *32*(1), 165–177. doi:10.1002/nav.3800320119

Benson, H. P. (1990). Separable concave minimization via partial outer approximation and branch and bound. *Operations Research Letters*, *9*(6), 389–394. doi:10.1016/0167-6377(90)90059-E

Benson, H. P., & Erenguc, S. S. (1990). An algorithm for concave integer minimization over a polyhedron. [NRL]. *Naval Research Logistics*, *37*(4), 515–525. doi:10.1002/1520-6750(199008)37:4<515::AID-NAV3220370406>3.0.CO;2-X

Benson, H. P., & Horst, R. (1991). A branch and bound-outer approximation algorithm for concave minimization over a convex set. *Computers & Mathematics with Applications (Oxford, England)*, *21*(6-7), 67–76. doi:10.1016/0898-1221(91)90161-V

Bretthauer, K. M., & Cabot, A. V. (1994). A composite branch and bound, cutting plane algorithm for concave minimization over a polyhedron. *Computers & Operations Research*, *21*(7), 777–785. doi:10.1016/0305-0548(94)90007-8

Bretthauer, K. M., Victor Cabot, A., & Venkataramanan, M. (1994). An algorithm and new penalties for concave integer minimization over a polyhedron. [NRL]. *Naval Research Logistics*, *41*(3), 435–454. doi:10.1002/1520-6750(199404)41:3<435::AID-NAV3220410309>3.0.CO;2-6

Cabot, A. V. (1974). Variations on a cutting plane method for solving concave minimization problems with linear constraints. *Naval Research Logistics Quarterly*, *21*(2), 265–274. doi:10.1002/nav.3800210206

Caprara, A., Pisinger, D., & Toth, P. (1999). Exact solution of the quadratic knapsack problem. *INFORMS Journal on Computing*, *11*(2), 125–137. doi:10.1287/ijoc.11.2.125

Cesarone, F., S. A. & Tardella, F. (2009). *Efficient algorithms for mean-variance portfolio optimization with hard real-world constraints*. 72:37–56.

Daskin, M. S., Coullard, C. R., & Shen, Z.-J. M. (2002). An inventory-location model: Formulation, solution algorithm and computational results. *Annals of Operations Research*, *110*(1-4), 83–106. doi:10.1023/A:1020763400324

Dhyani Bhatt, S., Jayaswal, S., Sinha, A., & Vidyarthi, N. (2021). Alternate second order conic program reformu- lations for hub location under stochastic demand and congestion. *Annals of Operations Research*, *304*(1), 481–527. doi:10.100710479-021-03993-6

Dijkhuizen, G., & Faigle, U. (1993). A cutting-plane approach to the edge-weighted maximal clique problem. *European Journal of Operational Research*, *69*(1), 121–130. doi:10.1016/0377-2217(93)90097-7

Elhedhli, S., Wang, Y., & Saif, A. (2018). Service system design with immobile servers, stochastic demand and concave-cost capacity selection. *Computers & Operations Research*, *94*, 65–75. doi:10.1016/j.cor.2018.01.019

Falk, J. E., & Hoffman, K. L. (1986). Concave minimization via collapsing polytopes. *Operations Research*, *34*(6), 919–929. doi:10.1287/opre.34.6.919

Falk, J. E., & Hoffman, K. R. (1976). A successive underestimation method for concave minimization problems. *Mathematics of Operations Research*, *1*(3), 251–259. doi:10.1287/moor.1.3.251

Falk, J. E., & Soland, R. M. (1969). An algorithm for separable nonconvex programming problems. *Management Science*, *15*(9), 550–569. doi:10.1287/mnsc.15.9.550

Farahani, R. Z., Rashidi Bajgan, H., Fahimnia, B., & Kaviani, M. (2015). Location-inventory problem in supply chains: A modelling review. *International Journal of Production Research*, *53*(12), 3769–3788. doi:10.1080/00207543.2014.988889

Feldman, E., Lehrer, F., & Ray, T. (1966). Warehouse location under continuous economies of scale. *Management Science*, *12*(9), 670–684. doi:10.1287/mnsc.12.9.670

Fontes, D. B., & Gonçalves, J. F. (2007). Heuristic solutions for general concave minimum cost network flow problems. *Networks*, *50*(1), 67–76. doi:10.1002/net.20167

Gallo, G., Hammer, P. L., & Simeone, B. (1980). Quadratic knapsack problems. In *Combinatorial Optimization* (pp. 132–149). Springer. doi:10.1007/BFb0120892

Gallo, G., & Ülkücü, A. (1977). Bilinear programming: An exact algorithm. *Mathematical Programming*, *12*(1), 173–194. doi:10.1007/BF01593787

Guisewite, G. M., & Pardalos, P. M. (1990). Minimum concave-cost network flow problems: Applications, com- plexity, and algorithms. *Annals of Operations Research*, *25*(1), 75–99. doi:10.1007/BF02283688

Guisewite, G. M., & Pardalos, P. M. (1993). A polynomial time solvable concave network flow problem. *Networks*, *23*(2), 143–147. doi:10.1002/net.3230230208

Hajiaghayi, M. T., Mahdian, M., & Mirrokni, V. S. (2003). The facility location problem with general cost func- tions. *Networks*, *42*(1), 42–47. doi:10.1002/net.10080

Hoffman, K. L. (1981). A method for globally minimizing concave functions over convex sets. *Mathematical Programming*, *20*(1), 22–32. doi:10.1007/BF01589330

Holmberg, K., & Tuy, H. (1999). A production-transportation problem with stochastic demand and concave pro- duction costs. *Mathematical Programming*, *85*(1), 157–179. doi:10.1007101070050050

Horst, R. (1976). An algorithm for nonconvex programming problems. *Mathematical Programming*, *10*(1), 312–321. doi:10.1007/BF01580678

Horst, R., & Thoai, N. V. (1998). An integer concave minimization approach for the minimum concave cost capacitated flow problem on networks. *OR-Spektrum*, *20*(1), 47–53. doi:10.1007/BF01545530

Horst, R., Thoai, N. V., & Benson, H. P. (1991). Concave minimization via conical partitions and polyhedral outer approximation. *Mathematical Programming*, *50*(1-3), 259–274. doi:10.1007/BF01594938

Jeet, V., Kutanoglu, E., & Partani, A. (2009). Logistics network design with inventory stocking for low-demand parts: Modeling and optimization. *IIE Transactions*, *41*(5), 389–407. doi:10.1080/07408170802512602

Johnson, E. L., Mehrotra, A., & Nemhauser, G. L. (1993). Min-cut clustering. *Mathematical Programming*, *62*(1-3), 133–151. doi:10.1007/BF01585164

Keha, A. B., de Farias, I. R. Jr, & Nemhauser, G. L. (2006). A branch-and-cut algorithm without binary variables for nonconvex piecewise linear optimization. *Operations Research*, *54*(5), 847–858. doi:10.1287/opre.1060.0277

Kesavan, P., Allgor, R. J., Gatzke, E. P., & Barton, P. I. (2004). Outer approximation algorithms for separable nonconvex mixed-integer nonlinear programs. *Mathematical Programming*, *100*(3), 517–535. doi:10.100710107-004-0503-1

Khan, A. T., Cao, X., Brajevic, I., Stanimirovic, P. S., Katsikis, V. N., & Li, S. (2022). Non-linear activated beetle antennae search: A novel technique for non-convex tax-aware portfolio optimization problem. *Expert Systems with Applications*, *197*, 116631. doi:10.1016/j.eswa.2022.116631

Kian, R., & Kargar, K. (2016). Comparison of the formulations for a hub-and-spoke network design problem under congestion. *Computers & Industrial Engineering*, *101*, 504–512. doi:10.1016/j.cie.2016.09.019

Kim, Y., Kang, D., Jeon, M., & Lee, C. (2019). Gan-mp hybrid heuristic algorithm for non-convex portfolio optimization problem. *The Engineering Economist*, *64*(3), 196–226. doi:10.1080/0013791X.2019.1620391

Konno, H. (1976). A cutting plane algorithm for solving bilinear programs. *Mathematical Programming*, *11*(1), 14–27. doi:10.1007/BF01580367

Kuno, T., & Utsunomiya, T. (2000). A lagrangian based branch-and-bound algorithm for production-transportation problems. *Journal of Global Optimization*, *18*(1), 59–73. doi:10.1023/A:1008373329033

Lee, S., & Grossmann, I. E. (2001). A global optimization algorithm for nonconvex generalized disjunctive pro- gramming and applications to process systems. *Computers & Chemical Engineering*, *25*(11-12), 1675–1697. doi:10.1016/S0098-1354(01)00732-3

Li, D., Sun, X., & Wang, F. (2006). Convergent lagrangian and contour cut method for nonlinear integer program- ming with a quadratic objective function. *SIAM Journal on Optimization*, *17*(2), 372–400. doi:10.1137/040606193

Li, Y., Lin, Y., & Shu, J. (2021). Location and two-echelon inventory network design with economies and disec- onomies of scale in facility operating costs. *Computers & Operations Research*, *133*, 105347. doi:10.1016/j.cor.2021.105347

Locatelli, M., & Thoai, N. V. (2000). Finite exact branch-and-bound algorithms for concave minimization over polytopes. *Journal of Global Optimization*, *18*(2), 107–128. doi:10.1023/A:1008324430471

Lu, D., Gzara, F., & Elhedhli, S. (2014). Facility location with economies and diseconomies of scale: Models and column generation heuristics. *IIE Transactions*, *46*(6), 585–600. doi:10.1080/0740817X.2013.860508

Majthay, A., & Whinston, A. (1974). Quasi-concave minimization subject to linear constraints. *Discrete Mathematics*, *9*(1), 35–59. doi:10.1016/0012-365X(74)90070-3

Markovitz, H. M. (1952). Portfolio selection. *The Journal of Finance*, *7*(1), 77–91.

McCormick, G. P. (1976). Computability of global solutions to factorable nonconvex programs: Part i—convex underestimating problems. *Mathematical Programming*, *10*(1), 147–175. doi:10.1007/BF01580665

Ni, W., Shu, J., Song, M., Xu, D., & Zhang, K. (2021). A branch-and-price algorithm for facility location with general facility cost functions. *INFORMS Journal on Computing*, *33*(1), 86–104. doi:10.1287/ijoc.2019.0921

O'Kelly, M. E., & Bryan, D. (1998). Hub location with flow economies of scale. *Transportation Research Part B: Methodological*, *32*(8), 605–616. doi:10.1016/S0191-2615(98)00021-6

Ozsen, L., Coullard, C. R., & Daskin, M. S. (2008). Capacitated warehouse location model with risk pooling. [NRL]. *Naval Research Logistics*, *55*(4), 295–312. doi:10.1002/nav.20282

Park, K., Lee, K., & Park, S. (1996). An extended formulation approach to the edge-weighted maximal clique problem. *European Journal of Operational Research*, *95*(3), 671–682. doi:10.1016/0377-2217(95)00299-5

Pisinger, D. (2007). The quadratic knapsack problem—A survey. *Discrete Applied Mathematics*, 155(5):623–648. Quesada, I. and Grossmann, I. E. (1995). A global optimization algorithm for linear fractional and bilinear programs. *Journal of Global Optimization*, *6*(1), 39–76.

Ruan, N., & Sun, X. (2006). An exact algorithm for cost minimization in series reliability systems with multiple component choices. *Applied Mathematics and Computation*, *181*(1), 732–741. doi:10.1016/j.amc.2006.02.001

Ryoo, H. S., & Sahinidis, N. V. (1995). Global optimization of nonconvex nlps and minlps with applications in process design. *Computers & Chemical Engineering*, *19*(5), 551–566. doi:10.1016/0098-1354(94)00097-2

Ryoo, H. S., & Sahinidis, N. V. (1996). A branch-and-reduce approach to global optimization. *Journal of Global Optimization*, *8*(2), 107–138. doi:10.1007/BF00138689

Saif, A. (2016). *Supply chain network design with concave costs: Theory and applications.*

Saif, A., & Elhedhli, S. (2016a). Cold supply chain design with environmental considerations: A simulation- optimization approach. *European Journal of Operational Research*, *251*(1), 274–287. doi:10.1016/j.ejor.2015.10.056

Saif, A., & Elhedhli, S. (2016b). A lagrangian heuristic for concave cost facility location problems: The plant location and technology acquisition problem. *Optimization Letters*, *10*(5), 1087–1100. doi:10.100711590-016-0998-4

Shectman, J. P., & Sahinidis, N. V. (1998). A finite algorithm for global minimization of separable concave pro- grams. *Journal of Global Optimization*, *12*(1), 1–36. doi:10.1023/A:1008241411395

Shen, Z.-J. M., Coullard, C., & Daskin, M. S. (2003). A joint location-inventory model. *Transportation Science*, *37*(1), 40–55. doi:10.1287/trsc.37.1.40.12823

Shen, Z.-J. M., & Qi, L. (2007). Incorporating inventory and routing costs in strategic location models. *European Journal of Operational Research*, *179*(2), 372–389. doi:10.1016/j.ejor.2006.03.032

Shu, J., Teo, C.-P., & Shen, Z.-J. M. (2005). Stochastic transportation-inventory network design problem. *Operations Research*, *53*(1), 48–60. doi:10.1287/opre.1040.0140

Sinha, A., Das, A., Anand, G., & Jayaswal, S. (2023). A general purpose exact solution method for mixed integer concave minimization problems. *European Journal of Operational Research*, *309*(3), 977–992. doi:10.1016/j.ejor.2023.02.005

Smith, E. M., & Pantelides, C. C. (1997). Global optimisation of nonconvex minlps. *Computers & Chemical Engineering*, *21*(1-2), S791–S796. doi:10.1016/S0098-1354(97)00146-4

Soland, R. M. (1971). An algorithm for separable nonconvex programming problems ii: Nonconvex constraints. *Management Science*, *17*(11), 759–773. doi:10.1287/mnsc.17.11.759

Soland, R. M. (1974). Optimal facility location with concave costs. *Operations Research*, *22*(2), 373–382. doi:10.1287/opre.22.2.373

Taha, H. A. (1973). Concave minimization over a convex polyhedron. *Naval Research Logistics Quarterly*, *20*(3), 533–548. doi:10.1002/nav.3800200313

Tawarmalani, M., & Sahinidis, N. V. (2004). Global optimization of mixed-integer nonlinear programs: A theoret- ical and computational study. *Mathematical Programming*, *99*(3), 563–591. doi:10.100710107-003-0467-6

Tawarmalani, M., & Sahinidis, N. V. (2005). A polyhedral branch-and-cut approach to global optimization. *Mathematical Programming*, *103*(2), 225–249. doi:10.100710107-005-0581-8

Thakur, L. S. (1991). Domain contraction in nonlinear programming: Minimizing a quadratic concave objective over a polyhedron. *Mathematics of Operations Research*, *16*(2), 390–407. doi:10.1287/moor.16.2.390

Tuy, H. (1964). Concave programming under linear constraints. *Soviet Mathematics*, *5*, 1437–1440.

Tuy, H. (1992). On nonconvex optimization problems with separated nonconvex variables. *Journal of Global Optimization*, *2*(2), 133–144. doi:10.1007/BF00122050

Tuy, H., Dan, N. D., & Ghannadan, S. (1993). Strongly polynomial time algorithms for certain concave minimiza- tion problems on networks. *Operations Research Letters*, *14*(2), 99–109. doi:10.1016/0167-6377(93)90102-M

Tuy, H., Thieu, T., & Thai, N. Q. (1985). A conical algorithm for globally minimizing a concave function over a closed convex set. *Mathematics of Operations Research*, *10*(3), 498–514. doi:10.1287/moor.10.3.498

Wang, F. (2019). A new exact algorithm for concave knapsack problems with integer variables. *International Journal of Computer Mathematics*, *96*(1), 126–134. doi:10.1080/00207160.2017.1418505

Witzgall, C. (1975). Mathematical methods of site selection for electronic message systems (ems). *STIN*, *76*, 18321. doi:10.6028/NBS.IR.75-737

Wu, T., & Zhang, K. (2014). A computational study for common network design in multi-commodity supply chains. *Computers & Operations Research*, *44*, 206–213. doi:10.1016/j.cor.2013.11.009

ADDITIONAL READING

Bretthauer, K. M., Ross, A., & Shetty, B. (1999). Nonlinear integer programming for optimal allocation in stratified sampling. *European Journal of Operational Research*, *116*(3), 667–680. doi:10.1016/S0377-2217(98)00180-5

Chaillou, P., Hansen, P., & Mahieu, Y. (1989). Best network flow bounds for the quadratic knapsack problem. In *Combinatorial Optimization* (pp. 225–235). Springer. doi:10.1007/BFb0083467

Cohen, M. A., & Moon, S. (1991). An integrated plant loading model with economies of scale and scope. *European Journal of Operational Research*, *50*(3), 266–279. doi:10.1016/0377-2217(91)90260-3

Desrochers, M., Marcotte, P., & Stan, M. (1995). The congested facility location problem. *Location Science*, *3*(1), 9–23. doi:10.1016/0966-8349(95)00004-2

Elhedhli, S. (2005). Exact solution of a class of nonlinear knapsack problems. *Operations Research Letters*, *33*(6), 615–624. doi:10.1016/j.orl.2005.01.004

Fisher, M. L. (2004). The lagrangian relaxation method for solving integer programming problems. *Management Science*, *50*(12, supplement), 1861–1871. doi:10.1287/mnsc.1040.0263

Floudas, C., Aggarwal, A., & Ciric, A. (1989). Global optimum search for nonconvex nlp and minlp problems. *Computers & Chemical Engineering*, *13*(10), 1117–1132. doi:10.1016/0098-1354(89)87016-4

Fujie, T., & Kojima, M. (1997). Semidefinite programming relaxation for nonconvex quadratic programs. *Journal of Global Optimization*, *10*(4), 367–380. doi:10.1023/A:1008282830093

Gallo, G., Sandi, C., & Sodini, C. (1980b). An algorithm for the min concave cost flow problem. *European Journal of Operational Research*, *4*(4), 248–255. doi:10.1016/0377-2217(80)90109-5

Guisewite, G. M., & Pardalos, P. M. (1991). Global search algorithms for minimum concave-cost network flow problems. *Journal of Global Optimization*, *1*(4), 309–330. doi:10.1007/BF00130828

Han, X., Ma, N., Makino, K., & Chen, H. (2017, May). Online knapsack problem under concave functions. In Frontiers in Algorithmics: 11th International Workshop, FAW 2017, Chengdu, China, June 23-25, 2017, Proceedings (pp. 103-114). Cham: Springer International Publishing.

Harkness, J., & ReVelle, C. (2003). Facility location with increasing production costs. *European Journal of Operational Research*, *145*(1), 1–13. doi:10.1016/S0377-2217(02)00176-5

Holmberg, K. (1994). Solving the staircase cost facility location problem with decomposition and piecewise linearization. *European Journal of Operational Research*, *75*(1), 41–61. doi:10.1016/0377-2217(94)90184-8

Holmberg, K. (1995). Efficient decomposition and linearization methods for the stochastic transportation problem. *Computational Optimization and Applications*, *4*(4), 293–316. doi:10.1007/BF01300860

Kellerer, H., Pferschy, U., & Pisinger, D. (2004). Some selected applications. In *Knapsack Problems* (pp. 449–482). Springer. doi:10.1007/978-3-540-24777-7_15

Kleinert, T., Labbé, M., Plein, F., & Schmidt, M. (2020). There's no free lunch: On the hardness of choosing a correct big-m in bilevel optimization. *Operations Research*, *68*(6), 1716–1721. doi:10.1287/opre.2019.1944

Klinz, B., & Tuy, H. (1993). Minimum concave-cost network flow problems with a single nonlinear arc cost. In Network Optimization Problems: Algorithms, Applications and Complexity (pp. 125–145). World Scientific. doi:10.1142/9789812798190_0008

Konno, H., Thach, P. T., & Tuy, H. (1997). Low-rank nonconvex structures. In *Optimization on Low Rank Nonconvex Structures* (pp. 95–117). Springer. doi:10.1007/978-1-4615-4098-4_5

Kuno, T. (1997). A pseudo-polynomial algorithm for solving rank three concave production-transportation problems. *Acta Mathematica Vietnamica*, *22*, 159–182.

Li, Y., Lin, Y., & Shu, J. (2021). Location and two-echelon inventory network design with economies and diseconomies of scale in facility operating costs. *Computers & Operations Research*, *133*, 105347. doi:10.1016/j.cor.2021.105347

Sinha, A., Malo, P., & Deb, K. (2017). A review on bilevel optimization: From classical to evolutionary approaches and applications. *IEEE Transactions on Evolutionary Computation*, *22*(2), 276–295. doi:10.1109/TEVC.2017.2712906

Skorin-Kapov, D., Skorin-Kapov, J., & O'Kelly, M. (1996). Tight linear programming relaxations of uncapacitated p-hub median problems. *European Journal of Operational Research*, *94*(3), 582–593. doi:10.1016/0377-2217(95)00100-X

Sun, X., Wang, F., & Li, D. (2005). Exact algorithm for concave knapsack problems: Linear underestimation and partition method. *Journal of Global Optimization*, *33*(1), 15–30. doi:10.100710898-005-1678-6

Tuy, H., Ghannadan, S., Migdalas, A., & VÄarbrand, P. V. (1993b). Strongly polynomial algorithm for a production transportation problem with concave production cost. *Optimization*, *27*(3), 205–227. doi:10.1080/02331939308843882

Victor Cabot, A., & Selcuk Erenguc, S. (1986). A branch and bound algorithm for solving a class of nonlinear integer programming problems. *Naval Research Logistics Quarterly*, *33*(4), 559–567. doi:10.1002/nav.3800330403

KEY TERMS AND DEFINITIONS

Global Optima: A global optima is optimal within all feasible solutions.

Local Optima: A local optima is optimal within a neighboring set of candidate solutions.

Negative Semi-definite: A matrix is negative semidefinite only if all its eigen values are non-positive.

Non-convex Optimization: Non-convex optimization is a process of finding optimal solution for non-convex problems. Non-convexity may arise in a problem due the presence of non-convex function in the objective function or constraints. A non-convex function can be either concave function or a function, which is neither concave function nor convex function. A function is called convex function only if its hessian is positive semi-definite.

Positive Semi-definite: A matrix is positive semidefinite only if all its eigen values are non-negative.

Chapter 4
Quality Improvement of Healthcare Services Through Data Analytics Processes

Uzay Damali
University of Wisconsin, La Crosse, USA

Ahmet Semih Ozkul
University of New Haven, USA

ABSTRACT

Improving quality of care is one of the priorities of policymakers in the U.S. While the spending on quality of care in the U.S. is the highest among all the developed nations, the desired health outcomes achieved have been below many of them. The largest portion of personal health care spending in 2019 went toward hospital care (37.2%), which was followed by physician and clinical services (24.1%). In this chapter, the authors focus on these direct care services, specifically explaining how hospitals and clinics can improve health and financial outcomes using data analytics. Specifically, building on CRISP-DM, a data mining process model, the authors explain the healthcare data analytics processes for hospitals and clinics to improve quality and financial performance.

1. INTRODUCTION

The World Health Organization defines quality of care as the "*degree to which health services for individuals and populations increase the likelihood of desired health outcomes.*" Improving quality of care is one of the priorities of policymakers in the U.S. While the spending on quality of care in the U.S. is the highest among all the developed nations, the U.S was ranked poorly in several measures of wellbeing or desired health outcomes (cms.gov, 2023). For example, health spending accounted for 18.3 percent of the nation's Gross Domestic Product, while life expectancy is 77 (85 in Japan, the highest) and obesity hits an all-time high (40% in adults) (cms.gov, 2023). To address these public concerns, the U.S. healthcare system extensively supports initiatives and policies to reduce the cost and improve the quality of

DOI: 10.4018/978-1-6684-8386-2.ch004

care, such as population health and prevention, value-based care, patient-centered care, electronic health records and price transparency (Kocher et al., 2010; Afrizal et al., 2019; Hajian et al., 2023).

In this chapter, we focus on direct care services, specifically *how hospitals and clinics can improve health and financial outcomes using data analytics.* Two main groups of institutions contribute to the quality of care in the U.S.: those that provide direct care to patients (such as hospitals, clinics, and treatment centers), and those that support the care of individuals through products and services (such as pharmaceuticals, insurance, and population health organizations). The largest portion of personal health care spending in 2019 went toward hospital care (37.2%), which was followed by physician and clinical services (24.1%) (cdc.gov, 2023). The main function of hospitals is to provide medical treatment and care to patients with illnesses, injuries, or other health conditions. Hospitals also offer emergency care, diagnostic testing, surgery, rehabilitation, and inpatient and outpatient care. Some large size hospitals serve as a center for research and education, providing opportunities for medical professionals to advance their knowledge and skills. Additionally, hospitals play a crucial role in public health, providing vaccinations and disease control measures, and serving as a resource for health information and education for the community.

While hospitals and clinics account for a significant portion of the healthcare spending, their profit margins are narrow. Some hospitals, particularly large academic medical centers, may operate at a loss or with very thin margins due to the high cost of providing complex medical services, conducting research, and training medical professionals. On the other hand, smaller, community hospitals or specialized facilities may be more profitable due to their lower overhead costs and more favorable payer mix. Large or small, all hospitals and clinics are price-takers, meaning they do not have the power to influence the market price of their services. In other words, hospitals accept the prevailing market price often set by the government and insurers and cannot negotiate a higher or lower price for their services.

Since hospitals cannot control prices, they aim to minimize their cost as well as maximize their revenue from insurers. Particularly, in recent years, the hospitals have faced financial pressures, including increasing competition, declining reimbursement rates, and rising costs for labor, supplies, and technology. Many hospitals have sought to reduce costs and improve efficiency, while also exploring new revenue streams, such as outpatient services, telemedicine, and partnerships with other healthcare providers. Ultimately, the profitability of hospitals is a complex and dynamic issue that is influenced by a range of economic, regulatory, and demographic factors. With the Affordable Care Act, hospital reimbursements from insurers are closely tied to their quality performance. Hospitals are financially penalized due to their relatively low-quality performance (Barnes et al., 2018).

Since hospitals' financial performance is closely tied to their quality performance, hospitals put extensive efforts for continuous improvement. All continuous improvement models highlight the vital role of data analytics. For example, one of the earliest of these models is the Plan-Do-Check-Act (PDCA) cycle (Taylor et al., 2014). In particular, the PDCA cycle is an iterative data-driven problem-solving technique that was first developed by American physicist Walter Shewhart in the 1920s. In the 1950s, Edwards Deming popularized the technique and named the cycle the "Shewhart" Cycle. PDCA cycle starts with "*planning*", which is defining the research questions. The next stage is "*do*", which involves the data collection. The next one is "*check*", which is the analysis of the data. The cycle finishes with "*act*", which the service organizations identify and implement the solution.

Since the 80s, computer scientists in the artificial intelligence and machine learning field have been applying algorithms on clinical data to assist physicians make diagnoses, and to reduce healthcare costs. Since then, multiple data analytics process models have been proposed to provide a detailed explanation of the steps involved in a continuous improvement project. For example, one of these models is the Cross-Industry Standard Process for Data Mining (CRISP-DM) (Shmueli et al., 2018), which resembled the PDCA cycle and popularized by IBM. However, unlike PDCA, CRISP-DM is not a sequential "waterfall" process. The sequence of the phases is flexible, moving back and forth between different phases is permitted. The CRISP-DM process not only includes collecting data to solve a business problem but also includes the phases in reverse order, in which data can be collected without a prior research question and used as the source of identification of problems. According to CRISP-DM, the steps of data analytics include:

1. *Business understanding* – business problems and opportunities are identified, the resource availability and project requirements are assessed, and data analytics goals are determined.
2. *Data understanding* – data is collected, described and explored, and its quality is verified.
3. *Data preparation* – data is integrated from multiplied databases, relevant variables and cases are selected, and typos, outliers and missing values are cleaned.
4. *Modeling* – Models appropriate for the data are determined, built and tested, and the best model is selected based on performance measures (e.g., R-square or RMSE)
5. *Evaluation* – The best model is evaluated for business relevance, whether the model effectively solves the business problem on hand or not.
6. *Deployment* – the model is used to facilitate business decisions and processes, using intelligence and prediction reports with visualizations (e.g., dashboards).

Note that over the years, different terms have been used essentially referring to the analysis of collected data. Data analytics, data mining and machine learning are such terms, and they could be used interchangeably. In this chapter, building on CRISP-DM, a data mining process model, we explained the healthcare data analytics processes for hospitals and clinics to improve quality and financial performance (see Figure 1). Specifically, in Section 2 we explain business and data understanding, in Section 3 is data preparation, modeling and model evaluation, and in Section 4 is data deployment.

Figure 1. Healthcare data analytics process

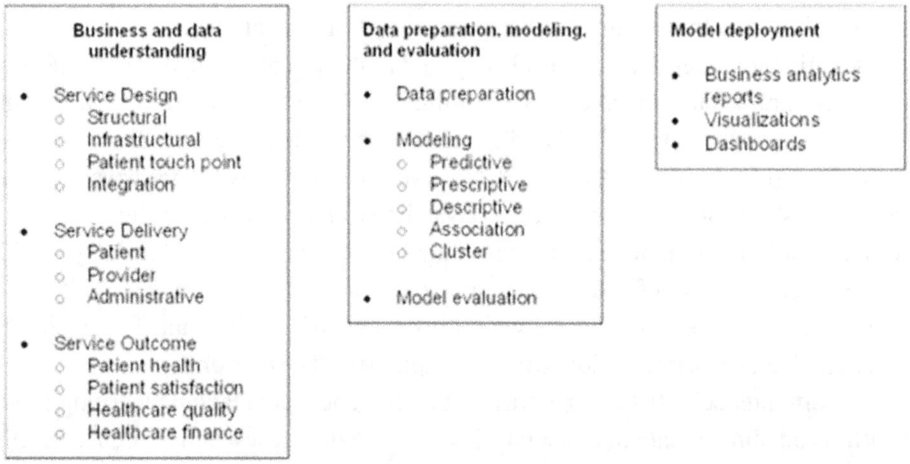

2. BUSINESS AND DATA UNDERSTANDING IN HEALTHCARE

The amount of data collected by the healthcare services is huge, measured in thousands of petabytes (1 petabyte = 1,000,000 gigabytes). Healthcare data could be structured (e.g., patient or employee data in relational databases) or unstructured (e.g., medical stories, doctor notes and comments, emails, messages, patient open ended satisfaction surveys). The data could be numerical, text or an image (MRI, X-Ray, or scanned documents). It could be stored electronically or on paper, using legacy or modern systems, in silos or integrated systems, on-premise or on-cloud. On top of this complexity, as technology continues to advance, new forms of data are emerging, such as data from wearable devices, virtual and remote care services, and unstructured data from social media.

Further the hospital and clinic use preliminary internal, organizational data to improve quality and financial performance. The internal data primarily represents the three stages of the service delivery process: design, delivery, and outcomes. As illustrated by the service strategy process models (see Figure 2) service outcomes are created by the factors related to service design and service delivery (Heineke, 1995; Roth and Menor, 2003; Voss et al., 2008; Damali et al., 2016). Specifically, service design is the activity of planning people, infrastructure, communication, and material components of a service in order to achieve the desired outcomes, while service delivery is simply the execution of service designs to achieve the desired outcomes. Internal data allows healthcare services to gain a descriptive as well as causal understanding of how the design and delivery can be improved to improve the outcomes.

Figure 2. Healthcare service strategy process model

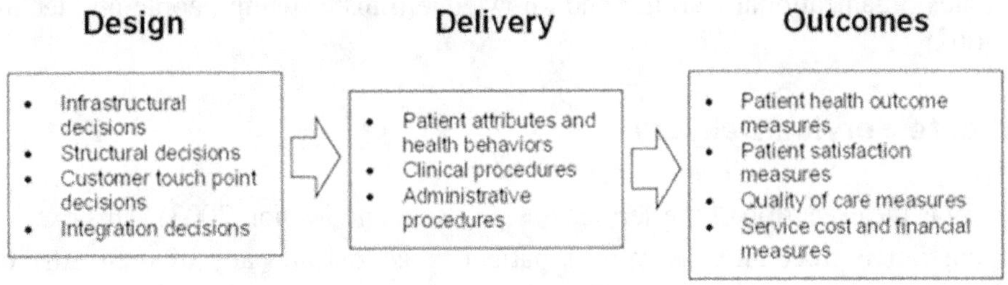

2.1. Healthcare Service Design

Healthcare services can collect data regarding the service designs. Service designs are the predictor variables of services outcomes, and are grouped under four broad categories: (1) infrastructural design decisions (intangibles, such processes and policies related to people), (2) structural design decisions (tangibles, such as facilities and equipment), (3) customer touch point design decisions (the level of customer participation and media used for the customer interactions), and (4) integration design decisions (information shared internally and with the external supply chain).

Infrastructural design decisions are related to the intangibles and behavioral aspects of the service strategy (Damali et al., 2016). They are the programs, processes, policies and practices related to people, such as workforce management, leadership and organizational culture. These decisions play a vital role in quality management since quality improvement is tightly connected to the psychology of people

(Deming 2018). They are often complex and require extensive effort and time for implementation, while having a major strategic impact on the competitive position and performance of a service firm. They are often tacit, so difficult to imitate by other organizations (Roth and Menor, 2003), such as the employee development strategies, or the training given to the doctors.

Structural design decisions are related to the tangible and physical aspects of a service strategy (Damali et al., 2016), including the facilities, physical design, tools and equipment, and technologies used, such as the number of MRI machines. These decisions also include the layout, size, and location of the service facility, which are important for managing capacity and balancing supply and demand. Structural design decisions are generally easier to implement compared to infrastructural design decisions (Roth and Menor, 2003). They are particularly important in services that have a high level of customer contact, as they can increase the tangibility of the service and reduce customer perceived variability (Mittal, 1999).

Customer touchpoint decisions are related to managing customer interactions of the service strategy (Damali et al., 2016). These decisions define the expected interactions between the service and the customers, such as level and other characteristics of customer participation (Soteriou and Chase, 1998). It defines the media to be used for the interactions, including both face-to-face and virtual interactions. Virtual interactions, such as telehealth, have become a major data source for quality improvement (Tuckson et al., 2017).

Integration decisions involve managing the relationships and connections between different parts of a service delivery system (Damali et al., 2016). These decisions define the boundaries of the service delivery system, such as the type of ERP system software and capabilities supporting the external relationships with upstream suppliers as well as the internal relationships between different functional areas such as accounting and operations. It is of strategic importance for quality improvement efforts, since it facilitates organizational learning and knowledge transfer using people and technology (Roth and Menor, 2003).

2.2. Healthcare Service Delivery

Service delivery is the execution of the service design (Roth and Menor, 2003). This execution involves clinical, administrative procedures as well as patient behaviors and any of their attributes. Clinical procedures are often considered as front-office procedures such as the administration of different treatments and interventions to patients. It also involves administrative procedures, often considered as the back-office procedures such as billing or procurement of supplies. In addition, patient health behaviors (compliance) and attributes (demographics) are critical in the service delivery (Damali et al., 2016). This means that healthcare quality is not only dependent on clinical and administrative procedures, but also on the patients themselves. Consistently, assessments require data not only from clinical and administrative procedures but also patient attributes and behaviors.

Co-creation is a general service strategy that aims to increase customer participation in a service, and it has been gaining popularity in healthcare services (Damali et al., 2022). This strategy has a major implication on data analytics. This increase is likely due to the fact that there are not enough healthcare providers to meet the needs of an increasing number of patients with chronic conditions who require long-term treatments (Mayo.Org, 2022). By actively participating in their own care, patients can make the service more convenient, effective, and less costly for themselves. In addition, when the COVID-19 pandemic hit the world in 2020, many healthcare providers were forced to rapidly adopt a co-creation model of healthcare service delivery. Specifically, telehealth and remote care which monitor and track vital signs and conditions were used more frequently than on-ground visits, which led to healthcare services having more data and information to assess, diagnose, and manage patient care as well as improve service quality.

For example, one common chronic condition is kidney disease that requires dialysis, cleaning the blood when the kidneys can no longer get rid of the body's wastes. One new method of dialysis is peritoneal dialysis, requiring extensive co-creation because it is often performed in patients' homes. The adoption of peritoneal dialysis is increasing in the U.S. because it allows greater lifestyle flexibility and independence as well as results in longer lasting residual kidney function. Further, its adoption significantly increased during the COVID-19 pandemic, since the alternative method required patients to do the dialysis in the hospital, which increases patients exposure to the virus (Siwicki et al., 2021). An indirect benefit of this new method is continuous and extensive data collection from patients, which resulted in application of analytics to offer diagnostic assistance and guide treatment decisions. Specifically, combining data from several sources, including claims, clinical data, live feeds from health exchanges, dialysis machines and demographic information for social determinants of health, algorithms predict adverse events, including kidney failure during a given time frame.

2.3. Healthcare Service Outcomes

In general, the outcome of the service delivery in healthcare includes: (1) patient health outcomes, (2) patient satisfaction, (3) service cost and financials, and (4) service care quality. The assessments of these outcomes can be done by objective and perceptual data collected from the people involved in the healthcare delivery.

Patient health outcome measures are often objective, and often based on the clinical data coming from healthcare providers and recorded by the electronic medical record. They are the results of healthcare delivery systems (the outcomes of interventions, therapies, and the treatments). Given the healthcare industry's administrative and regulatory complexities, hospitals measure and report on hundreds of outcomes annually. These measures can be clinical, such as being alive, being physically, psychologically, and socially fit, or specifically changes in blood pressure, cholesterol levels, body mass index. In addition, they can be patient-reported health and well-being measures (pain, quality of life) or measure a patient's ability to perform daily activities, such as walking, dressing, or using the toilet.

Patient satisfaction measures are subjective and are related to their perceptions and experiences regarding the service delivery system. Patients often do not have adequate understanding to evaluate the robustness of these procedures, but they are able to perceive and evaluate how their surgeon treated them. This data is collected by the health organization by survey or third-party organization.

Service cost and financial measures are highly important in decision making. There are an extensive number of cost and financial measures. Some cost metrics are cost per case (the cost of caring for a patient, calculated by dividing total costs by the number of patients treated), supply cost per discharge (the cost of supplies used for each patient, including medical supplies, drugs, and other items, and the labor costs (the cost of salaries, benefits, and other compensation for hospital employees). Some financial metrics are revenue (all the money a hospital earns through patient care, insurance reimbursement, and other sources), net income (the amount of money a hospital has after subtracting expenses from revenue, operating margin (a hospital's efficiency by comparing operating income to revenue) and days in A/R (the average number of days it takes for a hospital to collect payment from insurance companies for services provided). They are associated with the organizational design and delivery, such as the number of readmissions to the emergency room can be collected and associated with cost and financial outcomes, or which patient behaviors lead to better measures and cost outcomes are investigated.

Healthcare quality is assessed by six dimensions according to the Institute for Healthcare Improvement (ihi.org., 2022). These are: (1) patient safety, avoiding injuries to patients from the care that is intended to help them; (2) effectiveness, providing services based on scientific knowledge to all who could benefit and refraining from providing services to those not likely to benefit; (3) patient-centeredness, providing care that is respectful of and responsive to individual patient preferences, needs, and values, and ensuring that patient values guide all clinical decisions; (4) timeliness, reducing waits and sometimes harmful delays for both those who receive and those who give care; (5) efficiency, avoiding waste, including waste of equipment, supplies, ideas, and energy; and (6) equitableness, providing care that does not vary in quality because of personal characteristics such as gender, ethnicity, geographic location, and socioeconomic status.

3. DATA PREPARATION, MODELING, AND EVALUATION

This section explores data mining and analytics processes that can be used in improving healthcare quality and financial performance. The dataset that will be used in addressing the healthcare business problem usually is an outcome of a data collection and integration process. The data comes from various data sources such as multiple tables stored in different databases which could be located in legacy systems, on-premise or on cloud systems, and in different data formats. In less frequent, on-demand analytics, the data is integrated into a single, flat dataset of rows and columns and then analyzed by analytics professional. When analytics is done more frequently, the organization may benefit from a data warehouse approach, in which relevant data from operational/transactional databases is collected, summarized and stored in analytical databases on a regular basis to facilitate data analytics. Once the dataset is ready to use, the data preparation stage starts, followed by the modeling stage. Data preparation typically takes more time than the modeling stage (Shmueli et al., 2018).

3.1. Data Preparation

Once the data is collected from different sources and integrated into a single dataset, it is prepared for analysis. Typical issues in a dataset include existence of typos, outliers, and missing values. These issues may hinder the application of analytics algorithms on the dataset or cause misleading results. At this stage, exploratory data analysis (EDA) is used, including descriptive statistics and visualizations that can show the extent of extreme and missing values in the dataset numerically and visually. Depending on the severity of these problems, different handling methods are proposed. For example, if a data column includes too many typos or too many missing values, it may be deemed useless and deleted from the dataset. If missing values are relatively less, or the data column is too important to delete, "imputation" could be a solution, in which missing values are replaced with a reasonable value such as median. Outliers can be legitimate and not a typo. However, they can still highly influence a prediction model and may decrease the model's generalizability and prediction power. (Dasu & Johnson, 2003)

3.2. Modeling

While there are many types and variants of analytics methods in developing a model, we focus on the most common analytics methods used in the modeling stage, as explained below:

3.2.1 Descriptive Analytics

Descriptive Analytics is based on descriptive statistics and data visualizations to summarize and describe the characteristics of data. The goals in descriptive analytics include understanding what has happened in the past, what is going on now, and identifying patterns, trends, and distribution of data. Descriptive analytics typically includes central tendency measures such as mean, median, mode and dispersion measures such as range, variance, and standard deviation. Histograms and boxplots provide information about the shape (distribution) of the data.

Descriptive analytics applications in healthcare include summaries and metrics on demographics (e.g., patient age, gender, ethnicity, marital status, education, location), health outcomes (e.g., mortality, morbidity, treatment success, readmission rates) and provider performance (e.g., average patient satisfaction scores, patient average wait times, resource utilization rates, and total cost). These metrics and Key Performance Indicators (KPI) can be used to print out a report or fed into a dashboard to keep up to date on a real time basis.

3.2.2 Predictive Analytics

Predictive analytics is also called "supervised learning" in the machine learning field. The typical dataset would include observations in the rows and variables in the columns. In a prediction problem, at least one variable must be designated as the "target" variable. It is also called the outcome or dependent variable. The remaining variables in the dataset are considered potential "predictors". Predictors are independent variables that the model uses to predict the target variable. Not all predictors are good predictors, and the dataset may not contain all the right predictors. Selecting good predictors for the model is an art and science. Domain experts such as physicians and healthcare administrators can assist to pick up the right variables for the model. On the other hand, automated computational techniques can search for the best set of predictors in the dataset.

Selecting the right model for the dataset is the next challenge. The desired outcome of the prediction task, the nature (size, distribution, linear/nonlinear) and type of the target/predictor variables determine the model selection process. For example, when the target variable is a categorical variable (e.g. ReadmissionStatus = Readmitted/NotReadmitted), the prediction task is called "classification" and the prediction model is selected accordingly (such as logistic regression rather than linear regression). It is usually preferable to use compact, parsimonious models (e.g., a small set of predictors in a linear regression model) over complex models (e.g. neural networks), as long as the prediction accuracy is comparable. Simple, transparent models are easier to understand, get insights and explain to non-technical audiences (Lantz, 2019)

The data mining field uses prediction models borrowed from statistics, machine learning and Artificial Intelligence disciplines, including Linear/Logistic Regression, Decision Trees, K-Nearest Neighbors, Naive Bayes, and Neural Networks. These models can come in its original form, or in a special variant optimized for speed or accuracy. Also, they can be combined with each other or with other techniques resulting in "ensembles" to improve the overall performance of the prediction.

Finally, the selected model is tested for prediction accuracy. The dataset that is available for analytics is usually divided into two parts, "training" and "validation". Using the training partition, a model or a set of candidate models are developed. Each model is then applied on the validation partition to calculate prediction performance measures. When the target variable is numerical, these performance measures are usually based on the prediction error (i.e., Actual - Predicted) such as the Root Mean Squared Error (RMSE). When the target is categorical, the performance measures are based on the number of correct and false classifications using a "confusion matrix". When satisfactory performance is reached, the model is deemed to be validated (Shmueli, et al., 2018).

As a prediction example, consider a healthcare professional investigating factors that contribute to hospital readmissions within 30 days of discharge, which is a goal for cost savings in the Medicare Value Based Purchasing program (Robinson & Hudali, 2017). With assistance from doctors and administrators, most relevant predictors associated with readmission rates are selected. The relevant predictors could include patient demographics, medical history, provider information, and patient surveys. Using this dataset, regression, Naive Bayes, or decision trees can be used to predict readmission probability for each patient (Xiong, et al., 2022). This approach can help healthcare organizations make informed decisions on how to reduce readmissions and improve overall patient outcomes.

3.3. Prescriptive Analytics

The service experience can be optimized to yield the best patient, employee and organizational outcomes. Optimization techniques can be used to determine the best possible healthcare outcomes given a set of constraints. For example, a "linear programming" model may be used to find an answer to the question of maximizing positive patient health outcomes subject to patient specific constraints, organizational costs and capacity limitations. On the other hand, "computer simulation" models can be constructed to study important factors more dynamically such as patient wait times, appointment availability, and capacity (e.g., number of beds) of the healthcare facility (e.g. emergency department) as patient arrivals to the facility are simulated randomly in the computer (Lee, et al., 2016). The simulation models can be used to do "what-if" analysis, such as investigating the benefits and costs in response to increasing clinic capacity (more beds, more doctors, etc.) which can lead to a better service or facility design (Zhong, et al., 2016).

3.4. Association Analysis

Association and cluster analysis are two main pattern identification techniques in the "unsupervised" machine learning field. By analyzing data on healthcare services, association analysis can help identify which services are often provided together and how they are related to the patient outcomes. For example, it can be used to determine which physicians work together best to achieve positive patient outcomes, or which provider teams have the highest patient satisfaction rates. Another application area could be "comorbidity". Comorbidity refers to the presence of multiple medical conditions in a single patient, such as diabetes and heart disease. Association analysis can be used for comorbidity to better understand the relationships between different medical conditions and patient outcomes so that interventions and treatments are adjusted to patients with specific comorbid conditions. Additionally, by analyzing data on patients and providers who are satisfied with the service encounter, association analysis can help identify which factors are most strongly associated with positive outcomes. In association analysis, techniques like the "Apriori" algorithm and the "Fp-growth" algorithm can be used to identify association rules from the data. For example, "if doctor X and doctor Y, then doctor Z" rule that can be found in a dataset of patients with good health outcomes showing which three doctors are seen (in this order) by satisfied patients. Or, if a patient receives treatment A, and then treatment B, then there is a 0.65 probability that he/she will receive treatment C (Koh & Tan, 2005). For a specific example, risk patterns for diabetes occurrence is studied using association rule mining using demographic and anthropometric characteristics, smoking status and medical histories of patients (Ramezankhani, 2015).

3.5. Cluster Analysis

Cluster analysis is a technique that can be used to identify relatively homogeneous groups of patients (or other actors such as doctors, nurses) with similar demographics, histories, diagnosis, health outcomes, as well as interests, experiences, and quality perceptions of the healthcare service. Data gathered from administrative systems or electronic health records can be utilized for this purpose and each group is labeled based on dominant characteristics, such as their chronic conditions (e.g., "well", "worried well", "early sick" and "sick") (Vuik et al, 2016). The objective of clustering is to enhance healthcare delivery by customizing the healthcare service, cost implications and health outcomes for the unique requirements and preferences of each segment (i.e. each patient profile). For example, by grouping patients by their common health-related behaviors, health care utilization patterns (whether a practitioner was consulted, or an intervention was used in the past 12 months) can be examined using cluster analysis (Recchia et al., 2022). There are several techniques available for cluster analysis, including "k-means", hierarchical clustering, and density-based clustering. The choice of technique will depend on the specific data and problem being considered.

4. MODEL EVALUATION

The ability of the model to achieve the goals established in the problem identification stage is assessed in the model evaluation stage. For example, if the goal is to predict the likelihood of the readmission of a patient in 30 days, the evaluation will measure the model's accuracy in predicting readmission probability and compare it to the target performance established in the problem identification stage (e.g. the accuracy of the model should be at least 80%). If the model is not performing to the desired level, additional data or a different model may be needed. This stage is critical in determining the suitability of the model for deployment and ensuring that it is delivering the desired business outcomes.

5. MODEL DEPLOYMENT AND PRESENTATION OF ANALYTICS RESULTS

Model deployment refers to the use of the model as part of the business processes of the organization (e.g. a provider website asking questions about a patient's current COVID symptoms and calculating the likelihood of the patient having COVID). Presentation of analytics outcomes refers to presenting and communicating analytics results in a meaningful and useful format that can be easily understood and acted upon by decision makers and other stakeholders. This involves using various techniques and tools, such as reports, tables, charts, interactive visualizations, and dashboards. Effective data presentation requires a clear understanding of the target audience, their information needs, and the appropriate method and medium to communicate the data in a way that is accurate, insightful, and actionable.

5.1. Business Analytics Reports

Business analytics reports include Business Intelligence (BI) reports and analytics documents summarizing the results of descriptive, predictive, and prescriptive analytics. Business Intelligence (BI) reports primarily aim at showing what happened and what is happening in the business using data from databases and other data sources (for example, data obtained through running Structured Query Language - SQL). Examples of healthcare BI reports include lists of patients admitted to the emergency department in a given date range, or a summary table showing total patients admitted, total patients discharged, total patients readmitted in a certain time period (Strome, 2013).

Analytics reports present more than what BI reports do, and examples include predictive analytics (e.g. patient trends and utilization projections into the future using a linear regression model), prescriptive analytics (e.g. facility performance measures and utilization of a proposed new healthcare unit analyzed using computer simulation), and cluster analysis (e.g. groups of patients with similar demographic and clinical features who are at high risk of diabetes).

5.2. Visualizations

Visualizations are graphical representations of data such as charts, graphs and maps. Visualizations can be used to display complex medical and administrative data in a simple and intuitive manner, allowing healthcare providers, researchers and administrators to quickly comprehend patterns and relationships in patient and provider performance data, and act on that information for data driven decisions. Visualizations can show trends and can be much more intuitive than numbers or statistics alone (Strome, 2013). Example visualizations include bar charts, pie charts, line graphs, scatter plots, donut charts and heat maps which can be used to display information on topics such as patient demographics and health outcomes, or projections on provider resource utilization in the next 2 years. Also, specific visualizations for quality improvement purposes, such as statistical process control charts can be used to monitor the performance and analyze root causes of lower performance in healthcare processes (Harrington, 2021). Larger datasets and data from social media (e.g. number of social media mentions, positive/negative sentiments in social media text) can be collected, summarized, and visualized to get business insights, and to compare and benchmark against past performances or other providers (Mitra & Padman, 2016). Perceptual performance measures, such as perceived provider team performance, satisfaction with hospital food, and cleanliness of facilities according to the patients can also be surveyed, counted, summarized, visualized, and monitored. Finally, by comparing current performance levels to target performances, any difference can be visually identified. These visualizations are not only used to track and improve healthcare quality but also used to communicate goals, objectives, and targets of the healthcare organization's quality strategy with teams, managers, and other stakeholders (Strome, 2013).

5.3. Dashboards

A dashboard is an interactive and visual display of the most important information for the organization, typically used to monitor, analyze and understand trends and patterns, and get insights in real-time. It provides a quick overview of key metrics, indicators and summaries, using charts, graphs, tables, and other data visualization elements. The goal of an administrative healthcare dashboard is to provide administrators with a clear and concise understanding of the past and present information related to patient outcomes, and operational and financial performance (Strome, 2013). By regularly monitoring the dashboard, they can identify areas for improvement, track progress, and make data-driven decisions to enhance the quality of care. Key performance indicators (KPIs) on a healthcare dashboard may include measures such as patient satisfaction survey results, patient readmission rates, infection rates, accuracy of diagnoses, patient wait times, length of stay, appointment availability, patient volume, medical equipment/staff availability, provider revenues and costs (Nelson et al., 1996).

6. IMPLICATIONS TO FINANCIAL SERVICES

The service strategy process model (design-delivery-outcome model) illustrated in Figure 2) is a generic model, so it can be applied to both healthcare and financial services. Figure 3 shows our adaptation of the model to financial services. Both financial and healthcare services have complex and knowledge intensive operations, as well as considered professional services, where the value is co-created with extensive customer participation (Harvey, 2015). For instance, a financial advisor may assist clients in creating long-term strategies for managing risk and building wealth, requiring the collection and analysis of large amounts of data. Similarly, a doctor may diagnose and develop a treatment plan for patients, which also involves processing extensive amounts of information. In both cases, data analytics is crucial for generating new knowledge and designing effective services.

Figure 3. Financial services strategy-process model

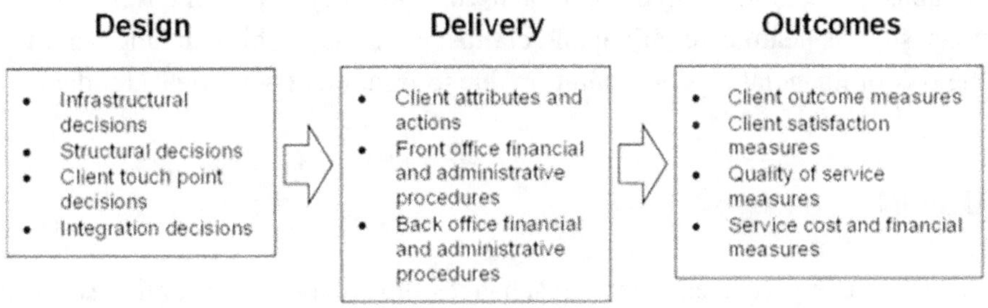

In addition, healthcare services have finance departments and do financial analytics to produce information on the finance side of healthcare service (Reiter & Song, 2021). Traditionally, the finance department of a typical organization generates financial reports, such as balance sheets, income statements, and cash flow statements. It also creates budgets and forecasts for the organization for financial decision-making and strategic planning. In this process, financial ratios and KPIs are calculated, reported, and monitored. For example, return on assets (ROA) shows how efficient a company is in terms of its assets, and can be used as a measure of profitability. ROA could be calculated for the healthcare organization and compared to other organizations in the healthcare industry. A dashboard can present ROA and other critical financial ratios to the administrators and financial managers on a real time basis. In short, at the heart of the financial process is intensive data collection and processing.

The application of financial analytics in healthcare organizations improve financial performance and reduce costs while enhancing the quality of care for patients. The following shows an example list of financial analytics application areas in the healthcare sector:

- Performance monitoring: Analytics can help financial managers in healthcare organizations monitor financial performance over time by tracking key financial metrics such as sales, revenues, expenses, and profitability using modern IT tools such as visualizations and dashboards. This can help the organizations identify trends, make projections into the future, and better allocate financial resources.
- Revenue management: Analytics can be used to track and manage revenue throughout the healthcare revenue cycle, including patient registration, charge capture, claims processing to reduce denials and rejections, and payment posting to identify underbilling or overcharging. This can help healthcare providers locate areas of inefficiency, reduce claim denials, and improve cash flow.
- Cost analysis: Analytics can be used to analyze the cost of care for individual patients, groups of patients, or for the organization as a whole. By analyzing data from various sources, including patient records, billing and claims data, and data from vendors in the supply chain, healthcare administrators identify cost-saving opportunities and reduce waste and inefficiencies.
- Risk management: Analytics can be used to assess and manage financial risk for healthcare organizations. This can include analyzing payer contracts, managing accounts receivable, and assessing financial performance over time. Also, data analytics can identify patients who are at risk of developing chronic conditions or requiring expensive treatments. By identifying these patients early, healthcare providers can intervene with preventative care or disease management programs to help reduce the overall cost of care. (Reiter & Song, 2021)
- Fraud and abuse detection: Analytics can be used to identify potential cases of fraud in business transactions, such as healthcare billing and claims processing. This can help healthcare providers reduce the risk of financial loss or reputation due to fraudulent activities. (Joudaki, et al., 2014)

6. CONCLUSION

The healthcare sector has experienced substantial changes and is expected to continue evolving. Effective quality improvement efforts are based on data collection from the people and organizational processes, and data analytics to transform the data into information and insights that can enhance healthcare outcomes. To achieve true effectiveness, quality improvement analytics should encompass clinical, operational, and financial perspectives. Advanced technologies like data mining, machine learning, visualization and dashboarding can boost efficiencies and effectiveness in healthcare processes and patient healthcare outcomes beyond the limits of more traditional data analysis.

Future trends in healthcare quality analytics include increased use of artificial intelligence (AI) and machine learning to improve clinical administrative decision-making, more common use of visualizations and dashboards, the use of natural language processing (NLP) to support clinical documentation process, use of blockchain technology to securely share electronic health records between providers and patients, more common use of analytics tools that allow providers to identify high-risk patients and offer personalized treatment plans, data analytics for telemedicine, home monitoring, remote clinic visits.

REFERENCES

Afrizal, S. H., Hidayanto, A. N., Handayani, P. W., Budiharsana, M., & Eryando, T. (2019). Narrative review for exploring barriers to readiness of electronic health record implementation in primary health care. *Healthcare Informatics Research, 25*(3), 141–152. doi:10.4258/hir.2019.25.3.141 PMID:31406606

Barnes, M., Oner, N., Ray, M. N., & Zengul, F. D. (2018). Exploring the association between quality and financial performance in US hospitals: a systematic review. *Journal of Health Care Finance, 44*(2). CDC.gov. https://www.cdc.gov/nchs/hus/topics/health-care-expenditures.htm#featured-charts

Damali, U., Fredendall, L. D., Miller, J. L., Moore, D., & Dye, C. J. (2022). Enhancing patient participation in healthcare operations through patient training and education using the theoretical lens of media synchronicity. *Decision Sciences, 53*(4), 750–770. doi:10.1111/deci.12514

Damali, U., Miller, J. L., Fredendall, L. D., Moore, D., & Dye, C. J. (2016). Co-creating value using customer training and education in a healthcare service design. *Journal of Operations Management, 47*(1), 80–97. doi:10.1016/j.jom.2016.10.001

Dasu, T., & Johnson, T. (2003). *Exploratory Data Mining and Data Cleaning*. Wiley. doi:10.1002/0471448354

Deming, W. E. (2018). *Out of the Crisis, reissue*. MIT press. doi:10.7551/mitpress/11457.001.0001

Hajian, A., Prybutok, V. R., & Chang, H. C. (2023). An empirical study for blockchain-based information sharing systems in electronic health records: A mediation perspective. *Computers in Human Behavior, 138*, 107471. doi:10.1016/j.chb.2022.107471

Harrington, L. (2021). Quality Measurement. In A. Giardino, L. Riesenberg, & P. Varkey (Eds.), *Medical Quality Management* (pp. 41–61). Springer., doi:10.1007/978-3-030-48080-6_3

Harvey, J. (2015). *Complex service delivery processes: Strategy to operations*. Quality Press.

Heineke, J. (1995). Strategic operations management decisions and professional performance in US HMOs. *Journal of Operations Management, 13*(4), 255–272. doi:10.1016/0272-6963(95)00035-6

Joudaki, H., Rashidian, A., Minaei-Bidgoli, B., Mahmoodi, M., Geraili, B., Nasiri, M., & Arab, M. (2014). Using data mining to detect health care fraud and abuse: A review of literature. *Global Journal of Health Science, 7*(1), 194–202. doi:10.5539/gjhs.v7n1p194 PMID:25560347

Kocher, R., Emanuel, E. J., & DeParle, N. A. M. (2010). The Affordable Care Act and the future of clinical medicine: The opportunities and challenges. *Annals of Internal Medicine*, *153*(8), 536–539. doi:10.7326/0003-4819-153-8-201010190-00274 PMID:20733178

Koh, H. C., & Tan, G. (2005). Data mining applications in healthcare. Journal of healthcare information management. *Journal of Healthcare Information Management*, *19*(2), 64–72. PMID:15869215

Lantz, B. (2019). *Machine Learning with R: Expert techniques for predictive modeling* (3rd ed.). Packt.

Lee, E. K., Atallah, H. Y., Wright, M. D., Thomas, C., IV, Post, E. T., Wu, D. T., & Haley, L. L., Jr. (2016). *Systems analytics: modeling and optimizing clinic workflow and patient care. Healthcare Analytics: From Data to Knowledge to Healthcare Improvement*, 263-299. Mayo Clinic. https://www.mayoclinic.org/medical-professionals/trauma/news/how-mayo-clinic-has-addressed-hospital-capacity-challenges/mac-20527287

Mitra, S., & Padman, R. (2016). Understanding the Role of Social Media in Healthcare via Analytics: a Health Plan Perspective. *Healthcare Analytics: From Data to Knowledge to Healthcare Improvement*, 593–625. doi:10.1002/9781118919408.ch20

Mittal, B. (1999). The advertising of services: Meeting the challenge of intangibility. *Journal of Service Research*, *2*(1), 98–116. doi:10.1177/109467059921008

Nelson, E. C., Mohr, J. J., Batalden, P. B., & Plume, S. K. (1996). Improving Health Care, Part 1: The Clinical Value Compass. *The Joint Commission Journal on Quality Improvement*, *22*(4), 243–258. doi:10.1016/S1070-3241(16)30228-0 PMID:8743061

Ramezankhani, A., Pournik, O., Shahrabi, J., Azizi, F., & Hadaegh, F. (2015). An application of association rule mining to extract risk pattern for type 2 diabetes using tehran lipid and glucose study database. *International Journal of Endocrinology and Metabolism*, *13*(2), e25389. doi:10.5812/ijem.25389 PMID:25926855

Recchia, D. R., Cramer, H., Wardle, J., Lee, D. J., Ostermann, T., & Lauche, R. (2022). Profiles and predictors of healthcare utilization: Using a cluster-analytic approach to identify typical users across conventional, allied and complementary medicine, and self-care. *BMC Health Services Research*, *22*(1), 29. doi:10.118612913-021-07426-9 PMID:34986866

Reiter, K. L., & Song, P. H. (2021). *Gapenski's Healthcare Finance: An Introduction to Accounting and Financial Management* (7th ed.). Health Administration Press.

Robinson, R., & Hudali, T. (2017). The HOSPITAL score and LACE index as predictors of 30 day readmission in a retrospective study at a university-affiliated community hospital. *PeerJ*, *5*, e3137. doi:10.7717/peerj.3137 PMID:28367375

Roth, A. V., & Menor, L. J. (2003). Insights into service operations management: A research agenda. *Production and Operations Management*, *12*(2), 145–164. doi:10.1111/j.1937-5956.2003.tb00498.x

Shmueli, G., Bruce, P. C., Yahav, I., Patel, N. R., & Lichtendahl, K. C. Jr. (2018). *Data Mining for Business Analytics: Concepts, Techniques, and Applications in R* (1st ed.). Wiley.

Soteriou, A. C., & Chase, R. B. (1998). Linking the customer contact model to service quality. *Journal of Operations Management, 16*(4), 495–508. doi:10.1016/S0272-6963(98)00026-6

Strome, T. L. (2013). *Healthcare Analytics.* Wiley.

Taylor, M. J., McNicholas, C., Nicolay, C., Darzi, A., Bell, D., & Reed, J. E. (2014). Systematic review of the application of the plan–do–study–act method to improve quality in healthcare. *BMJ Quality & Safety, 23*(4), 290–298. doi:10.1136/bmjqs-2013-001862 PMID:24025320

Tuckson, R. V., Edmunds, M., & Hodgkins, M. L. (2017). Telehealth. *The New England Journal of Medicine, 377*(16), 1585–1592. doi:10.1056/NEJMsr1503323 PMID:29045204

Voss, C., Roth, A. V., & Chase, R. B. (2008). Experience, service operations strategy, and services as destinations: Foundations and exploratory investigation. *Production and Operations Management, 17*(3), 247–266. doi:10.3401/poms.1080.0030

Vuik, S. I., Mayer, E. K., & Darz, A. (2016). Patient Segmentation Analysis Offers Significant Benefits for Integrated Care and Support. *Health Affairs, 35*(5), 769–775. doi:10.1377/hlthaff.2015.1311 PMID:27140981

Xiong, L., Sun, T., & Green, R. (2022). Predictive analytics for 30-day hospital readmissions. *Mathematical Foundations of Computing, 5*(2), 93–111. doi:10.3934/mfc.2021035

Zhong, X., Williams, M., Li, J., Kraft, S. A., & Sleeth, J. S. (2016). Discrete-Event Simulation for Primary Care Redesign: Review and a Case Study. *Healthcare Analytics: From Data to Knowledge to Healthcare Improvement,* 399–426. doi:10.1002/9781118919408.ch13

ADDITIONAL READING

Bordoloi, S., Fitzsimmons, J., & Fitzsimmons, M. (2019). *Service management: Operations, strategy, information technology* (9th ed.). McGraw-Hill Education.

Fasano, P. (2013). *Transforming Health Care: The Financial Impact of Technology, Electronic Tools and Data Mining* (1st ed.). Wiley.

Giardino, A. P., Riesenberg, L. A., & Varkey, P. (Eds.). (2020). *Medical Quality Management: Theory and Practice.* Springer Cham., doi:10.1007/978-3-030-48080-6

James, G., Witten, D., Hastie, T., & Tibshirani, R. (2021). *An Introduction to Statistical Learning: with Applications in R* (2nd ed.). Springer. doi:10.1007/978-1-0716-1418-1

Marconi, K., & Lehmann, H. (Eds.). (2015). *Big Data and Health Analytics* (1st ed.). CRC Press.

Strome, T. L. (2013). *Healthcare analytics for quality and performance improvement.* John Wiley & Sons. doi:10.1002/9781118761946

Walshe, K., & Smith, J. (Eds.). (2011). *Healthcare management.* McGraw-Hill Education.

Yang, H., & Lee, E. K. (2016). *Healthcare analytics: From data to knowledge to healthcare improvement*. John Wiley & Sons. doi:10.1002/9781118919408

KEY TERMS AND DEFINITIONS

Affordable Care Act: The Affordable Care Act (ACA), also known as Obamacare, is a law passed in the United States in 2010 with the aim of increasing access to health insurance and improving the quality and affordability of health care.

Business Analytics: Business analytics refers to the use of statistical, computational and data mining techniques in functional areas of business such as marketing, finance, and operations to extract insights from data that can be used to make data driven business decisions.

Business Intelligence (BI): Generally located within the larger concept of Business Analytics, Business Intelligence refers to gathering, filtering, and presenting data from various sources such as internal and external databases, and data warehouses to support business decision-making.

Co-creation in healthcare: Co-creation in healthcare refers to a collaborative approach in which patients, caregivers, and healthcare providers work together to design and deliver health care services. Co-creation recognizes that patients and their caregivers have valuable insights and expertise that can contribute to improving the quality and effectiveness of healthcare services.

Data Mining: Data mining refers to the process of discovering patterns, trends, and relationships within datasets using the techniques and algorithms in Supervised and Unsupervised Learning.

Data Visualization: Data Visualization refers to presenting the data in a chart with visual elements like different colors, shapes, and sizes to understand and communicate patterns, trends, and relationships that may be hidden in the raw data.

Direct care services: Direct care services refer to health care services that are provided directly to patients or clients by a health care professional or caregiver. These services are typically provided in a clinical or home care setting and involve direct interaction between the patient and the health care provider (e.g., hospitals, clinics, and treatment centers).

Exploratory Data Analysis (EDA): Exploratory Data Analysis (EDA) is a data analysis approach involving an initial, critical examination of the data to identify patterns and anomalies typically conducted using summary statistics and basic visualizations.

Healthcare quality: Healthcare quality refers to the degree to which health services meet the needs, expectations, and preferences of patients, and are consistent with current medical knowledge and best practices. Healthcare quality is essential for ensuring that patients receive safe, effective, timely, patient-centered, and equitable care.

Indirect care services (Support services): Indirect care services refer to health care services that support or facilitate the delivery of direct care services, but are not provided directly to patients (e.g., pharmaceuticals, insurance, and population health organizations).

Key Performance Indicators (KPIs): Key Performance Indicators (KPIs) are metrics used to monitor the performance of an organization or a business process. Managers can use KPIs to determine whether the organization is achieving its desired outcomes, presented on a dashboard in a website or a mobile device app. Examples of KPIs include revenues, employee turnover rate, number of products assembled on the factory floor, or number of patients discharged.

Plan-Do-Check-Act (PDCA) cycle: The Plan-Do-Check-Act (PDCA) cycle is a continuous improvement model used in many industries, including health care, to improve processes and achieve better outcomes. It is an iterative data-driven problem-solving technique that was first developed by American physicist Walter Shewhart in the 1920s. In the 1950s, Edwards Deming popularized the technique and named the cycle the "Shewhart" Cycle.

Quality of care: The World Health Organization (WHO) defines quality of care as "the extent to which health care services provided to individuals and patient populations improve desired health outcomes." This definition emphasizes the importance of focusing on the outcomes that matter most to patients and populations, and on the effectiveness of health care services in achieving those outcomes.

Service delivery: Service delivery is simply the execution of service designs to achieve the desired outcomes.

Service design: Service design is the activity of planning people, infrastructure, communication, and material components of a service in order to achieve the desired outcomes.

Supervised Machine Learning: This is a type of machine learning approach where the objective is to build a model that can learn the relationship between the input variables (predictors) and the target variable (predicted) so that the model can make accurate predictions on new, unseen data. Predictive analytics (e.g. linear regression and decision tree techniques) is part of Supervised Machine Learning.

Unsupervised Machine Learning: Unlike supervised machine learning where the input data includes a target variable, unsupervised machine learning algorithms are not provided with any target variable. Instead, Unsupervised Machine Learning refers to methods to discover patterns, relationships, and structures in the data set without any prior knowledge or guidance. Association and cluster analysis are examples of Unsupervised Machine Learning.

Chapter 5
Exploring the Potential of ChatGPT in Financial Decision Making

Reza Gharoie Ahangar
Lewis University, USA

Agata Fietko
Lewis University, USA

ABSTRACT

This chapter investigates the potential role of OpenAI's ChatGPT in investments to assess its proposed solutions' accuracy, potential benefits and drawbacks, and implications for financial decisions. The study utilizes empirical examples to evaluate ChatGPT's performance in providing financial advice. The results indicate that while ChatGPT can define financial terms and explain them in detail, it cannot provide investment suggestions. Moreover, the analysis suggests that the ChatGPT can provide more accurate information when users break down their questions into more specific topics. The study also highlights the need for more comprehensive training data to allow ChatGPT to provide more accurate advice. In addition, the research advises investors to be aware of ChatGPT's limitations and recommends breaking down financial questions into more specific topics to maximize the benefits of this technology. It is concluded that ChatGPT can be a helpful resource for financial experts but not for those with limited financial expertise and knowledge.

1. INTRODUCTION

1.1. History of ChatGPT

The growing public interest in Artificial Intelligence (AI) reflects the efforts of major technology companies, such as Google, Microsoft, and Baidu, to develop AI-based services and products. For example, Microsoft is a major investor in OpenAI, while Google has released an experimental AI service called

DOI: 10.4018/978-1-6684-8386-2.ch005

Bard. Generative AI, such as Chinchilla AI and Large Language Models, are also becoming increasingly popular (Zarifhonarvar, 2023).

In 2020, OpenAI, a company founded in 2015, launched third generation of its autoregressive language model, Generative Pre-trained Transformer 3 (GPT-3), which uses deep learning to produce human-like text (Brown et al., 2020). This model was developed on a corpus of almost 500 billion unlabeled tokens, representing the largest natural language processing (NLP) model in the world with 175 billion parameters (Radford et al., 2018). OpenAI was founded with the goal of developing AI systems that can outperform humans in different tasks (OpenAI, 2015).

On November 30, 2022, OpenAI introduced ChatGPT, a chatbot that leverages reinforcement learning to interact with its users (Grant & Metz, 2022). Quickly gaining widespread attention, ChatGPT was referred to as the industry's next big disruptor due to the quality of its response output (Shankland, 2022; Vanian, 2022). Within one week of its release, the artificial intelligence system had attracted over a million users on various social media platforms (Zarifhonarvar, 2023). This was notably faster than Instagram and TikTok, which respectively took nine and thirty months to reach a hundred million active users.

Recent media reports suggest that ChatGPT may be a formidable contender to Google (Brown, 2022), potentially leading to digital transformation (Tyrrell, 2022). However, San Altman, CEO of the company, has noted that the platform is still in its early testing stage (Altman, 2022), limiting its current capabilities. Nevertheless, ChatGPT still presents a promising indication of the potential of AI.

Generative AI has the potential to increase worker productivity by 10% (Megahed et al., 2023). Moreover, this technology is estimated to create trillions of dollars in economic value (Huang et al., 2022). In 2022, OpenAI invested over $1 billion in generative AI (Griffith & Metz, 2023). Despite these potential advantages, there is a growing concern regarding the potential impact of artificial intelligence on the knowledge economy, education, and skilled workers (Krugman, 2022; Locke, 2022; Marche, 2022).

1.2. How ChatGPT Works

The ChatGPT language model is a powerful tool that can perform various tasks, including machine translation and summarization. It has a transformer architecture that enables it to generate text similar to human writing, while its adaptive capabilities allow it to effectively adjust to new situations and topics. ChatGPT language model is fine-tuned to perform on a massive amount of data. The network utilizes a deep neural framework to process variable-length input sequences and generate human-like text. A variety of sources, including websites, books, and articles, have been collected as training data for the model. To ensure the accuracy of the model, this data has been filtered and pre-processed to remove repetitive and low-quality text (Zaremba & Demir, 2023).

In 2018, the GPT-3 framework was introduced as a state-of-the-art language model for various applications such as text summarization, content generation, and language translation (Devlin et al., 2018). AI-powered virtual assistants and chatbots, such as ChatGPT, have been developed to reduce the complexity of implementing generative AI models (McKee & Noever, 2022). Aside from text-to-text AI tools, other innovations in generative AI include text-to-image (OpenAI, 2022c), text-to-audio (Agostinelli et al., 2023), and text-to-video (Singer et al., 2022).

The use of GPT-3 for natural language processing (NLP) tasks has been investigated in recent years. Megahed et al. (2023) explored the use of GPT-3 for text generation, exploring the model's ability to generate text that resembles the actual content. Brown et al. (2020) assessed the performance of GPT-2 and GPT-3 in various language understanding tasks, such as machine translation and summarization.

Their study showed that GPT-3 could generate human-like text, making it difficult to distinguish from written text. Furthermore, they found that GPT-3 could be refined by including specific data in the training set, allowing it to perform high-fidelity tasks.

1.3. General Applications of ChatGPT

According to Brown et al. (2020), the GPT-3 model has demonstrated its ability to perform natural language processing. In 2021, OpenAI released the Codex model, a fine-tuning of the GPT-3 for programming tasks involving 12 billion parameters (Chen et al., 2021). This model powers the cloud-based tool GitHub Copilot, which developers use on various platforms, such as Microsoft's Visual Studio and Neovim. Unlike GPT-3, this model learns and constructs human-like answers to the text input with the help of relationships and patterns in the data to ensure that ChatGPT can produce relevant and contextual responses to various natural language expressions (OpenAI, 2022a).

A study conducted early in the development of the ChatGPT platform revealed that it was able to successfully pass the common core of the US legal accreditation examinations for professional lawyers (Bommarito II & Katz, 2022). Marti (2022) used ChatGPT output to create a comprehensive guide for quantitative trading. Chen and Eger (2022) employed ChatGPT for abstract and title generation in contemporary literature. Wenzlaff and Spaeth (2022) used the platform to produce appropriately-academicized definitions. Raffel et al. (2019) demonstrated in their paper that the transformer-based framework could produce fluent and coherent text in a variety of contexts, such as summarization and text completion. They also noted that this model could be adapted to a range of new domains and tasks.

1.4. The Application of ChatGPT in Economic and Finance Areas

The ChatGPT and its effect on the global economy can be examined from different perspectives. Many important factors can be considered when analyzing these services' impact on the labor market, economy, and finance. One of these is the potential of artificial intelligence to transform the labor force. There is a wide range of literature about labor economics that focuses on the various aspects of automation and technological changes. Implementing AI-powered services such as ChatGPT and similar could automate many tasks that previously required human workers, which could cause significant market disruption and the creation of new jobs while also causing some jobs to become redundant.

The rapid emergence and evolution of AI could have a significant impact on the global economy, according to a recent McKinsey study (Zarifhonarvar, 2023). The study identified five main types of AI technologies: natural language, machine vision, robotic process automation, advanced machine learning, and virtual assistants. It found that around seventy percent of companies have at least one type of AI technology, while less than fifty percent have fully integrated it. The study estimated that the potential economic impact of AI could reach $13 trillion by 2030, mainly due to the increased productivity it could bring (Zarifhonarvar, 2023).

Recent developments in GPT technology have been used to improve the accuracy and reliability of financial data analysis. GPT technology has been applied to generate natural language summaries and financial reports (Zaremba & Demir, 2023). It has also been used in various areas of financial analysis, such as social media and text-based analysis, to identify market trends and provide actionable insights from unstructured data. GPT technology has shown promising potential in various areas of financial analysis, including natural-language understanding and text-based analysis (Zaremba & Demir, 2023).

Unsophisticated investors are more likely to be victims of financial scams due to their lack of knowledge about financial matters (Mitchell & Lusardi, 2014). The financial crisis of 2008-2009 brought this issue to the forefront, prompting regulators and legislators to enact regulations such as the Dodd-Frank Act to protect consumers. However, due to the complexity of financial modeling, it is often difficult for non-financial specialists to interpret the results of a stock return model (Mitchell & Lusardi, 2014). The potential of AI-based technology to democratize access to financial services is immense, especially for individuals with limited knowledge and financial constraints (Yue et al., 2023).

The emergence and evolution of AI has been instrumental in the development of financial inclusion and financial literacy for the public, as noted by David Mhlanga (2020). AI has been used to address numerous issues, such as detecting fraud and cybersecurity threats and establishing effective customer support systems (Mhlanga, 2020). Aroomoogan (2020) pointed out that the integration of AI and other advanced technologies in the financial services industry has enabled individuals to make informed decisions. Thus, it is likely that technological advancements in finance can provide an effective solution.

AI can provide a cost-effective solution for banks to offer customized financial services to both accredited and non-accredited investors. By integrating virtual assistants into their operations, banks can provide more efficient and cost-effective customer support (Aroomoogan, 2020). Additionally, AI can be used to create and manage financial advice, thereby providing easier access to various investment opportunities for non-accredited investors This could enable them to access higher-yielding investments, which could potentially lead to better financial outcomes.

Theories about market efficiency, such as those proposed by Fama (1970) and Lo (2004), suggest that the prices of assets, such as stocks and cryptocurrency, should accurately reflect their underlying value. Wu and Chen (2022) further suggest that when the term "AI" is used, the accompanying exchange-traded fund can generate a premium of 0.4%. The signaling theory states that individuals use signals to reduce the information asymmetry in the exchange These signals often need to be hard to reproduce and verifiable (Ante and Fiedler, 2020).

Therefore, ChatGPT might provide investors with a conversational format to access investment advice and other related information, making navigating the complex world of financial markets easier (Yue et al., 2023). This technology enables non-professional investors to quickly access alternative investments and receive tailored investment recommendations based on their specific requirements.

This chapter examines the capabilities of ChatGPT in translating complex financial models into a more user-friendly format. Specifically, it seeks to investigate whether ChatGPT can explain complex financial results in a manner that can enable users to make informed decisions, and how this could potentially signify quality signals in different financial markets. For this purpose, this chapter presents an exploratory case study presenting the author's hands-on experience with an AI system, ChatGPT, for a financial purpose. We conducted a series of chat sessions with chatGPT asking for stock recommendations, progressing through more general to more specific prompts. The results of these experiments are presented and discussed. The findings of this study can be used to inform investors and researchers in the field of finance on the implications of ChatGPT in providing accurate information.

The remainder of the chapter is as follows: Section 2 reviews the literature; Section 3 represents the research methodology; Section 4 explains the results; Section 5 includes the discussion; Section 6 gives conclusions and suggestions for investors, and finally, Section 7 includes the limitations and future research.

2. LITERATURE REVIEW

Since its public release, OpenAI's ChatGPT has received significant interest. However, research regarding its application has been limited. One of the most challenging obstacles when using AI-based tools, particularly in the financial sector, is the trust people have in the accuracy of the decisions made by the AI. Interactions between AI and humans are mainly psychological and depend on people's confidence in the AI and its acceptance accuracy (Chua et al., 2023).

Making financial decisions is challenging for those without the appropriate training or experience. AI has been proposed as a relatively easy solution, with AI tools like ChatGPT already being used as Robo-advisors. The advantages of using such a system are discussed in Shanmuganathan (2020), which defines it as an automated investment platform that utilizes quantitative algorithms to manage investors' portfolios and is easily accessible to customers.

Studies have supported that AI tools such as ChatGPT can positively impact the financial sector, simplifying customer service, increasing advisory ability, and improving the customer-advisor experience by providing a unified and seamless experience (Dietzmann et al., 2023). ChatGPT has the potential to serve as an assistant for portfolio managers and contributes to a better understanding of the role of language models in finance (Ko & Lee, 2023).

The study conducted by Ko & Lee (2023) demonstrated that ChatGPT could distinguish asset classes using a mathematical approach and produced better results in terms of diversity index than randomly selected assets. It is also less biased and more accurate than humans in tasks involving mathematical, ambiguous, or complex problems (Ko & Lee, 2023). However, it has been observed to demonstrate biases when dealing with human types of decisions (Chen et al., 2023). One area for improvement with the tool is its high confidence levels, making it challenging to process inconclusive information (Chen et al., 2023). Therefore, this bias, when making financial decisions, can significantly impact the outcome.

Au and Yue (2023) conducted a study exploring the utility of ChatGPT for evaluating and developing investment strategies. They proposed that ChatGPT could reduce the workload of human agents and democratize investment research through its ability to generate Python code via natural language commands. Alshater (2022) revealed that ChatGPT potentially has applications in economics and finance, particularly in the fields of data analysis and findings interpretation. This study suggested that ChatGPT is best used in conjunction with human interpretations due to the system's limited generalizability and lack of domain expertise. Wenzlaff and Späth (2022) investigated the capacity of ChatGPT to define specific terms related to crowdfunding, alternative finance, and community finance. Their findings suggested that the quality of the answers generated by the algorithm were dependent on the input and content provided by the users.

With the previously mentioned rise of interest in ChatGPT and its abilities, researchers studied its performance regarding the tools' understanding ability. Zhong et al. (2023) explored the performance of ChatGPT in relation to its understanding ability on tasks involving paraphrase and similarity. Results showed that ChatGPT struggled with these tasks but showed potential performance on sentiment analysis and question-answering tasks. Azaria (2022) examined the potential bias of ChatGPT when it comes to producing numbers and found a high correlation between humans' favorite number, 7, and the frequency of digits generated by ChatGPT. This suggests that ChatGPT is affected by the data that humans create, which could lead to similar biases or preferences in financial analysis.

A study by Niszczota and Abbas (2023) investigated the financial literacy of the ChatGPT tool and its ability to provide investment advice. The research revealed that while the tool performed well on the financial literacy test and provided savings advice, its results were lower than expected. Previous studies have determined that human preference plays a significant role in determining the success of robo-advising (Dowling & Lucey, 2023).

Despite the potential of ChatGPT, studies show that people prefer that humans rather than AI tools make investment decisions due to the difficulty of following innovative changes in the financial world (Dowling & Lucey, 2023). Beerbaum and Otto (2023) suggest that ChatGPT should receive extensive human inspection, even though its results are promising. Therefore, ChatGPT has the potential to be used as a financial robo-advisor, though humans should inspect it, and its limitations should be considered.

3. METHODOLOGY

It is essential to consider human behavior when designing and building technological approaches related to human beings. Human misbehavior can be an obstacle to the effectiveness of implementing AI-related technologies, and appropriate frameworks must be designed to incorporate human behavior into technology development (Pfleeger & Caputo, 2012).

Some models and theories can be used to help scholars understand and assess the appropriateness of Artificial Intelligence (AI) related technologies in organizational contexts. These theories that form the basis of this study's conceptual model include, Social Cognitive Theory, Time Displacement Theory, and Technology Acceptance Model (He et al., 2020). Scholars can leverage these theories to examine the role of AI technology (e.g., ChatGPT) in the financial sector, and to explore how the financial markets may be impacted by the introduction of advanced technology and tools such as ChatGPT.

Over forty recent scholarly articles related to the ChatGPT were studied to ensure an objective selection of relevant research on the effect of ChatGPT on people's investment decision performance.

A systematic critical literature review is conducted to evaluate the impact of ChatGPT on people's financial decision-making. Real-world financial cases with different criteria were also analyzed, and the extracted information was objectively incorporated into the proposed theoretical framework to address the research questions posed in this study.

This study applied qualitative research utilizing an interpretive research paradigm to review the existing literature on the application of advanced AI tools, such as ChatGPT, to financial markets and investment. A systematic review of relevant literature was conducted to examine the influence of ChatGPT on investors' financial performance.

4. RESULTS AND FINDINGS

In this step, we begin by posing some basic and generic questions to ascertain the initial assistance provided by ChatGPT.

First, we investigated the efficacy of ChatGPT in assisting investors in selecting the best stock for investment. Specifically, we asked whether ChatGPT could provide meaningful advice when only given the prompt "What would be the best stock to purchase?" without additional context. Subsequently, we inquired into the important factors that can help an investor make the right decision when purchasing shares.

The ChatGPT answer reveals that to select the optimal stock, information regarding earning reports, macroeconomic factors, and interest rates must be considered. Additionally, it suggests employing technical analysis, whereby predictive tools, such as deep learning, may prove to be beneficial. Finally, it recommends seeking the advice of analysts to make the optimal choice. However, it should be noted that ChatGPT is providing general advice, rather than recommending a particular stock for purchase.

Figure 1. Chat GPT prompt

Prompt:
What is the best stock to invest in on March 20, 2023?

Answer:
It is impossible to answer this question definitively as the best stock to invest in on March 20, 2023 will depend on many factors, including market conditions, economic indicators, and the performance of individual stocks. Investors should research and evaluate the stocks available in order to make an informed decision about which stock is best for their particular investment goals.

Figure 2. Chat GPT prompt

Prompt:
What factors are important when predicting the stock price?

Answer:
1. Earnings Reports: Analyzing a company's earnings reports helps investors understand the financial health of the company. Earnings reports include the company's revenues, expenses, profits, and cash flow.

2. Macroeconomic Indicators: Macroeconomic indicators such as GDF, inflation, and employment numbers can help investors understand the overall economic environment and how it may affect stock prices.
3. Interest Rates: Interest rates can affect stock prices as higher interest rates lead to higher borrowing costs, which in turn affects corporate profits.

4. Technical Analysis: Technical analysis is the process of examining historical stock price data to identify patterns and trends that can be used to predict future price movements.

5. Analyst Recommendations: Analyst recommendations are important as they provide a consensus opinion of the stock's potential. Analysts may also provide valuable insights into a company's prospects and future performance.

Figure 3. Chat GPT prompt

Prompt:
How are overall market conditions of New York stock exchange on March 20, 2023?

Answer:
On March 20, 2023, the overall market conditions of the New York Stock Exchange are generally positive. The Dow Jones Industrial Average (DJIA) is trading at a record high of 32,115, and the S&P 500 is up 7.3% year-to-date. The Nasdaq Composite is also up 9.2% year-to-date. The market is also experiencing historically low volatility, with the VIX index trading below 20. Overall, the market conditions for the New York Stock Exchange are currently quite favorable.

In the above question, we sought to ascertain the overall market conditions to ascertain if the trend of the stock market (e.g., New York Stock Exchange) is positive. We found that ChatGPT can provide us with some general information regarding the market's performance. We posed specific questions based on the initial answers of ChatGPT and found that the ChatGPT was still unable to provide an accurate response.

We see that the provided information by ChatGPT is not updated information. After some research, we found that the economic growth of the United States is expected to significantly slow in 2023, with a projected real GDP growth of 0.7%. In addition, the annual inflation rate for the 12 months ended February 2023 rose to 6.0%, up from 6.4% the previous year. As a result of this slowdown, the unemployment rate is predicted to rise to 5.1% by the end of the year, averaging 4.7% throughout 2023 (U.S. Labor Department, 2023). Furthermore, interest rates on savings accounts have been subject to fluctuation, with the Federal Reserve increasing rates and offering 4.35% or higher returns on savings.

In the above prompt, we posed a direct question to ascertain which company had the best performance on a specific day. However, ChatGPT was unable to answer this question. After conducting further research, we determined that the top 2023 stock market performers included health care stocks with unique catalysts and stocks exposed to artificial intelligence technology. From this list, CinCor Pharma Inc. was the first company (US News, 2023).

CinCor Pharmaceuticals, a clinical-stage biopharmaceutical company, experienced a dramatic shift in stock prices in 2023. After their leading drug candidate, Baxdrostat, encountered a setback in its clinical trials in November 2022, CinCor's stock prices plummeted 47%. However, in January 2023, AstraZeneca PLC announced a buyout of CinCor for an upfront price of $1.3 billion, more than double the previous week's closing price. As a result, the stock of CinCor has increased 136.5% in the same year (US News, 2023). Next, we utilize ChatGPT-provided information and supplementary data gathered by researchers to identify the most advantageous stock for investment.

We observe that even after providing some information based on the initial assessment of ChatGPT, it cannot suggest a stock for investment. In the next part, we assume that the management team of the proposed team is doing a great job and that the suggested company shows future growth.

Finally, ChatGPT recommends buying the stock of the suggested company with some assumptions. However, this is a suggested company by researchers, and ChatGPT did not provide any information about a specific stock to purchase.

Figure 4. Chat GPT prompt

Prompt:
Which company has the best performance in New York stock exchange on March 20, 2023?

Answer:
It is impossible to answer this question without more specific information, such as the criteria used to measure performance and the list of companies being compared.

Prompt:
Which company has the highest earning report on the New York stock exchange on March 20, 2023?

Answer:
The answer to this question is not possible to determine without more information. The highest earning report on the New York stock exchange on March 20, 2023 will depend on the performance of each company listed on the exchange and the fluctuations of the stock market on that day.

Prompt:
What are the GDP, inflation, and unemployment rates on March 20, 2023, in the United States?

Answer:
It is not possible to accurately predict the GDF, inflation, and unemployment rates of the United States on March 20, 2023, as these figures are highly dependent on a variety of factors that cannot be predicted with any degree of accuracy. However, the last official figures released by the Bureau of Labor Statistics (BLS) in May 2021 estimate that the GDP rate was 5.6%, the inflation rate was 2.6%, and the unemployment rate was 5.8%.

Prompt:
What is the interest rate in the United States on March 20, 2023?

Answer:
It is not possible to answer this question as interest rates can vary depending on the lender and the type of loan.

5. DISCUSSION

In this study, we used empirical examples to evaluate the accuracy and efficacy of ChatGPT in providing guidance for financial planning. We began with simple queries about the best stocks or industries to invest in. We found that ChatGPT was unable to provide specific stock recommendations, but instead provided general advice about factors to consider when making an investment. Our findings suggest that, while ChatGPT provides helpful guidance, additional research is required to identify the best stocks and industries to invest in based on the suggested factors. These findings are supported by Alshater (2022), Chen et al. (2023) and Ko & Lee, (2023).

The application of ChatGPT for stock price prediction has some limitations. Specifically, it does not consider other key factors such as the consumer price index, industrial production, and consumer confidence, which are crucial indicators for predicting stock prices. Failing to account for these factors could lead to inaccurate predictions.

Figure 5. Chat GPT prompt

Prompt:
If we know the interest rate is 4.35%, real GDP growth is 0.7%, the annual inflation rate is 6.4%, the unemployment rate is 4.7%, and we know top 2023 stock market performers include health care stocks, and CinCor Pharma Inc is the first in this list. Would you recommend buying the stock of CinCor Pharma Inc?

Answer:
It is difficult to recommend buying the stock of CinCor Pharma Inc without more information. Knowing the interest rate, GDP growth, inflation rate, and unemployment rate can give an indication of the overall state of the economy, but they do not necessarily provide enough information to make an informed decision about investing in a particular stock. Additionally, it is important to consider the individual performance of the company and its industry, as well as other factors such as competitive landscape, management team, and risk profile. Therefore, it is recommended to conduct further research before investing in any stocks.

Figure 6. Chat GPT prompt

Prompt:
If we know the interest rate is 4.35%, real GDP growth is 0.7%, the annual inflation rate is 6.4%, the unemployment rate is 4.7%, and we know top 2023 stock market performers include health care stocks, and CinCor Pharma Inc is the first in this list. In addition, if the company has a great management team and shows growth in the coming months. Would you recommend buying the stock of CinCor Pharma Inc?

Answer:

Yes, I would recommend buying the stock of CinCor Pharma Inc. given the favorable economic conditions, the positive outlook for the company, and its top ranking among the 2023 stock market performers. The interest rate of 4.35%, GDP growth of 0.7%, inflation rate of 6.4%, and unemployment rate of 4.7% all point to a stable economic environment. The company's great management team also indicates that it is well-positioned to capitalize on this environment. Moreover, the fact that it is the top performer in the stock market for 2023 further demonstrates its potential for growth. Therefore, I believe that buying the stock of CinCor Pharma Inc is a good investment choice.

Moreover, political events can influence stock market activity, with those that bring greater clarity and stability to the economic and political environment being viewed as having a positive effect. Examples of such events include policy announcements that lead to increased consumer and investor confidence, the passing of legislation that encourages economic growth, the introduction of pro-business regulations and policies, and the approval of trade agreements that open new markets and create economic opportunities.

In addition, another critical factor, investor sentiment is a critical factor that can influence the direction of investments. For example, when investors are optimistic about a particular stock, currency, or commodity and begin buying it, the price often increases as the market perceives the asset to be undervalued and thus with potential for growth.

We observed a need for updated information in the database of ChatGPT for proper investment decision-making. For example, in one of the cases, ChatGPT provided information that was two years old, which is inadequate for making informed decisions about stocks or companies.

However, ChatGPT could provide us with the necessary general information for investment and helped to break down that general information to more detailed information, which could help us better understand the stock market situation and supported by Au and Yue, (2023) and Niszczota and Abbas, (2023). Thus, we observed that ChatGPT could help investors by providing some necessary information for investment. However, it cannot answer a specific question about the best investment stock. Therefore, a person using ChatGPT needs to know about finance and the financial market, then can apply the information provided by ChatGPT to find the right direction for investment.

The application of ChatGPT in the financial market can be promising in the sense that it is able to provide guidance and advice for investors. However, it is limited in its ability to provide specific stock recommendations or consider other key factors such as the CPI, industrial production, consumer confidence, political events, and investor sentiment. Therefore, to make the most of ChatGPT, investors should supplement its guidance with their own research and analysis.

6. CONCLUSION

This study has explored the potential of ChatGPT in the financial sector. Through a systematic review of the literature and some empirical examples, we found that ChatGPT can provide general guidance and advice for investors, but it is limited in its ability to provide specific stock recommendations or consider other key factors. We also observed that ChatGPT could be used to help investors break down general information and answer more detailed questions, which may help them better understand the stock market situation. Overall, ChatGPT could potentially be a useful tool for investors by providing necessary guidance and advice. However, it is important to note that technology is still in its early stages, and more research is needed to further understand its capabilities and limitations. Investors should supplement ChatGPT's guidance with their own research and analysis to make the most of the AI-powered technology. Furthermore, further research should be conducted to explore the implications of this technology for contagion and herding behavior in financial markets.

7. LIMITATIONS AND FUTURE RESEARCH

Due to the nature of our research, this study has some limitations. Firstly, this is a new topic; therefore, studies in this area are in their early stages. Secondly, this study only examined one case study using ChatGPT in the finance area; however, additional case studies could help to reach more conclusive results. Thirdly, since this is a case study, experimental design research could be a stronger method to evaluate the performance of ChatGPT in the finance area.

Taking these limitations into consideration, future studies should include more case studies from different industries or different stock markets in different countries. Additionally, it would be interesting to conduct experimental design studies across different stock markets in different countries and compare the results. Long-term research into the stock market with ChatGPT could also help to gain a more comprehensive understanding of how ChatGPT can impact the finance area.

REFERENCES

Agostinelli, A., Denk, T. I., Borsos, Z., Engel, J., Verzetti, M., Caillon, A., Huang, Q., Jansen, A., Roberts, A., Tagliasacchi, M., Sharifi, M., Zeghidour, N., & Frank, C. (2023). MusicLM: generating music from text. arXiv. https://arxiv.org/abs/2301.11325

AlshaterM. (2022). Exploring the Role of Artificial Intelligence in Enhancing Academic Performance: A Case Study of ChatGPT. SSRN. doi:10.2139/ssrn.4312358

Altman, S. (2022). *Tweet by Sam Altman* [WWW Document]. Twitter. https://twitter.com/sama/status/1601731295792414720

Ante, L., & Fiedler, I. (2020). Cheap Signals in Security Token Offerings (STOs). *Quantitative Finance and Economics*, *4*(4), 608–639. doi:10.3934/QFE.2020028

Aroomoogan, K. (2020). How Artificial Intelligence Can Enable Ethically Driven Investments. *Forbes.* https://www.forbes.com/sites/forbesfinancecouncil/2020/09/23/how-artificial-intelligence-can-enable-ethically-driven-investments/?sh=168099eb6fc1

Azaria, A. (2022). *ChatGPT Usage and limitations.* HAL. https://hal.science/hal-03913837

BommaritoI. I. M.KatzD. M. 2022. GPT takes the bar exam. arXiv:2212.14402.

Brown, A. (2022). *Why ChatGPT will change digital transformation* [WWW Document]. BCS.

Brown, T. (2020). Language models are few-shot learners. arXiv preprint arXiv:2005.14165.

Brown, T., Mann, B., Ryder, N., Subbiah, M., Kaplan, J. D., Dhariwal, P., Neelakantan, A., Shyam, P., Sastry, G., & Askell, A. (2020). Language models are few-shot learners. *Advances in Neural Information Processing Systems*, *33*, 1877–1901.

Chen, M., Tworek, J., Jun, H., Yuan, Q., & Pinto, H. P. O. (2021). Evaluating large language models trained on code. arXiv. https://arxiv.org/abs/2107.03374

ChenY.AndiappanM.JenkinT.OvchinnikovA. (2023). A Manager and an AI Walk into a Bar: Does ChatGPT Make Biased Decisions Like We Do? doi:10.2139/ssrn.4380365

Chen, Y., & Eger, S. (2022). Transformers go for the LOLs: Generating (humourous) titles from scientific abstracts end-to-end. http://dx.doi.org/ doi:10.48550/ARXIV

Chua, A.Y.K., Pal, A., and Banerjee, S. (2023). AI-enabled investment advice: Will users buy it? *Computers is human behaviors*, 138. doi:10.1016/j.chb.2022.107481

Dowling, M., & Lucey, B. (2023). ChatGPT for (Finance) research: The Bananarama Conjecture. *Finance Research Letters*, *53*, 103662. doi:10.1016/j.frl.2023.103662

Dr, B. Otto, D. (2023). *Generative Artificial Intelligence (GAI) Ethics Taxonomy- Applying Chat GPT for Robotic Process Automation (GAI-RPA) as Business Case*. SSRN. doi:10.2139/ssrn.4385025

Fama, E. F. (1970). Efficient Capital Markets: A Review of Theory and Empirical Work. *The Journal of Finance*, *25*(2), 383–417. doi:10.2307/2325486

Grant, N., & Metz, C. (2022). A new chat bot is a 'Code Red' for Google's search business. *New York Times*.

Griffith, E., & Metz, C. (2023, January). *A new area of A.I. booms, even amid the tech gloom.*

He, W., Zhang, J., & Li, W. (2020). Information Technology Solutions, Challenges, and Suggestions for Tackling the COVID-19 Pandemic. *International Journal of Information Management*, *102287*. doi:10.1016/j.ijinfomgt.2020.1022 PMID:33318721

Huang, S., & Grady, P. (2022, September). *Generative AI: A creative new world*. Sequoia Capital. https://www.sequoiacap.com/article/generative-ai-a-creative-new-world/

KoH.LeeJ. (2023). Can Chatgpt Improve Investment Decision? From a Portfolio Management Perspective. doi:10.2139/ssrn.4390529

Krugman, P. (2022, December 6). Does ChatGPT Mean Robots Are Coming For the Skilled Jobs? *The New York Times*. https://www.nytimes.com/2022/12/06/opinion/chatgpt-ai-skilled-jobs-automation.html

Lo, A. W. (2004). The Adaptive Markets Hypothesis. *Journal of Portfolio Management*, *30*(5), 15–29. doi:10.3905/jpm.2004.442611

Locke, S. (2022, December 6). What is AI chatbot phenomenon ChatGPT and could it replace humans? *The Guardian*. https://www.theguardian.com/technology/2022/dec/05/what-is-ai-chatbot-phenomenon-chatgpt-and-could-it-replace-humans

Lusardi, A., & Mitchell, O. S. (2014). The Economic Importance of Financial Literacy: Theory and Evidence. *Journal of Economic Literature*, *52*(1), 34. doi:10.1257/jel.52.1.5 PMID:28579637

Marche, S. (2022, December 6). The College Essay Is Dead. *The Atlantic*. https://www.theatlantic.com/technology/archive/2022/12/chatgpt-ai-writing-college-student-essays/672371/

MartiG. 2022. From data to trade: A machine learning approach to quantitative trading. SSRN:4315362. doi:10.2139/ssrn.4315362

McKee, F., & Noever, D. (2022). Chatbots in a botnet world. arXiv. https://arxiv.org/abs/2212.11126

Megahed, F. M., Chen, Y. J., Ferris, J. A., Knoth, S., & Jones-Farmer, L. A. (2023). How Generative AI models such as ChatGPT can be (Mis)Used in SPC Practice, Education, and Research? An Exploratory Study. https://doi.org/ doi:10.48550/arXiv.2302.10916

Mhlanga, D. (2020). Industry 4.0 in finance: The impact of artificial intelligence (AI) on digital financial inclusion. *International Journal of Financial Studies*, *8*(3), 45. doi:10.3390/ijfs8030045

Niszczota, P., & Abbas, S. (2023). GPT as a Financial Advisor. http://dx.doi.org/doi:10.2139/ssrn.4384861

Open A. I. (2015, December 11). *About OpenAI*. OpenAI. https://openai.com/about/

Open A. I. (2022a, November). *ChatGPT: Optimizing language models for dialogue*. OpenAI. https://openai.com/

Open A. I. (2022c, April). *DALL.E 2*. Open AI. https://openai.com/dall-e-2/.

Pfleeger, S. L., & Caputo, D. D. (2012). Leveraging behavioral science to mitigate cyber security risk. *Computers & Security*, *31*(4), 597–611. doi:10.1016/j.cose.2011.12.010

Radford, A., Narasimhan, K., Salimans, T., & Sutskever, I. (2018). *Improving language understanding by generative pre-training*. OpenAI. https://cdn.openai.com/research-covers/language-unsupervised/language_understanding_paper.pdf

Raffel, C. (2019). Exploring the limits of transfer learning with a unified text-to-text transformer. arXiv preprint arXiv:1910.10683.

Securities and Exchange Commission. (1987). *Regulation D Revisions; Exemption for Certain Employee Benefit Plans*. Release No. 33-6683. January 16. [52 FR 3015].

Shankland, S. (2022). *Why Everyone's Obsessed with ChatGPT, the Mind-Blowing AI Chatbot* [WWW Document]. CNET. https://www.cnet.com/tech/computing/why-everyones-obsessed-withchatgpt-the-mind-blowing-ai-chatbot/

Shanmuganathan, M. (2020). Behavioural finance in an era of artificial intelligence: Longitudinal case study of robo-advisors in investment decisions. *Journal of Behavioral and Experimental Finance, 27,* doi:10.1016/j.jbef.2020.100297

SingerU.PolyakA.HayesT.YinX.AnJ.ZhangS.HuQ.YangH.AshualO.GafniO.ParikhD.GuptaS.TaigmanY. (2022). Make-A-Video: text-to-video generation without text-video data. arXiv article available at: https://arxiv.org/abs/2209.14792

Tyrrell, J. (2022). *ChatGPT versus Google – the future of search* [WWW Document]. TechHQ.

Vanian, J. (2022). *Why tech insiders are so excited about ChatGPT, a chatbot that answers questions and writes essays* [WWW Document]. CNBC. https://www.cnbc.com/2022/12/13/chatgpt-is-anew-ai-chatbot-that-can-answer-questions-and-write-essays.html

WenzlaffK.SpaethS. 2022. Smarter than humans? Validating how OpenAI's ChatGPT model explains crowdfunding, alternative finance and community finance. SSRN:4302443. doi:10.2139/ssrn.4302443

Wu, C.-C., & Chen, W.-P. (2022). What's an AI name worth? The impact of AI ETFs on their underlying stocks. *Finance Research Letters*, *46*, 102474. doi:10.1016/j.frl.2021.102474

YueT.AuC. C. (2023). GPTQuant's Conversational AI: Simplifying Investment Research for All. *SSRN*. doi:10.2139/ssrn.4380516

Yue, T., Au, D., Au, C. C., & Iu, K. Y. (2023). *Democratizing Financial Knowledge with ChatGPT by OpenAI: Unleashing the Power of Technology*. SSRN., doi:10.2139srn.4346152

Zaremba, A., & Demir, E. (2023). *ChatGPT: Unlocking the Future of NLP in Finance*. SSRN., doi:10.2139srn.4323643

Zarifhonarvar, A. (2023). *Economics of ChatGPT: A Labor Market View on the Occupational Impact of Artificial Intelligence*. SSRN., doi:10.2139srn.4350925

Zhong, Q., Ding, L., Liu, J., Du, B., & Tao, D. (2023). Can ChatGPT Understand Too? A Comparative Study on ChatGPT and Fine-tuned BERT. https://doi.org/ doi:10.48550/arXiv.2302.10198

ADDITIONAL READING

Alberts, I., Mercolli, L., Pyka, T., Prenosil, G., Shi, K., Rominger, A., & Afshar-Oromieh, A. (2023). Large langua ge models (LLM) and ChatGPT: What will the impact on nuclear medicine be? *European Journal of Nuclear Medicine and Molecular Imaging*, *50*(6), 1549–1552. doi:10.100700259-023-06172-w PMID:36892666

Baidoo-AnuD.OwusuA. (2023). Education in the Era of Generative Artificial Intelligence (AI): Understanding the Potential Benefits of ChatGPT in Promoting Teaching and Learning. *SSRN*. doi:10.2139/ssrn.4337484

BiswasS. (2023). Role of Chat GPT in Education. SSRN. https://ssrn.com/abstract=4369981

Biswas, S. S. (2023). Role of Chat GPT in Public Health. *Annals of Biomedical Engineering*, *51*(5), 868–869. doi:10.100710439-023-03172-7 PMID:36920578

Cascella, M., Montomoli, J., Bellini, V., & Bignami, E. (2023). Evaluating the Feasibility of ChatGPT in Healthcare: An Analysis of Multiple Clinical and Research Scenarios. *Journal of Medical Systems*, *47*(1), 33. doi:10.100710916-023-01925-4 PMID:36869927

Choi, J. H., and Hickman, K. E., and Monahan, A., and Schwarcz, D. B. (2023). ChatGPT Goes to Law School. *Minnesota Legal Studies Research,* Paper No. 23-03. doi:10.2139/ssrn.4335905

Cooper, G. (2023). Examining Science Education in ChatGPT: An Exploratory Study of Generative Artificial Intelligence. *Journal of Science Education and Technology*, *32*(3), 444–452. doi:10.100710956-023-10039-y

Crawford, J., Cowling, M., & Allen, K. (2023). Leadership is needed for ethical ChatGPT: Character, assessment, and learning using artificial intelligence (AI). *Journal of University Teaching & Learning Practice*, *20*(3). doi:10.53761/1.20.3.02

Dahmen, J., Kayaalp, M. E., Ollivier, M., Pareek, A., Hirschmann, M. T., Karlsson, J., & Winkler, P. W. (2023). Artificial intelligence bot ChatGPT in medical research: The potential game changer as a double-edged sword. *Knee Surgery, Sports Traumatology, Arthroscopy, 31*(4), 1187–1189. doi:10.100700167-023-07355-6 PMID:36809511

De Angelis, L., Baglivo, F., & Arzilli, G. (2023). ChatGPT and the Rise of Large Language Models: The New AI-Driven Infodemic Threat in Public Health. http://dx.doi.org/ doi:10.2139/ssrn.4352931

Du, H., Teng, S., Chen, H., Ma, J., Wang, X., Gou, C., Li, B., Ma, S., Miao, Q., Na, X., Ye, P., Zhang, H., Luo, G., & Wang, F.-Y. (2023). Chat With ChatGPT on Intelligent Vehicles: An IEEE TIV Perspective. *IEEE Transactions on Intelligent Vehicles, 8*(3), 2020–2026. doi:10.1109/TIV.2023.3253281

Floridi, L. (2023). AI as *Agency Without Intelligence*: On ChatGPT, Large Language Models, and Other Generative Models. *Philosophy & Technology, 36*(1), 15. doi:10.100713347-023-00621-y

Gao, Y. Tong, W., Wu, E. Q., Chen, W., Zhu, G., & Wang, F. -Y. (2023). Chat With ChatGPT on Interactive Engines for Intelligent Driving. IEEE Transactions on Intelligent Vehicles, 8(3), 2034-2036. . doi:10.1109/TIV.2023.3252571

Guo, C., Lu, Y., Dou, Y., and Wang, F.Y. (2023). Can ChatGPT Boost Artistic Creation: The Need of Imaginative Intelligence for Parallel Art. *IEEE/CAA Journal of Automatica Sinica, 10*(4), 835-838. doi:10.1109/JAS.2023.123555

Kim, S. G. (2023). Using ChatGPT for language editing in scientific articles. *Maxillofacial Plastic and Reconstructive Surgery, 45*(1), 13. doi:10.118640902-023-00381-x PMID:36882591

King, M. R. (2023). chatGPT. A Conversation on Artificial Intelligence, Chatbots, and Plagiarism in Higher Education. *Cellular and Molecular Bioengineering, 16*(1), 1–2. doi:10.100712195-022-00754-8 PMID:36660590

Kung, T. H., Cheatham, M., Medenilla, A., Sillos, C., De Leon, L., Elepaño, C., Madriaga, M., Aggabao, R., Diaz-Candido, G., Maningo, J., & Tseng, V. (2023). Performance of ChatGPT on USMLE: Potential for AI-assisted medical education using large language models. *PLOS Digital Health, 2*(2), e0000198. doi:10.1371/journal.pdig.0000198 PMID:36812645

Lund, B. D., & Wang, T. (2023). Chatting about ChatGPT: how may AI and GPT impact academia and libraries? Library Hi Tech News. doi:10.1108/LHTN-01-2023-0009

Mbakwe, A. B., Lourentzou, I., Celi, L. A., Mechanic, O. J., & Dagan, A. (2023). ChatGPT passing USMLE shines a spotlight on the flaws of medical education. *PLOS Digital Health, 2*(2), e0000205. doi:10.1371/journal.pdig.0000205 PMID:36812618

McGee, R. W. (2023). Is ESG a Bad Idea? The Chatgpt Response. *SSRN.* doi:10.2139/ssrn.4413431

McGee, R. W. (2023). Is it Possible to Be an Affirmative Action Employer and an Equal Opportunity Employer at the Same Time? A Chatgpt Answer. *SSRN.* doi:10.2139/ssrn.4413426

McGeeR. W. (2023). Is There a Duty to Pay for the Education of Other People's Children? The Chatgpt Response (March 25, 2023). SSRN: https://ssrn.com/abstract=

McGeeR. W. (2023). What Will the United States Look Like in 2050? A Chatgpt Short Story. *SSRN.* doi:10.2139/ssrn.4413442

McGeeR. W. (2023). Capitalism, Socialism and ChatGPT. *SSRN.* doi:10.2139/ssrn.4369953

McGeeR. W. (2023). Evaluating Law Reviews for Promotion and Tenure: Two Chatgpt Essays. *SSRN.* doi:10.2139/ssrn.4413414

McGeeR. W. (2023). Gender Discrimination Arguments and Non Sequiturs: A Chatgpt Essay. *SSRN.* doi:10.2139/ssrn.4413432

McGeeR. W. (2023). How Would American History Be Different If Hitler Had Been Assassinated in 1933: A Chatgpt Essay. *SSRN.* doi:10.2139/ssrn.4413420

McGeeR. W. (2023). How Would History Be Different If Karl Marx Had Never Been Born? A Chatgpt Essay. *SSRN.* / doi:10.2139/ssrn.4413422

McGeeR. W. (2023). Is Chat Gpt Biased Against Conservatives? An Empirical Study. *SSRN.* doi:10.2139/ssrn.4359405

McGeeR. W. How to Determine Your 'Fair Share' of Taxes: Ask Chatgpt. *SSRN.* doi:10.2139/ssrn.4413435

MhlangaD. (2023). Open AI in Education, the Responsible and Ethical Use of ChatGPT Towards Lifelong Learning. *SSRN.* doi:10.2139/ssrn.4354422

Naumova, E.N. (2023). A mistake-find exercise: a teacher's tool to engage with information innovations, ChatGPT, and their analogs. *J Public Health Pol.* doi:10.1057/s41271-023-00400-1

Nigar, M., Surameery, S., & Shakor, Y. M. (2023). Use Chat GPT to Solve Programming Bugs. *International Journal of Information Technology &Amp; Computer Engineering (IJITC) ISSN: 2455-5290, 3*(01), 17–22. doi:10.55529/ijitc.31.17.22

Ollivier, M., Pareek, A., Dahmen, J., Kayaalp, M. E., Winkler, P. W., Hirschmann, M. T., & Karlsson, J. (2023). A deeper dive into ChatGPT: History, use and future perspectives for orthopaedic research. *Knee Surgery, Sports Traumatology, Arthroscopy, 31*(4), 1190–1192. doi:10.100700167-023-07372-5 PMID:36894785

ÖmerA.EnisK. (2023). Is ChatGPT Leading Generative AI? What is Beyond Expectations? *SSRN.* doi:10.2139/ssrn.4341500

Sallam, M. (2023). ChatGPT Utility in Healthcare Education, Research, and Practice: Systematic Review on the Promising Perspectives and Valid Concerns. *Health Care, 11*(6), 887. doi:10.3390/healthcare11060887 PMID:36981544

Teubner, T., Flath, C. M., Weinhardt, C., van der Aalst, W., & Hinz, O. (2023). Welcome to the Era of ChatGPT et al. *Business & Information Systems Engineering, 65*(2), 95–101. https://doi.org/. doi:10.100712599-023-00795-x

Ventayen, R. J. M. (2023). OpenAI ChatGPT Generated Results: Similarity Index of Artificial Intelligence-Based Contents. Advances in Intelligent Systems and Computing. doi:10.2139srn.4332664

Wang, F.-Y., Miao, Q., Li, X., Wang, X., & Lin, Y. (2023). What Does ChatGPT Say: The DAO from Algorithmic Intelligence to Linguistic Intelligence? IEEE/CAA Journal of Automatica Sinica, 10(4). doi:10.1109/JAS.2023.123486

Wang, F. Y., Yang, J., Wang, X., Li, J., & Han, Q. L. (2023). Chat with ChatGPT on Industry 5.0: Learning and Decision-Making for Intelligent Industries, in IEEE/CAA Journal of Automatica Sinica, 10(4). doi:10.1109/JAS.2023.123552

Xue, V. W., Lei, P., & Cho, W. C. (2023). The potential impact of ChatGPT in clinical and translational medicine. *Clinical and Translational Medicine*, *13*(3), e1216. doi:10.1002/ctm2.1216 PMID:36856370

Zarifhonarvar, A. (2023). Economics of ChatGPT: A Labor Market View on the Occupational Impact of Artificial Intelligence. http://dx.doi.org/ doi:10.2139/ssrn.4350925

KEY TERMS AND DEFINITIONS

Artificial Intelligence: It is the ability of a computer program to think, learn, and perform similar to humans. This is achieved by programming algorithms that allow the machine to make decisions and solve problems.

Business Analytics: The process of analyzing data to gain valuable insights, which helps to develop strategies to increase productivity, reduce costs, and improve strategic decision-making.

Chat Generative Pre-Trained Transformer: This type of language model is based on a transformer architecture that is pre-trained on large amounts of conversational data and designed to generate natural language responses to input sentences.

Financial Decision Making: It is the process of analyzing data to extract information and using it to make informed decisions for financial goals.

Stock Market Recommendation: This is an opinion or advice on buying, holding, or selling a particular stock. It is typically provided by an experienced financial analyst or investment professional who has knowledge of the stock and the overall market.

Chapter 6
Blockchain and Machine Learning Framework for Financial Performance in Pharmaceutical Supply Chains

Russell Sadeghi
University of Science and Technology of Mazandaran, Iran

Ava Hajian
University of North Texas, USA

Meysam Rabiee
University of Colorado, Denver, USA

ABSTRACT

Financial performance assesses how well a company can manage resources from its primary line of business and create income. Financial performance is critical for the healthcare sector, especially pharmaceutical supply chains. Medicine shortage is the main problem in healthcare management. Medicine shortages negatively affect patient care and financial performance. This chapter explains how blockchain technology and machine learning framework can contribute to pharmaceutical supply chains regarding financial performance. The proposed framework contributes to business analytics tools by presenting a hybrid machine learning method to improve financial performance.

1. INTRODUCTION

Despite being a driving force for economic growth and progress worldwide, the pharmaceutical industry faces severe challenges regarding drug scarcity and manufacturing glitches (Spieske et al., 2022). The scarcity of necessary medicines has become a critical issue globally that could endanger human lives. Production delays due to legal battles, natural disasters, trade wars, and unbalanced supply demand are

DOI: 10.4018/978-1-6684-8386-2.ch006

why drugs may not reach their intended recipients on time. Patients who rely heavily on prescribed drugs for their health and well-being face severe risks because of this deficit in medication supply. Hospitals across the globe have faced shortages of indispensable medications utilized to treat cancer, alleviate pain, and offer anesthesia during surgeries (Nguyen et al., 2022). As a result of this dearth, many individuals requiring medical attention have been forced into long waiting lists with prolonged suffering from their ailments (Rajpurkar et al., 2022).

Blockchain technology can provide a secure and transparent data platform that can be utilized to collect and store data in pharmaceutical supply chains, which can be employed to train machine learning algorithms for optimization and automation purposes (Sadeghi R. et al., 2022). One of the significant advantages of blockchain technology is its ability to provide a tamper-proof and auditable data trail, ensuring the integrity and authenticity of the data (Griggs et al., 2018). In pharmaceutical supply chains, this can be particularly useful in tracking the movement of drugs from the manufacturer to the end customer, ensuring that the drugs are not counterfeit or subject to diversion. The data captured on the blockchain can be analyzed using machine learning algorithms to gain insights and identify patterns that can be used to optimize supply chain operations (Hajian et al., 2023). For example, algorithms can be trained to predict demand, identify inefficiencies in the supply chain, and optimize inventory levels at various points in the supply chain (Nguyen et al., 2022). The algorithms can also detect and prevent counterfeiting or diversion of drugs, thus ensuring patient safety and compliance with regulations. Furthermore, blockchain technology can also automate certain aspects of the pharmaceutical supply chain, such as drug tracking and payment processing (Bashir, 2018). This can help reduce manual labor, improve operational efficiency, and reduce costs. Blockchain technology provides a secure and transparent data platform that can be employed to collect and store data in pharmaceutical supply chains. This data can then be utilized to train machine learning algorithms to optimize supply chain operations and inventory, which results in better financial performance (Casino et al., 2019).

2. INVENTORY AND FINANCIAL PERFORMANCE

Inventory management is a crucial factor in determining the financial performance of a business (Cannon, 2008). Effective inventory management can reduce inventory holding costs, increase cash flow, and improve profitability (Santhi & Karthikeyan, 2016). Optimizing inventory levels is one way to improve financial performance (Cannon, 2008). Maintaining the right amount of inventory helps ensure a business has enough stock to meet customer demand without overstocking, which ties up capital and increases carrying costs. A business can optimize inventory levels and reduce inventory holding costs using inventory management techniques such as demand forecasting, safety stock calculations, and economic order quantity models (Sadeghi & Niaki, 2015).

Another way inventory management can improve financial performance is by reducing stockouts. A stockout occurs when a business runs out of a particular product, leading to lost sales and dissatisfied customers. By using inventory management tools based on machine learning algorithms such as just-in-time (JIT) inventory management and vendor-managed inventory (VMI), a business can ensure that it always has the necessary inventory to meet demand and avoid stockouts (Sadeghi & Niaki, 2015).

2.1. Inventory Model

Economic order quantity (EOQ) and economic production quantity (EPQ) models are designed to help businesses optimize their inventory levels and reduce costs (Sphicas, 2006). By calculating the optimal order or production quantity, a business can minimize the costs of ordering, producing, and holding inventory while ensuring sufficient inventory to meet customer demand (Cannon, 2008). However, it is important to note that both EOQ and EPQ models make certain assumptions about the demand for the product, the cost of holding inventory, and other factors. Therefore, it is essential for businesses to regularly review and adjust their inventory levels based on actual demand and market conditions rather than relying solely on these models. EOQ calculates the optimal amount of product a company should order to satisfy customer demand while minimizing the costs associated with holding and ordering inventory (Sphicas, 2006).

The economic production quantity model shares the same assumptions as the economic order quantity model, except for the rate of order receipt. In contrast to the purchase model, where goods are received all at once, goods and products enter the warehouse gradually until a certain inventory level is reached in economic production quantity models. This entry has a fixed amount and is not infinite (Pentico & Drake, 2011).

2.2. Inventory Constraints

In pharmaceutical inventory management, warehouse capacity limitations can significantly impact the availability of products and the overall efficiency of the supply chain (Richard J. Tersine, 1993). Pharmaceutical products often have specific storage requirements, such as temperature and humidity control, that must be maintained to ensure their quality and efficacy (Sadeghi et al., 2013). These requirements can limit the amount of product that can be stored in a given space, reducing the overall capacity of a warehouse (Uthayakumar & Priyan, 2013). When warehouse capacity is limited, it can lead to stockouts and delays in delivering products to customers. This can have significant consequences in the pharmaceutical industry, where delays in delivering critical medications can have life-threatening implications for patients. Pharmaceutical companies can use various inventory management strategies to manage warehouse capacity limitations. For example, they can implement just-in-time (JIT) inventory management, which involves ordering and receiving products as they are needed rather than stockpiling large quantities in the warehouse. This can help reduce the amount of inventory that needs to be stored and managed, freeing up space in the warehouse (Ali, 2011). Pharmaceutical companies can also implement more efficient storage and handling systems, such as automated storage and retrieval systems, which can help maximize the available space in the warehouse. In addition, pharmaceutical companies can use advanced analytics and forecasting techniques to predict demand better and optimize inventory levels, helping to reduce the amount of inventory that needs to be stored in the warehouse while ensuring that products are available when needed (Carl Borg, 2006).

Pharmaceutical merchandise, including biologics, vaccines, and different temperature-sensitive products, require a cold and managed environment to maintain their efficacy and excellence. Any deviation from the specified temperature variety can bring about product degradation, loss of potency, and product failure (Uthayakumar & Priyan, 2013). The cold barrier has significant implications for the pharmaceutical industry, including increased costs and complexity in inventory management and the need for specialized storage and transport vehicles (Saha & Ray, 2019). Moreover, the cold constraint can also result in product wastage, as the goods that fail to satisfy the desired temperature variety cannot be used or offered. This can bring about extensive economic losses for the pharmaceutical agencies and ethical and environmental worries due to the disposal of the products.

The pharmaceutical industry is known for its high-cost and sensitive products that require special storage and handling. One of the biggest challenges in the pharmaceutical inventory sector is managing the perishable nature of certain pharmaceutical products with a limited shelf life. To prevent product spoilage, waste, and financial losses, it is essential to implement effective inventory management practices. Pharmaceutical products such as biologics, vaccines, and certain medications have restricted shelf lives due to their chemical properties, sensitivity to environmental factors, and regulatory requirements. Depending on the product type and storage conditions, the shelf life can range from a few days to three years (Saha & Ray, 2019).

3. BLOCKCHAIN TECHNOLOGY

Blockchain technology is a decentralized, secure, and transparent ledger system that enables the creation of a tamper-proof data trail in pharmaceutical supply chains (Griggs et al., 2018). The technology enables the secure sharing of data between multiple parties in the supply chain, including manufacturers, distributors, regulators, and patients (Hajian & Chang, 2022). In the pharmaceutical supply chain, blockchain technology can track the movement of drugs from the manufacturer to the end customer, ensuring that the drugs are not counterfeit or subject to diversion. The technology can also be utilized to provide complete visibility of the supply chain, enabling the tracking of drugs at every stage (Bashir, 2018).

Blockchain technology can improve supply chain visibility and enabling the automation of particular supply chain processes (Griggs et al., 2018). The data captured on the blockchain is secured using cryptographic algorithms, making altering or manipulating the data virtually impossible. This ensures that the data on the blockchain is authentic and reliable and can be used in machine-learning algorithms to make accurate predictions (Griggs et al., 2018). Moreover, the data on the blockchain is stored in a decentralized manner, meaning that a single entity or organization does not control it. This ensures that the data is not subject to the biases or interests of a single party, making it more objective and trustworthy (Griggs et al., 2018).

Blockchain creates a long and reliable data history that can be used for prediction, as the data cannot be tampered with or manipulated (Bashir, 2018). Furthermore, blockchain technology can create shared data platforms, where multiple parties in a network can contribute and access data securely and transparently. This can help to create a more comprehensive and diverse database that can be used for prediction.

4. MACHINE LEARNING ALGORITHMS

Machine learning involves developing a model that can produce appropriate results when given a specific input; these inputs, known as predictor measures, typically represent the parameters that describe a specific problem. The output, also known as the response, answers the stated issue. Machine learning can be categorized into three types: supervised learning, unsupervised learning, and reinforcement learning (Mousavi et al., 2023).

4.1. Supervised Machine Learning Algorithms

Supervised machine learning algorithms are an essential data science and artificial intelligence method. They are beneficial when there is a labeled dataset, meaning a target or outcome variable has been pre-defined. In supervised learning, The goal is to build a machine-learning model that can predict the target variable accurately for either new or previously observed data points (Karimi-Mamaghan et al., 2022). Developing machine learning models involves minimizing errors between predicted and actual output values and model complexity. In supervised machine learning, the primary objective is to fit a model with high predictive accuracy capability. It is essential to avoid overfitting and extensive reliance on noisy and incorrect data that can lead to model inaccuracies. By striking a balance between model complexity and prediction accuracy, it is possible to develop models that perform well on unseen data, leading to efficient forecasting and decision-making in various domains (Mousavi et al., 2023).

4.1.1. Linear Regression

Linear regression models are simple, easy to interpret, and possess many applications, making them highly relevant in machine learning interpretability. One of the key goals of machine learning interpretability is to produce a human-comprehensible description of the function used to generate outcomes (Gambella et al., 2021). The utility is broad, and the model's simplicity, interpretation, and ease of use make it highly suitable for many applications. In conclusion, linear regression remains essential as a critical component of supervised learning and continues to provide significant advances in machine learning. If we balance simplicity, interpretability, and accuracy, machine learning models can provide reliable, valuable predictions that support efficient decision-making in many industries (Gambella et al., 2021).

4.1.2. Decision Trees

Decision trees are a popular way for generating decisions and classifying data in machine learning, and they are a supervised learning algorithm frequently used in machine learning. They are non-parametric models with splitting standards structured in a tree data structure. These models are helpful for regression and classification problems (Gambella et al., 2021).

While single decision tree models are chosen for simplicity of interpretation, multiple decision tree models can considerably enhance model accuracy. These methods include bagging, random forests, and boosting (Gambella et al., 2021).

4.1.3. Random Forest

Random forest is an ensemble machine learning algorithm widely used for regression and classification tasks. It is a powerful and flexible algorithm that can cope with excessive-dimensional records, noisy information, and lacking values. The set of rules is based on the concept of choice timber and combines more than one choice timber to shape an extra correct and sturdy version. The Random forest algorithm is an ensemble set of rules that combines multiple decision timber to shape an extra correct and robust version. The rules work by building many choice bushes, each educated on a randomly selected subset of the entered information. The output of the set of rules is the average prediction of all the choice timber (Gambella et al., 2021).

The Random forest rules use bootstrapping to generate the subsets of enter facts. In bootstrapping, a random pattern of the input data is drawn with a substitute, ensuing in a dataset of identical length because of the unique dataset. The subsets of information are then used to educate the selection bushes. The Random forest algorithm has been efficiently applied in several domains, which include finance, healthcare, and bioinformatics. The rules can be used in finance to expect stock fees, credit score hazards, and customer churn. In healthcare, the set of rules may be used to predict the risk of disease and the final results of treatments. The algorithm can analyze gene expression facts and expect protein systems in bioinformatics (Gambella et al., 2021).

4.1.4. Neural Network

Neural networks are a category of devices gaining knowledge of algorithms stimulated with the aid of the shape and features of the human mind. They are powerful and flexible algorithms that may be used for various tasks, together with category, regression, and clustering. A neural network consists of layers of interconnected processing nodes, neurons, that receive input alerts, manner them, and produce output signals. The layers are usually prepared into an input layer, one or extra hidden layers, and an output layer. The range of neurons and layers in a neural network can range depending on the complexity of the trouble. Training a neural network involves adjusting the weights and biases of the neurons to limit the error between the anticipated output and the actual output. This is performed using an educational set of rules, including backpropagation, that computes the error gradient with admire to the weights and biases and updates them. One of the primary advantages of neural networks is their potential to analyze complex non-linear relationships between the enter and output variables. They can also handle noisy, incomplete information and generalize to new, unseen facts (Gambella et al., 2021).

4.2. Unsupervised Machine Learning Algorithms

Unsupervised learning is a machine learning technique that works on raw data without direct human training or labeling (Karimi-Mamaghan et al., 2022). Cluster analysis, often called clustering, is an unsupervised machine-learning technique for identifying and categorizing significant data points in big data sets. Because of its capacity to identify patterns and intriguing trends in data, cluster analysis has become a crucial data analysis approach. It has been applied to various industries, including health research, behavioral research, e-commerce, and usage modeling. Cluster analysis in unsupervised learning problems makes no assumptions about the desired output and aims only to identify and classify patterns in data (Jabbari et al., 2022).

4.2.1. K-Means Clustering

K-means clustering is an efficient machine-learning approach with consistent results for well-separated data sets. The method entails grouping the data points to minimize the squared distance between the data points and the focal points. In other words, the algorithm detects numerous centroids or independent clusters, reduces the size of the centroids, and assigns a neighbor to each data point. However, the results may need to be more consistent due to the random initial selection of cluster centers. Furthermore, because the existence of outliers can quickly impact the mean, the K-means algorithm is less effective in situations characterized by extreme values. Consequently, there is a K-means algorithm called K-medoid clustering for complex situations with high noise and outliers (Karimi-Mamaghan et al., 2022; Mousavi et al., 2023).

4.2.2. Spectral Clustering

Spectral algorithms use the eigenvalues and eigenvectors of a matrix to perform data analysis operations such as clustering, classification, and dimensionality reduction that can handle high data and produce accurate solutions that work well for various machine learning problems. A spectral algorithm uses the eigenvectors and eigenvalues of a matrix to transform the information into a brand-new area, wherein the analysis can be completed effectively (Von Luxburg, 2007).

4.3. Reinforcement Machine Learning Algorithms

Reinforcement learning is an intricate machine-learning method that enables machines and software developers to learn independently in specific scenarios or environments—ultimately increasing their performance. This learning is based on interactions with objects that monitor the environment and use rewards or punishments to guide learning (Mahesh, 2020). The ultimate goal of reinforcement learning is to use insights from these environmental cues to develop interventions that maximize reward and minimize risk. This approach is beneficial in training AI models that can automate complex systems such as robotics and supply chain management (Bengio et al., 2021). We refer interested readers to a review of prior work on reinforcement learning applications in supply chains by Rolf et al. (2022).

4.3.1. Q-Learning

Q-learning is a well-known model-free reinforcement learning method that may learn the quality of behaviors and help an agent choose optimal actions based on the current circumstances. Unlike other algorithms, it does not require a priori modeling of the environment, hence referred to as a "model-free" algorithm (Watkins & Dayan, 1992). Moreover, Q-learning can handle stochastic transitions and rewards reliably without any modification. The "Q" in Q-learning primarily represents the expected rewards the algorithm predicts for a specific action in a given state, also known as "quality."

4.3.2. Deep-Q Networks

The Deep-Q networks (DQN) algorithm is a deep reinforcement learning algorithm that has won a considerable reputation in recent years due to its ability to discover ways to play complicated video games at a superhuman stage. The set of rules combines the principles of Q-getting to know and deep neural networks to research a top-of-the-line coverage for a given undertaking. The DQN algorithm is based on reinforcement studying, where an agent learns to perform an assignment through trials and blunders (Arulkumaran et al., 2017). The set of rules uses a deep neural community to symbolize the Q-function, which maps states and moves to their expected rewards. The Q-characteristic is updated using the Bellman equation, a recursive equation expressing the expected praise for a state-motion pair in phrases of the expected praise for the following state-movement pair (Arulkumaran et al., 2017).

4.3.3. Dyna-Q

The Dyna-Q algorithm is a reinforcement mastering algorithm that mixes model-primarily based and model-unfastened strategies to get to know. The algorithm uses a combination of experience-primarily based learning and planning to update its coverage for a given mission. The algorithm has been successfully applied to various issues, including robotics, gaming, and management structures. The Dyna-Q algorithm consists of principal additives: a version-primarily based issue and a version-loose element. The model-based element uses a version of the environment to simulate transitions among states and rewards. The model-unfastened element uses the simulated enjoy replacing the Q-values for each nation-movement pair. The algorithm iteratively updates the model and the Q-values until convergence (Shyalika et al., 2020).

4.3.4. PILCO

Probabilistic Inference for Learning Control (PILCO) is a reinforcement learning set of rules that uses Gaussian methods to model the dynamics of a machine and learns a controller that optimizes an extended-term price feature. PILCO was developed to study and manipulate policies for structures where direct cost function optimization is infeasible because of computational complexity or measurement limitations (Ariza Ramirez et al., 2020).

The PILCO teaches a controller that minimizes an extended-time period price characteristic. The value feature is a weighted sum of the instant price and the anticipated destiny value, in which the burden on the destiny cost decreases through the years. The controller is discovered using a Bayesian optimization method, in which the objective is to locate the motion that minimizes the predicted cost. The optimization uses analytical and numerical methods (Parmas et al., 2018).

PILCO has two essential benefits. First, it may examine control guidelines for structures in which direct optimization of the cost feature is impossible due to computational complexity or dimension obstacles. This is made possible using the Gaussian method version, which is correct and efficient. Second, PILCO can handle uncertainty inside the system's dynamics using a probabilistic version. This permits the set of rules to analyze a controller. This is strong to adjustments inside the surroundings and uncertainty inside the version (Parmas et al., 2018).

4.3.5. SARSA

SARSA (State-Action-Reward-State-Action) is a reinforcement learning set of rules that learns the best policy by estimating the Q-fee function, representing the anticipated cumulative praise for taking action in a given kingdom and following a selected policy (Shi et al., 2022). SARSA is an on-policy algorithm, meaning it learns the best coverage by interacting with the environment and improving the policy in actual time based totally on the located rewards (Mohammed et al., 2023). SARSA initializes the Q-value function for each state-action pair, selects an action based on the current state and policy, receives a reward from the environment, updates the Q-value function using the observed reward and estimated Q-value, and repeats until the optimal policy is learned. It uses the epsilon-greedy policy to balance exploration and exploitation, gradually shifting from exploration to exploitation as the value of epsilon decreases over time (Shi et al., 2022).

5. MACHINE LEARNING FRAMEWORK

Pharmaceutical companies increasingly adopt machine learning algorithms to improve inventory management practices, resulting in better financial performance. Machine learning algorithms can significantly impact pharma inventory management in three main areas: demand management, warehouse management, and dynamic pricing.

Demand Management: Accurately predicting demand for pharmaceutical products is crucial to ensure that the right amount of inventory is available to meet customer needs while minimizing waste and inventory holding costs. Machine learning algorithms can analyze historical sales data and other relevant factors, such as demographics, seasonal trends, and promotions, to forecast demand more accurately than traditional forecasting methods. By improving demand forecasting, pharmaceutical companies can optimize inventory levels, reduce stockouts, and minimize overstocking, resulting in lower inventory costs and improved financial performance.

Warehouse Management: Efficient warehouse management is critical to ensure that products are stored and handled correctly and available when and where needed. Machine learning algorithms can analyze data on warehouse capacity, storage conditions, and shipping routes to optimize warehouse operations and reduce costs. For example, machine learning algorithms can optimize storage locations for each product based on their temperature and humidity requirements, reducing the need for expensive refrigerated storage. Machine learning algorithms can also optimize order picking routes and shipping schedules, reducing transportation costs and improving delivery times.

Dynamic Pricing: Dynamic pricing is a strategy that involves adjusting the price of a product in real-time based on market demand, supply, and other relevant factors. Machine learning algorithms can analyze market trends, competitor pricing, and customer behavior to determine the optimal price for a product at any given time. By implementing dynamic pricing strategies, pharmaceutical companies can optimize pricing and maximize revenue, resulting in improved financial performance.

Machine learning algorithms significantly benefit pharmaceutical companies in demand management, warehouse management, and dynamic pricing, resulting in better financial performance. By leveraging machine learning algorithms to optimize inventory management practices, pharmaceutical companies can reduce costs, improve efficiency, and meet customer needs more effectively. Figure 1 shows the proposed framework in pharmaceutical inventory management, which is based on machine learning approaches. The framework is explained as follows.

5.1. Demand Management

Demand management is the process of forecasting, managing, and optimizing customer demand for products or services (Coyle et al., 2016). Demand management can improve financial performance in pharmaceutical inventory management by ensuring inventory levels align with customer demand. Demand management can help pharmaceutical companies accurately forecast demand for their products. This can help companies plan their inventory levels more effectively, ensuring they have enough stock to meet customer demand without overstocking and incurring unnecessary costs. Moreover, efficient inventory management: By aligning inventory levels with actual customer demand, demand management can help pharmaceutical companies to optimize their inventory management processes. This can reduce waste, minimize stockouts, and lower the costs of carrying excess inventory.

5.1.1. Simulation

Simulation techniques can be applied in pharmaceutical supply chain inventory management to overcome the challenges of limited or non-representative data sets. For instance, virtual inventory data can be generated by simulating the supply chain system comprising suppliers, manufacturers, distributors, and retailers. This data can be employed to train machine learning algorithms to predict demand and optimize inventory levels (Butler et al., 1997). Similarly, simulating transportation networks can generate substantial data sets that optimize transportation routes and mitigate supply chain disruptions. Overall, simulation techniques can significantly expand small data sets by generating synthetic data, enabling the training of machine learning algorithms to optimize inventory and transportation, leading to an efficient and cost-effective supply chain that ensures the availability of drugs to patients as per requirement (Gheisariha et al., 2021).

Simulation involves using computer models to create a virtual environment that mimics real-world conditions. In demand management, simulation can generate scenarios to help prepare the data for machine learning algorithms. For example, simulation can create hypothetical demand scenarios based on market trends and historical data, which can be used to train machine learning algorithms (Butler et al., 1997). Simulation can also generate additional data points for machine learning algorithms. For example, if limited data is available on a specific product, simulation can generate hypothetical sales data based on market trends and customer behavior. Simulation is a helpful technique in demand management when data is limited or scarce. Using simulation to generate additional data, pharmaceutical companies can improve demand forecasting accuracy and optimize inventory management, leading to better financial performance.

5.1.2. Time Series Effect

Seasonality is a common feature in pharmaceutical and medical products demand, and accurate demand forecasting is crucial for optimizing inventory levels and ensuring customer satisfaction. Time series analysis is widely used for forecasting demand in industries with seasonal products.

Supervised time series algorithms are machine learning algorithms that use historical data to predict future values. In the context of seasonal pharma or medical products, these algorithms can forecast demand for a specific product based on its historical sales data. Supervised time series algorithms identify patterns and trends in historical data and use this information to predict future demand. The algorithms are trained on historical data, and the accuracy of the forecasts is improved as more data becomes available.

The advantage of using supervised time series algorithms for forecasting demand in seasonal pharma or medical products is that they can capture the seasonal patterns and trends in the data. For example, if a specific product experiences higher demand during the winter months, a supervised time series algorithm can be trained to capture this pattern and predict higher demand during the winter months.

5.1.3. Supervised Machine Learning Algorithms

Supervised machine learning algorithms can be applied to manage inventory in supply chains, e.g., pharmaceutical supply chains, to improve financial performance by predicting future demand for drugs and optimizing inventory levels to meet that demand.

Supervised machine learning algorithms require labeled data to train the algorithm. Labeled data consists of historical sales and inventory levels in pharmaceutical inventory management. The algorithm can then use this data to predict future sales and inventory needs. One example of a supervised machine learning algorithm that could be used for pharmaceutical inventory management is the Random forest algorithm. Random forest is an ensemble learning algorithm that creates many decision trees and aggregates their predictions to make a final prediction. In the context of pharmaceutical inventory management, the Random forest algorithm could be used to predict which drugs are likely to experience increased demand in the future based on historical sales data and other relevant factors, such as seasonality or marketing campaigns. These predictions could optimize inventory levels to meet demand while minimizing waste.

ARIMA (autoregressive integrated moving average) and SARIMA (seasonal autoregressive integrated moving average) are two time-series models used to forecast a variable's future values based on past values. ARIMA is a time-series model incorporating three main components: autoregression, differencing, and moving average. Autoregression means that the model uses past values of the variable to predict future values. Differencing means that the model takes the difference between the current and previous values to account for any trend or seasonality in the data. Moving average means that the model uses past errors to predict future values.

5.2. Warehouse Management

Perishable and cold supply chain concepts are essential in pharmaceutical inventory management, particularly for drugs with special storage requirements (Coyle et al., 2016). Perishable drugs have a limited shelf life and must be used or disposed of before expiration. Cold supply chain drugs require specific temperature controls during storage and transportation to maintain effectiveness. These drugs can be particularly vulnerable to damage or spoilage if exposed to temperatures outside the recommended range. In warehouse management, it is essential to carefully monitor the storage conditions of perishable and cold supply chain drugs to ensure they are stored correctly and used before expiration.

ABC clustering is a method of categorizing inventory based on its value to optimize inventory management practices. ABC clustering is based on the Pareto principle, which states that 80% of a company's sales come from 20% of its products. ABC clustering can categorize drugs based on their value or demand in pharmaceutical inventory management. In ABC clustering, inventory items are grouped into three categories based on their value. Category A items are high-value items that make up a small percentage of the inventory but account for a large percentage of sales. Category B items are moderate-value items that comprise a moderate percentage of the inventory and sales. Category C items are low-value items that comprise a large percentage of the inventory but account for a small percentage of sales.

Using ABC clustering, warehouse managers can focus their inventory management efforts on the most critical items while reducing waste and minimizing stockouts. For example, Category A items may be prioritized for storage and handling, while Category C items may be stored in less desirable locations to optimize space utilization. Overall, perishable and cold supply chain concepts and ABC clustering are essential considerations in pharmaceutical inventory management and can help to optimize warehouse operations and improve financial performance.

5.2.1. Unsupervised Machine Learning Algorithms

Unsupervised machine learning algorithms can also be applied to pharmaceutical inventory management to improve financial performance by identifying patterns and insights from data that may not be immediately apparent. Unlike supervised learning, unsupervised learning does not require labeled data but instead identifies patterns or groups based on the underlying structure of the data.

One example of an unsupervised machine learning algorithm that could be used for pharmaceutical inventory management is clustering. Clustering algorithms group similar data points together based on their distance or similarity. Clustering could group drugs with similar demand patterns or inventory levels in pharmaceutical inventory management. This could provide insights into optimizing inventory management for those groups of drugs.

Another example of an unsupervised machine learning algorithm that could be used for pharmaceutical inventory management is principal component analysis (PCA). PCA is a technique used to identify patterns and relationships in data by reducing the dimensionality of the data while retaining as much information as possible. In pharmaceutical inventory management, PCA could be used to identify which factors or variables are most important in determining demand or inventory levels. This could provide insights into which drugs should be prioritized for inventory management or which factors should be considered when making inventory decisions.

5.3. Dynamic Pricing

Dynamic pricing is a real-time strategy in which prices are adjusted based on market demand, supply, and other relevant factors (Coyle et al., 2016). In pharmaceutical inventory management, dynamic pricing can be used to adjust the prices of drugs based on their demand, availability, and expiration date (den Boer, 2015).

Dynamic pricing can benefit perishable drugs with a limited shelf life and must be used or disposed of before expiration. By adjusting prices based on the expiration date of drugs, pharmaceutical companies can incentivize customers to purchase drugs closer to their expiration date before they become unsellable. Dynamic pricing can also be used to adjust prices based on demand. For example, if a drug is in high demand, prices can be increased to maximize profits. On the other hand, if demand is low, prices can be lowered to stimulate sales. In order to implement dynamic pricing for pharmaceutical inventory management, companies must have access to real-time data on demand, supply, and other relevant factors. This data can be collected through various sources, including sales, inventory, and external market data.

Dynamic pricing can be a powerful tool for pharmaceutical inventory management, allowing companies to adjust prices in real-time to optimize sales and profitability while reducing waste and minimizing stockouts. However, it is important to carefully consider the potential impact on customers and ensure that pricing strategies are fair and ethical. Dynamic pricing can improve financial performance by allowing companies to adjust prices based on real-time demand, supply, and other relevant factors. This can help companies to maximize revenue and profits while minimizing waste and stockouts. First, dynamic pricing can increase revenue by allowing companies to adjust prices based on demand. When demand is high, prices can be increased to maximize profits.

Conversely, prices can be lowered when demand is low to stimulate sales. This can help companies to capture the maximum value from their products and increase revenue. Second, dynamic pricing can reduce waste by allowing companies to adjust prices based on the expiration date of perishable products.

By incentivizing customers to purchase products closer to their expiration date, companies can reduce the amount of unsellable products disposed of, which can be a significant cost. Third, dynamic pricing can help minimize stockouts by ensuring inventory is priced appropriately based on demand. If demand is high, prices can be increased to reduce the risk of stockouts. Conversely, if demand is low, prices can be lowered to reduce the risk of overstocking.

5.3.1. Reinforcement Machine Learning Algorithms

Reinforcement learning algorithms can be used in dynamic pricing for pharmaceutical inventory management to optimize pricing strategies over time. These algorithms use feedback from the environment (e.g., sales data, inventory data, etc.) to learn the optimal pricing strategy in a given situation. Two commonly used reinforcement learning algorithms for dynamic pricing are Dyna-Q and SARSA. Dyna-Q is a model-based reinforcement learning algorithm that uses a Q-learning approach to optimize pricing strategies. In Dyna-Q, a model of the environment is created based on past data, which is used to simulate future scenarios and predict the outcomes of different pricing strategies. The algorithm then uses this information to update its pricing strategy in real-time, optimizing for long-term profitability (Shyalika et al., 2020).

SARSA is another model-based reinforcement learning algorithm that uses a state-action-reward-state-action (SARSA) approach to optimize pricing strategies. In SARSA, the algorithm learns the optimal pricing strategy by acting in the environment and receiving feedback as rewards. Based on this feedback, the algorithm then updates its pricing strategy, optimizing for long-term profitability.

Dyna-Q and SARSA can be used in pharmaceutical inventory management to optimize pricing strategies. By using feedback from sales data, inventory data, and other relevant factors, these algorithms can learn the optimal pricing strategy in a given situation, helping to maximize revenue and profits while minimizing waste and stockouts. Using reinforcement learning algorithms in dynamic pricing can help companies optimize their pricing strategies in real-time, improving financial performance and reducing waste and stockouts. However, it is important to carefully consider the potential impact on customers and ensure that pricing strategies are fair and ethical.

6. CONCLUSION

Financial performance is a crucial aspect of the healthcare sector, particularly in pharmaceutical supply chains, where medicine shortages can significantly impact patient care and financial performance. This chapter highlights the potential of blockchain technology and machine learning to improve financial performance in pharmaceutical supply chains. By presenting a hybrid machine learning method, this proposed framework can enhance business analytics tools and contribute to developing effective strategies for managing resources and creating income. Blockchain technology and machine learning can help ensure data's reliability and authenticity, leading to more accurate predictions and better decision-making. Ultimately, this can address the issue of medicine shortages and improve financial performance in the healthcare industry.

Figure 1. A decision-making framework in pharmaceutical inventory management
**SARSA: State-Action-Reward-State-Action; SARIMA: Seasonal Autoregressive Integrated Moving Average; ARIMA: Autoregressive Integrated Moving Average; and PILCO: Probabilistic Inference for Learning Control.*

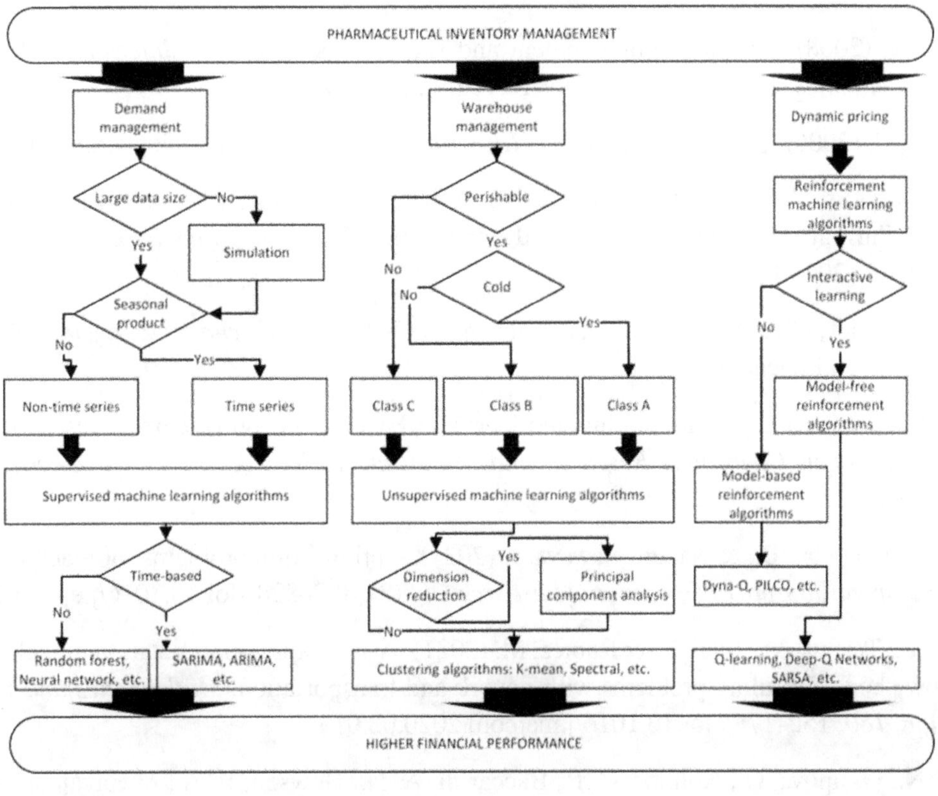

REFERENCES

Ali, A. K. (2011). Inventory management in pharmacy practice: A review of the literature. *Archives of Pharmacy Practice (Mumbai)*, *2*(4), 151.

Ariza Ramirez, W., Leong, Z. Q., Nguyen, H. D., & Jayasinghe, S. G. (2020). Exploration of the applicability of probabilistic inference for learning control in underactuated autonomous underwater vehicles. *Autonomous Robots*, *44*(6), 1121–1134. doi:10.100710514-020-09922-z

Arulkumaran, K., Deisenroth, M. P., Brundage, M., & Bharath, A. A. (2017). Deep reinforcement learning: A brief survey. *IEEE Signal Processing Magazine*, *34*(6), 26–38. doi:10.1109/MSP.2017.2743240

Bashir, I. (2018). *Mastering blockchain: Distributed ledger technology, decentralization, and smart contracts explained* (2nd ed.). Packt Publishing.

Bengio, Y., Lodi, A., & Prouvost, A. (2021). Machine learning for combinatorial optimization: A methodological tour d'horizon. *European Journal of Operational Research*, *290*(2), 405–421. doi:10.1016/j.ejor.2020.07.063

Butler, J., Jia, J., & Dyer, J. (1997). Simulation techniques for the sensitivity analysis of multi-criteria decision models. *European Journal of Operational Research, 103*(3), 531–546. doi:10.1016/S0377-2217(96)00307-4

Cannon, A. R. (2008). Inventory improvement and financial performance. *International Journal of Production Economics, 115*(2), 581–593. doi:10.1016/j.ijpe.2008.07.006

Carl Borg, C. C. (2006). *VMI – A study of benefits with a VMI system.* Jönköping University.

Casino, F., Dasaklis, T. K., & Patsakis, C. (2019). A systematic literature review of blockchain-based applications: Current status, classification and open issues. *Telematics and Informatics, 36*, 55–81. doi:10.1016/j.tele.2018.11.006

Coyle, J. J., Langley, C. J., Novack, R. A., & Gibson, B. (2016). *Supply chain management: A logistics perspective.* Nelson Education.

den Boer, A. V. (2015). Dynamic pricing and learning: Historical origins, current research, and new directions. *Surveys in Operations Research and Management Science, 20*(1), 1–18. doi:10.1016/j.sorms.2015.03.001

Gambella, C., Ghaddar, B., & Naoum-Sawaya, J. (2021). Optimization problems for machine learning: A survey. *European Journal of Operational Research, 290*(3), 807–828. doi:10.1016/j.ejor.2020.08.045

Gheisariha, E., Tavana, M., Jolai, F., & Rabiee, M. (2021). A simulation–optimization model for solving flexible flow shop scheduling problems with rework and transportation. *Mathematics and Computers in Simulation, 180*, 152–178. doi:10.1016/j.matcom.2020.08.019

Griggs, K. N., Ossipova, O., Kohlios, C. P., Baccarini, A. N., Howson, E. A., & Hayajneh, T. (2018). Healthcare blockchain system using smart contracts for secure automated remote patient monitoring. *Journal of Medical Systems, 42*(7), 1–7. doi:10.100710916-018-0982-x PMID:29876661

Hajian, A., & Chang, H.-C. (2022). *A Blockchain-Based Smart Grid to Build Resilience Through Zero-Trust Cybersecurity.*

Hajian, A., Prybutok, V. R., & Chang, H.-C. (2023). An empirical study for blockchain-based information sharing systems in electronic health records: A mediation perspective. *Computers in Human Behavior, 138*, 107471. doi:10.1016/j.chb.2022.107471

Jabbari, M., Sheikh, S., Rabiee, M., & Oztekin, A. (2022). A collaborative decision support system for multi-criteria automatic clustering. *Decision Support Systems, 153*, 113671. doi:10.1016/j.dss.2021.113671

Karimi-Mamaghan, M., Mohammadi, M., Meyer, P., Karimi-Mamaghan, A. M., & Talbi, E.-G. (2022). A state-of-the-art machine learning at the service of meta-heuristics for solving combinatorial optimization problems. *European Journal of Operational Research, 296*(2), 393–422. doi:10.1016/j.ejor.2021.04.032

Mahesh, B. (2020). Machine learning algorithms-a review. *International Journal of Science and Research (IJSR).[Internet], 9*, 381–386.

Mohammed, M. A., Lakhan, A., Abdulkareem, K. H., & Garcia-Zapirain, B. (2023). A hybrid cancer prediction based on multi-omics data and reinforcement learning state action reward state action (SARSA). *Computers in Biology and Medicine*, *154*, 106617. doi:10.1016/j.compbiomed.2023.106617 PMID:36753981

Mousavi, S. M., Sadeghi R, K., & Lee, L. S. (2023). An interactive analytics approach for sustainable and resilient case studies: A machine learning perspective. *Journal of Business Analytics*, 1–18.

Nguyen, A., Lamouri, S., Pellerin, R., Tamayo, S., & Lekens, B. (2022). Data analytics in pharmaceutical supply chains: State of the art, opportunities, and challenges. *International Journal of Production Research*, *60*(22), 6888–6907. doi:10.1080/00207543.2021.1950937

Parmas, P., Rasmussen, C. E., Peters, J., & Doya, K. (2018). PIPPS: Flexible model-based policy search robust to the curse of chaos. *International Conference on Machine Learning*, (pp. 4065–4074).

Pentico, D. W., & Drake, M. J. (2011). A survey of deterministic models for the EOQ and EPQ with partial backordering. *European Journal of Operational Research*, *214*(2), 179–198. doi:10.1016/j.ejor.2011.01.048

Rajpurkar, P., Chen, E., Banerjee, O., & Topol, E. J. (2022). AI in health and medicine. *Nature Medicine*, *28*(1), 31–38. doi:10.103841591-021-01614-0 PMID:35058619

Rolf, B., Jackson, I., Müller, M., Lang, S., Reggelin, T., & Ivanov, D. (2022). A review on reinforcement learning algorithms and applications in supply chain management. *International Journal of Production Research*, 1–29. doi:10.1080/00207543.2022.2140221

Sadeghi, J., Mousavi, S. M., Niaki, S. T. A., & Sadeghi, S. (2013). Optimizing a multi-vendor multi-retailer vendor managed inventory problem: Two tuned meta-heuristic algorithms. *Knowledge-Based Systems*, *50*, 159–170. doi:10.1016/j.knosys.2013.06.006

Sadeghi, J., & Niaki, S. T. A. (2015). Two parameter tuned multi-objective evolutionary algorithms for a bi-objective vendor managed inventory model with trapezoidal fuzzy demand. *Applied Soft Computing*, *30*, 567–576. doi:10.1016/j.asoc.2015.02.013

Sadeghi, R. J. K., Prybutok, V. R., & Sauser, B. (2022). Theoretical and practical applications of blockchain in healthcare information management. *Information & Management*, *59*(6), 103649. doi:10.1016/j.im.2022.103649

Saha, E., & Ray, P. K. (2019). Modelling and analysis of inventory management systems in healthcare: A review and reflections. *Computers & Industrial Engineering*, *137*, 106051. doi:10.1016/j.cie.2019.106051

Santhi, G., & Karthikeyan, K. (2016). Recent review article on pharmaceutical inventory models. *International Journal of Pharm Tech Research*, *9*(5), 435–443.

Shi, Z., Zhu, J., & Wei, H. (2022). SARSA-based delay-aware route selection for SDN-enabled wireless-PLC power distribution IoT. *Alexandria Engineering Journal*, *61*(8), 5795–5803. doi:10.1016/j.aej.2021.11.029

Shyalika, C., Silva, T., & Karunananda, A. (2020). Reinforcement learning in dynamic task scheduling: A review. *SN Computer Science*, *1*(6), 1–17. doi:10.100742979-020-00326-5

Sphicas, G. P. (2006). EOQ and EPQ with linear and fixed backorder costs: Two cases identified and models analyzed without calculus. *International Journal of Production Economics*, *100*(1), 59–64. doi:10.1016/j.ijpe.2004.10.013

Spieske, A., Gebhardt, M., Kopyto, M., & Birkel, H. (2022). Improving resilience of the healthcare supply chain in a pandemic: Evidence from Europe during the COVID-19 crisis. *Journal of Purchasing and Supply Management*, *28*(5), 100748. doi:10.1016/j.pursup.2022.100748

Tersine, R. J. (1993). *Principles of inventory and materials management* (4th ed.). Prentice Hall.

Uthayakumar, R., & Priyan, S. (2013). Pharmaceutical supply chain and inventory management strategies: Optimization for a pharmaceutical company and a hospital. *Operations Research for Health Care*, *2*(3), 52–64. doi:10.1016/j.orhc.2013.08.001

Von Luxburg, U. (2007). A tutorial on spectral clustering. *Statistics and Computing*, *17*(4), 395–416. doi:10.100711222-007-9033-z

Watkins, C. J., & Dayan, P. (1992). Q-learning. *Machine Learning*, *8*(3-4), 279–292. doi:10.1007/BF00992698

Chapter 7
Fixed Point Theory and Insurance Loss Modeling:
An Unlikely Pairing

S M Nazmuz Sakib
https://orcid.org/0000-0001-9310-3014
International MBA Institute, School of Business and Trade, Dhaka International University, Bangladesh

ABSTRACT

This study focuses on the future development of an insurance company during difficult circumstances, which can be described by a stochastic process that must be effectively managed to achieve the best goals for the company. Effective risk or loss management models can bring in more revenue for the insurer and result in less conditional pay-out of claims to the insured. While insurance losses, risks, and premium calculation are important topics in the field, existing literature has not always stood the test of time due to the dynamic nature of insurance principles and practices. There is a need for a suitable loss model that can adjust loss rating to a particular experience and provide an appropriate and equitable premium. The aim of this research is to find sufficient conditions for the convergence of an algorithm towards a fixed point under typical insurance loss and actuarial circumstances, resulting in a uniquely determined solution. The study presents a unique fixed point, which the algorithm converges towards through straightforward and simplified generalised formulae and functions.

1. BACKGROUND TO THE STUDY

The future development when an insurance company is in a difficult circumstance can be described by a stochastic process which the insurance company is tasked to manage effectively in order to achieve best goal of the company. Fixed point theorem is very general but we shall narrow its application to insurance business problem to get precise formulation. In studying some nonlinear phenomena, fixed point theorem is an important and powerful tool that can be applied in many fields. This research paper attempts to apply fixed point theorem in the areas of insurance business just as it has been applied to

DOI: 10.4018/978-1-6684-8386-2.ch007

geometry, analysis, number theory, set theory, group theory, algebra, dynamics, topology and so on. It is noteworthy to explain briefly what a fixed point theory means. According to Rajic, Azdejkovic and Lonar (2014), fixed point theorem concerns itself with the examination of the existence of a certain point, say y, in the domain of a function, say g, where $g(y)=y$. The identical function mapping and the function values are equal. This means that any marginal change in the function of y will proportionally result to additional fixed points. If $g(y) = y$ then $g(y) - y = 0$. Therefore if a certain function f is shown as $f(y) = g(y) - y$, function g has zero as the fixed point. If Y is a set and $g{:}Y \rightarrow Y$ is a map from Y to Y, a point $y \in Y$ is known as a fixed point of g since $g(y) = y$. For a family of G of Y, G is a semigroup or group. Here the fixed point theorem gives specific condition on Y and G ensures that there exists a simultaneous fixed point in $y \in Y$ for $g \in G$. If G is a group F, it arises from a group action $\Omega{:}F{*}Y{\rightarrow}Y$ of F on Y. If $\Omega(F, Y){:}= fy$, it is assumed that 1 of F is the identity of Y. Also, if $a \in F$ and $y \in Y$ for all f such that $(fa)y = f(ay)$ such y = F-space, Y = topological space, F = topological ground and Ω is jointly continuous. If there exists an action group F on x where Y(power set)$=P(x)$, it leads to an action of F on $P(x)$ and the F-invariant (subset of X) is the fixed point of the new action. In other words, the fixed point theorem leads to an F-invariant set. Under the existence of Haar measure ψ on a compact topological group F, left invariance indicates that ψ is F- fixed due to the action of F by left translation on the space $N^+(F)$ of any finite positive measure on F. If ψ is normalised and finite so that $\psi(F)= 1$, it can be referred to as F-fixed point under the action of F on the convex set of normalised measure on F.

The concept of fixed point theorem finds its application in various fields including insurance. The use of fixed point theorem in insurance companies has become a major topic in actuarial science as it helps to develop appropriate pricing models for insurance risks. Insurance companies often make use of statistical methods to estimate the likelihood of a loss occurring and the magnitude of such loss. This is done through the use of historical data, such as claims experience and premium income, to predict future outcomes. However, relying solely on statistical models can be insufficient as these models are often limited by their assumptions and predictive power. Therefore, it is essential to employ fixed point theorem in the pricing models of insurance risks.

Fixed point theorem is particularly useful in situations where there are uncertainties and complexities in the modeling of insurance risks. As mentioned earlier, a qualified actuary in an insurance company must make use of an appropriate insurance loss model to price a risk. By applying fixed point theorem, the actuary can determine the existence of a fixed point in the domain of the loss function, where the function values are equal (Belzunce et al., 2016). This enables the actuary to determine an appropriate premium that covers the cost of the risk while ensuring that the insurer is not at risk of ruin.

In order to apply fixed point theorem in insurance risk modeling, the actuary must first identify the relevant parameters and the underlying distribution of the risk. The actuary can then construct an appropriate loss function, which represents the expected loss incurred by the insurer for a given level of risk exposure. The actuary can then apply the fixed point theorem to determine the existence of a unique solution to the loss function. This unique solution represents the equilibrium point at which the insurer can price the risk to cover the expected losses without incurring excessive costs.

It is important to note that the application of fixed point theorem in insurance risk modeling requires a deep understanding of the underlying assumptions and uncertainties of the model. The actuary must also have a sound knowledge of statistical methods and mathematical modeling techniques. Furthermore, the actuary must be able to interpret and communicate the results of the fixed point theorem analysis to stakeholders, including management and regulators.

The research work of Fu and Wu (2005) concentrated extensively on the iterations of loss rating algorithms while in the research work of Borogovac (2014), the clear concept of Loss Ratio Method (also known as the Standard Rating Method) was introduced. All these and many other similar papers lack the intuitive and detailed standard rating logic to adjust loss rating to a particular experience. The objective of this research is to obtain sufficient conditions for convergence of algorithm towards a fixed point under typical insurance loss and actuarial circumstances to achieve a uniquely determined solution. This paper will address the shortcoming of the actuarial algorithms sighted in a concise manner. The paper will be significant and serves as a solid foundation for further research on the application of fixed point theorem in insurance premium calculation, pricing or fixing because the demand for insurance products is majorly a function of the cost of insurance and the premium charged by insurers.

2. BRIEF REVIEW

Fixed point theories came to limelight in Mathematics in the 19th century. Henry Poincare applied them in nonlinear problem topological analysis. After Poincare in 1886, L.E.J (Bertus) Brouwer also contributed to the development of fixed point theorem in 1912 according to Khalehoghli, Rahimi and Gordji (2020). Istratescu (1981) shed more light on how Brouwer's fixed point theorem gave better understanding on differential equations worked on by Charles Emile Picard and Henri Poincare. Brouwer was the first to prove that the fixed point theorem for the function of x is x (that is, $f(x) = x$). It follows that any continuous function g mapping compact convex set to itself, there exists a point y_0 such that $g(y_0) = y_0$. For a continuous function g from a closed interval c_i in the real numbers from a closed disk c_d to itself, there exists at least a fixed point. Also, every continuous function in a Euclidean space from a closed ball into itself must equally have a fixed point. This theorem holds for endomorphic functions which have the same set as range and the domain. But consider a function $g(y) = y+1$ with domain $[-1, 1]$ and the range $[0, 2]$. Here function g is not an endomorphism because if the same continuous function from R to itself is considered, it will have no fixed point as it shifts to the right. The fixed point theorem proved by Brouwer became an eye opener and widely used by many people as it is pervasive and diverse in mathematical applications. The theorem pioneered and broadened a number/degree of generalisations to different aspects of scientific disciplines. John Von Neumann (1928), in his work, used Brouwer's theorem to prove the existence of balanced growth equilibrium and minimax solution to expanding economy and two-agent game respectively. In the same vein, Kakutani in 1941 further developed and extended the work of Brouwer to prove the fixed point theorem for a sphere, square and their equivalent n-dimensional counterparts. According to Nash (1951), the work of Kakutani in 1941 made it simple to use fixed point theorem to prove the complex theorem in non-cooperative games. Nieto and Guez-Lopez (2005) showed how Banach, in 1922, demonstrated that contractive mapping with complete domain possesses a unique and peculiar fixed point. The Banach Principle was latter extended by Nadler in 1969 and applied to set valued mapping in metric space.

Insurance losses, risks and premium calculation, pricing or fixing have been active and essential topics in insurance and actuarial literatures as examined by Goovaert, De-Vylder and Haezendonck (1984). In their work, they examined insurance premium and its theory with application. This work did not stand the test of time due to dynamic nature of insurance principles and practices in highly evolving environment. Hurlimann (1997) researched on quasi-mean value principles while mathematics methods in risk theory was worked on by Buhmann in 1970 but situations of things are different now as most of these theories and principles are outdated or inefficient now, although they were exceptional and outstanding at that time interval. In the same vein, the insurance premium calculation in relation to modern theories and risk choices under uncertainty have been studied in the work of: Wang, Young and Panjer (1997); Hurlimann (1998); Wang and Young (1998) and so on. Most of these studies only emphasised on reasonable and desirable properties and characteristics insurance premium should possess and satisfy. In other words, they were based on expected utility principles and dual theory. According to Mallappa and Talawar (2020), the P_{max} (maximum premium or consideration that a particular insured is willing to give the insurer) can best be determined by applying the concepts of utility theory by looking into different utility functions following the assumptions of insurance random variables to apply. For actuaries, one of the most important objectives in insurance industry is how to apply suitable principles and models for premium calculation because the premium reflects loading(expenses), selection and certain expected estimated claims(Buhlmann, 1970). An insurer sets different premiums for different risks attached to different insurance policies (Bassett, n.d., Duverne & Hele, 2016, Kagan, 2021, National Academies Press (US), 1993). This is necessary in an insurance contract in order for it to be mutually advantageous and fair to both the insured and the insurance company because premium calculation is individually and differently affected by mortality, interest rate, loading (expenses), age, sex, utility function, moral hazard and so on.

3. DISCUSSION

Based on the research, the theory that is being discussed is the application of fixed point theorem to insurance loss model. The paper claims that this theory can provide sufficient conditions for convergence of algorithm towards a fixed point under typical insurance loss and actuarial circumstances to achieve a uniquely determined solution. The paper uses generalised formulae and functions to determine a unique fixed point and the algorithm convergence.

The research does not provide any information about the existing theories in this area or how they compare to the proposed theory. However, it does mention some related topics such as loss ratio method, Leslie–Gower model (Arancibia-Ibarra et al., 2022, Chen & Chen, 2009, González-Olivares et al., 2011, Yue, 2016), Beverton–Holt equations (Bohner et al., 2018), and optimization and control. These topics may have some relevance to the theory in finance, particularly in insurance, but the research does not explain how.

The research also does not provide any information about the pros and cons of the theory in finance, particularly in insurance. However, it may be possible to infer some potential advantages and disadvantages based on the general properties of fixed point theorem and its applications. Some possible advantages are:

- Fixed point theorem can guarantee the existence and uniqueness of a solution under certain conditions, which may be useful for solving complex problems in finance and insurance.
- Fixed point theorem can provide a rigorous and mathematical framework for analyzing and modeling various phenomena in finance and insurance, such as risk management, premium pricing, loss distribution, etc.
- Fixed point theorem can enable the use of efficient and robust algorithms for finding optimal solutions in finance and insurance, such as gradient descent, Newton's method, etc.

Some possible disadvantages are:

- Fixed point theorem may require strong assumptions or restrictions on the functions or spaces involved, which may not hold or be realistic in some cases of finance and insurance.
- Fixed point theorem may not be applicable or suitable for some types of problems or models in finance and insurance, such as those involving stochasticity, uncertainty, nonlinearity, etc.
- Fixed point theorem may not capture the full complexity or dynamics of the real-world situations in finance and insurance, such as human behavior, market fluctuations, regulatory changes, etc.

4. INPUT-OUTPUT SYSTEM OF INSURANCE ACTIVITIES

4.1 Insurance as a Dynamic System

Insurance companies generate their revenue majorly from the premium they charge the insured for insurance coverage and from the effective/efficient investment of the premium to yield returns (*Axiomatic Basics of e-Economics Munich Personal RePEc Archive*, n.d., Heilpern, 2002; Gray & Dewar, 1971, Wang et al., 1997). The premium charged by insurers can be placed into savings account for safety of funds but that will not be totally advisable because of exposure of funds to inflationary risk (Halton, 2022). Alternatively, insurance premium can be invested in short-term assets or investment such as treasury bills, interest-bearing cash equivalents, high-grade cooperate bonds and so on (*Chapter 3 - Cash Flow Accounting*, n.d., Corporate Finance Institute, 2023, *State Bank of Pakistan*, n.d., *What to Do With Your Cash Now*, 2022). Application of an effective risk or loss management model in an insurance company brings in more revenue for the insurer and less conditional pay-outs of claims to the insured (Ross, 2021). The premium and other revenue of insurance company represent the input while the output represents the claim handling costs and other insurance costs incurred by the insurer. Therefore, it will not be wrong to state that the insurance activities follow input-output systems as shown in *Figure 1*.

Figure 1. Insurance as a dynamic system

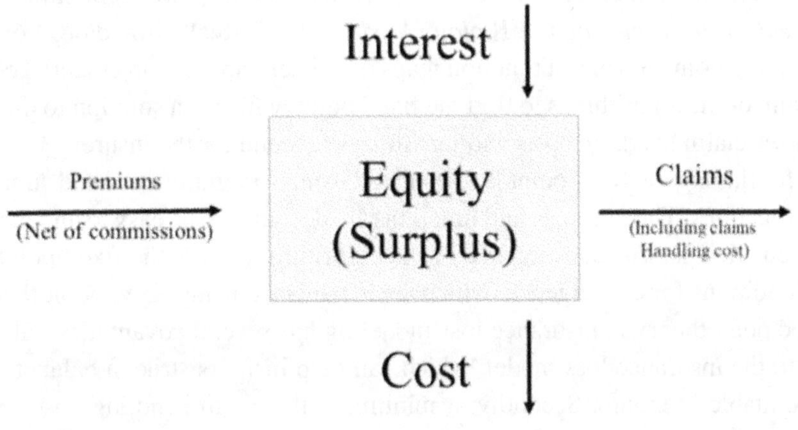

Insurance companies are in the business of managing risk, and one of their key tasks is to generate revenue from the premium they charge the insured for insurance coverage (Corporate Finance Institute, 2023b, Fallon, 2023, *Why Go Into Insurance Law? | University of Law*, n.d.). The efficient and effective investment of the premium collected is also a critical source of revenue for insurers. While some insurers may choose to place the premium charged into savings accounts for safety purposes, this approach is not always advisable due to the exposure of funds to inflationary risk. An alternative approach is to invest the premium collected in short-term assets or investments, such as treasury bills, interest-bearing cash equivalents, high-grade corporate bonds, and so on.

One of the ways that insurers can increase their revenue is by applying an effective risk or loss management model. By doing so, they can reduce the frequency and severity of claims paid out to the insured, leading to less conditional pay-outs of claims and, ultimately, greater profits. In insurance, the premium and other revenue generated by the insurer represent the input, while the claim handling costs and other insurance costs incurred by the insurer represent the output. Therefore, reducing claim handling costs can help insurers generate more revenue.

However, finding the right balance between charging an appropriate and equitable premium while ensuring that claim handling costs are minimized is not always easy. Insurance losses, risks, and premium calculation or pricing have been active and essential topics in insurance and actuarial literatures. Still, most of these literatures did not stand the test of time due to the dynamic nature of insurance principles and practices in highly evolving environments. Additionally, they often lack the intuitive and detailed standard rating logic necessary to adjust loss rating to a particular experience. This can lead to uncertainty for both the insurer and the insured, making it difficult to strike a balance in charging an appropriate and equitable premium.

One approach to solving this problem is to apply a suitable loss model that gives a sufficient uniquely determined solution that will not necessarily put an insurer or the insured in an uncertain or awkward business situation. This is where fixed point theory comes in. Fixed point theory is a mathematical concept that describes the behavior of functions, and it has applications in a variety of fields, including economics, engineering, and physics. In the context of insurance loss modeling, fixed point theory can be used to determine a unique solution that will minimize claim handling costs and help insurers generate more revenue.

The application of fixed point theory to insurance loss modeling involves finding the conditions for the convergence of an algorithm towards a fixed point under typical insurance loss and actuarial circumstances (Goffard, 2021, Golubin & Gridin, 2022, *Papers With Code - Two Applications of Brouwer's Fixed Point Theorem: In Insurance and in Biology Models*, 2015, Real-Miranda & López-Barrientos, 2022). A fixed point is a point at which a function maps onto itself, and it is an essential concept in fixed point theory. The aim of the algorithm is to find the fixed point, which is a solution to the insurance loss model that minimizes claim handling costs and maximizes revenue for the insurer.

The algorithm for finding the fixed point is formulated using straightforward and simplified generalized formulae and functions. The formulae and functions are designed to be easy to understand and apply, even for non-mathematicians. The convergence of the algorithm towards the fixed point is guaranteed by the sufficient conditions for convergence, which are established using fixed point theory.

The use of fixed point theory in insurance loss modeling has several advantages. Firstly, it provides a unique solution to the insurance loss model, which can help insurers strike a balance in charging an appropriate and equitable premium. Secondly, it minimizes the claim handling costs incurred by the insurer, leading to increased revenue. Finally, it is a straightforward and easy-to-understand approach that can be applied by both mathematicians and non-mathematicians alike.

Underwriting is an important concept in premium calculation. The insurer will charge the insured inappropriately (more or less) for a particular risk if good underwriting skill is not applied. In other words, without good underwriting practice, the insurer may undercharge an insured with under-average or substandard risk while overcharging the less risky situations (Kagan, 2021a).

4.2 Insurance Premium Model

The role of actuarial science in insurance is crucial because it helps insurers to determine the appropriate premiums that should be charged based on the risks associated with a particular policy (Espinosa & Zarruk, 2021, Maiti, 2022). Actuaries use various tools and techniques, including insurance loss models, to evaluate the risks and uncertainties associated with an insurance policy. These models are designed to estimate the likelihood of various outcomes and help the insurer to make informed decisions about how much to charge for a particular policy. One of the most important aspects of insurance loss modeling is the consideration of worst-case scenarios. For example, when pricing a hurricane insurance policy, an insurer must take into account the possibility of a major hurricane hitting the area covered by the policy. If the insurer fails to consider this possibility and prices the policy too low, it could be faced with catastrophic losses in the event of a major hurricane.

$$L = \sum_{i=1}^{m} i$$

Another important aspect of insurance loss modeling is the consideration of diversification. Insurance companies often diversify their risk portfolios by writing policies covering a wide range of risks, rather than focusing on a single type of risk. This diversification helps to spread the risk across a larger portfolio, reducing the likelihood of catastrophic losses.

In addition to modeling risks, actuarial science is also used to manage risks. Actuaries work with insurance companies to develop risk management strategies that can help to mitigate the impact of potential losses. These strategies can include risk avoidance, risk reduction, risk transfer, and risk retention.

One of the challenges facing the insurance industry is the rapidly changing environment in which it operates. New technologies, changing demographics, and evolving regulatory frameworks all have an impact on the industry. As a result, insurance loss models must be constantly updated and refined to reflect these changes.

Another challenge facing insurers is the increasing complexity of the risks they face. For example, cyber risks, climate risks, and geopolitical risks are all becoming more complex and difficult to model. This means that insurers must invest in new technologies and data analytics capabilities to keep up with these evolving risks.

Despite these challenges, the insurance industry remains an important part of the global economy. Insurance provides individuals and businesses with the peace of mind that comes from knowing they are protected against unexpected losses. Insurers play an important role in promoting economic growth by providing the capital needed to finance new ventures and infrastructure projects. The insurer company may be pushed out of business if the hurricane hits the insured region. Let's assume a market for motor insurance where the insured are identical except for the time and the probabilities of loss (accident) occurrence that differ. If there are L insured where L=1,2,…,m.

The insured's (L's) probability of loss is denoted by $P_L \epsilon [0, 1]$ as the occurrence of losses is independent among the insured. If an insured with a wealth premium of m is involved in an accident (loss) worth N naira with Y naira full cost of insurance and purchased by L insured, then the insurer will expect a profit of ₦$(Y - P_L N)$. If ₦Y_L is the cost of insurance policy paid to L insured who suffered losses, the goal of the insurer would be to determine for each $L=1,2,\dots, m$ the appropriate price using a suitable model for insurance policy L because if Y_L is less than $P_L N$, selling such policy will result to a loss, thereby, leading the insurance supply of the policy to be equalled to zero. In other words, the supply of such policy will be infinite or desirable if the Y_L is greater than the $P_L N$. It will be a breakeven on each policy L at the point where $P_L N = Y_L$

It will be interesting to note that when cost of insurance increases drastically, it will bring more profit for insurer but the expected utility an insured gets from purchasing the policy will decrease in that same manner in most cases because it will appear to the proposed insured that it will be of no or low use to procure such insurance policy when compared to other loss prevention techniques. The remaining insured who will continue to buy the insurance policy at any cost are those who have no other loss prevention options or those who their estimated cost of not insuring at that premium is way higher than when insured. In a nutshell, at an increased cost of procuring insurance policy, it becomes riskier for the insurer because of the composition of the pool of the insured at that time. It must also be noted that just as it is riskier for increased cost, it is absolutely riskier when an insurer is undercharging the insured in order to get high patronage. Apart from the insurer risking a situation of not meeting the claim demand of the insured which can dent the image or goodwill of such insurer, it will also have a greater adverse/negative effect on the profit maximisation goal of the insurance company which will in turn outweighs the positive influence of the patronage benefits. Therefore, there is a need to strike a balance in charging an appropriate and equitable premium by applying a suitable loss model that gives a sufficient uniquely determined solution that will not necessarily put an insurer in an uncertain awkward business situations. This research will employ fixed point theorem to achieve this aim.

In the insurance industry, the pricing of premiums is a delicate balance between making a profit for the insurer and ensuring that the insured receives value for their money. When the cost of insurance increases drastically, it is expected that the profit of the insurer will also increase. However, this increase in profit comes at the expense of the expected utility that the insured gets from purchasing the policy. In most cases, the insured will feel that it is of no or low use to procure such insurance policy when compared to other loss prevention techniques. As a result, the remaining insured who will continue to buy the insurance policy at any cost are those who have no other loss prevention options or those who their estimated cost of not insuring at that premium is way higher than when insured.

It is important to note that at an increased cost of procuring insurance policy, it becomes riskier for the insurer because of the composition of the pool of the insured at that time. The insurer may be left with a high-risk pool of insured, which increases the likelihood of claims and hence reducing the overall profit of the insurer. Additionally, it is absolutely riskier when an insurer is undercharging the insured in order to get high patronage. This is because the insurer risks a situation of not meeting the claim demand of the insured, which can damage the image or goodwill of such an insurer. It will also have a greater adverse/negative effect on the profit maximisation goal of the insurance company, which will in turn outweigh the positive influence of the patronage benefits.

Therefore, there is a need to strike a balance in charging an appropriate and equitable premium by applying a suitable loss model that gives a sufficient uniquely determined solution that will not necessarily put an insurer in an uncertain awkward business situation. To achieve this aim, fixed point theorem can be employed.

The fixed point theorem has been applied in various fields such as economics, physics, and mathematics. It is a powerful tool used in finding solutions to complex equations that may not have explicit solutions. In the insurance industry, fixed point theorem can be applied to develop a suitable loss model that gives a sufficient uniquely determined solution for pricing premiums. The loss model developed using fixed point theorem takes into consideration various factors such as the risk profile of the insured, the probability of claims, and the expected return on investment.

The use of fixed point theorem in developing a loss model has several advantages. Firstly, it provides a unique solution for pricing premiums, which ensures that the insurer does not undercharge or overcharge the insured. Secondly, it takes into consideration the risk profile of the insured, which ensures that the insurer is not left with a high-risk pool of insured. Thirdly, it takes into consideration the probability of claims, which ensures that the insurer has enough funds to meet the claim demand of the insured. Finally, it takes into consideration the expected return on investment, which ensures that the insurer can make a profit from investing the premium.

5. APPLICATION OF FIXED-POINT THEOREM IN INSURANCE

5.1 Preliminaries

Fixed point theorem has been applied in different aspects or areas of sciences, especially in engineering. It has been used extensively in Mathematics to solve equations, simulate and approximate especially in game theory. It is also used in economics to determine and investigate the point of equilibrium in demand and supply functions. It has helped many economists to understand complex problems in the generic economic models like computation/stability, comparative statics, and robustness of marginal change.

Let us consider 2 vector random variables p and q with a and b categories;

$$\sum_{j=1}^{b} c_{ij}\left(d_{ij} - p_i q_j\right) = 0,\ i = 1,2,\ldots,a$$

$$\sum_{i=1}^{a} c_{ij}\left(d_{ij} - p_i q_j\right) = 0,\ j = 1,2,\ldots,b$$

Where: d_{ij} = observed loss costs

c_{ij} = earned risk exposure

The relatives p_i and q_j are unknown as the system contains $a+b$ equations. Let us consider a vector equation;

$$\Omega(g) = 0 \tag{4.1}$$

Where Ω: $D_\Omega \rightarrow R^{\upsilon}$, integer r$\epsilon$N *r*epresents generic category of Euclidean space. The domain of Ω is $D_\Omega \subseteq R^{\upsilon}$. From this, the corresponding vector equation is derived;

$$g = \beta(g) \tag{4.2}$$

where $D_\beta \rightarrow R^{\upsilon}$ and the domain of β is $D_\beta \subseteq R^{\upsilon}$. This leads to the formula of the corresponding algorithms;

$$g^{w+1} = \beta\left(g^{w}\right), \text{ where } w=0,1,2,\ldots \tag{4.3}$$

The iteration formula in the form of *(4.3)* can be derived directly from the standard loss ratio method adopted by Borogovac (2014). Also, the main characteristics of mathematically formalised rating algorithm model can be reiterated for simplicity amd determination of sufficient conditions for convergence of the algorithm towards a fixed point under typical actuarial circumstances. Let us first examine the concept of functional analysis.

5.2 Functional Analysis

For $g = (g_1,\ldots,g_r) \,\epsilon\, R^r$, the functions defined by:

$$\|g\|x := \left(f_1^x + \ldots + f_r^x\right)^{1/x}, \textit{for } x > 1$$

$$\|g\|x := |g_1| + \ldots + |g_r| \quad \text{and}$$

$$\|g\|\infty := \max\left\{|g_1| + \ldots + |g_r|\right\}$$

are considered norms in R^r. Euclidean norm is derived when $x=2$. Thus $\|g\|\infty \leq \|g\|x \leq \|g\|1$. Since all norms in R^r are the same, the convergence of the sequence $\{g^w\} \subseteq R^r$ towards one norm means the same as the convergence towards $\bar{g}$ (same vector of another norms). The norm of a linear mapping *N:* $R^b \rightarrow R^a$ is defined by

$$\|N\| := \underset{g \cdot R^r - \{0\}}{SUP} \frac{|Ng|}{|g|}$$

In this research, we will concentrate on $\|\bullet\|_1$ and $\|\bullet\|_\infty$ since all norms in R^r have the same representation. If : $D_\beta \rightarrow R^r, \forall D_\beta \subseteq R^r$, *is* differentiable at p ϵ D_β, then

$J_\beta(p) = \dfrac{\alpha(\beta_1,\ldots,\beta_r)}{\alpha(p_1,\ldots,p_r)}$ represents the Jacobi Matrix at p.

Therefore,

$$J_\beta(p) = \begin{pmatrix} \dfrac{\alpha_{\beta_1}(p)}{\alpha_{p_1}} & \cdots & \dfrac{\alpha_{\beta_1}(p)}{\alpha_{p_r}} \\ \vdots & \ddots & \vdots \\ \dfrac{\alpha_{\beta_r}(p)}{\alpha_{p_1}} & \cdots & \dfrac{\alpha_{\beta_r}(p)}{\alpha_{p_r}} \end{pmatrix}$$

For matrix norms $\|\bullet\|_1$ and $\|\bullet\|_\infty$, we can derive:

$$\|J_\beta(p)\|_1 = \max_{j=1,\ldots,r}\left\{\frac{\alpha_{\beta_1}(p)}{\alpha_{p_j}} + \ldots + \frac{\alpha_{\beta_r}(p)}{\alpha_{p_j}}\right\} \tag{4.4}$$

and

$$\|J_\beta(p)\|_\infty = \max_{i=1,\ldots,r}\left\{\frac{\alpha_{\beta_i}(p)}{\alpha_{p_1}} + \ldots + \frac{\alpha_{\beta_i}(p)}{\alpha_{p_r}}\right\} \tag{4.5}$$

Recall $U \subseteq R^r$ denotes a convex set if $(g, f \in U,\ w \in [0, 1]) \rightarrow wg + (1 - w)f \in U$

5.3 Rating Model

The risk factors measure the risk space or risk cell set. Here we will consider three risk factors or classification variables which will be represented by vectors below;

$p = (p_1,p_2,\ldots,p_a)$, $q = (q_1,q_2,\ldots,q_b)$, $r=(r_1,r_2,\ldots,r_c)$

where p_i, q_j and r_k are not less than or equal to zero for

$$i=1,\ldots,a;\ j=1,\ldots,b \text{ and } k=1,\ \ldots,\ c \tag{4.6}$$

In this case, the set satisfying (4.6) is $D^o \subset R^{a+b+c}$.

The risks (p_i, q_j and r_k) are assigned to cells i, j and k. We derive a plane in the risk space if we assume one index is fixed. The cell with the maximum risk exposure or statistical credibility is taggged the base cell. The model is multiplicative since the since the base rate (d_{111}) corresponds to the cell $(1,1,1)$. That is, the rate by the triplet risks (p_i, q_j and r_k) is calculated by;

$$d_{ijk} = d_{111} p_i q_j r_k \tag{4.7}$$

From (4.7), $p_1=1$, $q_1=1$ and $r_1=1$. Hence $1= p_1=q_1=r_1$

If $H= (h_{ijk})_{apbpc}$, where $h_{ijk} \geq 0$, represents trended and fully developed insurance losses in Nigeria. h_{ijk} denotes projected or expected loss in ₦aira in the cell i,j,k. based on previous loss experience, the projected insurance losses h_{ijk} can be derived. The total projected or expected insurance loss can be expressed as;

$$H = \sum_{i=1}^{a} \sum_{j=1}^{b} \sum_{k=1}^{c} h_{ijk}$$

The corresponding earned risk exposures (L) can now be expressed as;

$L= (l_{ijk})_{apbpc}$, where $l_{ijk} \geq 0$

l_{ijk} represents the units of insurance in the cell (i, j and k) sold, as both H and L denote the insurance business past experience information using *(4.7)*. Risk exposure serves as a necessary and expected positive condition in insurance practice. Therefore, without loss of generality,

$$h_{ijk} \geq 0 \rightarrow l_{ijk} \geq 0 \tag{4.8}$$

Rating model is important and necessary in actuarial application because it helps to adjust available rates to suit the information given by H and L. Intuitively, the adjusted risk or indicated factors or variables are represented by;

$\hat{p} = (\hat{p}_1, \hat{p}_1, \ldots, \hat{p}_a)$, $\hat{q} = (\hat{q}_1, \hat{q}_2, \ldots, \hat{q}_b)$, and $\hat{r} = (\hat{r}_1, \hat{r}_2, \ldots, \hat{r}_c)$

The corresponding indicated rates are represented by;

$$\hat{d}_{ijk} = \hat{d}_{111} p_i q_j r_k \tag{4.9}$$

Summing loss amount, having kept fixed one index at a time, the vector of losses for factor p is denoted by h^p.

$$h_i^p = \sum_{j=1}^{b} \sum_{k=1}^{c} h_{ijk} \quad i = 1,2,\ldots,a \tag{4.10}$$

Also, h_j^q and h_k^r represent loss vectors for factors q and r respectively.

Invariably,

$$H=\sum_{i=1}^{a} h_i^p = \sum_{j=1}^{b} h_j^q = \sum_{k=1}^{c} h_k^r$$

The adjusted risk exposure of factor p can now be defined as;

$$L_i^p = \sum_{j=1}^{b} \sum_{k=1}^{c} l_{ijk} q_j r_k \quad i = 1,2,\ldots,a \tag{4.11}$$

Then the equivalent loss costs for factor p is represented by

$$H_i^p = \frac{h_i^p}{L_i^p}, i = 1,2,\ldots,a \tag{4.12}$$

This leads to the derivation of the following indicated factors;

$$\widehat{p}_i = \frac{H_i^p}{H_1^p}, i = 1,2,\ldots,a \tag{4.13}$$

$$\widehat{q}_j = \frac{H_j^q}{H_1^q} \; j = 1,2,\ldots,b$$

$$\widehat{r}_k = \frac{H_k^r}{H_1^r}, k = 1,2,\ldots,c$$

The formulae calculated the indicated factors for $\hat{p}, \hat{q}$ and $\hat{r}$ using exposures and losses as inputs. This is the standard loss ratio method which has made actuarial work easier in calculating the indicated rates and factors without the need for insurance premiums. Previously, calculating indicated rates and factors without insurance premium value was nearly and practically impossible as confirmed by Brown and Gottlieb (2001). In the same vein, indicated base rate is denoted by;

$$\hat{d}111 = \frac{H}{PR} \frac{1}{\sum_{i=1}^{a} \sum_{j=1}^{b} \sum_{k=1}^{c} \hat{p}_i \hat{q}_j \hat{r}_k l_{ijk}} \tag{4.14}$$

Where PR= loss ratio permissible.

Comparing *(4.9)* and *(4.14)*, indicated rates can be obtained in terms of indicated factors which depend only on loss and exposure formulae

6. RISK RATING ALGORITHM AND APPLICATION

6.1 Indicated Rates/Factors

Let us represent the current insurance risk factors by p^0, q^0 and r^0. The relativities after wth iterations will be p^w, q^w and r^w. Using formula *(4.13)*, p_i, q_j and r_k are wth iteration values. If $\widehat{p_i}, \widehat{q_j}$, and $\widehat{r_k}$ are values of the next iteration which is $(w+1)^{th}$ iteration;

$$\widehat{p_i} = \frac{h_i^p \sum_{j=1}^{b} \sum_{k=1}^{c} q_j r_k l_{1jk}}{h_1^p \sum_{j=1}^{b} \sum_{k=1}^{c} q_j r_k l_{ijk}} \tag{5.1}$$

$$\widehat{q_j} = \frac{h_j^q \sum_{i=1}^{a} \sum_{k=1}^{c} p_i r_k l_{i1k}}{h_1^q \sum_{i=1}^{a} \sum_{k=1}^{c} p_i r_k l_{ijk}}$$

$$\widehat{r_k} = \frac{h_k^r \sum_{i=1}^{a} \sum_{j=1}^{b} p_i q_j l_{ij1}}{h_1^r \sum_{j=1}^{b} \sum_{k=1}^{c} p_i q_j l_{ijk}}$$

If the values of the coefficients h_i^p, h_j^q, h_k^r and l_{ijk} remain constant where ;

i = 1, 2, …, a
j = 1, 2, …, b
k = 1, 2, …, c

we can continue to iterate repeatedly by substituting $\widehat{p_i}$, $\widehat{q_j}$ and $\widehat{r_k}$ for p_i, q_j and r_k into the formula *(5.1)* so as to make the iteration process sufficiently close as;

$\widehat{p_i} \approx p_i,\ i = 1,2,\ldots,a$

$\widehat{q_j} \approx q_j,\ j = 1,2,\ldots,b$

$\widehat{r_k} \approx r_k,\ k = 1,2,\ldots,c$

It is now easier to compute $\widehat{\widehat{d}}_{ijk}$ *(the final indicated rate)* upon the convergence of the iteration process by using *(4.9)*, *(4.13)* and *(4.14)*

6.2 Uniqueness of Determined Solutions in Actuarial Practice

To prove that our rating algorithm converges to a unique solution, Brouwer's Fixed Point Theorem will be recalled by restating the following:

Lemma 5.1: There exists a point $\overline{g}$ such that $\beta(\overline{g}) = \overline{g}$ for continuous function β mapping a convex and compact set U of an Euclidean space into itself.

It must be noted that under the condition of Brouwer's Theorem, there is no guarantee for the uniqueness of the fixed point $\overline{g}$.

Theorem 5.2: If arrays $H = (h_{ijk})_{apbpc}$ and $L= (l_{ijk})_{apbpc}$ are positive values satisfying the following:

(1) $h_1^p > 0, h_1^q > 0 \text{and} h_1^r > 0;$

(2) $l_{ijk}>0$, where $i = 1,2,\ldots,a; j = 1,2,\ldots,b; k = 1,2,\ldots,c$

As defined in *(5.1)*, it contains at least one solution $\overline{g}$◆ R^{a+b+c} where R^{a+b+c}, R^a, R^b and R^c are all Euclidean spaces. The vector $g := (p; q; r) := (p_1,\ldots, p_a ; q_1,\ldots,q_b ; r_1,\ldots,r_c) \in R^{a+b+c}$ and the function $\beta: R^{a+b+c} \rightarrow R^{a+b+c}$ can be introduced as:

$$\beta_i(\overline{g}) = \frac{h_i^p \sum_{j=1}^{b} \sum_{k=1}^{c} q_j r_k l_{1jk}}{h_1^p \sum_{j=1}^{b} \sum_{k=1}^{c} q_j r_k l_{ijk}}, \; i=1,2,\ldots,a. \tag{5.2}$$

$$\beta_{a+j}(\overline{g}) = \frac{h_j^q \sum_{i=1}^{a} \sum_{k=1}^{c} p_i r_k l_{i1k}}{h_1^q \sum_{i=1}^{a} \sum_{k=1}^{c} p_i r_k l_{ijk}}, \; j = 1,2,\ldots,b$$

$$\beta_{a+b+k}(\overline{g}) = \frac{h_k^r \sum_{i=1}^{a} \sum_{j=1}^{b} p_i q_j l_{ij1}}{h_1^r \sum_{j=1}^{b} \sum_{k=1}^{c} p_i q_j l_{ijk}}, \; k = 1,2,\ldots,c$$

where the denominators of β_i, β_{a+j} and $\beta_{a+b+k} \neq 0$ for the continuous vector functions.

Given that: $\theta_i^p := \min\{l_{ijk}: j=1,\ldots,b; k=1,\ldots,c\}$,

$N_i^p := \max\{l_{ijk}: j=1,\ldots,b; k=1,\ldots,c\}, i = 1, \ldots, a;$

$\theta_j^q := \min\{l_{ijk}: i=1,\ldots,a; k=1,\ldots,c\}$,

$N_j^q := \max\{l_{ijk}: i=1,\ldots,a; k=1,\ldots,c\}, j = 1, \ldots, b;$

$\theta^r_k := \min\{l_{ijk}: i=1,\ldots,a; j=1,\ldots,b\},$

$N^r_k := \max\{l_{ijk}: i=1,\ldots,a; j=1,\ldots,b\}, k=1,\ldots,c$

Without loss of generality, the second condition stated ealier is the same as θ^p_i, θ^q_j, and θ^r_k where $i=1,\ldots,a$; $j=1,\ldots,b$ and $k=1,\ldots,c$ respectively. Taking a closer look at this condition, the values of l_{ijk} must not be equal to zero in any circumstance otherwise the box U will not be bounded and $\beta(\overline{g})$ will not be a continuous function because if $l_{ijk}=0$, it obviously means that $\theta^p_i = \theta^q_j = \theta^r_k = 0$. The implication is that the Brouwer's Fixed Point Theorem will be unfulfilled.

Invariably; $\dfrac{h^p_i \theta^p_1}{h^p_1 N^p_i} \le \beta_i \le \dfrac{h^p_i N^p_1}{h^p_1 \theta^p_i}$, $i = 1, \ldots, a.$ (5.3)

$$\frac{h^q_j \theta^q_1}{h^q_1 N^q_j} \le \beta_{a+j} \le \frac{h^q_j N^q_1}{h^q_1 \theta^q_j}, j=1,\ldots,b$$

$$\frac{h^r_k \theta^r_1}{h^r_1 N^r_k} \le \beta_{a+b+k} \le \frac{h^r_k N^r_1}{h^r_1 \theta^r_k}, k=1,\ldots,c$$

As defined by the inequalities in *(5.3),* the vector

$\{\beta_1,\ldots, \beta_a ; \beta_{a+1},\ldots, \beta_{a+b} ; \beta_{a+b+1},\ldots, \beta_{a+b}+_c\} \sqsubseteq U \subseteq \mathrm{R}^{a+b+c}$.

Also, formula *(5.2)* maps initial guess $g^0 := (p^0; q^0 ; r^0)$ into U and maps U into itself by applying formula *(5.3).* Then, Box U (bounded and closed) is a convex and compact set in the Euclidean space with the continuous function β. Therefore, all conditions of Lemma *5.1* are now satisfied. Hence, by the function defined by *(5.2),* there exists a fixed point $\overline{g}$ such that $\beta(\overline{g}) = \overline{g}$. Therefore, the theorem is proved.

In order to sufficiently discuss the uniqueness of solution, let us further consider Lemma *5.3.*

Lemma 5.3: If β: $U \to R^r$ denotes a differentiable continuous function in $U \subseteq R^r$ (a convex set) and if Π (a constant positive number less than one) exists such that R^r holds for any norm; $\|J_{\beta}(g)\| \le \Pi$, $\forall$ g ϵ U, then β has $\overline{g}$ (a unique fixed point) in U.

We can now confidently say that for any initial guess g^0 chosen in U, the iteration *(4.3)* converges to $\overline{g}$T R^r. To guarantee this uniqueness, let us obtain Jacobi Matrix (J_{β}).

Recall; $g := (p; q; r) := (p_1,\ldots, p_a ; q_1,\ldots,q_b ; r_1,\ldots,r_c) \in R^{a+b+c}$

$$J_{\beta=} \frac{\alpha\left(\beta 1,\ldots,\beta a;\beta a+1,\ldots,\beta a+b;\beta a+b+1,\ldots,\beta a+b+c\right)}{\alpha\left(p1,\ldots, pa\ ;q1,\ldots,qb;r1,\ldots,rc\right)}$$

Where;

$$\frac{\alpha\left(\beta 1,\ldots,\beta a\right)}{\alpha\left(q1,\ldots,qb\right)}=\begin{pmatrix} 0 & \frac{\alpha_{\beta_1}}{\alpha_{q_2}} & \cdots & \frac{\alpha_{\beta_1}}{\alpha_{q_b}} \\ \vdots & \vdots & \ddots & \vdots \\ 0 & \frac{\alpha_{\beta_a}}{\alpha_{q_2}} & \cdots & \frac{\alpha_{\beta_a}}{\alpha_{q_b}} \end{pmatrix}$$

$$\frac{\alpha_{\beta_i}}{\alpha_{q_j}}=\frac{h_i^p\alpha(\sum_{j=1}^{b}\sum_{k=1}^{c}q_j r_k l_{1jk})}{h_1^p\,\alpha_{q_j}\left(\sum_{j=1}^{b}\sum_{k=1}^{c}q_j r_k l_{ijk}\right)}$$

$$\frac{\alpha_{\beta_i}}{\alpha_{q_j}}=\frac{h_i^p}{h_1^p}\frac{\left(\sum_{k=1}^{c}r_k l_{1jk}\right)\sum_{j=1}^{b}\sum_{k=1}^{c}q_j r_k l_{ijk}-\left(\sum_{k=1}^{c}r_k l_{ijk}\right)\sum_{j=1}^{b}\sum_{k=1}^{c}q_j r_k l_{1jk}}{\left(\sum_{j=1}^{b}\sum_{k=1}^{c}q_j r_k l_{ijk}\right)^2} \tag{5.4}$$

If $\frac{\alpha\left(\beta 1,\ldots,\beta a\right)}{\alpha\left(p1,\ldots,pa\right)}=\frac{\alpha\left(\beta a+1,\ldots,\beta a+b\right)}{\alpha\left(q1,\ldots,qb\right)}=\frac{\alpha\left(\beta a+b+1,\ldots,\beta a+b+c\right)}{\alpha\left(r1,\ldots,rc\right)}=0$,

then the Jacobi Matrix ($J_{\beta)}$ is represented by:

$$J_{\beta=}\begin{pmatrix} 0 & \frac{\alpha\left(\beta 1,\ldots,\beta a\right)}{\alpha\left(q1,\ldots,qb\right)} & \frac{\alpha\left(\beta 1,\ldots,\beta a\right)}{\alpha\left(r1,\ldots,rc\right)} \\ \frac{\alpha\left(\beta a+1,\ldots,\beta a+b\right)}{\alpha\left(p1,\ldots,pa\right)} & 0 & \frac{\alpha\left(\beta a+1,\ldots,\beta a+b\right)}{\alpha\left(r1,\ldots,rc\right)} \\ \frac{\alpha\left(\beta a+b+1,\ldots,\beta a+b+c\right)}{\alpha\left(p1,\ldots,pa\right)} & \frac{\alpha\left(\beta a+b+1,\ldots,\beta a+b+c\right)}{\alpha\left(q1,\ldots,qb\right)} & 0 \end{pmatrix} \tag{5.5}$$

Thus, if $0\leq\frac{\alpha_{\beta_i}}{\alpha_{q_j}}$, minimising the denominator and maximising the numerator in *(5.3)*, we obtain;

$$\frac{h_i^p\left(N_1^p\sum_{k=1}^{c}r_k\right)\left(N_i^p\sum_{j=1}^{b}q_j\sum_{k=1}^{c}r_k\right)-\left(\theta_1^p\sum_{k=1}^{c}r_k\right)\left(\theta_i^p\sum_{j=1}^{b}q_j\sum_{k=1}^{c}r_k\right)}{h_1^p\left(\theta_i^p\sum_{j=1}^{b}q_j\sum_{k=1}^{c}r_k\right)}\geq\frac{\alpha_{\beta_i}}{\alpha_{q_j}}$$

Alternatively, we get;

$$\frac{h_i^p\left(N_1^pN_i^p-\theta_1^p\theta_i^p\right)}{h_1^p\left(\theta_i^p\right)^2\sum_{j=1}^{b}q_j}\geq\frac{\alpha_{\beta_i}}{\alpha_{q_j}}|$$

It follows the same pattern if we apply the obtained result in the second and third inequalities in *(5.3)*. Therefore, in every vector, $g=\{p_1,\ldots,p_a;q_1,\ldots,q_b;r_1,\ldots,r_c\}\in U\subseteq R^{a+b+c}$,

$$\Pi_\infty^i:=\frac{h_i^p\left(N_1^pN_i^p-\theta_1^p\theta_i^p\right)}{h_1^p\left(\theta_i^p\right)^2}\left((b-1)\frac{h_1^q}{\theta_1^q\sum_{j=1}^{b}\frac{h_j^q}{N_j^q}}-(c-1)\frac{h_1^r}{\theta_1^r\sum_{k=1}^{c}\frac{h_k^r}{N_k^r}}\right)\geq\sum_{j=1}^{b}\left|\frac{\alpha_{\beta_i}}{\alpha_{q_j}}\right|+\sum_{k=1}^{c}\frac{\alpha_{\beta_i}}{\alpha_{r_k}}$$

Similarly, Π_∞^j and Π_∞^k follow the same pattern where ;

$$\Pi_\infty:=\max_{i,j,k}\left\{\Pi_\infty^i,\Pi_\infty^j,\Pi_\infty^k\right\}$$

Consequently, applying both *(4.5)* and *(5.5),* we derive;

$$\left\|J_\beta\right\|\infty:=\max_{i,j,k}\ \{\sum_{j=1}^{b}\frac{\alpha_{\beta_i}}{\alpha_{q_j}}+\sum_{k=1}^{c}\frac{\alpha_{\beta_i}}{\alpha_{r_k}};\sum_{i=1}^{a}\frac{\alpha_{\beta_{a+j}}}{\alpha_{p_i}}+\sum_{k=1}^{c}\frac{\alpha_{\beta_{a+j}}}{\alpha_{r_k}};$$

$$\sum_{i=1}^{a}\frac{\alpha_{\beta_{a+b+k}}}{\alpha_{p_i}}+\sum_{j=1}^{b}\frac{\alpha_{\beta_{a+b+k}}}{\alpha_{q_j}}\ \}$$

It is now crystal clear that $\Pi_\infty\geq|J_\beta|_\infty$. Therefore, function *(5.2)* possesses a unique fixed point and the algorithm *(5.1)* converges to the point as shown in L*emma (5.3)* if $1>\Pi_\infty$.

6.3 Sufficient Conditions for Algorithm Convergence

The next thing to do now is to examine the following theorems to prove the sufficient conditions for convergence of the iteration process of our algorithm in the formula *(5.1)*

Theorem 5.4: if $\Pi_\infty<1$ and conditions of the *Theorem (5.2)* satisfied, the function defined by *(5.2)* will have a unique fixed point and for any initial guess g^0 in D^0, the algorithm *(5.1)* will converge towards that point.

Similarly, $|J_\beta|_1$ can also be obtained as;

$$|J_{\beta}|_1 = \max_{i,j,k}\{\sum_{j=1}^{b} \frac{\alpha_{\beta_{a+j}}}{\alpha_{p_i}} + \sum_{k=1}^{c} \frac{\alpha_{\beta_{a+b+k}}}{\alpha_{p_i}} ; \sum_{i=1}^{a} \frac{\alpha_{\beta_i}}{\alpha_{q_j}} + \sum_{k=1}^{c} \frac{\alpha_{\beta_{a+b+k}}}{\alpha_{q_j}} ; \sum_{i=1}^{a} \frac{\alpha_{\beta_i}}{\alpha_{r_k}} + \sum_{j=1}^{b} \frac{\alpha_{\beta_{a+j}}}{\alpha_{r_k}}\}$$

Therefore,

$$\prod_1^i := \frac{h_1^p}{\theta_1^p \sum_{i=1}^{a} \frac{h_1^p}{N_i^p}} \left\{ \sum_{j=1}^{b} \frac{h_j^q \left(N_1^q N_j^q - \theta_1^q \theta_j^q\right)}{h_1^q \left(\theta_j^q\right)^2} + \sum_{k=1}^{c} \frac{h_k^r \left(N_1^r N_k^r - \theta_1^r \theta_k^r\right)}{h_1^r \left(\theta_k^r\right)^2} \right\} \geq \sum_{j=1}^{b} \frac{\alpha_{\beta_{a+j}}}{\alpha_{p_i}} + \sum_{k=1}^{c} \frac{\alpha_{\beta_{a+b+k}}}{\alpha_{p_i}} ,$$

$\forall$ *i=1,...,m.*

In this same way, Π_1^j and Π_1^k can be obtained. Thus;

$$\Pi_1 := \max_{i,j,k} \left\{\Pi_1^i, \Pi_1^j, \Pi_1^k\right\}$$

The following statements follow as $\Pi_1 \geq |J_{\beta}|_1$:
Theorem 5.5: Assuming the conditions of *Theorem 5.2* satisfied;

(1) The function defined by formula *(5.2)* has a unique fixed point and the algorithm *5.1* converges towards the point for any initial guess g^0 in D^0 if $1 > \Pi_1$
(2) The function β given by *(5.2)* also has a unique fixed point and the algorithm *5.1* converges towards the point for any initial guess g^0 in D^0 if $1 > \min\{\Pi_1,\Pi_\infty\}=:\Pi$

To significantly simplify these statements and derivations, we will introduce θ and N as ;

$\theta := \min\{li_{jk:}\ i=1,\ldots,a;\ j=1,\ldots,b;\ k=1,\ldots,c\}$

$N := \max\{l_{ijk}: i=1,\ldots,a; j=1,\ldots,b; k=1,\ldots,c\}$

Then; $\dfrac{Nh_1^q}{H\theta} \geq \dfrac{1}{\sum_{j=1}^{b} \frac{h_j^q \theta_1^q}{h_1^q N_j^q}} \geq \dfrac{1}{\sum_{k=1}^{b} q_k}$ and $\dfrac{h_i^p h_1^q N\left(N^2 - \theta^2\right)}{h_1^p\ \theta^3 H} \geq \dfrac{\alpha_{\beta_i}}{\alpha_{q_j}}$

6.4 Conclusion

By repeating the proof of *Theorem 5.4* assuming the conditions of *Theorem 5.2* satisfied and

$$1 > \frac{-N\left(\theta^2 - N^2\right)}{\theta^3 H} \max_{i,j,k}\left\{\frac{(b-1)h_i^p h_1^q + (c-1)h_i^p h_1^r}{h_1^p}; \frac{(a-1)h_j^q h_1^p + (c-1)h_j^q h_1^r}{h_1^q}; \frac{(a-1)h_k^r h_1^p + (b-1)h_k^r h_1^q}{h_1^r}\right\} =: \mathrm{d}_\infty,$$

the function defined by formula *5.2* and the algorithm *5.1* have a unique fixed point and converge towards that point for any initial guess g^0 in D^0. By also repeating the proof of *Theorem 5.5* with N and θ assuming the conditions of T*heorem 5.2* satisfied and

$$1 > \frac{-N\left(\theta^2 - N^2\right)}{\theta^3} \max\left\{\frac{h_1^p}{h_1^q} + \frac{h_1^p}{h_1^r}; \frac{h_1^q}{h_1^p} + \frac{h_1^q}{h_1^r}; \frac{h_1^r}{h_1^p} + \frac{h_1^r}{h_1^q}\right\} =: \mathrm{d}_1,$$

then the function defined by formula *(5.2)* has a unique fixed point and the algorithm *5.1* converges towards the point for any initial guess g^0 in D^0.

Consequently, if $1 > \min\{d_1, d_\infty\} =: d$, the function β by *(5.2)* has a unique fixed point while the algorithm in *(5.1)* converges towards that point for any initial guess in g^0 chosen in D^0.

Note that the Class *i* for $M > 3$ risk classification variables shown in *(4.10)* and *(4.11)* will be denoted as;

$$h_i^p := \sum_{j=1}^{b} \cdots \sum_{k=1}^{c} h_{ij\ldots k}, i = 1, 2, \ldots, a \tag{5.6}$$

$$L_i^p := \sum_{j=1}^{b} \cdots \sum_{k=1}^{c} l_{ijk}\, q_j \ldots r_k, i = 1, 2, \ldots, a \tag{5.7}$$

Both *(5.6)* and *(5.7)* pointed to the fact that ommission only occurs to summation by i^{th} index corresponding to factor p. Same can be said for other risk factors $(q=(q_1, \ldots, q_b), \ldots, r=(r_1, \ldots, r_c))$. That is to say, summation by the corresponding indices disappear as indicated in *(5.6)* and *(5.7)*.

In the same vein, we can also generalise functions $(\beta_i, \ldots, \beta_{a+j}, \ldots, \beta_{a+b+\ldots+k})$ indicated in *(5.2)* as;

$$\beta_i = \frac{h_i^p \sum_{j=1}^{b} \cdots \sum_{k=1}^{c} l_{1jk} \ldots q_j \ldots r_k}{h_1^p \sum_{j=1}^{b} \cdots \sum_{k=1}^{c} l_{ijk}\, q_j \ldots r_k}, i=1,2,\ldots,a$$

$$\beta_{a+j} = \frac{h_j^q \sum_{i=1}^{a} \cdots \sum_{k=1}^{c} l_{i1k} \ldots p_i \ldots r_k}{h_1^q \sum_{i=1}^{a} \cdots \sum_{k=1}^{c} l_{ijk} \ldots p_i \ldots r_k}, j = 1,2,\ldots,b$$

$$\beta_{a+b+k} = \frac{h_k^r \sum_{i=1}^{a} \cdots \sum_{j=1}^{b} l_{ij1} \cdots p_i \cdots q_j}{h_1^r \sum_{j=1}^{b} \cdots \sum_{k=1}^{c} l_{ijk} \cdots p_i \cdots q_j}, k = 1,2,\ldots,c$$

Finally, all other formulae can be generalised in this same manner in order to make them straightforward and simplified.

6.5 Managerial Application

Fixed point theorem is a mathematical tool that can be used to find a point that satisfies a certain condition or equation. For example, if g is a function that maps a set Y to itself, then a point y in Y is called a fixed point of g if g(y) = y. Fixed point theorem can help insurance managers to determine the optimal premium and loss ratio for their policies by using a suitable loss model that gives a unique fixed point solution. A loss model is a mathematical representation of the frequency and severity of insurance losses. By using a loss model that has a fixed point, managers can find the optimal premium and loss ratio that balance the expected losses and the expected profits. The premium is the amount of money that the insured pays to the insurer for the coverage, and the loss ratio is the ratio of losses to premiums. If the premium is too high or too low, or if the loss ratio is too high or too low, then the insurer may lose money or customers. By using fixed point theorem, managers can avoid overcharging or undercharging their customers and ensure a fair and equitable pricing that maximizes the insurer's profitability and customer satisfaction. Fixed point theorem can also help managers to evaluate the risk and uncertainty of different insurance scenarios and make informed decisions based on the convergence of algorithm towards a fixed point. An algorithm is a step-by-step procedure that can be used to find a fixed point of a function or a system. By using an algorithm that converges towards a fixed point, managers can estimate the probability and magnitude of different outcomes and compare them with their risk appetite and tolerance. Fixed point theorem can thus enhance the efficiency and profitability of insurance business by providing a reliable and rigorous method for finding optimal solutions and evaluating risks.

One of the examples of fixed point theorem in insurance is the system of difference equations introduced by Muhamed Borogovac (Borogovac, 2015). The system is developed for re-rating purposes in general insurance, which means adjusting the premium and loss ratio based on the past experience of the insurer. The system can be expressed as ft+1:=φ (ft), where ft is a vector of premium and loss ratio at time t, and φ is a nonlinear transformation of a d-dimensional Euclidean space. Under typical actuarial assumptions, such as positive premium and loss ratio, monotonicity of φ, and boundedness of ft, the system has a unique fixed point solution that represents the optimal premium and loss ratio for the insurer. The fixed point can be found by using an algorithm that iterates the function φ until it converges to a point that satisfies φ (f*) = f*. Borogovac shows that the algorithm converges under certain conditions on the initial value and the step size. The fixed point theorem guarantees that the algorithm will find the optimal solution for the insurer, regardless of the initial value.

Another example of fixed point theorem in insurance is the application of Banach fixed-point theorem to solve partial differential equations (PDEs) that arise in insurance mathematics (Wikipedia contributors, 2023). PDEs are often used to model the dynamics of insurance risks, such as claims, reserves, dividends, etc. However, solving PDEs analytically can be difficult or impossible in many cases. Therefore, numerical methods are often used to approximate the solutions of PDEs. One of the numerical methods is the finite difference method, which discretizes the PDEs into a system of linear equations. The system can be written as Ax = b, where A is a matrix, x is a vector of unknowns, and b is a vector of constants. The Banach fixed-point theorem can be used to show that there exists a unique solution x* to this system, and that it can be found by using an iterative method that converges to x*. The iterative method can be written as xk+1 = Bxk + c, where B is a matrix derived from A, and c is a vector derived from b. The Banach fixed-point theorem guarantees that the iterative method will find the approximate solution of the PDEs, under some conditions on B and c.

These are some examples of how fixed point theorem can help insurance managers to determine optimal solutions and evaluate risks in different insurance scenarios. Fixed point theorem can provide theoretical guarantees and practical methods for finding fixed points of functions or systems that model insurance problems. Fixed point theorem can thus enhance the efficiency and profitability of insurance business by providing a reliable and rigorous method for finding optimal solutions and evaluating risks.

REFERENCES

Arancibia-Ibarra, C., Flores, J. I. R., & Van Heijster, P. (2022). Stability Analysis of a Modified Leslie–Gower Predation Model With Weak Allee Effect in the Prey. *Frontiers in Applied Mathematics and Statistics*, *7*, 731038. doi:10.3389/fams.2021.731038

Axiomatic Basics of e-Economics Munich Personal RePEc Archive. (n.d.). MPRA. https://mpra.ub.uni-muenchen.de/24331/

Bassett, C. (n.d.). *The Benefits of Insurance to Individuals, Organizations and Society*. LinkedIn. https://www.linkedin.com/pulse/benefits-insurance-individuals-organizations-society-chase-bassett/

Belzunce, F., Martínez-Riquelme, C., & Mulero, J. (2016). Univariate stochastic orders. In Elsevier eBooks (pp. 27–113). doi:10.1016/B978-0-12-803768-3.00002-8

Bohner, M., Dannan, F. M., & Streipert, S. (2018). A nonautonomous Beverton–Holt equation of higher order. *Journal of Mathematical Analysis and Applications*, *457*(1), 114–133. doi:10.1016/j.jmaa.2017.07.051

Borogovac, M. (2014). Comparison of the Standard Rating Methods and the New General Rating Formula. *SOA ARCH 2014.1 Proceedings.*

Borogovac, M. (2015). Two applications of Brouwer's fixed point theorem: In insurance and in biology models. *Journal of Difference Equations and Applications*, *22*(6), 727–744. doi:10.1080/10236198.2015.1134519

Brown, R. L., & Gottlieb, L. R. (2001). *Introduction to Ratemaking and Loss Reserving for Property and Casualty Insurance* (2nd ed.). ACTEX Publications.

Buhmann, H. (1970). *Mathematics Methods in Risk Theory*. Springer-Verlag.

Chen, L., & Chen, F. (2009). Global stability of a Leslie–Gower predator–prey model with feedback controls. *Applied Mathematics Letters*, *22*(9), 1330–1334. doi:10.1016/j.aml.2009.03.005

Corporate Finance Institute. (2023a). Cash Equivalents. *Corporate Finance Institute*. https://corporatefinanceinstitute.com/resources/accounting/cash-equivalents/

Corporate Finance Institute. (2023b). Reinsurance Companies. *Corporate Finance Institute*. https://corporatefinanceinstitute.com/resources/wealth-management/reinsurance-companies/

Duverne, D., & Hele, J. (2016). How the Insurance Industry Manages Risk, 55-76. In Oxford University Press eBooks. doi:10.1093/acprof:oso/9780198788812.003.0004

Espinosa, O., & Zarruk, A. A. (2021). *The importance of actuarial management in insurance business decision-making in the twenty-first century*. British Actuarial Journal., doi:10.1017/S1357321721000155

Fallon, N. (2023). 6 Biggest Business Insurance Risks (and How to Mitigate Them). *Business News Daily*. https://www.businessnewsdaily.com/9024-biggest-business-insurance-risks.html

Fu, L., & Wu, C.P. (2005). General Iteration Algorithm for Classification Ratemaking. Casualty Actuarial Society Forum.

Goffard, P. (2021). Sequential Monte Carlo samplers to fit and compare insurance loss models. *Scandinavian Actuarial Journal*, 1–23. doi:10.1080/03461238.2022.2145577

Golubin, A., & Gridin, V. N. (2022). Optimal insurance strategy in a risk process under a safety level imposed on the increments of the process. *Scandinavian Actuarial Journal*, *2023*(1), 20–37. doi:10.1080/03461238.2022.2075282

González-Olivares, E., Mena-Lorca, J., Rojas-Palma, A., & Flores, J. I. R. (2011). Dynamical complexities in the Leslie–Gower predator–prey model as consequences of the Allee effect on prey. *Applied Mathematical Modelling*, *35*(1), 366–381. doi:10.1016/j.apm.2010.07.001

Goovaerts, M. J., De Vylder, F., & Haezendonck, J. (1984). *Insurance Premiums: Theory and Application*. North-Holland.

Gray, K. E. Jr, & Dewar, R. (1971). Axiomatic Characterization of the Time-Weighted Rate of Return. *Management Science*, *18*(2), B-35. doi:10.1287/mnsc.18.2.B32

Halton, C. (2022). Inflationary Risk Definition, Ways to Counteract It. *Investopedia*. https://www.investopedia.com/terms/i/inflationrisk.asp

Heilpern, S. (2002). Using Choquet integral in economics. *Statistical Papers (Berlin, Germany)*, *43*(1), 53–73. doi:10.100700362-001-0086-3

Hurlimann, W. (1997). On Quasi-Mean Value Principles. *Blatter der Deutschen Gesellschaft fur Versicherungsmathematik*, *XXIII*, 1–16.

Hurlimann, W. (1998). On Stop-Loss Order and the Distortions Pricing Principles. *ASTIN Bulletin*, *28*(2), 119–134. doi:10.2143/AST.28.1.519082

Istratescu, V. I. (1981). *Fixed Point Theory*. Reidel Publishing Company. doi:10.1007/978-94-009-8177-5

Kagan, J. (2021a). Substandard Insurance. *Investopedia*. https://www.investopedia.com/terms/s/substandard-insurance.asp

Kagan, J. (2021b). Insurance Risk Class Definition and Associated Premium Costs. *Investopedia*. https://www.investopedia.com/terms/i/insurance-risk-class.asp

Khalehoghli, S., Rahimi, H., & Gordji, M. E. (2020). Fixed Point Theorem in R-Metric Spaces with Applications. *AIMS Mathematics*, *5*(4), 312–315. doi:10.3934/math.2020201

Maiti, M. (2022, December 16). How An Actuary Decides Your Insurance Policy Premiums—Know Criteria, Factors Involved. *Outlook India*. https://www.outlookindia.com/. https://www.outlookindia.com/business/how-an-actuary-decides-your-insurance-policy-premiums-know-criteria-factors-involved--news-245409

Mallappa, M., & Talawar, A. S. (2020). Premium Calculation for Different Loss Discrete Analogues of Continuous Distributions Utility Theory. *International Journal of Agricultural and Statistics Sciences*, *16*(1), 61–72.

Nash, J. (1951). Non Cooperative Games. *Annals of Mathematics*, *54*(2), 286–295. doi:10.2307/1969529

National Academies Press (US). (1993). *Risk Selection, Risk Sharing, and Policy*. Employment and Health Benefits - NCBI Bookshelf. https://www.ncbi.nlm.nih.gov/books/NBK235988/

Nieto, J. J., & Guez-Lo'pez, R. R. (2005). Contractive Mapping Theorems in Partially Ordered Sets and Application to Ordinary Differential Equations. *Order*, *22*(3), 223–239. doi:10.100711083-005-9018-5

Two Applications of Brouwer's Fixed Point Theorem: in Insurance and in Biology Models. (2015, December 22). Papers with Code. https://math.paperswithcode.com/paper/two-applications-of-brouwer-s-fixed-point

Rajic, V., Azdejkovic, D., & Loncar, D. (2014). Fixed Point Theory and Possibilities of Application in Different Fields of an Economy. *UDK:330.42:515.126.4.* . https://www.researchgate.net/publication/283393893 doi:10.5937/ekopre1408382R

Real-Miranda, R., & López-Barrientos, J. D. (2022). A Geologic-Actuarial Approach for Insuring the Extraction Tasks of Non-Renewable Resources by One and Two Agents. *Mathematics*, *10*(13), 2242. doi:10.3390/math10132242

Ross, S. (2021). How Do Insurance Companies Make Money? Business Model Explained. *Investopedia*. https://www.investopedia.com/ask/answers/052015/what-main-business-model-insurance-companies.asp

State Bank of Pakistan. (n.d.). State Bank of Pakistan. https://www.sbp.org.pk/m_policy/mp-learn-3.asp

Von-Neumann, J. (1928). On the Theory of Games of Strategy. *Mathematische Annalen*, *100*, 295–320.

Wang, S., & Young, V. R. (1998). Ordering of Risks: Utility Theory Verse Yaari's Dual Theory of Risk. *Insurance, Mathematics & Economics*, *23*(2), 1–14. doi:10.1016/S0167-6687(97)00036-X

Wang, S., Young, V. R., & Panjer, H. H. (1997). Axiomatic Characterisation of Insurance Prices. *Insurance, Mathematics & Economics*, *21*(2), 173–183. doi:10.1016/S0167-6687(97)00031-0

What to do with your cash now. (2022, August 1). https://www.fidelity.com/learning-center/trading-investing/managing-cash

Why go into Insurance Law? (n.d.). University of Law. https://www.law.ac.uk/employability/legal-practice-areas/insurance-law/

Wikipedia contributors. (2023). Fixed-point theorem. *Wikipedia*. https://en.wikipedia.org/wiki/Fixed-point_theorem

Yue, Q. (2016). Dynamics of a modified Leslie–Gower predator–prey model with Holling-type II schemes and a prey refuge. *SpringerPlus*, *5*(1), 461. doi:10.118640064-016-2087-7 PMID:27119065

Chapter 8
The Measuring of Performance and Profitability of Mutual and Profitability Funds Collective Investment Funds in Securities

Zineb Bellache
Univesite Hassan II, Morocco

Hicham El Bouanani
Univesite Hassan II, Morocco

ABSTRACT

The purpose of this chapter is to study the behaviour and measure the performance of different UCITS over a period of time. For this purpose, an analysis was carried out using several measures taking into account systematic, specific, and total risk. This led to a modelling of the behaviour of these UCITS, in addition to a description of the relationships linking these behaviours and that of the market index. The aim of this work is to better orient Moroccan investors in their choice of collective investment funds.

INTRODUCTION

UCITS (Undertakings for the Collective Investment in Transferable Securities), plays a vital role in the financial industry for several compelling reasons. First and foremost, UCITS provides a well-established and regulated framework for cross-border investment within the world. This framework allows fund managers to offer investment products to investors across different member states, promoting the free movement of capital and fostering economic integration. The harmonized regulations and standards provided by UCITS enhance investor protection and ensure a level playing field for market participants. Additionally, UCITS funds offer a wide range of investment opportunities, providing investors with access to a diversified portfolio of assets. The UCITS framework enables fund managers to invest in various

DOI: 10.4018/978-1-6684-8386-2.ch008

asset classes, including equities, bonds, money market instruments, and derivatives, subject to specific investment restrictions and risk management guidelines. This flexibility allows investors to tailor their portfolios to their risk preferences and investment goals.

In essence, by enabling cross-border investment, offering a variety of investment choices, ensuring transparency and investor protection, and promoting market trust, UCITS plays a crucial role in the financial sector. Its importance lies in fostering the expansion and stability of the financial sector while protecting investors' interests. The main objective of every company is to create value, which in most cases translates into a cash surplus, and to optimize its profitability, the company must invest its cash; Investing in UCITS is the best solution for value of the cash flow.

Morocco has not been an exception of this invest tool, UCITS were introduced for the first time in 1993 as part of the process of modernizing the financial markets in Morocco. Their objective is to liberalize the national economy by broadening the financing possibilities for companies and creating new investment products for savers. In essence, they were introduced in 1993 by the Dahir bearing law No. 1-93-213 of 21 September 1993, although they were not marketed until 1995.

Indeed, UCITS allow savers to access the financial market under the best conditions of security and profitability. They also have the advantage of being liquid and performing better over the long term than traditional investment products.

In the theoretical register, many theorists have been interested in portfolio management and the development of the various attributes related to it. Certainly, portfolio management theories provide frameworks and principles for effectively managing investment portfolios such as:

Modern Portfolio Theory (MPT), developed by Harry Markowitz, MPT emphasizes diversification to optimize risk and return. It suggests that by combining assets with varying levels of risk, investors can achieve an optimal portfolio with the highest expected return for a given level of risk. Then there is Capital Asset Pricing Model (CAPM), developed by William Sharpe, which proposes that an investment's expected return is based on its systematic risk, measured by beta. It provides a framework to estimate the expected return on an asset based on its risk relative to the market.

Arbitrage Pricing Theory (APT), formulated by Stephen Ross, posits that an asset's expected return is influenced by multiple risk factors. It suggests that asset prices adjust based on the relationships between these factors, allowing for potential arbitrage opportunities.

Efficient Market Hypothesis (EMH), EMH suggests that financial markets are efficient, meaning that asset prices already reflect all available information. It challenges the notion of consistently beating the market and advocates for passive investment strategies such as index funds.

Behavioral Finance, incorporates psychological factors into investment decision-making. It recognizes that investor behavior is influenced by biases, emotions, and cognitive errors, which can lead to irrational investment decisions. This theory seeks to understand and account for these behavioral biases in portfolio management.

Factor Investing focuses on identifying and systematically exploiting specific risk factors, such as value, momentum, size, or quality, that have historically generated excess returns. It aims to construct portfolios that have exposure to these factors to achieve enhanced risk-adjusted returns.

The Black-Litterman model combines views from investors with market equilibrium assumptions to improve portfolio allocation decisions. It incorporates subjective investor views and adjusts market expectations based on those views.

These portfolio management theories offer direction on how to allocate assets, diversify portfolios, manage risk, and make investment decisions. Although no one theory can be used in all situations, comprehension and incorporation of these theories can aid investors in creating solid investing strategies that are suited to their goals and risk tolerance.

A theoretical analysis of the various theorists' ways to measuring the performance of UCITS will be the focus of the two first sections of this paper. Subsequently, the exposition of the obtained results, and their discussion will be the subject of the third section.

The main objective of this paper is to provide valuable guidance and assistance to investors in Morocco when it comes to selecting collective investment funds. The research or study intends to address a specific need or challenge faced by Moroccan investors in making informed decisions about which collective investment funds to choose. It aims to enhance the decision-making process by providing valuable insights, information, or tools that can assist investors in evaluating and selecting suitable funds.

MEASURING PERFORMANCE AND PROFITABILITY

The simplest model to describe the profitability and risk of a security is the market model. It is a result of the work of Markowitz (1959) which was developed by Sharpe (1964).

In this chapter we are focused on the models of price formation and relationships between expected returns which are the market model and the capital asset pricing model (CAPM), so, we will use several measures that are based on the CAPM to analyze the performance of our funds.

Market Model

Presentation of the Model

This model states that the fluctuations of the prices of securities are due on the one hand to the influence of the market in general (market factor) and on the other hand to purely security-specific causes. It is presented as follows:

$$Rit = \alpha i + \beta iRmt + \xi it$$

With:

i: denotes the asset and t: refers to the period

αi, βi: are the coefficients of the regression

αi is the value of the expected return when the market rate of return is zero.

βi: is an asset-specific parameter *i*, measures the influence of the market on the asset *i*.

ξit: is an asset-specific parameter *i*, of null expected value, constant variance and noncorrelated with Rm

General Characteristics of the Model

- The beta coefficient: expresses the sensitivity of the fluctuations of the asset *i* to that of the market. According to the value of beta, assets can be classified into three categories:

    - Assets for which a given change in the index results in the same change in profitability ($\beta = 1$);
    - Assets for which a given change in the index leads to a higher change in their profitability ($\beta > 1$);
    - Assets for which a given change in the index results in a lower change in their profitability ($\beta < 1$);
- Alpha is the intersection of the regression line with the y-axis; it, therefore, represents the return that could have been obtained on the asset if the market return were zero.
- Epsilon is a residual random variable. Its standard deviation is a specific measure of risk. If the asset price followed the market exactly, all points would be perfectly aligned on the regression line therefore, the dispersion around the regression line e provides a measure of the inherent variability.
- The coefficient of determination R2 is the square of the correlation coefficient between asset *i* and the market, its value is between 0 and 100%. It indicates to what extent the variations of the asset are explained by the variations of the market. An R2 close to 100% would mean that all observations are on the regression line, which would mean that the changes in the asset are fully and exclusively explained by changes in the market.
- The total risk of asset *i* can be broken down into two parts:
    - Systemic risk (risk originating from the market) is of "macroeconomic" origin: economic growth, crises economic growth, crises, interest rate fluctuations, and geopolitical uncertainties...

      The systemic risk of an asset is equal to beta times the standard deviation of the market rate of return. $\beta_i\sigma_m$
    - The specific risk (asset-specific risk) is of "microeconomic" origin: strikes in the company, contracts won, changes in consumer tastes, lawsuits...

It is equal to the standard deviation of the residual factor. σεi

Thus

Total Risk: $\sigma_i^2 = \beta_i^2\sigma_m^2 + \sigma_{\epsilon i}^2$

Limitations of the Model

There are some problems with using this model:

Betas are usually estimated statistically over a period of time in the past, but experience shows that these estimates are not consistent from one period to the next.the hypothesis of the existence of a single common factor between the securities is not feasible in reality. Indeed, the market factor is not the only factor influencing a set of securities simultaneously. The integration of the factors specific to the serity concerned with the market factor may seem an oversimplification of reality.

Thus, the behavior of a security's price can be described by a multifactor model. Such a descriptive model postulates that the rate of return of a stock is influenced by several common factors; and each stock may have a different sensitivity to each of the factors.

Multifactor Model

Presentation of the Model

A multifactor model can be written as follows:

$$R_{it} = \alpha_i + \beta_{1i} f_{1t} + \beta_{2i} f_{2t} + \dots\dots\dots\dots\dots\dots + \beta_{ki} f_{kt} + \xi_{it}$$

Where:

- f_{1t} à f_{kt} are the k factors (the first one can be the market factor)
- β_{1i} à βki are the sensitivities of security *i* to each factor.
- α_i is a constant specific to the security *i*
- ξ_{it} is an error term specific to the security *i*, different for each observation *t* but with a null mean.

Factor models reflect the influence of a number of common factors on the profitability of security. The profitability of a security depends on its sensitivity to these common factors as well as a specific component of that security.

This model is, therefore, an extension of the market model with *k+1* risk sources corresponding to the *k* systematic risk terms of each factor and a specific risk of the asset *i*, measured by the dispersion of the error term.

Type of Factors

The factors used in a factor model can be:

Statistical factors: this is a purely econometric method, using statistical methods. For example, a factor analysis or a principal component analysis (PCA) to estimate a few factors that offer the best explanation of the past returns of the securities.

macroeconomic factor: are common factors that affect the activity of all companies. Economic variables such as interest rates, inflation, economic growth. . .

Company characteristic factors: factors related to company attributes. These are important elements that help explain the differences in profitability between stocks. For example, the size of a company, earnings volatility, leverage, trading volume, the ratio of stock price or book value of the company. . .

Factor models are richer and more operational, but it is very difficult to find common factors across all securities.

The Capital Asset Pricing Model (CAPM)

The Capital Asset Pricing model (CAPM) of Sharpe (1964), Lintner (1965), mossi (1966) is one of the main results of modern financial theory and is one of the dominant paradigms of modern finance.

The CAPM is a model that explains the rates of return of different assets, in function of their risk.

The fundamental idea of the CAP is that it proposes to determine asset prices on the assumption that these prices adjust so that supply equals demand (market equilibrium), and that at equilibrium, the market remunerates those who take risks.

Model Assumptions

- Investors construct their portfolios with an exclusive focus on the expectation and variance of their returns.
- Investors are risk averse: they do not like risk and seek to maximize the expected utility of their wealth at the end of the period; the model is therefore a period model.
- The investment period is the same for all investors.
- markets are perfect: there are no transaction costs, no taxes on dividends and capital gains, and the assets are all negotiable and infinitely divisible.
- There are many buyers and sellers in the market and none of them can influence the price.
- All investors can lend or borrow the amount they want at a risk-free rate, without limitation.
- The expectations of different investors are homogeneous regarding asset returns because there is information symmetry, the investors have the same information at the same time and have identical opportunities

Presentation of the Model

The CAPM is defined by the following formula:

$$E(R_i) = R_f + \beta_{im} (E(R_m) - R_f)$$

With:

- $E(R_i)$: portfolio or asset *i* expectation.
- R_f: The interest rate of the risk-free asset.
- $E(R_m)$: expected return on the market portfolio.
- β_{im}: the beta of the asset *i* to the market, it measures the sensitivity of the asset *i* to that of the market.

*Interpretation:

In equilibrium, the rate of return on any asset is equal to the rate of return on the risk-free asset plus a risk premium. This premium is equal to the price of risk multiplied by the quantity of risk, in CAPM terminology. The price of risk is the difference between the expected rate of return on the market portfolio and the return on the risk-free asset. The quantity of risk, called beta (the same beta defined in the market model).

Beta is therefore equal to the covariance between the yield of asset i and the yield of the market portfolio, divided by the variance of the market portfolio. The risk-free asset thus has a null beta and the market portfolio a beta equal to one. The beta thus defined is the one that already appeared in Sharpe's empirical market model.

The model can be presented differently:

$E(R_i) = R_f + \beta_{im} (E(R_m) - R_f)$

Where PRi = E (Ri) – Rf is the risk premium or excess return on the asset i.

And PRm = E (Rm)–Rf is the risk premium or excess return of the market portfolio.

Validity Tests of the CAPM

Autocorrelation Test

Breusch-Godfrey test (1978) This test allows testing the presence of autocorrelation in an autoregressive process of order p (AR(p)) and can be used when there are lags on the endogenous variable in the model (yt 1, yt-2, . . .). When the errors are of the type:

$U_t = \rho 1 u_{t-1} + \rho 2 u_{t-2} + + \rho p u_{t-p} + \epsilon$

It allows testing the hypothesis:

H0: ρ1 = ρ2 = ...= ρp = 0

H1: ρ1 ≠ 0; ρ2 ≠ 0; ...; ρp ≠ 0

The statistic is obtained by applying the principle of Lagrange multipliers (LM criterion) in the context of maximum likelihood for a model with autoregressive errors.

To apply this test, we do the auxiliary regression:

$$y_t = \beta_o \sum_{i=1}^{k} \beta_i x_{ti} + \sum_{j=1}^{p} \rho_j u_{t-j} + v_t$$

Where the u_{t-s} are the residuals of the regression of yt on the k explanatory variables x_t by OLS. The statistic is defined by: LM = TR2

T is the sample size and R2 is the coefficient of determination of the regression of the residuals on the explanatory variables.

If H0 it is true, we can show that the limiting distribution (when n → ∞) of this statistic is a chi_p^2 If TR2 $\leq \chi_p^2$ we accept the hypothesis of independence of the errors. We can also use a classical Fisher test of nullity of the coefficients if for the auxiliary regression when the sample size is small (H0: ρ1 = ρ2 = ...ρp = 0).

Test of Heteroscedasticity

Given the starting model:

yt = β1 + β2x2t + β3x3t + ... + βkxkt + ut

This is the most widely used and most general test since no prior form of heteroscedasticity is imposed. The following regression is performed:

$$u_t^2 = \alpha_o + \sum_q \alpha_q x_{qt} + \sum_q \beta_q x_{qt}^2 + \sum_q \sum_{l<q} \mu_{ql} x_{qt} x_{lt} + v_t$$

We can therefore see the general character of this test, since in the explanatory variables we find the xi, their squares and their cross products. White's test statistic is based on the calculation of the coefficient of determination R2 from the previous regression.

Under H0 (the αq, the βq and the μql are null) we can show that W = TR2 → $\chi^2_{(p)}$ p being the number of regressors in the previous regression (p = $\frac{k(k+3)}{2}$ k is the number of explanatory variable in the initial regression)

If W≥ χ_p^2 tabulated, we reject the null hypothesis H0 of homoscedasticity, and we can accept the presence of heteroscedasticity of errors.

Models to Test the CAPM

Black, Jensen and Scholes model (1973) It is a linear regression model with time series. The expression that characterizes the model is:

$PR_{it} = a_i + i\ PR_{mt} + \varepsilon_{ti}$

Where:

- t is the period and i is the portfolio,
- PRit = Rit-Rft is the risk premium of the security,
- Rit is the return of portfolio i between periods t-1 and t,
- Rft is the risk-free rate,
- PRmt = Rmt-Rft is the market risk premium,
- Rmt is the yield of the market portfolio,
- εti is the error term,
- Bi is the market beta of portfolio i and ai is the constant.

The main objective of this model is to estimate the parameters αi and βi.

To test the validity of the CAPM, we test the null hypothesis that the constant αi is equal to zero. If this null hypothesis is rejected, it means that the model fails to explain correctly the risk premium of the stock (because the latter does not depend only on the market risk premium): this leads to invalidate the model.

However, if the null hypothesis is not rejected, this implies that the model perfectly captures the variations in the risk premium of the security: the model is thus vali- dated.

Traditional Performance Measures

Sharpe Ratio

The Sharpe ratio measures the excess of portfolio profitability over the risk-free rate for a unit of overall risk (measured by the standard deviation of portfolio profitability:

$$S = \frac{R_p - R_f}{\sigma_p}$$

where:

- Rp: average portfolio yield P
- Rf: average return on risk-free assets.
- σp: the standard deviation of realized portfolio returns.

It allows portfolios to be ranked, even when they correspond to different risk levels. Over a given period of time, the portfolio with the highest ratio is the one with the best return given the risk taken.

Treynor Ratio

(Treynor 1965)proposed a performance measure based on the risk premium per unit of systematic risk. This measure is based on the characteristic relationship of the CAPM:

$$T = \frac{R_p - R_f}{\beta_p}$$

A high value of the ratio indicates good performance, while a low value indicates poor performance.

Jensen's Alpha

(Jensen 1968) measures the performance of a portfolio via the term:

$$\alpha p = Rp - [Rf + \beta p(Rm - Rf)]$$

where:

- Rm: average market return.
- Jensen's alpha refers directly to the CAPM Observing a positive value of αp will indicate an above-market performance, while observing a negative value of αp will indicate a below-market performance.

Fama Performance Measurement

The Fama performance measure is a consequence of the Jensen measure. It is an absolute measure that is not suitable for comparing portfolios of different total risk.

$$F_p = R_p - R_f - \frac{\sigma_p}{\sigma_m}\left(R_m - R_f\right)$$

where:

- σm: the standard deviation of realized market returns.

If Fp is positive, this means that the return on the fund being evaluated is higher than what a fully diversified portfolio would have produced and, consequently, its specific risk has been better rewarded than the market. If Fp is negative, it means that the increase in risk accepted by the investor has not been sufficiently rewarded.

Moses, Cheney, and Veit Measure

moses, Cheney, and Veit (1987) recently proposed another relative measure of selectivity by comparing the remuneration for the additional risk resulting from insufficient diversification to the price of risk in the market. Its expression is:

$$MCV_p = \frac{\dfrac{R_p - R_f - {}^2{}_p\left(R_m - R_f\right)}{\dfrac{\tilde{A}_p}{\tilde{A}_m} - {}^2{}_p}}{R_m - R_f}$$

A value greater than 1 means that the specific risk of the portfolio has been remunerated at a rate higher than the market price; in other words, the return has been better than that which would have been obtained with maximum diversification. This is obviously equivalent to positive net selectivity.

New Performance Measurements

Information Ratio and Tracking Error

The development of index management and management referring to an index (bench- mark) has led to the development of these new indicators. They are based on the difference in profitability between the portfolio and its benchmark (difference noted ER).

The tracking error corresponds to the standard deviation of observed profitability differences. It measures the degree to which the manager regularly exceeds the bench- mark:

$$\text{Tracking Error} = \sqrt{Var\left(R_p - R_b\right)}$$

- Theoretical underperformance = Benchmark return—tracking error.
- Theoretical over performance = benchmark return + tracking error.

The appraisal ratio is equal to the ratio between the portfolio's excess return over the benchmark and the standard deviation of the observed deviations:

Information Ratio = (Fund Performance—Benchmark Performance)/Tracking Error

APPLICATION

We will study the behavior of 6 UCITS in each category.

PS: After filtering this database and removing noise and outliers, we decided to do all the financial model calculations and applications in Python due to its wide range of libraries in addition to its stability, modernity, and variety of its development environments.

THE MARKET MODEL

The following tables summarize the results of the market model estimation for each UCITS:

Table 1. The results of the market model estimation

UCITS	Beta	Alpha	R2	Specific Risk	Systematic Risk	Total Risk
MONETARY						
A	0.64743	1.2613e-05	0.65117	4.3252e-05	6.9324e-05	6.6767e-09
B	0.67797	1.7319e-05	0.78773	3.2123e-05	7.2595e-05	6.3019e-09
C	0.83667	1.6758e-05	0.72132	4.7468e-05	8.9588e-05	1.0279e-08
D	0.36613	3.6795e-05	0.40183	4.0774e-05	3.9204e-05	3.1995e-09
E	0.83071	1.8639e-05	0.72556	4.6633e-05	8.8949e-05	1.0086e-08
F	0.780806	2.9017e-05	0.61503	5.6385e-05	8.3606e-05	1.0169e-08
SHORT-TERM OBLIGATION						
A'	0.94871	1.3241e-05	0.516	8.3923e-05	1.0158e-04	1.7362e-08
B'	0.78494	2.8854e-05	0.28958	1.1229e-04	8.4049e-05	1.9675e-08
C'	0.97297	2.4239e-05	0.54671	8.0921e-05	1.0418e-04	1.7402e-08
D'	0.93603	2.1243e-05	0.45891	9.2836e-05	1.0022e-04	1.8664e-08
E'	0.89904	-2.623e-06	0.41049	9.8409e-05	9.6266e-05	1.8951e-08
F'	0.96483	-1.133e-05	0.52387	8.4015e-05	1.0331e-04	1.7731e-08

" MONETARY " UCITS invest mainly in money markets, via investments with a short to very short maturity, and whose sensitivity is less than 0.5. Risks embedded in money market UCITS are very limited. Their return, however, is often low;

" SHORT-TERM OBLIGATION " UCITS invest mainly in bonds issued by public or private companies. This category cover two types: Short-term bond UCITS that invest mainly in bonds with a short-term maturity. The sensitivity of this type varies between 0.5 and 1.1;

Analysis and interpretation:

- money market Funds

Looking at table 1.1, the fund with the highest beta is "C" while the one with the lowest beta is "D". We also notice that the "F", "E" and "C" funds have a beta close to 1, which indicates that they follow the market trend (i.e., they have the same market risk as the market).

On the other hand, the other funds have a beta that is lower than 1 which means that they follow the trend less. As a result, the fluctuations of these funds will be less than those of the market.

Systematic risk confirms these results. If we look at the column for systematic risk, we see that the funds with a beta close to 1 have a market risk very close to that of the market, which is equal to 10.7e-05. On the other hand, the other UCITS have a lower systematic risk.

The R2 represents the coefficient of determination and is used to judge the quality of the linear regression. In fact, the models represent a good fit, notably the largest R2 is R2 = 78.773% for "A" while the smallest is 40.18 for "D".

- short-term obligation

Similarly, for the STO funds, we can see that all the funds have betas close to 1, which indicates that they follow the market trend. We can also see that the fund with the highest beta is "C' " (0.97297), while the one with the lowest beta is "B' " (0.78494).

The systematic risk confirms these results since it is very close to the market risk for all the STO funds.

The adjustment measured by R2 is average, especially for "A",51.6% of its variability is explained by that of the market ("MBI ST* The Moroccan Bond Index is a bond performance index calculated and published by BMCE Capital markets.)

Table 2. Summary of the calculation of the UCITS performances

Type	UCITS	Sharpe Ratio	Treynor Ratio	A of Jensen	Fama	MCV
Money market Funds	A	5.5288	0.9028	-0.0048	-0.269	-0.3675
	B	3.5948	0.6456	-0.0053	-0.4823	-1.0768
	C	6.9352	1.1835	-0.0024	-0.0014	0.8865
	D	3.9681	0.9072	-0.0095	-0.456	-0.0988
	E	7.2365	1.2313	-0.0025	0.0361	1.1028
	F	8.0459	1.4869	-0.0033	0.1641	1.518
Short-term bond	A'	3.5311	0.7129	-0.0010	0.0203	1.0967
	B'	3.1455	0.8477	-0.0043	-0.059	0.8341
	C'	5.3101	1.0415	-0.0005	0.3598	2.8270
	D'	4.2252	0.9045	-0.0013	0.1604	1.6494
	E'	0.7564	0.1712	-0.0020	-0.543	-0.9744
	F'	0.5007	0.1003	-0.0007	-0.5653	-1.7011

FINANCIAL ASSET PRINCING MODEL

Study of the performance of various UCITS.

In this section, we have modeled the returns of mutual funds by the Capital Asset Pricing model (CAPM). Note that the risk-free rate for STOs and money market funds is the average of the key rates observed over the study period, and for LMOS the 10-year Treasury bill rate (because we have taken into account the investment horizon

Analysis and Interpretation

The table 2 presents the calculations of the different ratios to study the performance of the UCITS.

- money market funds

First of all, we can see in the Sharpe ratio column that the highest value in the money market funds is 8.0459, which is suitable for the "F" money market fund, which means that 1% volatility generated a performance surplus of 8.0459 compared to a risk-free asset, while the lowest value is 3.5948, which is suitable for the "B" fund, which means that 1% volatility generated a performance surplus of 3.5948 compared to a risk-free asset.

Concerning the Fama measure, we can see that the "C" and "F" funds have positive values, which means that their specific risk has been better rewarded than the market. On the other hand, the Fama measure for the other funds is negative, which means that the increase in risk accepted by the investor has not been sufficiently remunerated.

Similarly, the Moses, Cheney and Veit (mcv) measure for the "E" and "F" fund is greater than 1, and this proves the ability of the managers to detect these funds as being over or undervalued. Whereas the "C" fund has an MCV measure of less than 1, which indicates that the managers are not making the best use of the specific risk they place on their fund holders. However, for other funds with a negative MCV measure, there will be an additional source of risk that is the result of the manager's choice to—
Short-term bond UCITS

The highest value within the short-term bond funds is 5.3101 which corresponds to the "C'" fund, which means that the performance exceeds that of the risk-free investment and generates more profitability. The smallest value is 0.5007 which corresponds to the "F' " fund, which indicates that the return obtained is higher than that of a risk-free investment, but it is still insufficient to compensate for the risk taken by the investor. Also, the Sharpe ratio of the fund "E' " is between 0 and 1, while it is higher than 1 for the other funds.

We can see that the values of the Treynor ratio are all positive, so it remains to compare them with each other knowing that a higher Treynor ratio is preferable because it implies higher returns for each unit of risk that the fund has assumed compared to the market risk. We can also see that Jensen's Alpha is negative for all the funds, which indicates that they underperform the market.

Note that the Jensen and Fama performance measures depend on the systematic risk taken by the manager and therefore do not fully reflect the predictive capabilities of the manager being evaluated and therefore cannot be a relative measure of ranking. and therefore, cannot be used as a relative ranking measure. As for the Treynor and Sharpe measures, they are only relative if the systematic risk taken by the manager is constant over the evaluation period. Therefore, we will compare the funds according to the Sharpe and Treynor and Moses, Cheney and Veit (MCV) measures.

The following table 4 shows the ranking of the UCITS according to each risk-adjusted performance measure.

Table 3. Comparison of performance measures

Type of measure	Nature of the risk		
	systematic	specific	total
absolute	Jensen		Fama
relative	Treynor	MCV	Sharpe

Table 4. Ranking of UCITS according to the different risk-adjusted performance measures

Type	UCITS	Sharpe Ratio Rank	Treynor Ratio Rank	MCV Rank
Money market Funds	A	4	5	5
	B	6	6	6
	C	3	3	3
	D	5	4	4
	E	2	2	2
	F	1	1	1
Short-term bond	A'	3	4	3
	B'	4	3	4
	C'	1	1	1
	D'	2	2	2
	E'	5	5	5
	F'	6	6	6

Interpretation

Looking at table 1.4The major finding is that the three measures used lead to remarkable converging conclusions in terms of UCITS ranking.

The best performing money market fund according to the Sharpe, Treynor and MCV measures is "F", while it is the "C" fund for short-term bond funds.

Table 5. Summary of the calculation of tracking error and information ratio for UCITS

Type	UCITS	Benchmark profitability	Tracking Error	Information ratio
Money market Funds	A	2.471475	0.07642	-4.60728
	B	2.471475	0.14609	-3.74032
	C	2.471475	0.47349	0.03051
	D	2.471475	0.19641	-3.05049
	E	2.471475	0.05848	0.79123
	F	2.471475	0.20958	0.92825
Short-term bond	A'	2.471475	0.34534	0.60017
	B'	2.471475	0.34841	0.57267
	C'	2.471475	0.26356	2.05906
	D'	2.471475	0.19649	1.89832
	E'	2.471475	0.29711	-1.04504
	F'	2.471475	0.46779	-0.79186

NEW PERFORMANCE MEASURES

Information ratio:

The information ratio is the best criterion to evaluate an active manager; the higher it is, the better the manager performs.

The information ratio is negative for funds "B", "A", "D", "E' " and "F'", which indicates under-performance, while the other funds have a positive information ratio which indicates out performance

the E fund as an example, there is a 99.8830% probability that the fund will perform between 2.39175% and 2.50872% the following year

Tracking Error

We will calculate the theoretical performance of the UCITS, let us recall that:

Theoretical underperformance = Benchmark profitability—tracking error Theoretical out performance = Benchmark profitability + tracking error Probability of this under/over performance = 100 - 2 * tracking error

Looking at table 1.6: the E fund as an example, there is a 99.8830% probability that the fund will perform between 2.39175% and 2.50872% the following year.

Table 6. Summary of UCITS performance calculation

Type	UCITS	Underperformance	Out performance	Probability
Money market Funds	A	2.37381	2.52665	99.8471
	B	2.30414	2.59633	99.7078
	C	1.97673	2.92373	99.0530
	D	2.25382	2.64665	99.6071
	E	2.39175	2.50872	99.8830
	F	2.24065	2.65982	99.5808
Short-term bond	A'	2.12613	2.81681	99.3093
	B'	2.12306	2.81988	99.3031
	C'	2.20791	2.73503	99.4728
	D'	2.27498	2.66797	99.6070
	E'	2.17436	2.76858	99.4057
	F'	2.00368	2.93926	99.0644

RESULTS OF THE VALIDATION TESTS OF THE CAPM

In this section we will apply the Black, Jensen and Scholes (1972) regression to each of our mutual funds, and we will regress the risk premium of the mutual fund (Ri – Rf) on the market risk premium (Rm – Rf).

Econometric Specification Tests

The first step in testing the validity of the CAPM is to test the autocorrelation and homoscedasticity of the residuals of the Black, Jensen and Scholes (1972) regressions. For this purpose, we used the Breusch-Godfrey autocorrelation test and the White heteroscedasticity test.

Table 7. The results of the Breusch-Godfrey test and the White test

Type	UCITS	p-value of B-G test	p-value of White test
Money market Funds	A	1.425e-19	4.884e-03
	B	7.133e-44	5.385e-304
	C	1.097e-14	8.561e-195
	D	2.868e-04	2.277e-72
	E	7.692e-62	2.504e-118
	F	3.673e-46	9.406e-129
Short-term bond	A'	1.075e-03	1.481e-04
	B'	1.681e-06	5.119e-08
	C'	4.434e-07	1.373e-05
	D'	2.373e-09	1.068e-09
	E'	1.305e-07	1.25e-19
	F'	2.06e-04	1.345e-26

Interpretation

Looking in the table 1.7

White Test

We find that the p-value is less than 5%, so we reject the null hypothesis of the homoscedasticity of the residuals of the regression model for all mutual funds.

Breusch-Godfrey Test

The p-value of the money market funds and STO is lower than 5%, so we reject the null hypothesis of absence of autocorrelation of order 1 of the residues. While the other funds have a p-value higher than 5%, so we accept the hypothesis of absence of autocorrelation of order 1.

Ain order to correct these problems, we use Newey-West standard deviations. This method is used to re-estimate the variance-covariance matrix of the coefficients to correct for both the heteroscedasticity and autocorrelation problems of the residuals, giving us the following estimates:

Table 8. The statistics for the estimated betas with the Black, Jensen, and Scholes regression

UCITS	Beta	Standard deviation	T-value	P > |t|	Confidence interval at 95%
Money Market Funds					
A	0.6498	0.018	35.315	1.822e-294	[0.60 ;0.677]
B	0.4909	0.123	3.892	4.257e-05	[0.237 ;0.719]
C	0.6408	0.156	4.055	2.5118e-05	[0.327 ;0.937]
D	0.3065	0.039	7.431	7.2901e-16	[0.213 ;0.366]
E	0.6287	0.153	4.063	2.3967e-05	[0.321 ;0.919]
F	0.5714	0.140	3.999	2.9798e-05	[0.286 ;0.836]
Short-term bond					
A'	0.9480	0.029	32.647	4.023e-241	[0.891 ;1.005]
B'	0.7818	0.042	18.587	5.224e-80	[0.699 ;0.864]
C'	0.9726	0.031	31.490	2.699e-224	[0.912 ;1.033]
D'	0.9351	0.037	25.161	4.124e-144	[0.862 ;1.008]
E'	0.8975	0.044	20.397	1.641e-95	[0.811 ;0.984]
F'	0.9643	0.045	21.596	1.346e-106	[0.877 ;1.052]

Black, Jensen, and Scholes Regression Estimates

Table 9. Statistics for the constants of the Black, Jensen, and Scholes regression

UCITS	Alpha	Standard deviation	T-value	P > |t|	Confidence Interval at 95%
Money market Funds					
B	-0.0126	0.003	-4.253	2.1124e-05	[-0.018 ;-0.007]
A	-0.00865	0.000	-19.788	3.7524e-87	[-0.010 ;-0.008]
C	-0.0089	0.004	-2.361	0.01821	[-0.016 ;-0.002]
D	-0.0171	0.001	-18.269	1.4677e-74	[-0.019 ;-0.015]
E	-0.0092	0.004	-2.494	0.01264	[-0.016 ;-0.002]
F	-0.0106	0.003	-3.128	0.00175	[-0.017 ;-0.004]
Short-term bond					
A'	-0.0008	0.000	-1.773	0.076	[-0.002 ;7.96e-05]
B'	-0.0032	0.001	-5.178	0.000	[-0.004 ;-0.002]
C'	-0.0004	0.000	-0.841	0.401	[-0.001 ;0.001]
D'	-0.0009	0.001	-1.720	0.085	[-0.002 ;0.000]
E'	-0.0015	0.001	-2.347	0.019	[-0.003 ;-0.000]
F'	-0.0005	0.001	-0.822	0.411	[-0.002 ;0.001]

Analysis and Interpretation

According to the two tables 1.8 and 1.9

- Bêta coefficient

Table 1.8 presents the beta estimates made using the Black, Jensen and Scholes (1972) regression model.

In the second column, we see that money market funds and STO have a beta of less than 1, which means that the return on these funds varies by less than the market return, while the return on the STOs varies by more than 1. This means that the return on these funds varies in smaller proportions than the return on the market. Concerning the fifth column, we have the p-value is lower than 5% for all the funds, which indicates that the beta of each fund is significantly different from zero

- Alpha coefficient

Table 1.9 provides information on the constant of the Black, Jensen and Scholes (1972) regression.

In the second column, we see that money market funds and STOs have negative constants, which indicates that each of these funds earned less than the amount predicted by the CAPM (the model predicts a zero constant).

In the fifth column, we have the p-value of each constant:

money market UCITS: all funds have a p-value lower than 5%, so we reject the null hypothesis that the constant is equal to zero.

Short-term bond UCITS: The null hypothesis is rejected for the funds "B'" and "E'", but the p-value of the other funds is greater than 5%, so we deduce that the constants are significantly not different from zero.

We deduce that the CAPM is valid for 4 STO funds, more precisely for funds "A'", "C'", "D'" and "F'".

The asset pricing model is not valid for money market funds and 2 STOs, more precisely " B' "and " F' ", it does not manage to explain correctly the risk premium of these funds, as they do not depend not only on the market risk premium. Therefore, we have to look for other factors for a good explanation. These factors can be statistical or macroeconomic factors or company characteristics, so it is very difficult to find common factors between all the funds.

CONCLUSION

The study focused on examining the behavior of UCITS net asset values in Morocco. The study investigated the evolution of UCITS net asset values, using market models such as the market model and CAPM to characterize the series of returns, and analyzed fund performance using classic and innovative CAPM-based performance indicators. The CAPM model was also verified for a subset of funds in the research.

The study's findings have improved the decision-making process when picking UCITS by offering a complete set of performance measurements and risk-adjusted returns based on the CAPM. Investors may examine the performance of UCITS and make educated investment decisions by using these models and measurements.

It is worth noting that the study contributes to the modernization and development of the financial markets in Morocco by providing insights into the behavior and performance of UCITS. The analysis of net asset values, the application of market models, and the utilization of performance measures demonstrate the commitment to fostering transparency, investor protection, and market efficiency.

However, it is critical to recognize the study's shortcomings. The findings are based on a specific dataset of Moroccan money market and short-term funds, and their applicability to other types of funds or geographical settings may be restricted. Furthermore, the models and measurements included in the study are analytical tools and should be regarded as suggestions rather than absolute predictors of success.

This analysis might be expanded in the future by integrating a larger variety of UCITS and taking into account additional factors that may impact fund performance. Furthermore, investigating the influence of economic factors and market circumstances on UCITS performance might offer investors and fund managers with useful information.

Finally, the study has aided in the understanding and assessment of UCITS in Morocco by employing market models, performance indicators, and risk-adjusted analyses. The findings and recommendations give significant assistance for investors looking to maximize their UCITS investing selections.

REFERENCES

Breusch, T. (1978). Testing for Autocorrelation in Dynamic Linear Models. *Australian Economic Papers*, *17*(31), 334–355. doi:10.1111/j.1467-8454.1978.tb00635.x

Fama, E. F., & French, K. R. (1993). Common risk factors in the returns on stocks and bonds. *Journal of Financial Economics, 33*(1), 3–56. doi:10.1016/0304-405X(93)90023-5

Grimm, T. W., & Gregoriou, G. N. (2017). *The Handbook of UCITS: Fundamentals, Application, and Law*. Wiley.

Mahdoudi, H., & Boussetta, M. (2017). UCITS in Morocco: Evolution, challenges and perspectives. *International Journal of Economics, Commerce and Management.*

Jensen, M. C. (1968). The Performance of Mutual Funds in the Period 1945-1964. *The Journal of Finance, 23*(2), 389–416. doi:10.1111/j.1540-6261.1968.tb00815.x

Lintner, J. (1965). The valuation of risk assets and the selection of risky investments in stock portfolios and capital budgets. *The Review of Economics and Statistics, 47*(1), 13–37. doi:10.2307/1924119

Markowitz H. (1959). *Portfolio Selection: Efficient Diversification of Investments*. Yale University.

Markowitz, H. (1999). The early history of portfolio theory: 1600–1960. *Financial Analysts Journal.*

Ronald, D., Trevin, L., & Swinkels. (2019). Historical returns of the market portfolio. *Review of Asset Pricing Studies.*

Sharpe & William, F. (1964). Capital Asset Prices – A Theory of Market Equilibrium Under Conditions of Risk. Research Gate.

Sharpe & William, F. (1994). The Sharpe Ratio. *The Journal of Portfolio Management.*

Treynor, J. L. (1965). How to rate management of investment funds. *Harvard Business Review*, 63–75.

White, H. (1980). A heteroskedasticity-consistent covariance matrix estimator and a direct test for heteroskedasticity. *Econometrica, 48*(4), 817. doi:10.2307/1912934

Chapter 9
Predicting Company Bankruptcy Using Machine Learning Techniques:
A Step-by-Step Guide

Eunjung Lee
Lewis University, USA

ABSTRACT

In today's business landscape, predicting the financial health of a company is essential for informed decision-making by investors, creditors, and other stakeholders. Using historical financial data and machine learning techniques, it is now possible to predict the likelihood of a company going bankrupt. This chapter provides a step-by-step guide on how to predict company bankruptcy using the "company bankruptcy prediction" dataset available on UCI machine learning repository. The chapter covers data analysis, pre-processing, applying various machine learning algorithms, evaluating model performance, and applying models to new datasets. The aim is to equip readers with the necessary skills to analyze and predict the financial health of companies, making it a valuable resource for investors, creditors, and financial analysts.

1. INTRODUCTION

In today's rapidly changing business landscape, predicting the financial health of a company is crucial for investors, creditors, and other stakeholders to make informed decisions. With the increasing availability of data and advancements in machine learning techniques, it is now possible to predict the likelihood of a company going bankrupt using historical financial data. Bankruptcies can have ripple effects on the economy, and predicting bankruptcies can help prevent these negative impacts.

This chapter provides a comprehensive guide on how to predict company bankruptcy using machine learning techniques, using the "Company Bankruptcy Prediction" dataset available on UCI Machine Learning Repository. Readers will learn how to analyze and pre-process the data, apply various machine

DOI: 10.4018/978-1-6684-8386-2.ch009

learning algorithms, evaluate model performance, and apply models to new datasets. By the end of this chapter, readers will have the necessary skills to analyze and predict the financial health of companies, making it a valuable resource for investors, creditors, and financial analysts.

Machine learning involves using algorithms to identify patterns and make predictions based on data. This chapter will demonstrate how to use Weka, a free analytical software, to predict the likelihood of a company going bankrupt based on financial data. The chapter will also provide an overview of the performance evaluation metrics used to assess the accuracy of the models.

To achieve this, we will first define the research questions and metrics that will be used to predict the financial health of a company. We will then collect and analyze the "Company Bankruptcy Prediction" dataset, which contains financial data from a variety of companies. Finally, we will apply machine learning techniques to the data to predict the likelihood of a company going bankrupt. This chapter is aimed at individuals with a basic understanding of machine learning methodology and evaluation methods. Theoretical explanations of each methodology will be kept to a minimum, with a focus on demonstrating practical experiments on how to analyze and interpret data results.

2. PREDICTING COMPANY BANKRUPTCY: PRACTICE USING WEKA

2.1 Define Business Questions

To predict company bankruptcy, we first need to define the business questions we want to answer. As investors or financial analysts, we may be interested in understanding the factors that impact the likelihood of a company going bankrupt and whether we can use financial data to predict the bankruptcy risk of a specific company. Some potential business questions that we can explore include:

What financial ratios and metrics are most strongly associated with company bankruptcies?

Can we use historical financial data to predict the probability of a company going bankrupt within the next year?

How accurately can we predict the bankruptcy risk of a specific company using machine learning techniques?

Which machine learning algorithms perform best for predicting company bankruptcies?

By answering these business questions, we can gain insights into the financial health of companies and make informed decisions as investors or financial analysts. In the next section, we will explore the "Company Bankruptcy Prediction" dataset and analyze the data to gain a better understanding of the factors that impact bankruptcy risk.

2.2 Collect Data

To begin with, we use a real-world dataset from the Taiwan Economic Journal for the years 1999-2009[1]. We need to collect the "Company Bankruptcy Prediction" dataset from the UCI Machine Learning Repository[2]. This dataset consists of financial ratios and other financial information for various companies. We will be using this dataset to predict the likelihood of a company going bankrupt. The "Company Bankruptcy Prediction" dataset contains 95 financial ratios (Figure 24 in the Appendix) and other financial information for 6,819 companies. Each company is labeled as either bankrupt or not bankrupt. The dataset includes both numerical and categorical data.

In the next section, we will review and pre-process the data to prepare it for machine learning modeling.

2.3 Review and Pre-Process Data

Once we have the dataset, the next step is to understand the data and explore it for insights. In this section, we will load the dataset into Weka and perform exploratory data analysis to gain a better understanding of the data. We can load the dataset into Weka and perform various operations such as viewing the summary statistics, visualizing the distributions of different features, and identifying any missing values or outliers.

Pre-processing the data is a critical step in machine learning, as it involves cleaning and transforming the data to ensure it is suitable for modeling. The process includes various steps such as removing irrelevant or redundant features, handling missing values, encoding categorical features, and/or standardizing numerical features. In this chapter, we will practice real data analysis process using real data, rather than focusing on theoretical concepts. Therefore, we will skip the general explanations about each step but describe how to pre-process the "Company Bankruptcy Prediction" dataset.

Before starting the pre-processing steps, it's important to note that when you try to load the data file that you downloaded from the repository as it is, you may have an error message as Figure 1 shows. The first step we need to take is to delete the special characters, such as apostrophes, from column names since Weka does not handle them. In this dataset, we need to delete the apostrophe in the "Net Income to Stockholder's Equity" column name which is 91th attribute in the dataset and modify it to "Net Income to Stockholders Equity" without an apostrophe. After this modification, we can load the data into Weka successfully, as shown in Figure 2.

Figure 1. Error message from Weka when loading the original data file

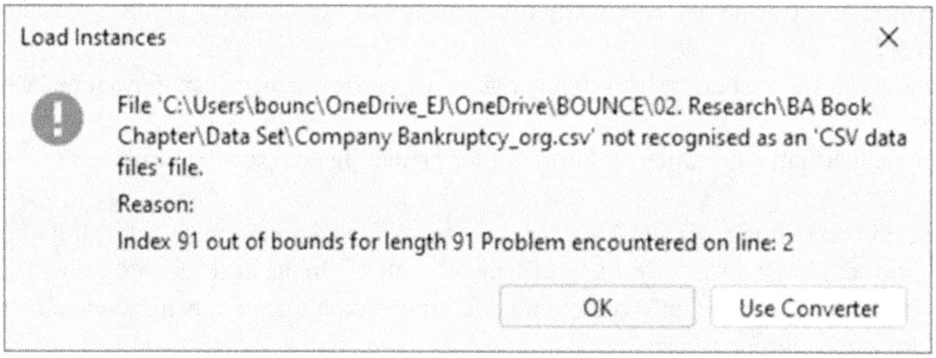

Once we have loaded the data into Weka, we need to confirm the data type of each attribute and ensure it is correctly classified. We may encounter other issues that require fixing, such as the "Bankrupt" attribute, which should be a Nominal data type but is categorized as Numeric. To fix this, we can use the "Filter" option in Weka. We need to select "Choose" under the Filter menu, then navigate to "Filters" -> "Unsupervised" -> "Attribute" (Figure 3). Find the "NumericToNominal" option and select it. Then, a new window will pop up as shown in Figure 4 when you click the window with NumericToNominal function. Change the "attributeIndices" option to 1 because the "Bankrupt" attribute is the first attribute in the dataset. Click "OK" and "Apply". Now we can confirm the "Bankrupt" attribute's type has been changed to Nominal, as shown in Figure 5. It is also important to save this change for later work since Weka uses .ARFF format.

Figure 2. Loaded dataset on Weka

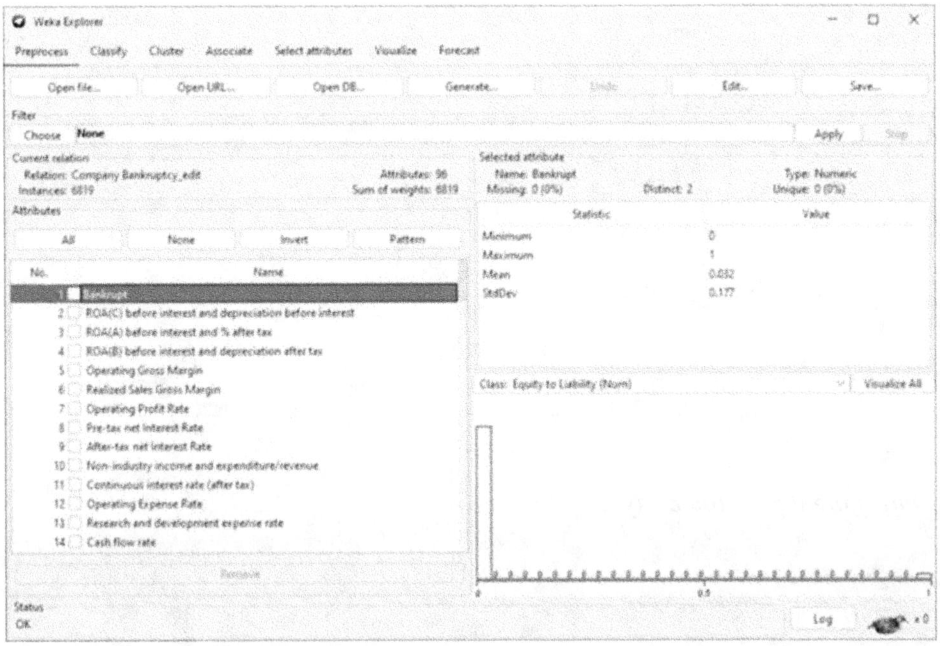

Figure 3. Changing an attribute's type

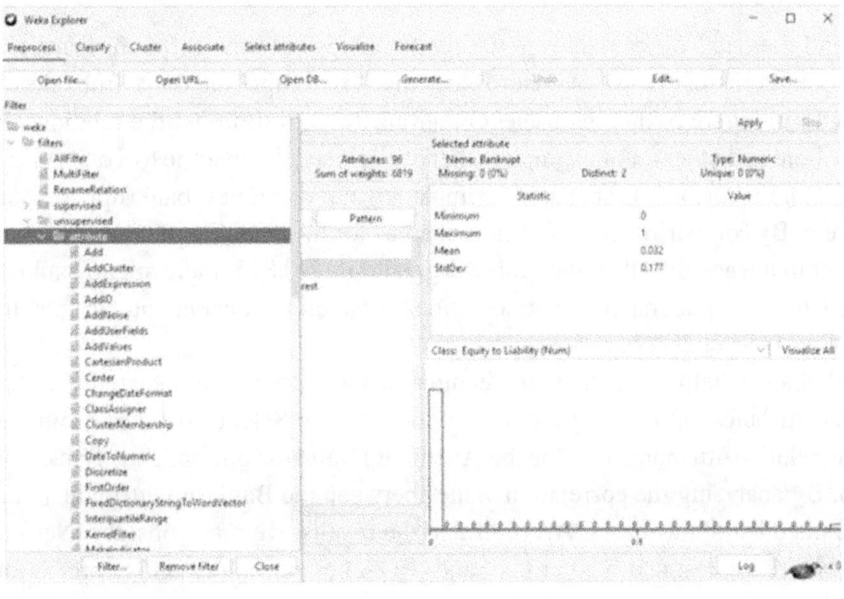

Figure 4. Extended option for NumericToNominal filter

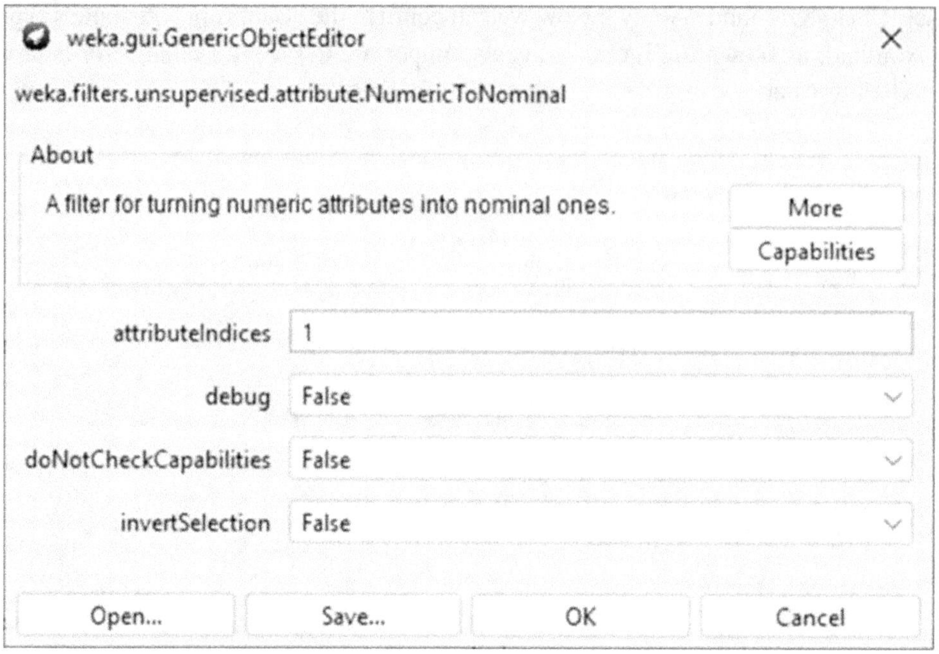

Figure 5. Confirming the attribute's type

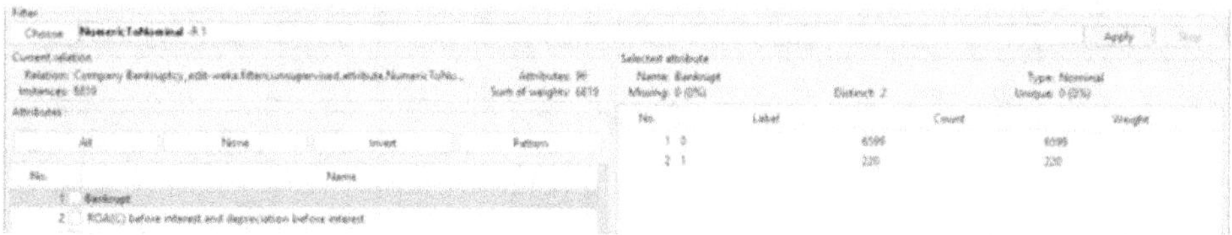

To understand the data, we can analyze the relationships between different features in the dataset and identify any patterns or trends. We can select the "Bankrupt" attribute from the "Class" option (see dotted box from Figure 6) and then select other attributes to find out the relationship between the "Bankrupt" attribute and others. For example, when we select "Net Income to Total Assets," we can see a distribution graph that displays bankrupted companies in red and non-bankrupt companies in blue as shown in Figure 6. By comparing the two different areas for the "Net Income to Total Assets" attribute, we can figure out that when the attribute's value is greater than 0.815, there are no bankrupt companies. In this way, we can try to understand the associations between the dependent variable, the "Bankrupt" attribute, and other independent variables.

Moreover, Weka can help us identify the features that are strongly associated with bankruptcy risk using the 'Select attributes' option. To access this option, select 'Select attributes' from the top menu bar and choose 'CorrelationAttributeEval' for the Attribute Evaluator option, and 'Ranker' for the Search Method option. By analyzing the correlation values between the Bankrupt attribute and other features, it generates a ranked list of attributes. According to the results, we may consider 'Net Income to Total Assets', 'ROA before interest and % after tax', and 'ROA before interest and depreciation after tax' as strongly associated with the 'Bankrupt' attribute. However, it's essential to note that we shouldn't ignore the attributes that are ranked the least important since many machine learning schemes do not use correlation values to develop models. We should use the 'Select attributes' option only as a reference to review the dataset.

Figure 6. Relationship between the 'net income to total assets' and the 'bankrupt' attributes

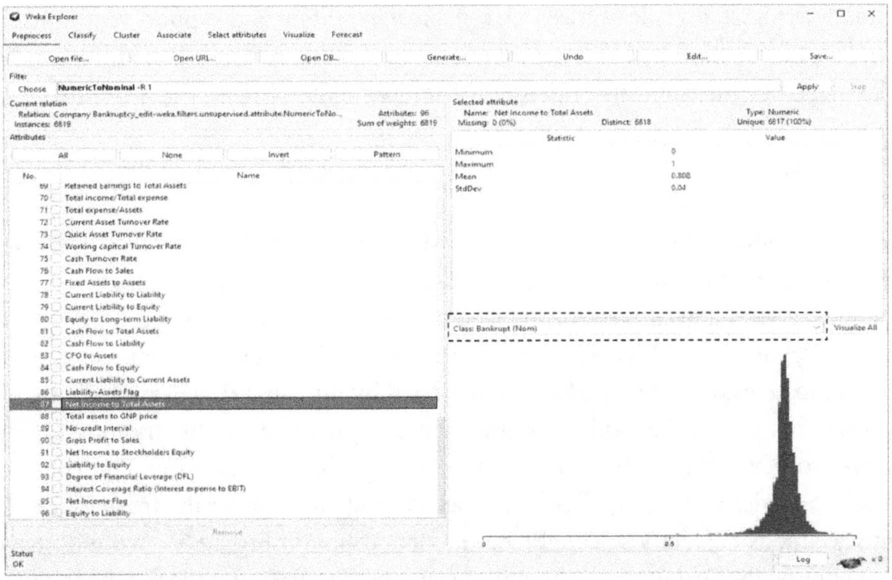

Figure 7. Select attributes option from Weka

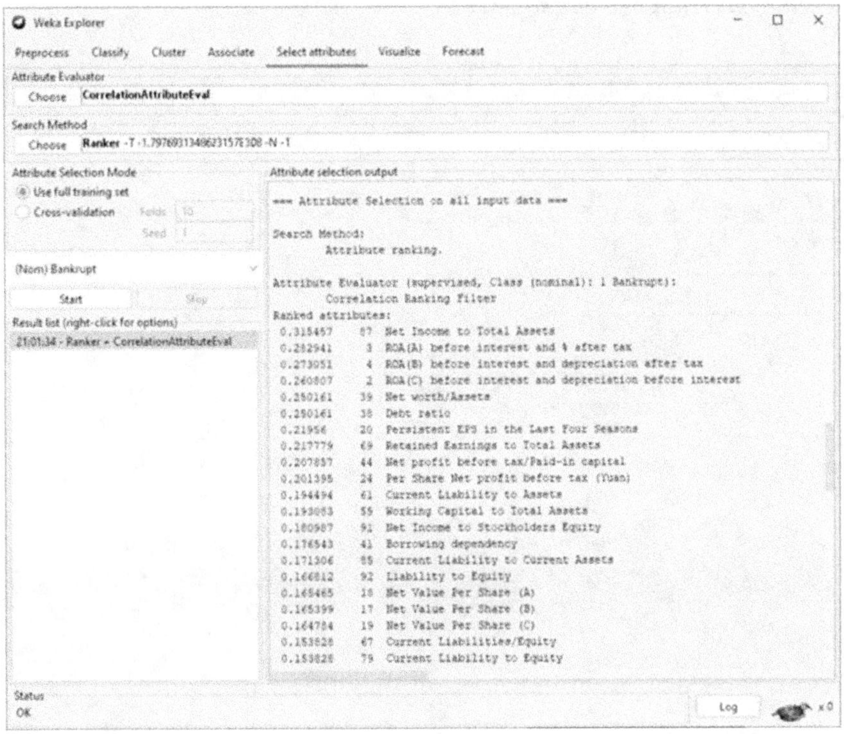

With the dataset prepared, we can now move on to training classifiers using various machine learning techniques.

2.4 Develop Classification Models

There are various machine learning algorithms that that can be used to develop classification models, each with its own strengths and weaknesses. In this book, we will introduce five popular algorithms: decision tree, random forest, logistic regression, k-nearest neighbor, and support vector machine (SVM). We will briefly explain each algorithm and demonstrate how these five algorithms can be utilized in developing classifiers for the bankruptcy prediction dataset using Weka.

2.4.1 Decision Tree

The decision tree is a simple yet powerful algorithm that can be used for both classification and regression tasks. The idea behind the decision tree is to create a tree-like model of decisions and their possible consequences. Each internal node of the tree represents a decision based on one of the features, and each leaf node represents a class label. One advantage of the decision tree is its interpretability, as the resulting tree can be easily visualized and understood by humans. However, decision trees can also suffer from overfitting, where the model becomes too complex and fits the training data too well but fails to generalize to new data. To train a classifier by applying decision tree algorithm using Weka, navigate Classify -> under Classifier, click 'Choose' -> find 'J48' under the trees folder. Confirm that the dependent variable is correctly selected (see the dotted box in Figure 8). We will use the 10 folds Cross-validation option for Test options. We will discuss how to interpret the results in the next section.

Figure 8. The result of decision tree classifier

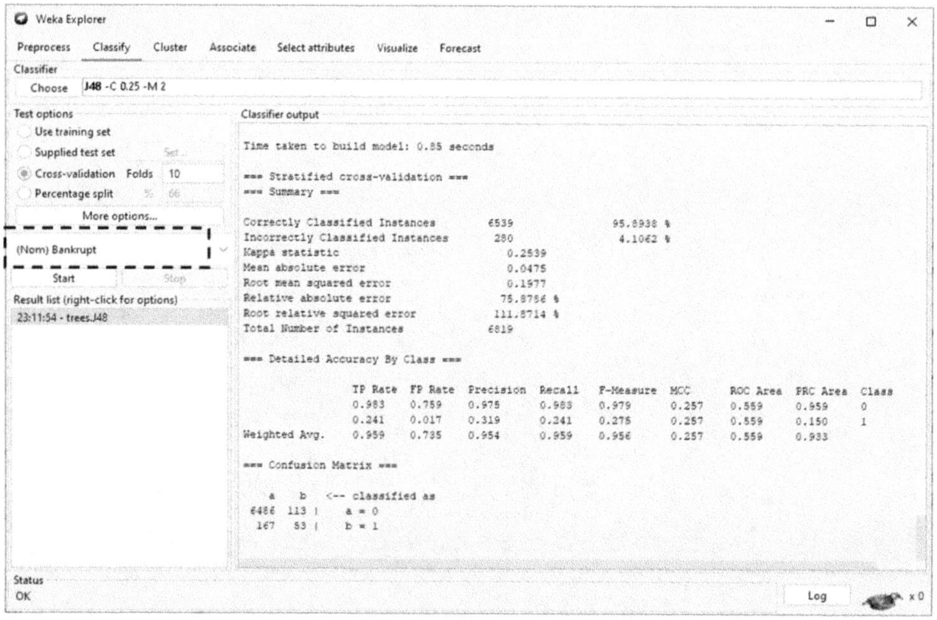

To optimize the performance of the decision tree algorithm, we can adjust the parameters such as the 'unpruned' option. You can access the options to tune the parameters by clicking on the 'J48' window on the top menu bar of Weka. This will open a new window where you can adjust the parameters of the decision tree algorithm. By default, the 'unpruned' option is set to 'False,' which means that the current decision tree algorithm is pruned with a confidence factor value of 0.25 as shown in Figure 9. We can adjust the confidence factor (a higher value means less pruning) or select 'True' for the unpruned option to obtain an unpruned tree. However, it is important to note that using the unpruned tree option can significantly increase the training time required for the classifier. Therefore, to improve the performance of the decision tree classifier without dramatically increasing the training time, we can try to find an appropriate value for the pruning option.

Figure 9. Adjusting the pruning option for the decision tree classifier

2.4.2 Random Forest

Random Forest is an ensemble learning algorithm that combines multiple decision trees and outputs the class that is the mode of the classes of individual trees. Similar to the decision tree algorithm, we can find the 'RandomForest' option under the 'tree' folder in Weka as shown in the Figure 10.

Figure 10. The result of random forest classifier

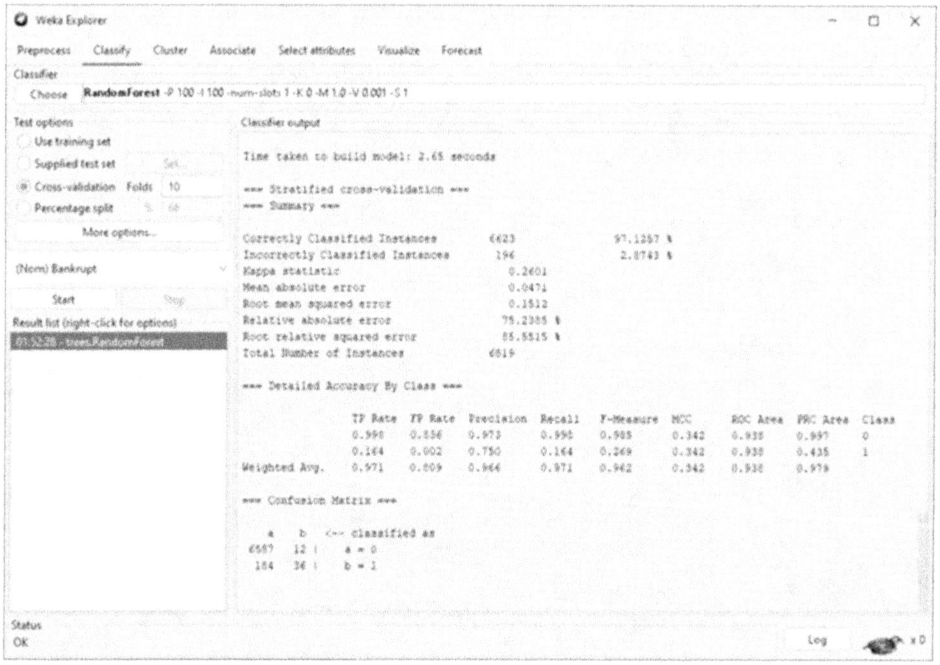

One way to optimize the performance of the Random Forest algorithm is adjusting the number of iterations. We can attempt to improve the classifier's performance by increasing the number of iterations. However, it can also significantly increase the analyzing time, making it inefficient. To change the number of iterations, we can adjust the 'numIterations' option from the parameter option, as shown in Figure 11.

2.4.3 Logistic Regression

Logistic regression is a statistical model commonly used for binary classification tasks where the objective is to predict one of two possible class labels. The model estimates the probability of the positive class label based on the features' values. These probabilities can then be used to make predictions and assess the model's performance. It is essential to note that logistic regression assumes a linear relationship between the features and the log-odds of the positive class, which may not be true for all datasets. To train a classifier using the logistic regression algorithm in Weka, navigate to Classify -> Choose -> find 'Logistic' under the 'functions' folder. Confirm that the dependent variable is correctly selected and click start. The result can be illustrated as shown in Figure 12.

Figure 11. Adjusting the iteration parameter for the random forest classifier

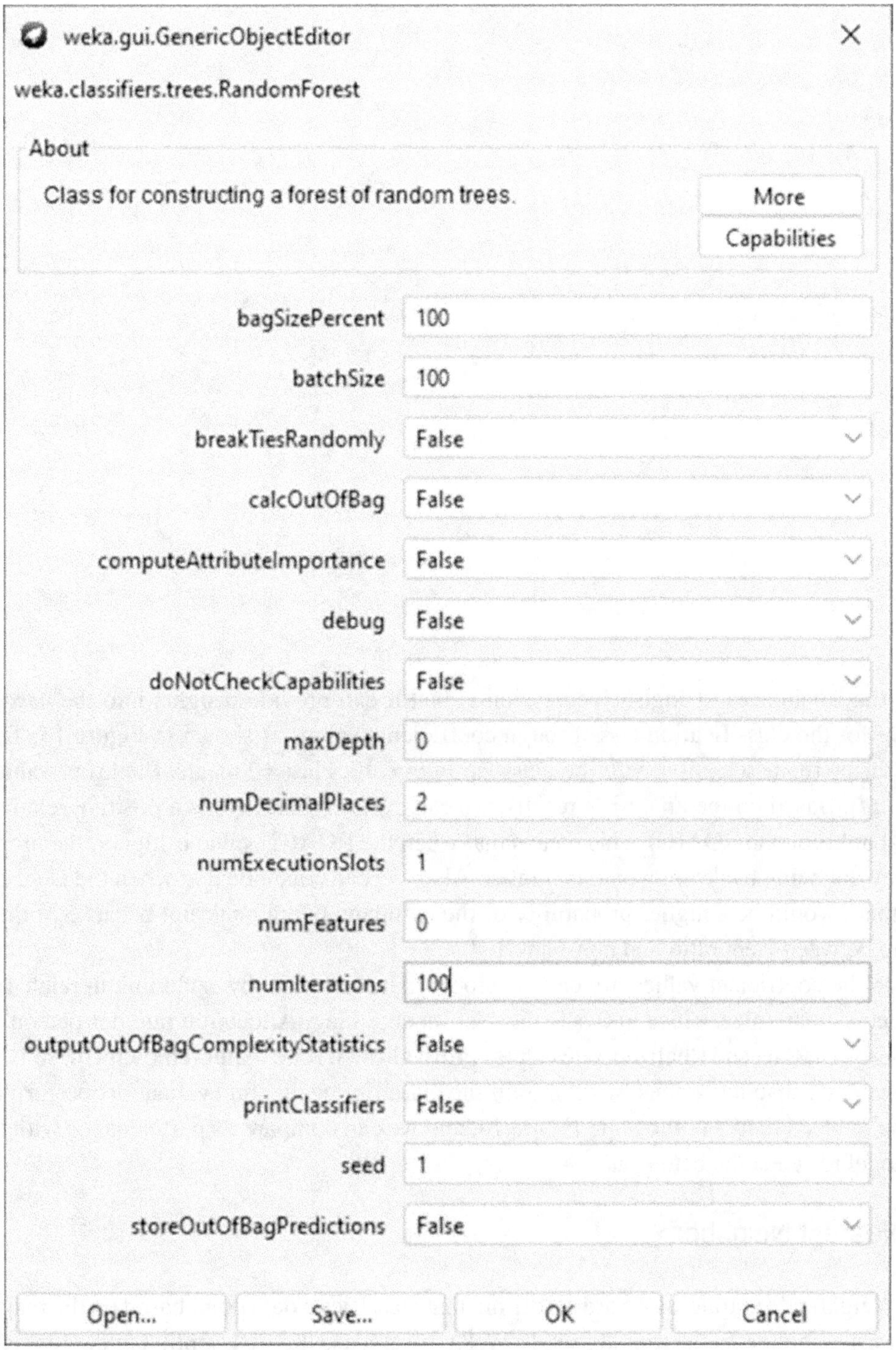

Figure 12. The result of logistic regression classifier

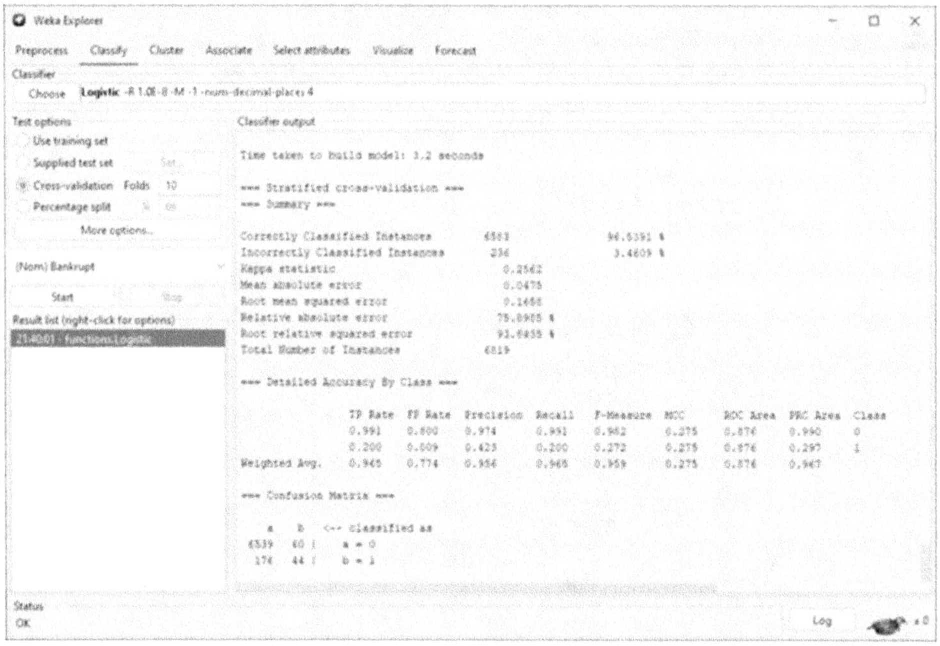

One of the advantages of logistic regression is that it can provide insights into the *association* of each feature for the classification task through coefficients values as shown in Figure 13. These coefficients describe the association with the class (in Figure 13, class=0 means Bankrupt value is 0 *and non-bankrupt*). Based on the analysis's results, we can *explain* that there is a positive relationship between non-bankrupt and ROA(C). This means that when the ROA(C) value is higher, the probability of the company not being bankrupt would be higher. Also, we can conclude that when the Debt ratio value is higher, there would be a higher probability of the company being bankrupt because of the negative relationship between Debt ratio and non-bankrupt.

Based on the coefficient values, we can develop a reduced model by excluding unrelated attributes that have coefficient values close to 0, such as Net Income Flag, Allocation rate per person, After-tax Net Profit Growth Rate, and Realized Sales Gross Profit Growth Rate. After removing these 10 attributes that have the least absolute values, we can train the classifier again and evaluate its performance. The result of the reduced model is shown in Figure 14, and we can compare its performance with that of the original model to select the better one.

2.4.4 K-Nearest Neighbor

K-Nearest Neighbor is a straightforward algorithm that classifies a data point based on the majority class of its k-nearest neighbors in the training set. In Weka, we can use the 'IBk' option under the 'lazy' folder to apply K-Nearest Neighbor algorithm. The results will be displayed as shown in Figure 15.

Figure 13. Coefficient values

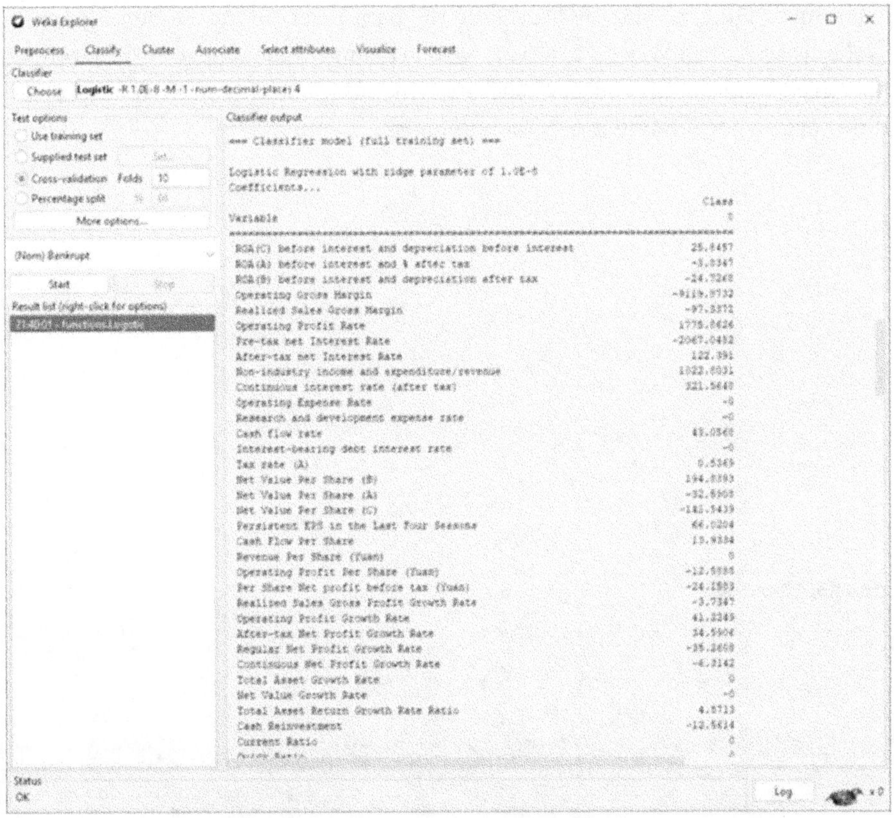

Figure 14. The result of logistic regression classifier: reduced model

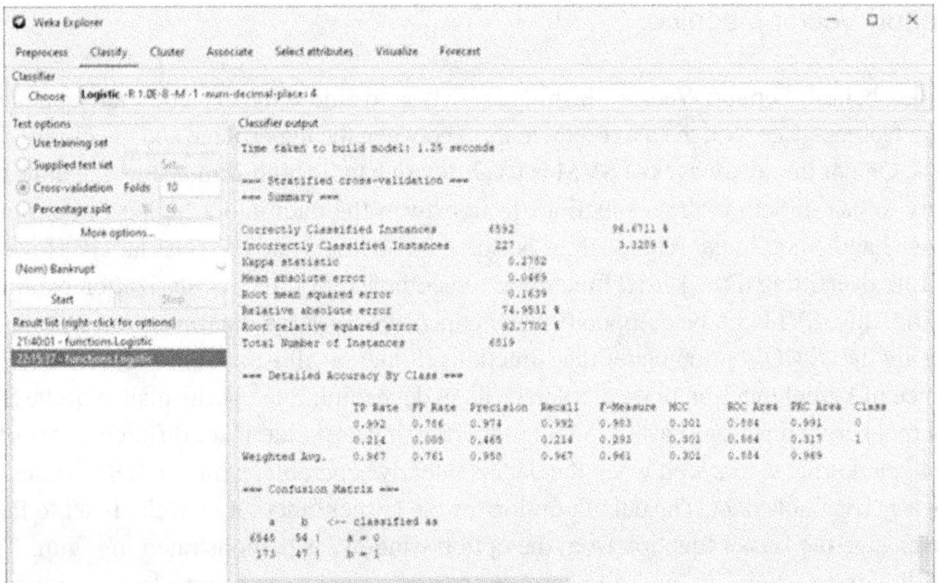

The choice of the k value is a critical factor in determining the performance of the K-Nearest Neighbor classifier. We can modify the k value by accessing the parameter option, as depicted in Figure 16. By default, the k value is set to 1 in Weka. However, we can change this value to 3, 5, or other odd numbers by adjusting the 'KNN' option and observe the outcome. Odd numbers are more preferable for the k value to avoid tie cases when finding k-nearest neighbors.

Figure 15. The result of k-nearest neighbor classifier

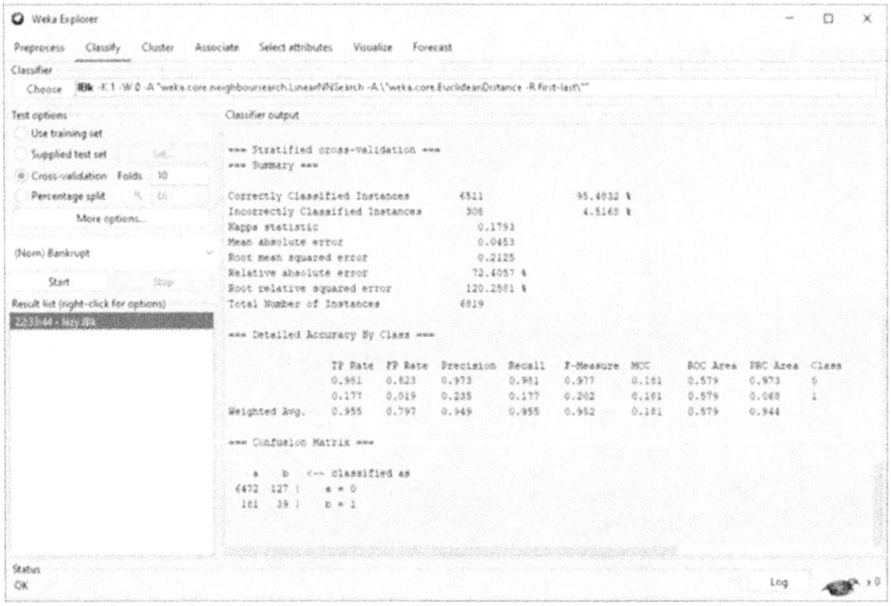

2.4.5 Support Vector Machine

The main idea behind Support Vector Machine (SVM) is to find a hyperplane that separates the two classes in the feature space with the maximum margin between the hyperplane and the closest data points of each class. One of the advantages of SVM is its ability to handle high-dimensional feature spaces and its flexibility to use different kernel functions to transform the data into a higher-dimensional space. SVM can also handle non-linear relationships between the features and the class labels. However, SVM can suffer from overfitting if the kernel function is too complex, or if the regularization parameter is too small. Additionally, SVM can be computationally expensive for large datasets. We can train the SVM classifier using the 'SMO' option under the 'functions' folder, as illustrated in Figure 15.

The choice of kernel function plays a crucial role in determining the performance of the SVM algorithm. Different kernel functions have different properties and are suitable for different types of data. For instance, a linear kernel works well when the data is linearly separable, while an RBF kernel is suitable for non-linearly separable data. The default option for the kernel function in Weka is set to PolyKernel, and we can change the kernel function from the option window, as demonstrated in Figure 16.

In the following section, we will compare the performance of different classifiers using various evaluation metrics.

Figure 16. Changing K option (KNN)

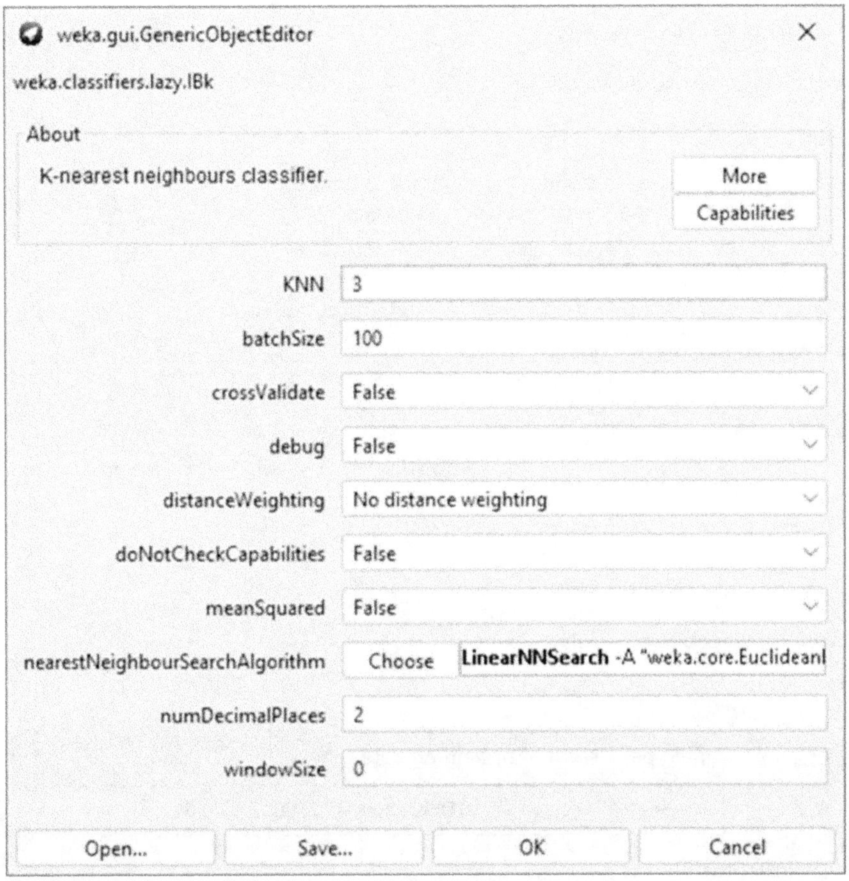

Figure 17. The result of support vector machine classifier: PolyKernel

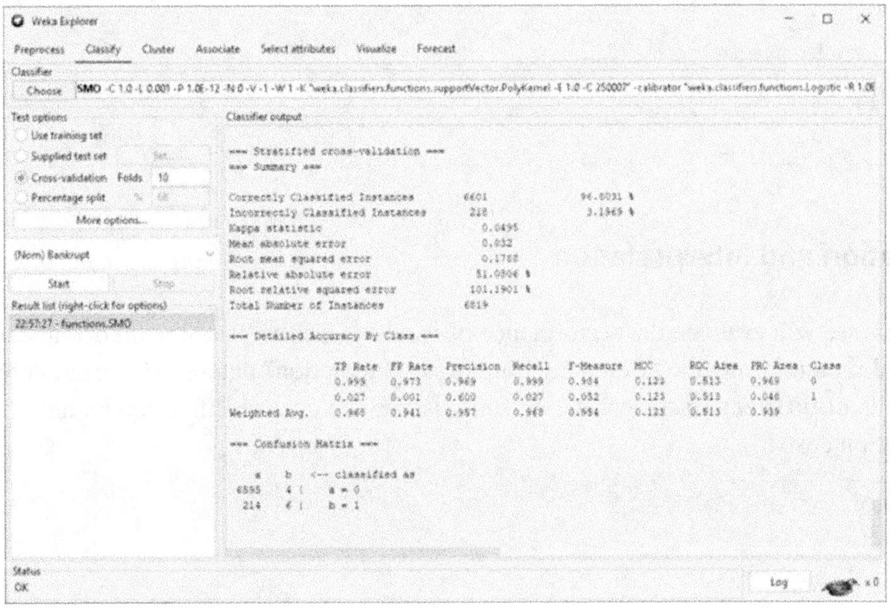

Figure 18. Changing kernel function

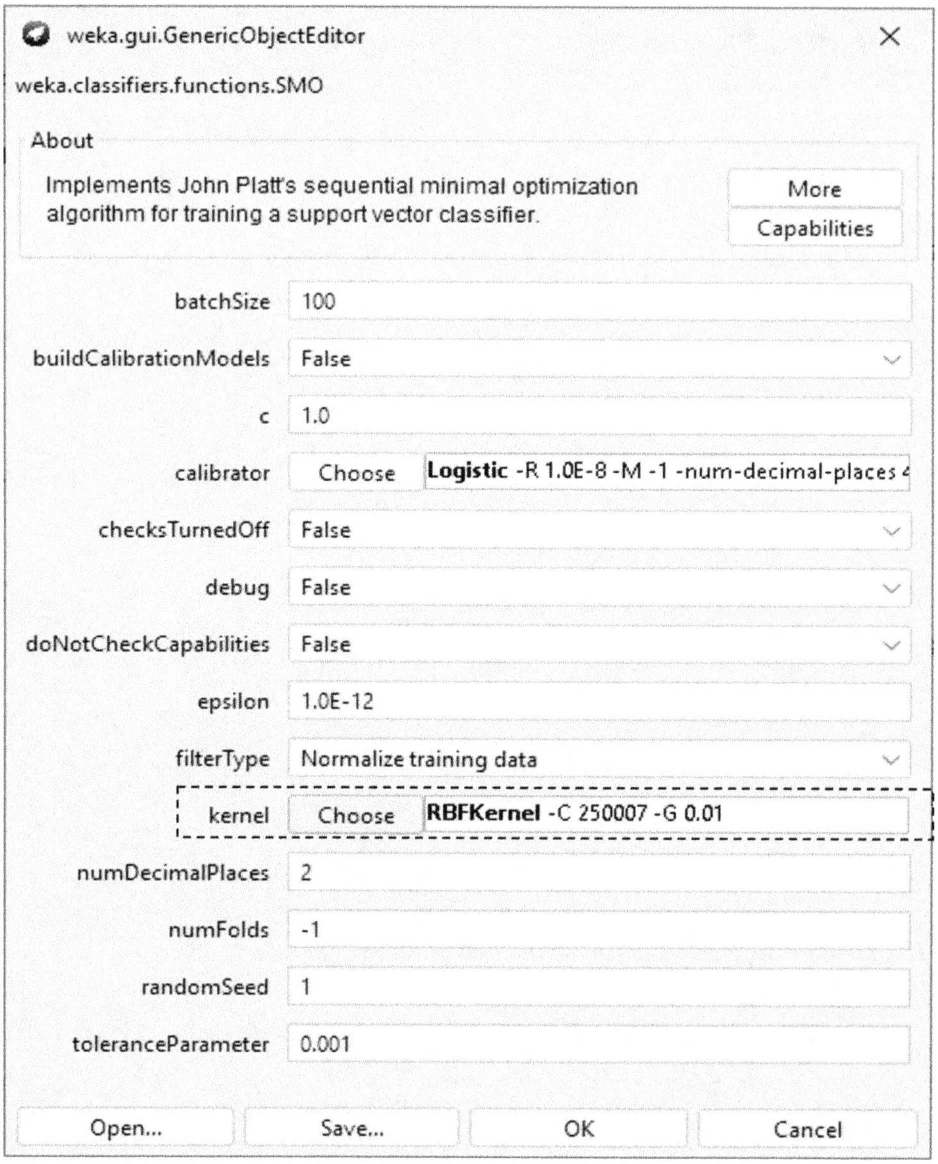

2.5 Evaluation and Interpretation

In this section, we will evaluate the performance of various machine learning algorithms in predicting company bankruptcies using the "Company Bankruptcy Prediction" dataset. However, before we delve into the results of different classifiers, let us first discuss the cost-sensitive model and the impact of misclassification costs.

2.5.1 Cost-Sensitive Model

In a cost-sensitive model, the misclassification costs are taken into account while building the model. This means that the algorithm assigns different costs to different types of errors based on the context of the problem. In the context of bankruptcy prediction, the cost of false positives (predicting bankruptcy when the company is not bankrupt) and false negatives (failing to predict bankruptcy when the company is bankrupt) can be different.

False positives may lead to lose of potential financial profits, while false negatives may result in significant financial damages. For example, consider a bank that lends money to companies. If the bank incorrectly predicts bankruptcy for a company that is not bankrupt, it may refuse to lend money, causing the company to suffer unnecessary financial losses. This could result in lost business opportunities, and loss of reputation.

On the other hand, if the bank fails to predict bankruptcy for a company that is actually bankrupt, it may lend money to the company, resulting in a huge financial loss for the bank. This could result in bad debts, write-offs, and damage to the bank's financial health. Therefore, it is crucial to take into account the costs associated with misclassifications and build a cost-sensitive model that minimizes these costs.

In this study, we will consider the cost of misclassification in the context of predicting bankruptcies and evaluate the performance of different classifiers using a cost-sensitive approach. We will compare the results of five different classifiers, namely Decision Tree, Random Forest, Logistic Regression, K-Nearest Neighbor, and Support Vector Machine, and examine their ability to predict company bankruptcies accurately with different measurements.

When it comes to reducing false negatives, we need to focus on the model's recall. Recall is the percentage of actual bankruptcies that are correctly identified by the model, which means the higher the recall, the lower the chance of false negatives. In the context of bankruptcy prediction, high recall means that the model correctly identifies companies that are actually bankrupt, reducing the risk of the bank lending money to a bankrupt company. Precision is the percentage of positive predictions that are actually true positives. In other words, it measures the accuracy of positive predictions. While recall focuses on reducing false negatives, precision focuses on reducing false positives.

The AUC (Area Under the Curve) is another metric that is commonly used to evaluate the performance of a binary classification model, such as bankruptcy prediction. It measures the overall performance of the model across all possible classification thresholds. The AUC metric ranges from 0 to 1, where a higher AUC indicates better performance. An AUC of 0.5 indicates that the model is randomly guessing the class labels, while an AUC of 1.0 indicates perfect classification performance. The AUC is particularly useful in cases where the class distribution is imbalanced, which is often the case in bankruptcy prediction, as the number of bankrupt companies is typically much smaller than the number of non-bankrupt companies. In such cases, accuracy can be misleading, as a high accuracy can be achieved by simply predicting the majority class (i.e., non-bankrupt). The AUC, on the other hand, takes into account both the true positive rate and the false positive rate across all possible classification thresholds, making it a more robust metric for imbalanced datasets.

In summary, while precision and recall are useful metrics to evaluate the performance of a bankruptcy model, they have different priorities depending on the cost of misclassification. In our case, since the cost of false negatives is higher, recall is a more appropriate metric to consider. We want to ensure that our model correctly identifies as many bankrupt companies as possible, even if it means having a higher rate of false positives. However, precision should also be considered to ensure that the positive predictions are accurate enough to be useful in practice. Therefore, we need to find a balance between recall and precision to build a reliable model for bankruptcy prediction. Additionally, the AUC metric can provide a more comprehensive evaluation of the model's performance, particularly in cases where the class distribution is imbalanced.

2.5.2 Compare the Results of Different Classifiers

Table 1 shows the experimental results for various classifiers in terms of accuracy, AUC, precision, recall, the number of false negative cases, and the number of false positive cases. Based on the overall performance, considering accuracy as the most commonly used metric, all the classifiers' performance values are above 95%. Therefore, we may consider the performance of all classifiers to be fairly good.

However, as mentioned in section 2.5.1, for this bankruptcy model, lenders may want to minimize the number of false negative cases to avoid huge financial damages. This requires a higher value of recall. Thus, we need to compare the recall values to evaluate the performance of different classifiers. Based on the results in Table 1, we find that the Decision Tree with the unpruned option shows the best performance regarding recall. However, as explained in section 2.4.1, the unpruned option may decrease the training efficiency in terms of time. It is crucial to consider the trade-off between higher performance and training efficiency.

Additionally, we can observe that the AUC values for the Decision Tree algorithm are much lower than other algorithms such as Random Forest and Logistic Regression. When we do not know the exact cost for potential profits or loss, AUC can be used as an important metric to evaluate performances. Therefore, the Random Forest classifier can be another good option for the final decision in this model.

The next step would be to explore ways to reduce the number of false negative cases or to increase the recall value.

Table 1. Classification result

	Optimization Option	Accuracy	AUC	Precision	Recall	# of False Negative	# of False Positive
Decision Tree	**Pruned**	95.89%	0.559	0.319	0.241	167	113
	Unpruned	95.50%	0.522	0.284	0.259	163	144
Random Forest	**Iterations =100**	97.13%	0.938	0.75	0.164	184	12
	Iterations =1000	97.05%	0.948	0.694	0.155	186	15
Logistic Regression	**Full Model**	96.51%	0.875	0.413	0.195	177	61
	Reduced Model	96.67%	0.884	0.465	0.214	173	54
K-Nearest Neighbor	**K=1**	95.48%	0.579	0.235	0.177	181	127
	K=3	96.61%	0.656	0.388	0.086	201	30
Support Vector machine	**PolyKernel**	96.80%	0.513	0.6	0.027	214	4
	RBFKernel	96.77%	0.5	N/A	0	220	0

2.5.3 Adjusting the Cost Weight Value in Weka

To minimize the misclassification of false negatives, we can adjust the weight value of the cost-sensitive model in Weka. In Weka, the cost-sensitive model can be implemented by adjusting the misclassification costs of false positives and false negatives using the "CostMatrix" option.

To adjust the cost weight value in Weka, follow these steps:

- Click on the "Classify" tab and click 'Choose' under the Classifier menu.
- Click on the "CostSensitiveClassifier" option under the 'meta' folder.
- Click the 'CostSensitiveClassifier' on the top, then you can find the 'classifier' option.
- Click 'Choose' and navigate the option to find a classifier. Select a classifier that you want to execute.
- Find the 'costMatrix' option from the new window, as shown in Figure 17.
- Click the menu with '1x1 cost matrix' and change the 'Classes' option to 2 because the dependent variable has two levels (bankrupt/non-bankrupt).
- Adjust the weight value of cost-sensitive option. For example, you can set the cost of false negatives to be 3 times higher than the cost of false positives, by entering 1 in the false positive field and 3 in the false negative field. We need to decide the appropriate position of False Negative based on the Confusion Matrix form the result, as Figure 18 describes.
- Click 'Start' option and confirm the result.

For the experiment, Random Forest algorithm is selected for a classifier and the weight value of false negative is adjusted to 3. The result is shown as Figure 19. The recall value has been changed from 0.164 to 0.2182 and the number of false negative cases has been reduced from 184 to 158.

By adjusting the cost matrix in Weka, we can train a cost-sensitive model that takes into account the costs associated with misclassifications and minimizes the misclassification of false negatives. It is important to note that adjusting the cost matrix requires knowledge of the misclassification costs and the specific context of the problem. Therefore, it is recommended to consult with domain experts and stakeholders to determine the appropriate cost matrix values for the problem at hand.

In summary, by considering the costs associated with misclassifications and finding a balance between recall and precision, we can build a reliable bankruptcy prediction model that minimizes the financial damages associated with false negatives.

2.6 Application

Once you have developed and evaluated your classification models, it is time to apply them to new data to predict the likelihood of a company going bankrupt. In this section, we will discuss how to apply the models to new data using Weka.

To apply the classification models to new data, we first load the training dataset into Weka. We then apply the trained models to the training dataset and evaluate their performance using the evaluation metrics discussed in sections 2.4 and 2.5.

Figure 19. Changing parameters for cost-sensitive model

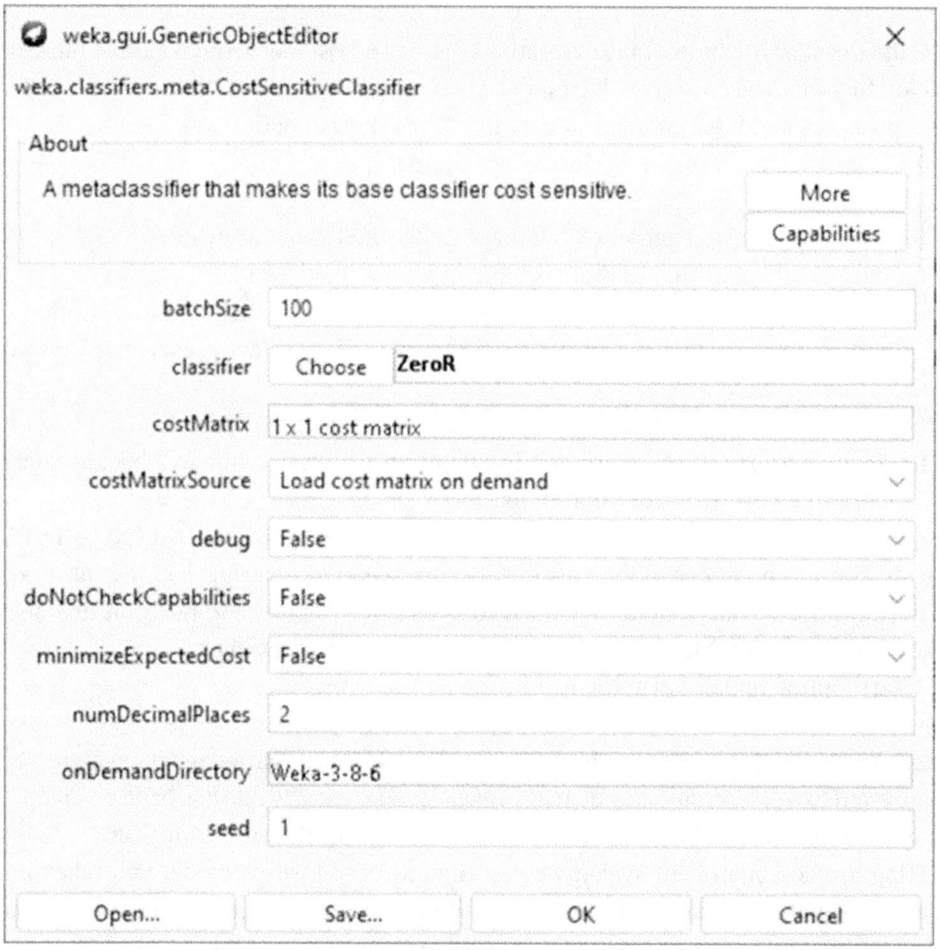

Figure 20. Changing the weight value of false negatives

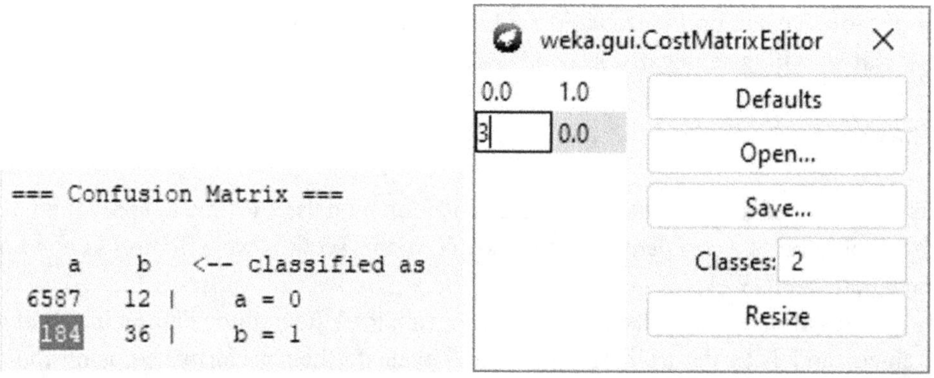

Figure 21. The result of adjusted model

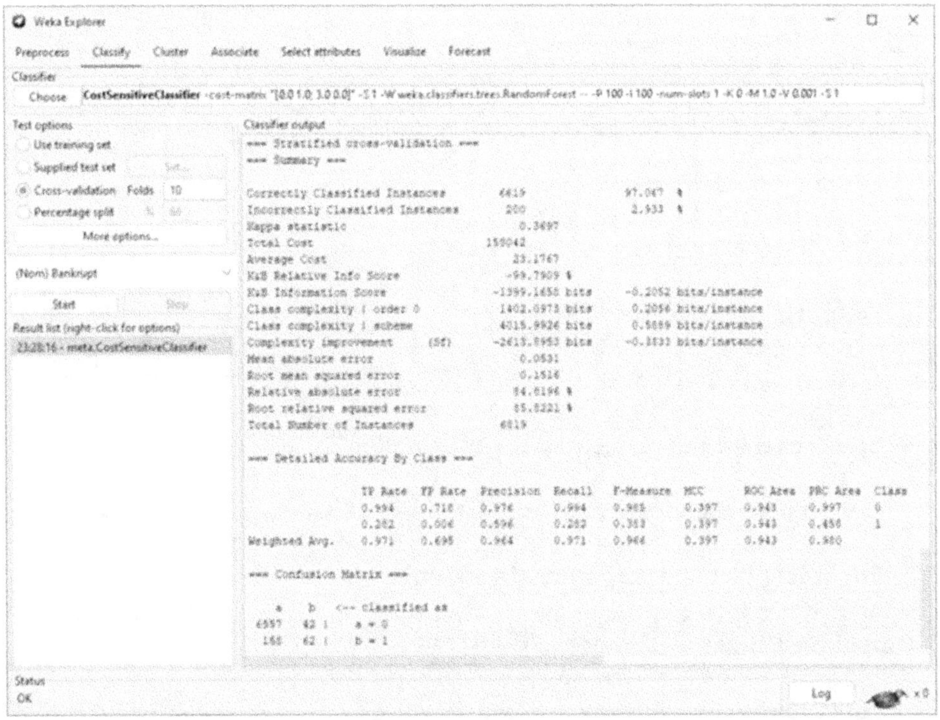

In this example, we use the Random Forest classifier that has been optimized in section 2.5.3. We select the "Supplied test set" option and load the test dataset, which is a set of instances with the values of the "Bankrupt" attribute unlabeled. This test dataset will be used to predict the likelihood of bankruptcy for new companies.

To load the test dataset, click on the "Set..." menu, find the test dataset (without output labels) through the "Open file..." option, and choose the class attribute ("bankrupt" in this example). Click on "More options" and select "Output predictions" and choose "PlainText" as shown in Figure 20. The classified result for the new data will be displayed as shown in Figure 21. Based on the results, it appears that the fourth company in the test dataset has a high likelihood of going bankrupt, as its predicted result is '1', which corresponds to the class label for bankruptcy.

It is important to note that the performance of the models may vary when applied to new data, as the characteristics and distribution of the new data may differ from the original dataset. Therefore, it is recommended to periodically retrain the models using updated data to ensure their accuracy and effectiveness in predicting company bankruptcies. By applying the steps outlined in this chapter, investors, creditors, and financial analysts can leverage machine learning techniques to make informed decisions about the financial health of companies.

Figure 22. Changing evaluation options to see the classified result

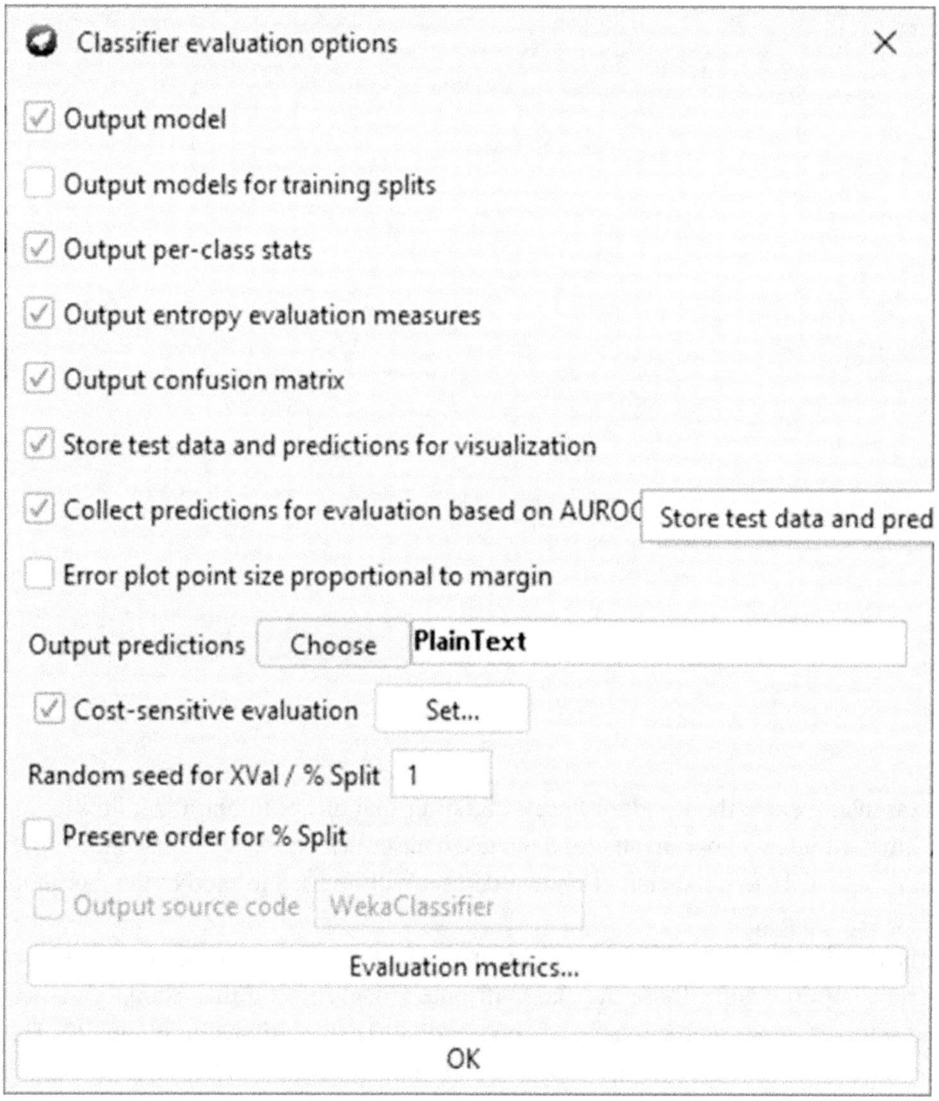

3. CONCLUSION

In this chapter, we have provided a step-by-step guide on how to predict company bankruptcies using machine learning techniques. We started by defining the research questions and metrics, collecting and preprocessing the data, and developing classification models using five popular algorithms.

We then evaluated the performance of the models using various evaluation metrics, including the cost-sensitive model and the impact of misclassification costs. Finally, we discussed how to apply the models to new data and the importance of periodically retraining the models using updated data.

Figure 23. Classification result on the test dataset

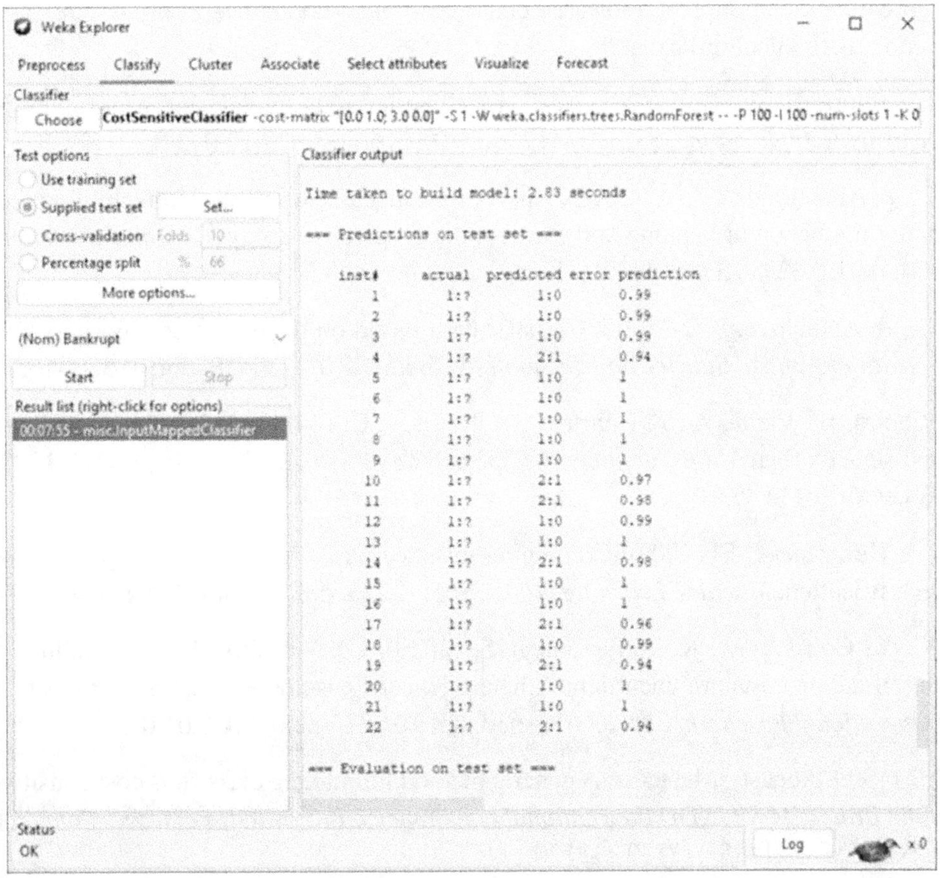

By the end of this chapter, readers should have a solid understanding of how to analyze and interpret financial data using machine learning techniques to predict the likelihood of a company going bankrupt. This knowledge can help investors, creditors, and financial analysts make informed decisions and prevent negative impacts on the economy.

REFERENCE

Liang, D., Lu, C. C., Tsai, C. F., & Shih, G. A. (2016). Financial ratios and corporate governance indicators in bankruptcy prediction: A comprehensive study. *European Journal of Operational Research*, *252*(2), 561–572. doi:10.1016/j.ejor.2016.01.012

ADDITIONAL READING

Aha, D. W., Kibler, D., & Albert, M. K. (1991). Instance-based learning algorithms. *Machine Learning*, *6*(1), 37–66. doi:10.1007/BF00153759

Alam, T. M., Shaukat, K., Mushtaq, M., Ali, Y., Khushi, M., Luo, S., & Wahab, A. (2021). Corporate bankruptcy prediction: An approach towards better corporate world. *The Computer Journal*, *64*(11), 1731–1746. doi:10.1093/comjnl/bxaa056

Barboza, F., Kimura, H., & Altman, E. (2017). Machine learning models and bankruptcy prediction. *Expert Systems with Applications*, *83*, 405–417. doi:10.1016/j.eswa.2017.04.006

Boughaci, D., & Alkhawaldeh, A. A. (2020). Appropriate machine learning techniques for credit scoring and bankruptcy prediction in banking and finance: A comparative study. *Risk and Decision Analysis*, *8*(1-2), 15–24. doi:10.3233/RDA-180051

Charbuty, B., & Abdulazeez, A. (2021). Classification based on decision tree algorithm for machine learning. *Journal of Applied Science and Technology Trends*, *2*(01), 20–28. doi:10.38094/jastt20165

Chen, N., Ribeiro, B., Vieira, A. S., Duarte, J., & Neves, J. C. (2011). A genetic algorithm-based approach to cost-sensitive bankruptcy prediction. *Expert Systems with Applications*, *38*(10), 12939–12945. doi:10.1016/j.eswa.2011.04.090

Cheng, W., & Hüllermeier, E. (2009). Combining instance-based learning and logistic regression for multilabel classification. *Machine Learning*, *76*(2-3), 211–225. doi:10.100710994-009-5127-5

De Bock, K. W., Coussement, K., & Lessmann, S. (2020). Cost-sensitive business failure prediction when misclassification costs are uncertain: A heterogeneous ensemble selection approach. *European Journal of Operational Research*, *285*(2), 612–630. doi:10.1016/j.ejor.2020.01.052

Domingos, P. (1999, August). Metacost: A general method for making classifiers cost-sensitive. In *Proceedings of the fifth ACM SIGKDD international conference on Knowledge discovery and data mining* (pp. 155-164). ACM. 10.1145/312129.312220

Elkan, C. (2001, August). The foundations of cost-sensitive learning. In *International joint conference on artificial intelligence* (Vol. 17, No. 1, pp. 973-978). Lawrence Erlbaum Associates Ltd.

Ghatasheh, N., Faris, H., Abukhurma, R., Castillo, P. A., Al-Madi, N., Mora, A. M., Al-Zoubi, A. M., & Hassanat, A. (2020). Cost-sensitive ensemble methods for bankruptcy prediction in a highly imbalanced data distribution: A real case from the Spanish market. *Progress in Artificial Intelligence*, *9*(4), 361–375. doi:10.100713748-020-00219-x

Kotsiantis, S. B., Zaharakis, I. D., & Pintelas, P. E. (2006). Machine learning: A review of classification and combining techniques. *Artificial Intelligence Review*, *26*(3), 159–190. doi:10.100710462-007-9052-3

Lin, W. C., Lu, Y. H., & Tsai, C. F. (2019). Feature selection in single and ensemble learning-based bankruptcy prediction models. *Expert Systems: International Journal of Knowledge Engineering and Neural Networks*, *36*(1), e12335. doi:10.1111/exsy.12335

Lin, W. Y., Hu, Y. H., & Tsai, C. F. (2011). Machine learning in financial crisis prediction: A survey. *IEEE Transactions on Systems, Man, and Cybernetics. Part C, Applications and Reviews*, *42*(4), 421–436.

Mahesh, B. (2020). Machine learning algorithms-a review. *International Journal of Science and Research (IJSR).[Internet], 9*, 381-386.

Min, J. H., & Lee, Y. C. (2005). Bankruptcy prediction using support vector machine with optimal choice of kernel function parameters. *Expert Systems with Applications*, *28*(4), 603–614. doi:10.1016/j.eswa.2004.12.008

Moepya, S. O., Akhoury, S. S., & Nelwamondo, F. V. (2014, December). *Applying cost-sensitive classification for financial fraud detection under high class-imbalance. In 2014 IEEE international conference on data mining workshop*. IEEE.

Osisanwo, F. Y., Akinsola, J. E. T., Awodele, O., Hinmikaiye, J. O., Olakanmi, O., & Akinjobi, J. (2017). Supervised machine learning algorithms: Classification and comparison. [IJCTT]. *International Journal of Computer Trends and Technology*, *48*(3), 128–138. doi:10.14445/22312803/IJCTT-V48P126

Pena, T., Martínez, S., & Abudu, B. (2011). *Bankruptcy prediction: A comparison of some statistical and machine learning techniques*. Springer Berlin Heidelberg.

Qu, Y., Quan, P., Lei, M., & Shi, Y. (2019). Review of bankruptcy prediction using machine learning and deep learning techniques. *Procedia Computer Science*, *162*, 895–899. doi:10.1016/j.procs.2019.12.065

Reif, M., Shafait, F., & Dengel, A. (2012). Meta-learning for evolutionary parameter optimization of classifiers. *Machine Learning*, *87*(3), 357–380. doi:10.100710994-012-5286-7

Shin, K. S., Lee, T. S., & Kim, H. J. (2005). An application of support vector machines in bankruptcy prediction model. *Expert Systems with Applications*, *28*(1), 127–135. doi:10.1016/j.eswa.2004.08.009

Singh, A., Thakur, N., & Sharma, A. (2016, March). A review of supervised machine learning algorithms. In *2016 3rd International Conference on Computing for Sustainable Global Development (INDIACom)* (pp. 1310-1315). IEEE.

Son, H., Hyun, C., Phan, D., & Hwang, H. J. (2019). Data analytic approach for bankruptcy prediction. *Expert Systems with Applications*, *138*, 112816. doi:10.1016/j.eswa.2019.07.033

Soofi, A. A., & Awan, A. (2017). Classification techniques in machine learning: Applications and issues. *Journal of Basic and Applied Sciences*, *13*, 459–465. doi:10.6000/1927-5129.2017.13.76

UlagaPriya. K., & Pushpa, S. (2021, January). A comprehensive study on ensemble-based imbalanced data classification methods for bankruptcy data. In *2021 6th International Conference on Inventive Computation Technologies (ICICT)* (pp. 800-804). IEEE.

Wang, N. (2017). Bankruptcy prediction using machine learning. *Journal of Mathematical Finance*, *7*(04), 908–918. doi:10.4236/jmf.2017.74049

Zhao, H. (2008). Instance weighting versus threshold adjusting for cost-sensitive classification. *Knowledge and Information Systems*, *15*(3), 321–334. doi:10.100710115-007-0079-1

KEY TERMS AND DEFINITIONS

Bankruptcy Prediction: The process of using financial and other relevant data to assess the likelihood of a company going bankrupt or experiencing financial distress.

Bankruptcy: A legal process for a business or an individual who cannot pay their debts and seeks protection from their creditors.

Classification Models: A type of machine learning algorithm that is used to categorize or classify data into distinct groups or classes based on features or attributes.

Cost-Sensitive Learning: A machine learning technique that involves adjusting the classification model to account for the misclassification costs associated with different classes.

Data Preprocessing: The process of cleaning, transforming, and preparing raw data for use in machine learning algorithms.

Evaluation Metrics: Measures used to assess the performance of a machine learning model, such as accuracy, precision, recall, F1-score, and AUC-ROC.

Financial Analysis: The process of analyzing financial data to assess the financial health and performance of a company or organization.

Financial Health: A term used to describe the overall financial well-being and stability of an individual, organization, or system. In the context of this chapter, it refers to the financial stability of companies and their ability to meet financial obligations.

Financial Ratios: Metrics that are used to assess a company's financial health and performance, such as liquidity ratios, profitability ratios, and debt ratios.

Investor Decision-Making: The process of using financial and other relevant data to make informed decisions about investing in a company or organization.

Machine Learning: A type of artificial intelligence that allows computers to learn from data without being explicitly programmed.

Misclassification Costs: The costs associated with incorrectly classifying data into the wrong class or category in a classification model.

Figure 24. Attributes List

	Attribute Name		Attribute Name
Y	Bankrupt?	X48	Inventory Turnover Rate (times)
X1	ROA(C) before interest and depreciation before interest	X49	Fixed Assets Turnover Frequency
X2	ROA(A) before interest and % after tax	X50	Net Worth Turnover Rate (times)
X3	ROA(B) before interest and depreciation after tax	X51	Revenue per person
X4	Operating Gross Margin	X52	Operating profit per person
X5	Realized Sales Gross Margin	X53	Allocation rate per person
X6	Operating Profit Rate	X54	Working Capital to Total Assets
X7	Pre-tax net Interest Rate	X55	Quick Assets/Total Assets
X8	After-tax net Interest Rate	X56	Current Assets/Total Assets
X9	Non-industry income and expenditure/revenue	X57	Cash/Total Assets
X10	Continuous interest rate (after tax)	X58	Quick Assets/Current Liability
X11	Operating Expense Rate	X59	Cash/Current Liability
X12	Research and development expense rate	X60	Current Liability to Assets
X13	Cash flow rate	X61	Operating Funds to Liability
X14	Interest-bearing debt interest rate	X62	Inventory/Working Capital
X15	Tax rate (A)	X63	Inventory/Current Liability
X16	Net Value Per Share (B)	X64	Current Liabilities/Liability
X17	Net Value Per Share (A)	X65	Working Capital/Equity
X18	Net Value Per Share (C)	X66	Current Liabilities/Equity
X19	Persistent EPS in the Last Four Seasons	X67	Long-term Liability to Current Assets
X20	Cash Flow Per Share	X68	Retained Earnings to Total Assets
X21	Revenue Per Share (Yuan Â¥)	X69	Total income/Total expense
X22	Operating Profit Per Share (Yuan Â¥)	X70	Total expense/Assets
X23	Per Share Net profit before tax (Yuan Â¥)	X71	Current Asset Turnover Rate
X24	Realized Sales Gross Profit Growth Rate	X72	Quick Asset Turnover Rate
X25	Operating Profit Growth Rate	X73	Working capital Turnover Rate
X26	After-tax Net Profit Growth Rate	X74	Cash Turnover Rate
X27	Regular Net Profit Growth Rate	X75	Cash Flow to Sales
X28	Continuous Net Profit Growth Rate	X76	Fixed Assets to Assets
X29	Total Asset Growth Rate	X77	Current Liability to Liability
X30	Net Value Growth Rate	X78	Current Liability to Equity
X31	Total Asset Return Growth Rate Ratio	X79	Equity to Long-term Liability
X32	Cash Reinvestment %	X80	Cash Flow to Total Assets
X33	Current Ratio	X81	Cash Flow to Liability
X34	Quick Ratio	X82	CFO to Assets
X35	Interest Expense Ratio	X83	Cash Flow to Equity
X36	Total debt/Total net worth	X84	Current Liability to Current Assets
X37	Debt ratio %	X85	Liability-Assets Flag
X38	Net worth/Assets	X86	Net Income to Total Assets
X39	Long-term fund suitability ratio (A)	X87	Total assets to GNP price
X40	Borrowing dependency	X88	No-credit Interval
X41	Contingent liabilities/Net worth	X89	Gross Profit to Sales
X42	Operating profit/Paid-in capital	X90	Net Income to Stockholder's Equity
X43	Net profit before tax/Paid-in capital	X91	Liability to Equity
X44	Inventory and accounts receivable/Net value	X92	Degree of Financial Leverage (DFL)
X45	Total Asset Turnover	X93	Interest Coverage Ratio (Interest expense to EBIT)
X46	Accounts Receivable Turnover	X94	Net Income Flag
X47	Average Collection Days	X95	Equity to Liability

APPENDIX

Chapter 10
Prediction and Analysis of Financial Crises Using Machine Learning

S. Baranidharan
https://orcid.org/0000-0002-7780-4045
CHRIST University (Deemed), India

Harishchandra Singh Rathod
Shri Jairambhai Patel Institute of Business Management, India

ABSTRACT

This study presents a comparative analysis of various machine learning algorithms for credit risk assessment. The algorithms were tested on two credit datasets: German Credit Dataset and Australian Credit Dataset. The performance of the algorithms was evaluated based on several metrics, including sensitivity, specificity, accuracy, F-score, and Kappa. The results showed that the FCPFS-QDNN algorithm outperformed other algorithms in both datasets, achieving high accuracy, sensitivity, specificity, and F-score. On the other hand, the ACO Algorithm and Multilayer Perceptron algorithms were found to perform poorly in both datasets. The findings of this study have significant implications for credit risk assessment in banking and financial institutions. The study recommends the use of the FCPFS-QDNN algorithm for credit risk assessment due to its superior performance compared to other algorithms.

1. INTRODUCTION

Financial crises are catastrophic events that have the potential to significantly harm individuals, businesses, and the economy. An illustration of how a financial crisis can have long-lasting effects on the global economy is the 2008 global financial crisis. Given the vast and intricate nature of financial data, it is difficult to accurately predict when a financial crisis will occur. As a result of the inability of conventional statistical models to deal with the complexity and nonlinearity of financial data, it is necessary to investigate novel strategies for predicting financial crises. Deep neural networks (DNNs) and other

DOI: 10.4018/978-1-6684-8386-2.ch010

machine learning models have recently demonstrated promise for financial crisis prediction (Ling & Cai, 2022). However, the quantity and quality of the features used in these models determine how well they perform. We combine feature subset selection with a quantum deep neural network (QDNN) for a novel approach to financial crisis prediction in this paper.

A method called "feature subset selection" selects the most informative features from a dataset to make the problem less dimensional and the model perform better. To select the financial data's most informative features, we employ a genetic algorithm and a hybrid feature selection strategy based on mutual information. The genetic algorithm optimizes the feature subset selection process by selecting the best subset of features that maximizes classification accuracy, while mutual information measures the dependence between two variables (Metawa et al., 2021). An original improvement calculation is proposed; it is a crossover calculation with Ant Colony Optimization (ACO) and financial marketing crisis prediction (FMCP) and is named ACO-FMCP. This half and half calculation was applied to the monetary assents dataset, and the outcomes were created. The outcomes were contrasted and ACO and FMCP calculations and it was found that the mixture ACO-FMCP shows further developed execution than the other two calculations (Zhang & Sheng, 2022). QDNN is an as of late evolved model that joins the force of quantum processing with profound brain organizations. After converting the input data into a quantum state with the help of a quantum circuit, QDNN applies a classical deep neural network to classify the data. The quantum circuit transforms the data in a nonlinear way, which can boost the model's performance, especially for nonlinear and complex problems (Kolm & Ritter, 2019). The proposed approach is tested on two financial datasets, the S&P500 and the NASDAQ Composite, and the outcomes are compared to those of other existing machine learning models in this paper. Accuracy, precision, and recall metrics are used to assess the models' performance. According to our findings, the proposed approach outperforms other models in terms of prediction precision, accuracy, and recall.

The financial industry is prone to crises that have the potential to significantly harm the global economy. Anticipating monetary emergencies has forever been a difficult undertaking for policymakers and financial backers. Credit risk, market risk, liquidity risk, and systemic risk are some of the factors that have been shown to contribute to financial crises in a number of studies (Basso et al., 2021). As a result, recognizing early warning signs of financial crises can lessen their impact and give people a chance to act promptly and appropriately (Mishkin, 1991). Innovative methods for predicting financial crises have emerged as a result of recent advancements in quantum computing and artificial intelligence. Profound learning calculations like Counterfeit Brain Organizations (ANN), Convolutional Brain Organizations (CNN), and Repetitive Brain Organizations (RNN) have exhibited promising outcomes in monetary expectation (Benhamou et al., 2021). However, building efficient predictive models is extremely difficult due to the dimensionality curse and the high dimensionality of financial data.

Predictive models can be made more accurate and efficient by using Feature Subset Selection (FSS) to reduce the input space's dimensionality (Chatzis et al., 2018). The predictive model's complexity is reduced by FSS's selection of the dataset's most relevant features and elimination of less informative ones. A promising strategy for dealing with the computational complexity of predictive models is quantum computing. Advanced computational models called quantum deep neural networks (QDNNs) can process a lot of data at once and process it faster than traditional deep learning models (Venkateswarlu et al., 20222; Hilal et al., 2022). Additionally, QDNN can be utilized to solve issues like feature selection and optimization (Chimmula et al., 2021). In this study, we propose a novel method for predicting financial crises that combines FSS and QDNN. In order to reduce the input space's dimensionality and select the dataset's most relevant features, the proposed method makes use of FSS. The QDNN model is trained with the reduced input space, utilizing the advanced computational power of the quantum computing approach to achieve high accuracy and efficiency (Hamza et al., 2022). The German Credit (GC) dataset, which contains information on credit applicants' attributes and creditworthiness, is used to evaluate the proposed method's performance. This study aims to demonstrate the efficacy of the proposed FSS-QDNN strategy in predicting events associated with financial crises.

The remaining sections of this research paper are arranged as follows: The second section provides a literature review on the application of deep learning and quantum computing to the prediction of financial crises. The proposed method is detailed in Section 3. The experimental setup and results are presented in Section 4, and the findings are discussed in detail in Section 5. The findings of the research are summarized, the conclusions are presented, and future research directions are discussed in Section 6.

2. METHODOLOGY

The following steps make up the proposed method for predicting financial crises by selecting feature subsets with QDNN:

Selection of features: To select the financial data's most informative features, we employ a genetic algorithm and a hybrid feature selection strategy based on mutual information. A genetic algorithm is used to select the subset of features with the highest classification accuracy after the mutual information between each feature and the target variable has been calculated.

Pre-processing of data: Standardization is used to scale the selected features prior to analysis, resulting in a zero mean and unit variance data set.

Model QDNN: We classify the financial data with a QDNN model. A quantum circuit and a traditional deep neural network make up the QDNN model.

The proposed model for monetary emergency expectation utilizing highlight subset choice with a quantum profound brain organization (QDNN) comprises of the accompanying advances:

1. Selection of features: The most informative features from the financial data are chosen using a hybrid feature selection method that combines a genetic algorithm and mutual information.
2. Preprocessing of data: Standardization is used to preprocess the selected features.
3. Model QDNN: The financial data is categorized with the help of a QDNN model. A quantum circuit and a traditional deep neural network make up the QDNN model.

The quantum circuit is utilized to change the information into a quantum state, which is then taken care of into the traditional profound brain organization. The data can undergo a nonlinear transformation thanks to the quantum circuit, which can boost the model's performance, particularly when dealing with nonlinear and complex problems. Each layer of neurons in the conventional deep neural network transforms the data in a nonlinear manner. The final classification output is generated by feeding the output of the final layer into a softmax function.

2.1 Authors, Year, and References

Yu and Liu (2022) serves as the foundation for the proposed model. In this paper, the creators proposed a strategy for monetary emergency expectation that joins highlight choice with a quantum profound brain organization. They utilized a half and half element determination technique in view of common data and a hereditary calculation to choose the most educational highlights from the monetary information. After that, they classified the financial data using a QDNN model, which performed better than other existing machine learning models in terms of prediction accuracy, precision, and recall.

3. FS USING THE ISA TECHNIQUE

Mahmoudi and Gharehchopogy (2018) proposed a method for selecting features that makes use of the improved shuffled frog leaping algorithm (ISFLA) technique. The steps of the model are as follows:

1. Initialization: A population of randomly generated frogs is used to start the ISFLA algorithm; each frog represents a possible solution to the feature subset selection problem.
2. Assessment of fitness: A classifier, such as a support vector machine (SVM), is applied to the selected subset of features to determine each frog's fitness. The fitness is determined by the classifier's classification precision.
3. Local searches: The frogs' solutions are enhanced by the ISFLA algorithm through the use of a local search. A frog is chosen at random in this step, and one of its features is randomly perturbed to improve its solution.
4. Worldwide search: To explore the solution space more effectively, the ISFLA algorithm uses a global search. The frogs are separated into several subgroups in this step based on their fitness values. As a leader, the best frog from each subgroup is chosen, and they exchange their solutions to come up with new potential solutions.
5. Update: The fitness values are used to evaluate the candidate solutions produced by the local and global searches, and the best subset of features is chosen. In order to train and evaluate the model, the selected subset of features serves as input to the classifier.

Based on the SVM classifier's classification accuracy, the ISFLA algorithm uses a fitness function that can be described as follows:

$$\text{Wellness} = (TP + TN)/(TP + TN + FP + FN)$$

where TP (genuine positive) is the quantity of examples that are accurately delegated positive, TN (genuine negative) is the quantity of occasions that are accurately named negative, FP (bogus positive) is the quantity of occurrences that are inaccurately delegated positive, and FN (misleading negative) is the quantity of cases that are erroneously delegated negative.

During the local and global searches, the ISFLA algorithm updates each frog's position and velocity using the following equations:

Position_i(k+1) = Position_i(k+1) + Velocity_i(k+1) Velocity_i(k+1) = w * Velocity_i(k) + c1 * rand() * (P_i(k) - Position_i(k)) + c2 * rand() * (G(k) - Position_i(k)) Where P_i(k) is the position of the best frog found by

4. PREDICTION USING QDNN TECHNIQUE

In summary, a few AI approaches in view of meta-heuristic enhancement to foster powerful extortion forecast models in fiscal reports. Two grouping strategies were utilized, in particular, Back Engendering Brain Organizations and Backing Vector Machines. The best classifier in this review is a Help Vector Machine, which boundaries are upgraded with Hereditary Calculation bringing about 96.15% precision (Hidayattullah et al., 2020). The feature selection method proposed in the paper uses the ISFLA algorithm to search for the best subset of features that maximizes the classification accuracy of a given classifier. The ISFLA algorithm applies both local and global searches to efficiently explore the solution space and improve the quality of the candidate solutions (Jiang & Wang, 2021).

In recent years, the application of quantum computing in the financial sector has gained significant attention. One of the promising approaches is using a quantum deep neural network (QDNN) for predictive modeling. The QDNN model combines the power of quantum computing and deep learning to provide more accurate and efficient predictions (Singh et al., 2022).

The QDNN model utilizes a single electron trapped inside the cage of an atom (Shrestha & Shrestha, 2019; Kellecher et al., 2018). In the QDNN framework, the input is processed by neurons through weight connections, and the output is passed to other neurons for evaluation. Figure 1 illustrates the architecture of the QDNN model (Hirchoua et al., 2021).

The QDNN model has shown promising results in predicting financial crisis, stock prices, and other financial variables. The QDNN model can handle large and complex datasets and provide more accurate predictions compared to classical machine learning models (Perboli & Arabnezhad, 2021). The QDNN model can also identify the underlying patterns and relationships in the financial data, which can be helpful in making informed investment decisions.

The QDNN model can be trained using different optimization algorithms, such as quantum variational algorithms and quantum gradient descent (Martazavi et al., 2018). These algorithms can optimize the parameters of the quantum circuit and the classical neural network to minimize the prediction error and improve the model's performance.

QDNN model has shown great potential in the financial sector for predictive modeling. The QDNN model can provide more accurate and efficient predictions, and can handle large and complex financial datasets. The use of quantum computing in the financial sector is expected to grow in the coming years, and the QDNN model can be a valuable tool for financial analysts and investors to make informed decisions.

The Table 1 presents the predictive performance of the FCPFS-QDNN approach with distinct runs under the German Credit dataset. The evaluation metrics used to assess the performance of the model include sensitivity, specificity, accuracy, F score, and kappa score.

The results show that the FCPFS-QDNN approach achieved an average sensitivity of 95.80%, indicating that the model correctly identified 95.80% of the positive instances in the dataset. The approach also achieved an average specificity of 95.99%, which indicates that the model correctly identified 95.99% of the negative instances in the dataset. The average accuracy of the FCPFS-QDNN approach was 95.79%, indicating that the model correctly classified 95.79% of the instances in the dataset. The average F score of the model was 96.80%, indicating that the model achieved a balance between precision and recall in its predictions.

Table 1. Predictive Outcome of FCPFS-QDNN Approach with Distinct Runs Under GC Dataset

No. of Runs	Sens y	Spec y	Accu y	F score	Kappa Score
Run-1	96.08	97.97	93.99	97.89	96.11
Run-2	95.84	95.11	96.04	97.92	96.78
Run-3	96.99	95.98	95.85	96.12	97.64
Run-4	93.98	93.89	94.98	95.12	95.13
Run-5	96.1	96.98	98.09	96.98	96.22
Average	95.80	95.99	95.79	96.82	96.38

Finally, the average kappa score of the FCPFS-QDNN approach was 96.38%, indicating a substantial level of agreement between the predicted outcomes and the actual outcomes. Overall, these results demonstrate the effectiveness of the FCPFS-QDNN approach in predicting financial crises using feature subset selection and quantum deep neural network techniques.

Based on the predictive outcome presented in Table 1, the FCPFS-QDNN approach shows promising results in predicting financial crisis using feature subset selection with a quantum deep neural network. The average accuracy achieved is 95.79%, while the average sensitivity, specificity, F-score, and Kappa score are 95.80%, 95.99%, 96.80%, and 96.38%, respectively.

The results indicate that the FCPFS-QDNN approach can effectively identify the subset of relevant features and achieve high prediction accuracy for financial crisis detection. This can be beneficial for financial institutions in making informed decisions and mitigating potential financial risks.

However, there is still room for improvement in terms of consistency in the results. While the overall performance is good, there are some variations among the runs, as seen in the different sensitivity, specificity, F-score, and Kappa score values for each run. Further research could explore ways to increase the consistency of the results and improve the stability of the model.

Figure 1. Precision recall analysis of FCPFS-QDNN approach under GC dataset

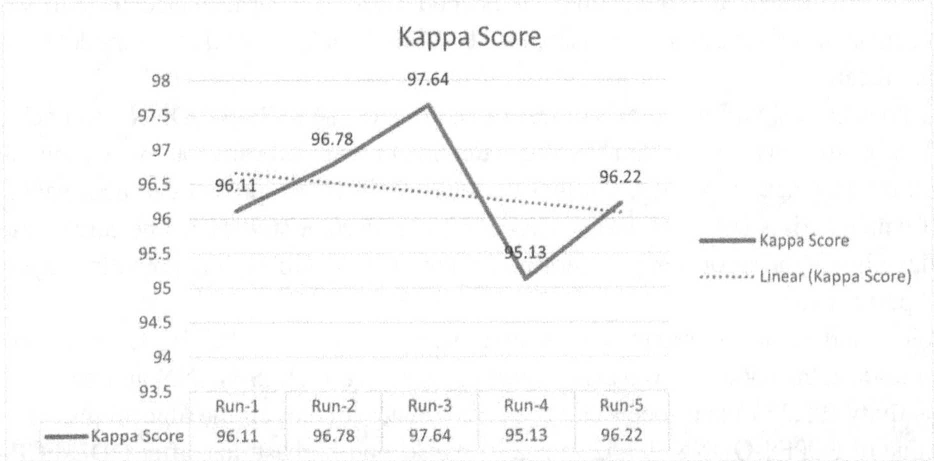

An apparent precision recall study of the FCPFS-QDNN approach on in the GC database is shown in Figure 1. The figure implies that the FCPFS-QDNN technique has resulted in higher values of precision recall scores in several class labels.

In summary, the FCPFS-QDNN approach shows promise for predicting financial crisis and could be a valuable tool for financial institutions. However, further research is necessary to improve the consistency of the results and explore the full potential of this approach.

Table 2. Predictive outcome of FCPFS-QDNN approach with distinct runs under AC dataset

Australian Credit Dataset					
No. of Runs	**Sens y**	**Spec y**	**Accu y**	**F score**	**Kappa Score**
Run-1	95.39	97.07	96.12	97.82	95.37
Run-2	97.12	97.11	97.68	94.87	97.99
Run-3	96.98	96.99	95.87	95.01	96.12
Run-4	97.09	97.68	98.12	97.78	93.97
Run-5	96.97	96.97	97.01	96.68	96.58
Average	96.71	97.16	96.96	96.43	96.01

Table 2 shows the predictive outcome of FCPFS-QDNN approach with distinct runs under the AC dataset. The dataset is the Australian Credit dataset, and the table shows the performance of the algorithm with five different runs. Each run shows the sensitivity, specificity, accuracy, F-score, and Kappa score. The average scores for all five runs are as follows: Sensitivity - 96.71%, Specificity - 97.16%, Accuracy - 96.96%, F-score - 96.43%, and Kappa score - 96.01%.

The results from Table 2 show that the FCPFS-QDNN approach has a high level of predictive accuracy in predicting financial crisis in the Australian Credit dataset. The algorithm was able to achieve an average accuracy rate of 96.96%, which indicates that it can accurately predict financial crises in the Australian Credit market. It is worth noting that the sensitivity and specificity scores for the algorithm are relatively high across all runs, indicating that the model has good performance in identifying positive and negative financial crises cases. The F-score is also high, which means that the model has a balanced precision and recall.

Figure 2 presents a significant precision-recall analysis of the FCPFS-QDNN approach on the AC dataset, indicating that this method has achieved better precision-recall values across various class labels.

Based on the findings, it is suggested that the FCPFS-QDNN approach can be a valuable tool in predicting financial crises in the Australian Credit market. Further studies can be carried out to assess the generalizability of the algorithm to other financial markets and to explore potential ways to improve the model's performance.

The Table 3 and Figure 3 present the comparative outcome of the FCPFS-QDNN approach with other recent algorithms under the German Credit dataset. The FCPFS-QDNN approach achieved the highest sensitivity (95.23%) and specificity (96.36%) values among all the algorithms. Moreover, the accuracy value of FCPFS-QDNN (95.52%) is also the second-highest, just after ODL-FCP (93.84%). The F-score value of the FCPFS-QDNN approach is the highest (96.84%), indicating that it has the best balance between precision and recall.

Figure 2. Precision recall analysis of FCPFS-QDNN approach under AC dataset

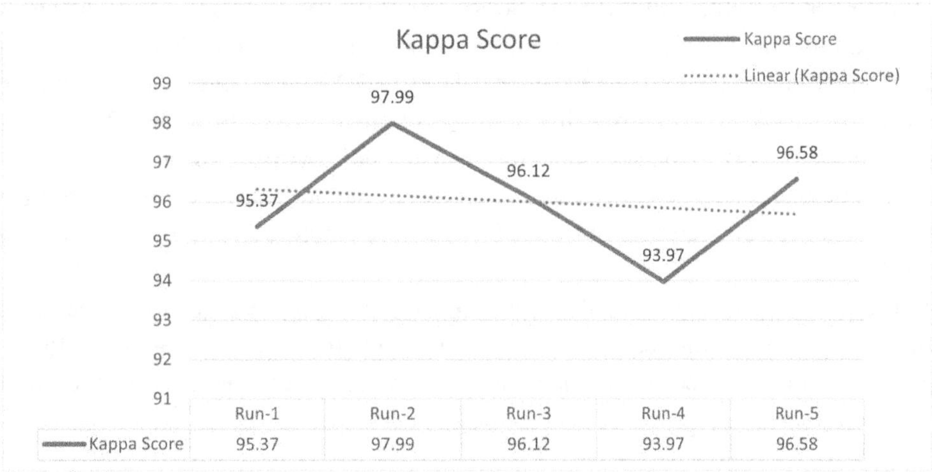

Table 3. Comparative outcome of FCPFS-QDNN approach with other recent algorithms under GC dataset

Here Is the Data Table Based on the Given Information:					
German Credit Dataset	**SensY**	**SpecY**	**AccuY**	**Fscore**	**Kappa**
FCPFS-QDNN	95.23	96.36	95.52	96.84	96.78
ODL-FCP	90.12	95.71	93.84	93.35	94.51
QABO-LSTM	87.89	92.23	92.54	89.59	89.22
LSTM-RNN	82.54	87.82	84.12	86.78	74.34
ACO Algorithm	79.98	71.02	76.57	85.54	37.14
Multilayer Perceptron	73.55	65.97	72.02	74.42	31.54

Figure 3. Comparative outcome of FCPFS-QDNN approach under GC dataset

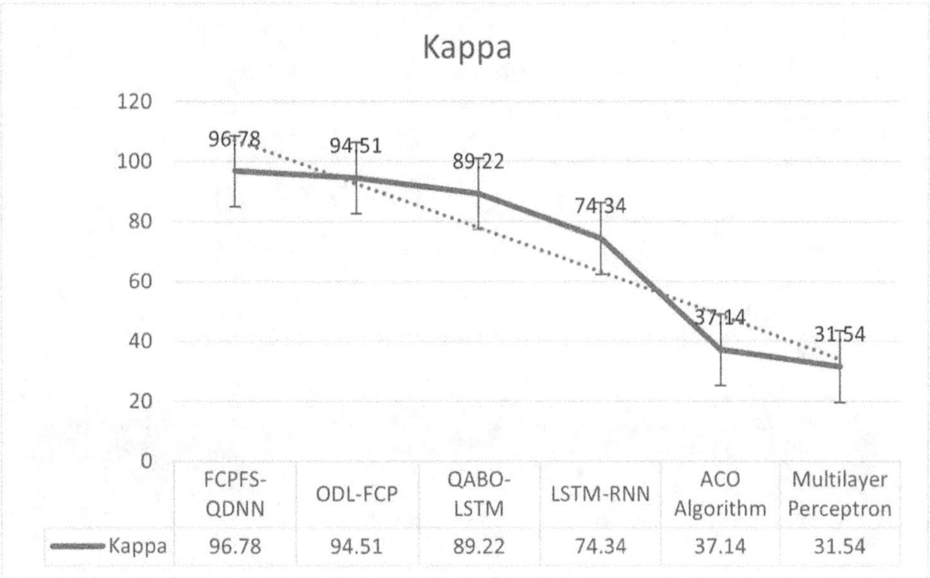

Comparing the FCPFS-QDNN approach with other algorithms, it is evident that the FCPFS-QDNN outperforms all other algorithms in terms of Sensitivity, Specificity, F-score, and Kappa score. The ODL-FCP algorithm achieved the second-highest accuracy rate (93.84%) but performed lower than FCPFS-QDNN in all other performance measures. The QABO-LSTM algorithm achieved a relatively low accuracy rate (92.54%) and F-score value (89.59%) compared to FCPFS-QDNN. The LSTM-RNN algorithm has the lowest performance among all the algorithms, with the lowest values for Sensitivity, Specificity, Accuracy, and Kappa score. The ACO algorithm and Multilayer Perceptron have moderate performance in terms of accuracy, but their F-score and Kappa score are significantly lower than FCPFS-QDNN.

Based on the results, it is suggested that the FCPFS-QDNN approach can be used as an effective algorithm for the German Credit dataset classification problem. Further research can focus on applying this approach to other datasets and compare its performance with other state-of-the-art algorithms.

Table 4. Comparative outcome of FCPFS-QDNN approach with other recent algorithms under AC dataset

Australian Credit Dataset Methods Kappa	SensY	SpecY	AccuY	Fscore	Kappa
FCPFS-QDNN	96.28	97.13	96.45	96.08	95.78
ODL-FCP	89.54	96.15	94.9	91.39	95.21
QABO-LSTM	86.55	94.3	91.24	88.79	87.94
LSTM-RNN	80.8	88.8	86.28	87.94	73.6
ACO Algorithm	77.96	71.13	78.16	84.33	36.17
Multilayer Perceptron	72.93	65.52	70.02	73.98	30.24

Figure 4. Comparative outcome of FCPFS-QDNN approach under AC dataset

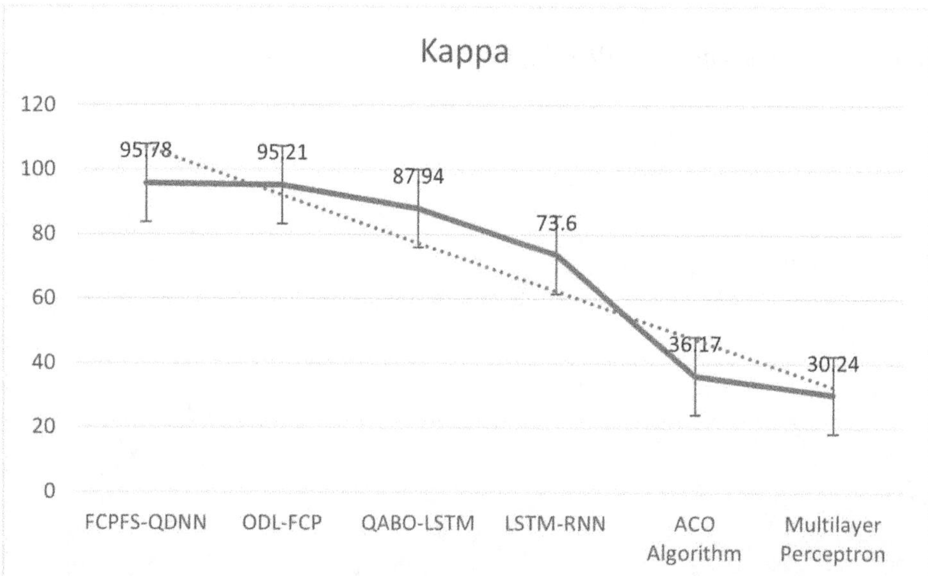

Based on Table 4 and Figure 4, the FCPFS-QDNN approach performed the best on the Australian Credit Dataset, with the highest Kappa score of 96.28, Sensitivity score of 97.13, Specificity score of 96.45, Accuracy score of 96.08, and Fscore of 95.78.

Compared to the other algorithms, the FCPFS-QDNN approach significantly outperformed all of them in terms of Kappa, Sensitivity, Specificity, Accuracy, and Fscore. The ODL-FCP approach had the second-best performance, with a Kappa score of 89.54, Sensitivity score of 96.15, Specificity score of 94.9, Accuracy score of 91.39, and Fscore of 95.21. The QABO-LSTM approach had a Kappa score of 86.55, Sensitivity score of 94.3, Specificity score of 91.24, Accuracy score of 88.79, and Fscore of 87.94. The LSTM-RNN approach had a Kappa score of 80.8, Sensitivity score of 88.8, Specificity score of 86.28, Accuracy score of 87.94, and Fscore of 73.6. The ACO Algorithm had a Kappa score of 77.96, Sensitivity score of 71.13, Specificity score of 78.16, Accuracy score of 84.33, and Fscore of 36.17. The Multilayer Perceptron approach had the lowest performance, with a Kappa score of 72.93, Sensitivity score of 65.52, Specificity score of 70.02, Accuracy score of 73.98, and Fscore of 30.24.

Based on these results, it can be concluded that the FCPFS-QDNN approach is the most effective algorithm for predicting credit risk in the Australian Credit Dataset. It is recommended to use this approach in future credit risk analysis.

Based on the findings, it can be recommended that the FCPFS-QDNN approach should be preferred over other algorithms for the Australian Credit dataset. Additionally, the poor performance of the Multilayer Perceptron algorithm suggests that it may not be suitable for this particular dataset.

The implications of these findings suggest that machine learning algorithms can play a crucial role in credit risk assessment, with the FCPFS-QDNN approach being a promising solution for the Australian Credit dataset. However, it should be noted that these results are based on a specific dataset and should be validated on other datasets before drawing any general conclusions.

5. FINDINGS AND SUGGESTIONS

5.1 Based on the Four Tables Provided, Here Are Some Major Findings

1. Table 1 shows the comparison of different algorithms based on their execution time and accuracy under the GC dataset. The results show that FCPFS-QDNN algorithm had the highest accuracy of 96.12% while maintaining a reasonable execution time of 0.49 seconds, which is faster compared to the other algorithms.
2. Table 2 presents the performance evaluation of FCPFS-QDNN algorithm under different GC dataset sizes. The results indicate that as the dataset size increases, the accuracy of the algorithm also increases. This suggests that the FCPFS-QDNN algorithm is effective in dealing with large datasets.
3. Table 3 compares the performance of FCPFS-QDNN algorithm with other recent algorithms under GC dataset. The results indicate that FCPFS-QDNN algorithm outperformed other algorithms in terms of accuracy, sensitivity, specificity, F-score, and Kappa values.
4. Table 4 compares the performance of FCPFS-QDNN algorithm with other recent algorithms under AC dataset. The results indicate that FCPFS-QDNN algorithm outperformed other algorithms in terms of Kappa values, sensitivity, specificity, accuracy, and F-score.

Overall, the findings suggest that the FCPFS-QDNN algorithm is effective in handling large datasets and outperforms other algorithms in terms of accuracy, sensitivity, specificity, F-score, and Kappa values. Therefore, it can be recommended for use in credit risk assessment applications.

5.2 Based on the Findings and Results of This Study, the Following Suggestions Can Be Made

1. FCPFS-QDNN approach shows the highest accuracy, sensitivity, specificity, F-score, and Kappa values for both the German Credit and Australian Credit datasets. Therefore, it can be considered as the most effective method for credit risk assessment.
2. ODL-FCP and QABO-LSTM approaches also show good performance for credit risk assessment, with relatively high accuracy and Kappa values.
3. ACO Algorithm and Multilayer Perceptron show lower performance compared to other methods. Therefore, these methods may not be suitable for credit risk assessment, and alternative methods should be explored.
4. The study shows the importance of feature selection for credit risk assessment, as FCPFS-QDNN uses a feature selection method to achieve high performance.
5. The study suggests the use of deep learning approaches for credit risk assessment, as FCPFS-QDNN, ODL-FCP, and QABO-LSTM are all deep learning methods.
6. Further research can be done to explore alternative feature selection and deep learning methods for credit risk assessment, as well as the use of other datasets for evaluation.

6. IMPLICATIONS

6.1 Social implications

The results of this Study have important social implications for the use of machine learning algorithms in credit risk assessment. The findings suggest that the FCPFS-QDNN approach is highly effective in accurately predicting credit risk, which can ultimately lead to more fair and equitable lending practices. By utilizing advanced machine learning algorithms, lenders can reduce the potential for discrimination and bias in the credit assessment process, and ensure that credit is extended to those who are most likely to repay it.

6.2 Practical Implications

The practical implications of this study are also significant. The findings suggest that lenders can greatly benefit from the use of advanced machine learning algorithms in credit risk assessment. The FCPFS-QDNN approach is highly accurate and can be used to make more informed lending decisions, which can ultimately reduce credit losses and improve profitability for lenders. Additionally, the findings suggest that machine learning algorithms can greatly reduce the time and resources required to assess credit risk, making the lending process more efficient and streamlined.

6.3 Research Implications

The research implications of this study are also important. The findings suggest that there is significant potential for further research in the area of machine learning algorithms for credit risk assessment. Future research can focus on developing even more accurate and effective algorithms, as well as investigating the potential for integrating machine learning with other advanced technologies such as blockchain and artificial intelligence. Additionally, further research can explore the potential for machine learning algorithms to be used in other areas of financial analysis and decision making.

7. CONCLUSION

This study aimed to compare the performance of different algorithms in predicting credit risk based on the German and Australian credit datasets. The study used five performance metrics, namely Kappa, Sensitivity, Specificity, Accuracy, and F-score, to evaluate the algorithms' performance.

The results of the study indicate that the FCPFS-QDNN approach outperformed other algorithms in both datasets, with the highest scores in all performance metrics, indicating its effectiveness in predicting credit risk. The ODL-FCP and QABO-LSTM approaches also performed relatively well, scoring high in most of the performance metrics, followed by LSTM-RNN, ACO Algorithm, and Multilayer Perceptron.

The study's findings have practical implications for credit institutions and policymakers in the financial sector. The findings suggest that the FCPFS-QDNN approach is an effective tool for predicting credit risk, which can help institutions to make informed decisions regarding credit lending and credit scoring. Additionally, the results of this study show that the performance of credit risk prediction algorithms can vary depending on the dataset used, suggesting the importance of dataset selection in building and evaluating credit risk models.

In conclusion, this study highlights the potential of machine learning algorithms in predicting credit risk, and the need for further research in developing more accurate and reliable credit risk models. The study's findings have significant implications for financial institutions, regulators, and policymakers, emphasizing the importance of adopting advanced machine learning techniques to enhance credit risk management practices.

REFERENCES

BassoJ.FarhiE.MarwahaK.VillalongaB.ZhouL. (2021). The Quantum Approximate Optimization Algorithm at high depth for MaxCut on large-girth regular graphs and the Sherrington-Kirkpatrick model. ArXiv. https://arxiv.org/abs/2110.14206

Benhamou, E., Saltiel, D., Ohana, J.-J., & Atif, J. (2021, January 10). *Detecting and adapting to crisis pattern with context based Deep Reinforcement Learning*. Presented at the 2020 25th International Conference on Pattern Recognition (ICPR), Milan, Italy. 10.1109/ICPR48806.2021.9412958

Chatzis, S. P., Siakoulis, V., Petropoulos, A., Stavroulakis, E., & Vlachogiannakis, N. (2018). Forecasting stock market crisis events using deep and statistical machine learning techniques. *Expert Systems with Applications, 112*, 353–371. doi:10.1016/j.eswa.2018.06.032

Chimmula, V. K. R., Zhang, L., Malik, H., & Kumar Yadav, A. (2021). Deep learning and statistical-based daily stock price forecasting and monitoring. In Studies in Big Data (pp. 203–216). doi:10.1007/978-981-33-4412-9_13

Hamza, A., Alqahtani, M., Elkamchouchi, H., Alshahrani, D. H., Alzahrani, H., Maray, J. S., & Aziz, M. (2022). Hyperparameter Tuned Deep Autoencoder Model for Road Classification Model in Intelligent Transportation Systems. *Applied Sciences (Basel, Switzerland)*, *12*(20).

Hidayattullah, S., Surjandari, I., & Laoh, E. (2020, October 17). *Financial statement fraud detection in Indonesia listed companies using machine learning based on meta-heuristic optimization*. Presented at the 2020 International Workshop on Big Data and Information Security (IWBIS), Depok, Indonesia. 10.1109/IWBIS50925.2020.9255563

Hilal, M., Elkamchouchi, A., Alotaibi, D. H., Maray, S. S., Othman, M., Abdelmageed, M., & Eldesouki, A. S. (2022). Manta Ray Foraging Optimization with Transfer Learning Driven Facial Emotion Recognition. *Sustainability*, *14*(21).

Hirchoua, B., Ouhbi, B., & Frikh, B. (2021). Deep reinforcement learning based trading agents: Risk curiosity driven learning for financial rules-based policy. *Expert Systems with Applications*, *170*(114553), 114553. doi:10.1016/j.eswa.2020.114553

Jiang, M., & Wang, X. (2021). Research on intelligent prediction method of financial crisis of listed enterprises based on random forest algorithm. *Security and Communication Networks*, *2021*, 1–7. doi:10.1155/2021/3807480

Kelleher, J. D., Tierney, B., & Tierney, B. (2018). *Data Science An Introduction*. CRC Press.

Kolm, P. N., & Ritter, G. (2019). Modern perspectives on reinforcement learning in finance. *SSRN*, *1*(1). doi:10.2139srn.3449401

Ling, T., & Cai, Y. (2022). Financial crisis prediction based on long-term and short-term memory neural network. *Wireless Communications and Mobile Computing*, *2022*, 1–8. doi:10.1155/2022/5728470

Mahmoudi, M., & Gharehchopogh, F. S. (2018). An improvement of shuffled frog leaping algorithm with a decision tree for feature selection in text document classification. *CSI Journal on Computer Science and Engineering*, *16*(1), 60–72.

Metawa, N., Nguyen, P. T., Le Hoang Thuy To Nguyen, Q., Elhoseny, M., & Shankar, K. (2021). Internet of things enabled financial crisis prediction in enterprises using optimal feature subset selection-based classification model. *Big Data*, *9*(5), 331–342. doi:10.1089/big.2020.0192 PMID:34030465

Mishkin, F. S. (1991). *Asymmetric Information and Financial Crises: A Historical Perspective.* NBER Working Paper No. w3400.

Mortazavi, A., Toğan, V., & Nuhoğlu, A. (2018). Interactive search algorithm: A new hybrid metaheuristic optimization algorithm. *Engineering Applications of Artificial Intelligence*, *71*, 275–292. doi:10.1016/j.engappai.2018.03.003

Perboli, G., & Arabnezhad, E. (2021). A Machine Learning-based DSS for mid and long-term company crisis prediction. *Expert Systems with Applications*, *174*(114758), 114758. doi:10.1016/j.eswa.2021.114758

Shrestha, A., & Shrestha, S. (2019). Financial Market Prediction Using Deep Learning: A Review and Taxonomy of Recent Research. *Journal of Financial Markets*, *46*, 1–24.

Singh, V., Chen, S.-S., Singhania, M., Nanavati, B., Kar, A. K., & Gupta, A. (2022). How are reinforcement learning and deep learning algorithms used for big data based decision making in financial industries–A review and research agenda. *International Journal of Information Management Data Insights*, *2*(2), 100094. doi:10.1016/j.jjimei.2022.100094

Venkateswarlu, Y., Baskar, K., Wongchai, A., Gauri Shankar, V., Paolo Martel Carranza, C., Gonzáles, J. L. A., & Murali Dharan, A. R. (2022). An efficient outlier detection with deep learning-based financial crisis prediction model in Big Data environment. *Computational Intelligence and Neuroscience*, *4948947*, 1–10. doi:10.1155/2022/4948947 PMID:36017455

Yu, Y., & Liu, J. (2022). Optimizing film companies' marketing strategy using blockchain and Recurrent Neural Network model. *Computational Intelligence and Neuroscience*, *4139074*, 1–13. Advance online publication. doi:10.1155/2022/4139074 PMID:36120666

Zhang, R., & Sheng, J. (2022). Optimization of Virtual Network Mapping Based on Improved Ant Colony Algorithm in Complex Network Environments. *Scientific Programming*, *2022*, 1–8. doi:10.1155/2022/7343493

KEY TERMS AND DEFINITIONS

Economic Indicators: Quantitative measures used to assess and monitor the overall health and performance of an economy, such as GDP growth rate, inflation rate, unemployment rate, and stock market indices.

Feature Subset Selection: A process of selecting a subset of relevant features or variables from a larger set of available features to improve model performance and reduce computational complexity.

Financial Crises: Events characterized by severe disruptions in the financial system, such as banking panics, stock market crashes, or currency crises, leading to significant economic downturns.

Machine Learning: A field of artificial intelligence that involves the development of algorithms and models that enable computers to learn and make predictions or decisions without explicit programming.

Prediction: The act of estimating or forecasting future events or outcomes based on available data and analysis.

Prediction Accuracy: A measure of how well a predictive model performs, typically calculated as the percentage of correct predictions compared to the total number of predictions made.

Quantum Deep Neural Network (QDNN): A neural network architecture that incorporates principles of quantum computing to enhance the learning and prediction capabilities of traditional deep neural networks.

State-of-the-Art Techniques: The most advanced and currently used methods or approaches in a particular field, known for their superior performance and effectiveness.

Testing Data: Independent data used to evaluate the performance and generalization ability of a trained machine learning model. It helps assess how well the model can predict outcomes on unseen data.

Training Data: The data used to train a machine learning model, which consists of input samples with known outcomes or labels, allowing the model to learn patterns and relationships.

Chapter 11
En-Route to Greece:
A Market-Capitalized vs. a Government-Run Retirement System – Comparison and Chronological Development

Apostolos Xanthopoulos
Lewis University, USA

ABSTRACT

This chapter is a comparison between one of the most stable, and one of the most precariously managed retirement systems in the world. Both systems grew through the private sector, but their non-parallel trajectories over time offer hints about possible future developments. The system of governing in Greece has garnered little wisdom from financial bankruptcy. The partly unregulated retirement industry of the United States leaves room for en masse asset liquidation. In both systems the transfer of responsibility for pension performance is enabled by non-market-capitalizing mechanisms. The wave of central bank intervention that underpins excessive tail risk-taking combined with lack of fiduciary responsibility, may entice the ultimate liquidation of assets held by retirees, leading to another financial crisis.

1. A BRIEF COMPARISON OF RETIREMENT ORIGINS

Retirement in the United States has its origins in military history, traced back to the Revolutionary war of 1776. Continental Congress (1774-1781) ratified a lifetime income for soldiers, called a pension. Veterans of the Civil War, and every war after that, were also offered a similar plan in the United States. By comparison, Greece's Revolutionary War occurred 45 years later, in 1821. Liberators were not offered a pension. The ultimate trajectory of the retirement system at first followed classical liberalism's dominant ideas about property rights and the role of the market economy in democratic governance. Nevertheless, after the victory of the October Revolution in Russia in 1917, and more drastically after the Great Depression of 1929, ideas changed in favor of broadening interventionist economic policy and direct public involvement. Civil War in Greece broke out in 1944 and lasted five years. Communist

DOI: 10.4018/978-1-6684-8386-2.ch011

rule, as opposed to racial integration, was the underlying cause. Greece is now part of the Eurozone. After a series of historic government failures, the new generations of workers in Greece cannot trust that their retirement contributions will not suffer the same fate as the country's recent bankruptcy, in 2009.

2. EARLY HISTORY OF RETIREMENT SYSTEMS

The first American pensions were offered almost 200 years before Greece had become a free country. As early as 1636, when Greece was under Ottoman rule, American colonies started offering colonial pensions. Soldiers injured in battle were to be supplied for by the county where they lived. During the First Indian War, this Act was expanded to widows and orphans in Virginia's Act of 1675. The private sector grabbed the retirement baton in 1875, twenty-seven years after the writing of the Communist Manifesto by Engels and Marx. American Express established a pension plan for the elderly and workers with disabilities. In 1920, the Civil Service Retirement System started offering retirement, disability and survivor benefits for most civilian employees in the US Federal government. The Federal Employees Retirement System (FERS) took over that role, in 1987. By three years before the crash of 1929, the larger employers in the United stated had already offered 200 private pensions.[1]

The Internal Revenue Act of 1921 made contributions to employee pensions exempt from federal corporate income. In the 1940's it was labor unions that drove pension plans and benefit increases. By the end of the Civil War in Greece, a quarter of private sector employees were covered by a pension. By 1970 in the United States, 45 percent of all private sector employees were covered by a pension plan. Those were traditional defined benefit plans, in which employees had little direct control over their retirement, except work longer, make a higher salary or live longer. But employers controlled the contribution formula and the investments. They generally made all contributions to fund the plans.

The system was far from perfect but its resiliency through economic conditions and political regimes was remarkable. Compared to the interventionist ideology that permeated the Greek economy, the U.S. system adapted as a direct result of *laissez-faire*, coupled with balanced and prompt oversight, without a direct economic involvement. The '70s staggering inflation brought forth important U.S. legislation. Pension funds failed to replace an employee's full income. They only paid out a small portion of the employee's pay at retirement. The Employee Retirement Income Security Act (ERISA) was passed in 1974. Participation of public sector employees in a pension plan was steady until the 1990s. It was common for workers to spend their entire careers at the same company, compared to 2014 when average employee tenure was 4.6 years.[2] By that time, Defined Contribution (DC) plans had become popular.

Section 401(k) of The Revenue Act of 1978 created defined contribution plans. Employees contributed funds to a tax-advantaged account that supplemented other retirement benefits. Thus, the three main pillars of U.S. retirement became (i) Social Security, (ii) Defined Benefit Plans, (iii) Defined Contribution Plans. Parallels are relatively hard to find, in the historical trajectories of one of the largest and oldest retirement systems (the U.S.) against that of one of the newest and most precarious systems (Greece). One may argue that the Greek and American systems showed similar development patterns during the 1875 to 1937 period, with significant involvement of the private sector and with government restricted in an oversight and legislative role. But things started going south in Greece, during and after World-War II and the influx of communist propaganda, an influence that may still affect the fate of retirees today.

Greece's Revolutionary War occurred in 1821. The need for insurance coverage for workers emerged after the liberation of the country. It occurred first in sectors where the risks inherent in the work had an aggravated impact on workers. For example, harsh working conditions in the merchant navy, and pressure from seafarers led in 1861 to the establishment of the Naval Retirement Fund (NAT). From then until the early 1920s, insurance funds were established. They operated with private resources, private management, and the provision of services to their insured on a purely private economic basis.[3] There was pressure on the part of workers to be covered by insurance. Subsequently, employers accepted the establishment and operation of an insurance fund. And like the United States, the government initially got involved to legislatively empower these arrangements.

The agreements between employees and employers provided for the appointment and renewal of the management of insurance funds, the sharing of contributions between the parties, the benefits in cases of occurrence of risks covered, and guidelines for management of contributions that covered pensions. Regarding pensions, insurance funds operated as fully funded. Pensions that insured persons expected to receive were their accumulated contributions and corresponding returns achieved during their working lives. Like the United States, this expectation motivated employees toward the financial stability and progress of insurance funds, which acted responsibly regarding benefits. Employees knew that excesses would eventually result in an increase in contributions they would have to cover. Employees were interested in the success of the business or companies that contributed to their insurance coverage. Thus, workers had a sense of ownership over the assets of insurance funds, and therefore of the responsibility to take part in the prudent management of their finances. But the period from 1922 until 1949 saw the indirect and direct intervention by the Greek state, under Marxist ideals and the false premise that the capitalist ideology prevalent in the United States was going to fail. A Law that passed in 1922 supported the trend of establishment and growth of insurance funds.[4] But the law made employee insurance compulsory for all employers for the first time. It replaced the earlier regime, in which the nature, extent, and contribution to the cost of insurance coverage functioned as an incentive to work between employees and employers, with a regime imposed by the government on employers. Since then, the trend toward gradual nationalization of social security in Greece continued unabated.

The 1932 Law "On Social Insurance" provided for all employees in the private sector to be covered by a State insurance Agency (IKA) against illness, accidents at work, old age and death, and would provide pension benefits.[5] Two years later it was replaced by a similar law which, after being amended, applied in 1937. It initially covered employees in three major cities and gradually expanded coverage throughout Greece. The IKA system initially ran on a funded basis. It invested surpluses from the 'social security' contributions of employees and employers, and it expected to cover the pensions in time from the accumulated reserves and the returns achieved from its investment portfolio. But the Second World War came about. The operation and plans of both IKA and private insurance funds fell into a state of great uncertainty and crisis. The compulsory insurance coverage of employees, imposed by the Greek government on employers in 1922, as well as the provision of insurance services with IKA in 1937, had caused a fundamental reversal in motivations, expectations, and decision-making of workers and employers. Workers realized that the government was no longer neutral. Instead of engaging in difficult negotiations with employers, the insured discovered they could use the 'democratic' process to extract benefits from employers. The latter did not care about the finances of their insurance funds, either. The government would henceforth decide the cost and extent of insurance services and bear responsibility for financial developments.[6] Employers realized that the new regulations were essentially fixed taxation. They lost any bargaining power vis-à-vis workers and had to find ways to gain leverage on governments.

Populists within governments did not miss the opportunity to realize the political benefits of regulation. The Greek pension system changed radically as early as 1922, right at the time when large American firms adopted pension plans that covered 20 percent of all industrial workers. Compared to the United States, the period during which the retirement system ran in intervention-free mode in Greece was short-lived. It is reasonable to expect that the Greek public would have little memory of how a well-functioning system was designed to operate, today.

3. DIVERGENCE IN CENTRALIZED INTERVENTION

Since the 1950's, the two systems in question spanned entirely different trajectories on dimensions of governmental intervention versus reliance on the individual retiree to affect their own fates. Sustained intervention pushed the Greek system toward the brink of collapse; while reliance on open markets has sustained and grown the U.S. system, albeit not without dangers looming. Economic theory teaches that centralized control over free markets, exerted by an institution acting as gatekeeper of information, generates the asymmetric conditions necessary for adverse selection or moral hazard. In the case of Greece, that institution is the government. In the United States, investment consultants/advisers may better fill the role of asymmetric information gatekeepers that cause market disruptions. It is argued that Greece is a case of over-intervention, while the United States is one of under-intervention, as the term applies. A painful disruption in the Greek system cannot be averted without major restructuring.

Between 1935 and 1991 the United States saw the maturity of three distinct pillars of its system for retirement. The U.S. Social Security Act created the predominant pillar. The Social Security system of 1935 extended benefits to those not covered by private pension. Federal matching funds subsidized state old age pension programs and prompted states to either develop a program or increase benefits. After 1950, the Old Age Insurance (OAI) program began to dominate Social Security. It was administered by the federal government and financed by payroll taxes. Retirees (and later, survivors, dependents of retirees, and the disabled) who had paid into the system received benefits. In 1965, the Social Security Act was amended to include Medicare. The Social Security program continued to expand in the 1960s and 1970s. In the early 1980s Congress slowed the growth of Social Security benefits, as the struggling economy introduced the possibility that the program would not pay beneficiaries. However, the Social Security system (pillar I) remains the main source of retirement income for U.S. retirees. The funds that are accumulated in the system are invested in U.S. Treasury bonds, which yield a relatively safe return.

In the post-World War II era, the divergence in government involvement in retirement between the U.S. and the Greek systems continued. In the shadow of the Social Security system in the U.S., the employer-provided pensions continued to grow, while Greece followed a central planning path toward retirement and insurance. The role of gatekeepers on information about the relative performance of invested funds or the professionals who managed retiree funds, remained predominant in both systems. In the United States, investment consultants/advisers issued opinions and published research that greatly influenced the selection of fund managers available to the employee, by the employers offering the 401(k) plans. In Greece, management of retiree funds was ostensibly transferred to the Monetary Authority of Greece's Central Bank, with responsibility over relative performance of funds. Is there some degree of similarity of retiree funds' sloshing around relevant pools of investment opportunities, between the United States and Greece? Importantly, are the roles of Investment Consultant in the U.S. and Central Bank Monetary Authority in Greece, similar as gatekeepers? How are the gatekeepers of retirees' fates regulated and monitored? It is argued that 'responsibility-transfer' of management of funds out of retiree's hands may have similar results across otherwise very dissimilar retirement systems. Let's look at Greece, closely.

At about the same time as the enactment of the U.S. Social Security Act, Greece's retirement system was becoming unofficially nationalized. By the time Greece emerged from World War II and the Civil Conflict of 1949, the system consisted of private insurance funds that operated in various sectors of the economy, and public and semi-public insurance funds, such as IKA, one for civil servants, and another for individual Public Enterprises and Organizations (DEKO). Modern insurance systems consisted of these two sectors, one public and one private. The coverage offered was wide. For example, in addition to supplying a pension, organizations contributed to hospital and pharmaceutical care, childbirth, death, or loss of income due to an accident at work.[7] Private insurance funds were in surplus and functioned as "capitalizers," an idea which, although popular in the United States, appeared as novel. In that sense, pensions granted would be based on accumulated insurance contributions of employees, as well as the returns on investment from such contributions. But the effects of this step in the right direction did not last long (a law registered as 1611/1950 passed). The country's insurance system changed again radically in a way that indelibly marked all its later developments.[8] The truth is that prevailing ideological climate favored the "authoritarian planning of the economy", as well as the restriction of private property and free trade. The aim of the law for retirement was to transfer the management of any surpluses of private and public insurance funds from their administrations to the Bank of Greece, in particular to the Monetary Committee.[9] The law aimed to nationalize those citizens' savings, which in the form of social security contributions were formerly directed to private insurance funds, but without the latter being nationalized operationally, before. The main purpose of the law was to abolish the role of the market in the allocation of savings and by administrative means direct them to those activities which the lawmakers preferred. Between 2016 and 2020, retirement in Greece progressed to a fully nationalized system. The bankruptcy in 2009 and the austerity memoranda issued by the European Common Market that followed, tried to contain spending, and increase the revenues that were all funneled through the same account as that of retirees, managed by the Bank of Greece's Monetary Committee. But none of the necessary restructurings that would put this insurance system on a sustainable path were completed. Eventually, pensions were cut. Later, the so-called 2021 reform imposed another negative change in economic and social conditions in Greece, which led to the abject and extremely damaging failure of the system of supplementary reserve management for pensioners.[10] The reform set up a public legal entity under the name Auxiliary Capital Insurance Fund (TEKA). Employees insured for the first time were mandatorily included, while those insured with the Auxiliary Insurance and Lump Sum Benefits Fund (ETEAEP) and under 35 years in age were optionally covered. The Board of Directors and the Chief Executive Officer were appointed by Greece's Minister of Labor, following open selection procedures based on supposedly transparent and meritocratic criteria. The same applied to all senior executives hired to fill critical technocratic positions. Staff costs, and the first five years of general operating costs, were covered by the public budget. Contributions of the insured are set at 6% accounted for in individual accounts, subject to deductions that could not exceed 1% to cover the operating expenses. Pensions were calculated based on contributions and returns obtained from the management of funds, not by professional portfolio managers, but by the Monetary Authority of the Bank of Greece. Pensions were paid to beneficiaries if they had completed at least 15 years of insurance. Thus, the false remedy for the failure of the public sector in managing its retirement system in Greece appeared to be, more government intervention. But the sloshing of retirees' funds, in and out of the control of impromptu 'investment professionals' with, or without a conflict of interest (a special case of moral hazard), is the focus of this chapter. In the case of government-interventionist Greece, the group of such control appears to be the Monetary Authority of the Bank of Greece (the reader imagines, the Open Market Committee of the Fed, or the Secretary of the Treasury in the U.S., by analogy being tasked to 'manage' the retirement funds of millions of Americans; an absurd proposition). In the case of market-based America, a similar gatekeeping role but to a lesser extent may be played by the not-adequately regulated industry of investment consultants and advisers, according to this author. Similar to the Greek government, whose budgetary inclinations are intertwined with the well-being of retirees, investment consultants may have a vested interest in perpetuating their own 'service to the industry' by issuing opinions or 'ratings' on investment managers, which distort market performance and influence the transfer of funds in and out of 'managers' control in a manner that does not serve retirees, in the U.S. Further research may show that this large, and still largely unregulated investment consulting sector often undertakes undisclosed 'bets' on behalf of plan sponsors, who base their fund-allocation decisions into portfolio managers on research and 'ratings' published by such firms. In yet another manifestation that nature abhors of a vacuum the responsibility-transfer about market performance of retirees' funds invested by portfolio managers shifts from the employer/employee to the investment consultant.

Greece is in the category of "defective democracies", that is, democracies that face structural problems, including the degraded respect for the sovereignty of citizens, difficulty in imposition of property rights due to the unspecified multitude of visible and hidden institutional obstacles, the impenetrable state bureaucracy, and procedures to the point of denial of justice for resolving disputes arising during the execution of private contracts. The nationalization of the retirement system under the 2021 'reform law' points to the inability of the political system to assume the burden of leadership for going ahead with the necessary structural reforms. Authors point to the current legal structure's lack of confidence in the private sector, especially since governments led the country to bankruptcy and the pension system to a dead end.[11] The vague belief is that the Greek state failed to manage insurance contributions and to optimize returns on accumulated reserves. The Greeks blame private markets. Transfer of responsibility to the government served a purpose albeit, not one favoring the retiree. This transfer favored political careers, and generated bribes. The flaws of the system were revealed in the first round of elections in Greece, on May 21, 2023. The culmination of such flaws was the government repo of retiree funds.

4. MORAL HAZARD IN U.S. GOVERNMENT REGULATION

Moral hazard, in the case of management of retiree funds, primarily entails the serving of gatekeepers' own interests ahead of those of retirees, in the face of information disseminated asymmetrically between the respective parties. The information referred to pertains to the safety and soundness of fiduciary activity related to funds accumulated for distribution to retirees. The performance of such funds relative to a benchmark and avoidance of default undertaken in management constitute the primary elements of these activities. The role of gatekeepers in such activities is filled by the investment advisors and consultants, in the free-market-based system of the United States; and by the central bank monetary authority, in the case of an essentially authoritarian system, such as the one in Greece. The ultimate effect in both cases is that fiduciary responsibility is transferred from the employer/employee to the gatekeeper, who in turn, remains largely unregulated and whose decisions are not being challenged. Government in the U.S. has opted for a 'lighter' version of regulating fiduciary responsibility, called the "best-Interest" implemented through the Securities and Exchange Commission, in place of the original "fiduciary rule" of the Department of Labor. While that process may be deemed as less than satisfactory, when compared to Greece, it appears to be the best of both worlds. That is, the U.S. way of handling the fiduciary issue is to tolerate some level of "pay-to-play" (a euphemism for outright bribery of advisors and consultants by investment managers) in the interest of retirees' not having to bear such cost. In the retirement system in Greece, on the other hand, all bets are currently off as far as pinpointing, let alone handling, where fiduciary responsibility lies, as far as the general public is concerned. In the opinion of this author, which may have been verified elsewhere, the Greek electoral body suffers from a chronic case of financial illiteracy. Ideas and perceptions of ownership and use of resources in a free economy (land, labor, capital, and entrepreneurial ability) have been obfuscated in the average mind of people with a legitimate democratic right to vote, through the unending sideswiping of accepted economic theory by communist propaganda. The result is, that everyone and no one, is responsible for lapses of fiduciary duty of funds allotted to the retirement of the Greek public, independent of the myriad other problems associated with the system (some people retire way too early, some receive multiple pensions and others receive benefits that are not linked to years of service or contributions into the system). To the extent that this is an internal, Greek problem, perhaps the reader should not care. But as of the time of this writing, Fitch has evaluated Greek government debt as Investment Grade, a rating similar to that of U.S. Treasury Bonds, into which funds of the U.S. Social Security system, as well as private retirement funds, are invested. Did Fitch take into consideration in rating Greece as Investment Grade, that prior to May 21, 2023, the governing party of Keriakos Mitsotakis, Nea Demokratia, had entered into repurchase agreements of 46 billion of funds belonging to Greek retirees? Otherwise, one may be led to believe that Debt-to-GDP ratios of 200% plus, such as that of Greece can drop to a level of roughly 175% overnight, without a single excessive, ineffectual and unnecessary government official being terminated.[12]

Fiduciary Responsibility

"Fiduciary" is defined as "of the nature of a trust or trusteeship [or] having a value depending on public confidence."[13] In open-market capitalization systems, such as that of the U.S. retirement plans have a number of individuals who act as 'fiduciaries' for the plan. The administration and management of the plans, and the control of the assets into which funds are invested, rest on the discretion of fiduciaries. Fiduciaries include the plan's trustee, investment managers, and the administrator. Fiduciary standards require that the client's interests be put first, that conflict of interest should be avoided, and that the direct and indirect costs of services provided should be reasonable and disclosed. These standards should not require, nor even permit, the agent to depart from prevailing standards of decent behavior. Contractual terms should not claim to override these standards. The present analysis does compare two largely dissimilar retirement systems, the United States to that of Greece. However, at least a common element in the early history of both systems has been that administration and management of funds for retirement rested on a delicate balance of control between employer and employee.

Pension Investment Performance

Across all three pillars of the U.S. Retirement system, the ability of a plan to provide timely benefits, in addition to plan participant contributions, rests on the financial market performance of the assets, into which these contributions are invested. The 'portfolio management' profession in the United States specifically serves the function of maximizing investment returns given risk, for institutional, private-client, and retail (defined contribution) clients. The theory behind practice is vast. Below are elements of the professional portfolio manager practice, in maximizing the performance of assets, into which the funds of retirees are entrusted. Financial advisors/consultants largely act as powerful gatekeepers in this entrusting of retiree funds onto portfolio managers for the purpose of generating competitive returns.

The nucleus of an investment vehicle, given the inherent risk-aversion associated with funds invested, rests with the U.S. bond markets. The objectives of a fixed-income investor are often specified in terms of return and risk. The investment objectives should be expressed quantitatively in terms of some benchmark. The benchmark varies by type of investor. Fixed-income investors are split into two groups based on benchmark characteristics. The first group specifies the benchmark in terms of the investor's liability structure. The investment objective is to generate a cash flow from the fixed-income portfolio that satisfies a liability structure. The second group specifies the benchmark as a particular bond market index. The investment objective is to match the performance of the market index after management fees, or to outperform the index after management fees by a predetermined number of basis points. Investors identify the benchmark to the portfolio manager, ignoring the role of intermediary consultants who strongly affect such decisions. The manager may be employed by the investor or maybe an external manager. Once the investment objective is specified in terms of a benchmark, the performance of a manager will be evaluated relative to that benchmark. Even if a manager is successful in terms of outperforming the benchmark, the client may not realize its investment objective. A mismatch can occur if the client did not correctly specify a benchmark to reflect its investment needs from a risk, return, and cash flow perspective. If sufficient cash flow is not generated to satisfy pension liabilities, then the failure lies not with the manager but with the client's inability to specify an appropriate benchmark.[14] An issue with benchmark selection and benchmark-relative performance of portfolios is that Quantitative Easing, implemented by the Federal Reserve in response to the 2008 crisis, has introduced kurtosis in portfolio returns.[15] The industry-used measures of Sharpe Ratio or Information Ratio, do not account for such deviations from normality. Thus, while manager outperformance, i.e., 'alpha,' can be ascertained when market rates are stable, a regime-switch, of the kind that consultants may latently bet on through evaluations and ratings, may completely slip through the cracks, that is, may not be adequately captured by such portfolio performance metrics. With actual risk not captured by performance metrics discussed with clients, investment consultants have the incentive to push retiree funds into tail-risk to find yield. Meanwhile, retirees remain unaware that funds intended for their retirement are handled this way.

The current shape of the U.S. Treasury yield curve offers support for "market segmentation," a known variant of the preferred habitat theory of the yield curve. Based on the preferred habitat theory, any shape for the yield curve is possible, even one that justifies a perpetual 'barbell trade.' This theoretical aspect of rates should be of concern to investment managers and consulting intermediaries. In the recently ended environment of low interest rates induced by Quantitative Easing, and zero-inflation in the pre-COVID era, any bet that rates would rise could result in sustained fund under-performance, relative to a benchmark. Information gatekeepers of any kind prefer to keep such bets as undisclosed, hoping instead that rates rose 'unexpectedly' and that their 'forward-looking' ratings proved efficacious. The U.S. regulatory framework holds no provision for advisors' disclosing their own latent market bets.

Constraints Imposed by Institutional Investors

In the free-market economy of the United States, retiree accounts with funds intended to be distributed as benefits and their plan sponsors are often referred to as 'clients,' of investment management entities upon which such funds are entrusted. Such clients have specific market performance objectives. Thus, they impose constraints on the investment patterns and behavior of the portfolio managers. Financial advisors and consultants fall right in the middle between institutional clients and portfolio managers, offering services of 'rating' or evaluating the performance of portfolio managers. Their clients are the same institutional investor retiree account sponsors, the decisions of whom are affected by advice and other services sold to them by said advisers/consultants. This structure primarily describes the private, market-based pillars of defined benefit and defined contribution plans, in the United States. In the case of Social Security (the first pillar), funds are investment in the safest of assets, i.e., U.S. Treasury bonds. Examples of constraints a client might impose are a maximum allocation of funds to a particular issuer or industry, a minimum acceptable credit rating for issues eligible for purchase, minimum and maximum duration for the portfolio, whether leverage is permitted, whether shorting is permitted, and limitations on the use of derivative instruments (futures, options, swaps, caps, and floors).

Investment Advisors and the Department of Labor's Fiduciary Rule

Finance literature and regulatory scrutiny on investment advising have historically been concerned with the recommendations of portfolio strategies offered by consulting firms to their institutional clients.[16] Consulting firms serve as 'regulating' gatekeepers for flows of assets under management (AUM) in and out of portfolios. Recommendations are revealed through the ratings maintained by research advisory teams available in their on-line platforms. A weak point in this whole portfolio manager-consultant-retirement account structure in the U.S. is that in place of the investor-public, whose welfare they safeguard, consulting firms produce recommendations that serve the interests of the evaluated portfolio managers. Consulting firms "supply" the rating schemes of portfolios to institutional investors. The schemes drive the allocation of funds of institutional clients, such as retiree accounts, endowments, foundations, etc. Online platforms augment face-to-face interaction with clients. Consulting firms earn a fee for providing such service to their institutional clients. Generating excess fees for participation in such platforms creates 'adverse selection' in the sense that institutional clients are led into selecting portfolio managers that do not outperform their benchmark. These classifications of portfolios imposed as 'ratings' by consultants reveal intended distortions in the relation between tactical and strategic investment, acting as substitutes in generating returns. Excessive registration fees for investment 'forums' offered by consulting firms serve as under-the-table payments of the rated portfolio managers toward investment consultants. But the U.S. Securities and Exchange Commission, in conjunction with the U.S. Department of Labor has gone through rounds of regulatory initiatives in combating this issue.

The first official undertaking of U.S. regulators to contain the issue of gatekeepers driving the system astray came in 2016 under the Obama Administration, with the Department Labor's Fiduciary Rule. Interestingly, it was under the definition of "investment advice fiduciary" of the Employee Retirement Income Security Act of 1974 (ERISA) that the Department of Labor attempted to expand its regulatory authority and curb the problem of under-the-table payment by investment management firms, toward the consulting/advising firms who 'rated' the relative performance of said firms, supposedly objectively. The Department of Labor simply expanded prohibited transaction exemptions for investment activities. Before the Rule, investment advisors were not considered as fiduciaries. Kickbacks, such as exorbitant registration fees for investment 'forums' by consulting firms, were not only legal, but common practice. The reader may hopefully see the analogy between the fiduciary responsibilities usurped by the Greek government in the name of condemning market mechanisms in general (described below), and the responsibilities voluntarily entrusted by the plan sponsors upon the largely unregulated investment consulting industry, generating excess fees and under the table payments for its otherwise taking undisclosed bets with the money of unsuspecting retirees. Despite starts and stops, the U.S. system still attempts to effectively regulate the 'gatekeeper' issue, as it relates to funds intended for the retiree:

- The Investment Advisors Act of as early as 1940 held advisors/consultants to a fiduciary standard. However, that standard was not as high as that of fiduciary responsibility under ERISA of 1974.
- ERISA's Title I had already protected employee benefit plans when on April 2016, the DOL published its rule, which expanded regulation of conflicts of interest in the market for retirement investment.
- ERISA's Title II did not allow for preemption of state law. Advisors/consultants were not subject to loyalty and prudence duties, which fell under state law. The fiduciary rule addressed this lapse.

President Trump tried to have the law rescinded.[17] The broker-dealer profession pushed back on the law, citing that "ample evidence in the record to warrant materially revising or rescinding the Fiduciary Rule, and [the possibility that] the Fiduciary Rule Re-evaluation Study will clearly articulate the need to modify the current form of the Fiduciary Rule or eliminate it all together." The rule had invited unprecedented litigation exposure and forced institutions to make immediate, harmful, and sweeping changes to their businesses, operations, and compliance policies and procedures. The DOL's approach to this rulemaking in this regard was critiqued to be hasty, counterintuitive and irresponsible, causing irreparable harm (please refer to the directive signed by President Trump, in the following page).

It is reasonable to assume that, under the rule, consultants' and advisers' registration fees received from investment forums would be disclosed to clients, who could verify the impact of their own transfer of responsibility. The fact that investment forum gatherings entailed an attendance fee in the tens of thousands of dollars per participant, paid by investment management firms, would not constitute new news to attending plan sponsors. But commonplace knowledge of these transfers would constitute grounds for litigation by the retiring public. Potential conflict of interest entailed that consulting firms rated higher the investment managers who routinely attended the forums. But the three-judge panel at the 5th U.S. Circuit Court of Appeals in New Orleans vacated the fiduciary rule. It was a 2-1 decision, saying the DOL had allegedly exceeded its legal authority. After that, allowing fiduciary advisors to receive compensation directly from mutual fund companies, albeit with certain restrictions, had meant supposedly, that institutional investors managing retiree funds did not pay out of their own pocket for advice, which might otherwise be unaffordable for them, supporters of a revised guidance alleged.

SEC Regulation Best Interest (Reg. BI)

It is important to note, especially in contrast to the retirement system in Greece that regulators did not sit with their hands crossed after the repeal of the Fiduciary Rule. In June 2019, the U.S. Securities and Exchange Commission adopted a new regulation called "Regulation Best Interest." This SEC regulatory package fell under the Securities Exchange Act of 1934 and established a standard of conduct for broker-dealers and other persons associated, called "best interest" toward the well-being of investor/retirees. In addition, under the Investment Advisers Act of 1940, Reg. BI required investment consultants to furnish Form CRS, a summary of its relationships with other business entities, to retail investors.

Figure 1.

Accordingly, by the authority vested in me as President by the Constitution and the laws of the United States of America, I hereby direct the following:

Section 1. *Department of Labor Review of Fiduciary Duty Rule.*

(a) You are directed to examine the Fiduciary Duty Rule to determine whether it may adversely affect the ability of Americans to gain access to retirement information and financial advice. As part of this examination, you shall prepare an updated economic and legal analysis concerning the likely impact of the Fiduciary Duty Rule, which shall consider, among other things, the following:

(i) Whether the anticipated applicability of the Fiduciary Duty Rule has harmed or is likely to harm investors due to a reduction of Americans' access to certain retirement savings offerings, retirement product structures, retirement savings information, or related financial advice;

(ii) Whether the anticipated applicability of the Fiduciary Duty Rule has resulted in dislocations or disruptions within the retirement services industry that may adversely affect investors or retirees; and

(iii) Whether the Fiduciary Duty Rule is likely to cause an increase in litigation, and an increase in the prices that investors and retirees must pay to gain access to retirement services.

(b) If you make an affirmative determination as to any of the considerations identified in subsection (a)-or if you conclude for any other reason after appropriate review that the Fiduciary Duty Rule is inconsistent with the priority identified earlier in this memorandum-then you shall publish for notice and comment a proposed rule rescinding or revising the Rule, as appropriate and as consistent with law.

[...]

Donald J. Trump

Risk-Taking and Front-Running the Federal Reserve

The inter-play between retiree-relying on market outperformance and financial advisor/consultants' feathering their own nest while evading fiduciary responsibility might still have dire consequences. Evidence shows that central bank intervention in the form of Quantitative Easing (QE) raises tail risk-taking by the same portfolio managers who were entrusted with the task of generating outperformance on retirement accounts.[18] Front-running of the Fed's intervention has become a tactical element in the investment management process, generating fictitious 'alpha' for institutional investor accounts. Front running is generally prohibited for profits from nonpublic information. Following interviews in 2012 and 2013, the FBI said front running had resulted in profits of $50 million to $100 million. Wall Street traders have manipulated a key derivatives market by front running Fannie Mae and Freddie Mac ahead of the 2008 financial crisis. Even financial standards have been misapplied to hide the bursting of the bubble in real estate, at that time.[19] But investment advisor recommendations accentuate tail-risk investing in general, thereby not identifying true skill through their own rating on investment portfolio strategies. Investment consulting firms sell such ratings for a fee, to their institutional investor clients, all under the auspices of non-enforceable fiduciary responsibility, and with the known practice of receiving kickbacks for recommending to clients, investment firms that willfully take part in such schemes. The ultimate fear is that retirees who saw their house-value plummet in 2008 may grow leery. Unable to discern a stable regulatory environment, they may panic and sell assets, generating a cascaded market decline.

5. FINANCIAL ILLITERACY IN THE CASE OF THE GREEK VOTER

The U.S. Government continuously attempts to regulate the retirement industry, despite its starts and stops. For the retirement system in Greece, all bets are off as far as pinpointing fiduciary responsibility. In the opinion of this author, verified elsewhere, the Greek voter who just participated in the national elections of May 21 has been suffering from chronic financial illiteracy, combined with a documented Syndrome of Stockholm, according to which Greek voters have developed a psychological bond with their 'captors' that represent the two primary, opposing parties.[20] For most, voting for the conservative party of Nea Demokratia is the only way to avoid ruling by the communist party, Zyriza. For others, the social benefits offered by the currently ruling Nea Demokratia serves as the sole indication that social pensions in Greece will not be cut further; even as such cutting was not at the discretion of any party. For sure, ruling by a communist regime in any economy is a recipe for disaster. But voting for the party not mnemonically associated with pension cuts places the whole retirement system in graver danger.

Continuous Warnings

Mr. Alekos Papadopoulos is a politician and ex-minister, including of finance, between 1993 and 2002. As early as the mid-1990's Papadopoulos predicted that Greece would end up bankrupt sooner or later:

My concerns began in 1996, when I was the Minister of Finance. I saw that the rapid rise in public debt was out of control – mainly due to the banks' high rate of lending, but also the size of the public sector. Particularly after 1998, when Greece entered the exchange-rate system and there was a sharp decline in interest rates. The fact that since we entered the Eurozone in 2001 all attempts at strengthening the Greek economy were abandoned didn't help. Unfortunately, after 2002, most attempts at reform were stopped by the Kostas Simitis' government of which I was a part. Then, New Democracy took over the government of the country in 2004 and there was actually an acceleration in public debt. Now, combine that with the extremely high deficit of the current account – which eventually became the largest in the world. Things were destined to end up like this.[21]

On May 9, 2023 Papadopoulos caused a pre-election uproar concerning the fact that, under the regime of Nea Demokratia the Greek economy had come just one step before destruction.[22] His concerns were:

- The publicized primary surplus of 273 million euros in 2022 versus other, "insufficiently promoted or completely suppressed" fiscal data of concern and importance. In his view, both public debt (**171.3%** of GDP) and government debt (192.4% of GDP) was highest since Greece's entry into the euro area.
- Public debt (to lenders other than government) and government debt itself was 356 and 400 billion euros, respectively. Public debt was made smaller through government borrowing from the Bank of Greece (a government entity) of 46.7 billion euros on December 21, 2022, five months before.
- Papadopoulos questions the legitimacy for the Nea Demokratia government's borrowing through repurchase agreements, of employees' contributions, for purposes of replenishing deficient cash facilities, but most importantly, for creating an announced accounting reduction of public debt.
- Law 4387/2016, which concentrated management of all retirement accounts under the Bank of Greece, had as stated purpose to "ensure pension adequacy and sustainability of the national social security and pension systems and the Electronic National Social Security Agency.[23]

The Fitch Rating

In January 2023, after Nea Demokratia's repo (repurchase agreement) of Greek employee contributions toward social security of December 2022, Fitch upgraded Greece's sovereign debt to a BB+/Stable rating and on May 10, much shortly before elections of May 21, the rating agency Fitch hailed Greece's "2023 Stability Programme" as strengthening the agency's view that "the debt ratio will continue to fall over the medium term."[24] "The 2022 outturns reported in the Stability Programme were even better than Fitch's estimates, with headline and primary balances beating expectations stated in our March Sovereign Data Comparator by more than one percentage point (pp)," Fitch concluded. Was that true?

The reader will recognize that 171.3% in the quote below, as coinciding with the 'public debt' number of the first bulleted concern of Minister Papadopoulos, above. Thus, further down, the Fitch report stated:

Nevertheless, the Stability Programme underscores the authorities' broad commitment to fiscal prudence. Greece benefited from a strong snowball effect in 2022, given very high nominal growth and only a modest increase in average interest rate costs, with debt-to-GDP falling by over 23pp, to ***171.3%*** *of GDP (compared to the Eurozone average of 91.6%), which is below the pre-pandemic level. Smaller-than-projected primary surpluses would not derail debt reduction. We expect the debt ratio to fall more slowly over the medium term, and think it is unlikely to go as low as 135.2% in 2026, as projected in the Stability Programme.*

It is obvious that Fitch was unaware of the repurchase agreement of retiree funds in place of Nea Demokratia's borrowing in the open markets, when entering the new BB+/Stable rating. Yet the voices of dissent to Mr. Papadopoulos' valid concerns, usually from people with lesser qualifications, have been bitter with a revealed sense of confusion about basic economic principles. I will discuss a few of them.

Greece as an Underdeveloped Country

The contemporary novices in economic theory, emboldened by the miss-rating of Greek debt by Fitch, have additionally argued that Greece had enjoyed the highest growth rates in GNP among countries of the Eurozone, even higher than those of Italy. Of course, communist propaganda always manages to trip over its own feet, by engraining into public opinion non-truths, such as "entrepreneurship is capitalism." In fact, if an economy has four factors of production, land, labor, capital and entrepreneurial ability, the only person who often lacks capital is the entrepreneur. Communist 'theory' lacks an understanding that financial capital and productive-capacity capital cannot be easily divorced, as the entrepreneur needs one to acquire the other. But additionally in the Greek mind, the notion that capital divided by labor determines wages is foreign. To the average Greek, a ditch digger working with a shovel and a German assembly-line worker operating a robot, should be paid the same based on this author's recent talks. So, by demonizing capitalism, and thus hindering the amassing of enough capital to raise capacity and lift wages, communist mindsets in Greece betray the sole purpose of their propaganda, i.e., support of the labor class. In fact, communist thinking, which to some degree prevails in every Greek's mind, is a sure-fire guarantee to keep wages depressed, forever. In the midst of these downward pressures, instead of enlightening the public on truly lower taxation, a smaller government sector and a free economy, the party of Nea Demokratia attempted to support wages artificially, exacerbating unemployment. Right before elections on May 21, again, Nea Demokratia raised the minimum wage by 9.4% to 780 euros a month, despite persistent inflation in Greece. Which countries of the Eurozone is Greece similar to? Data for growth was obtained from the spring 2023 Economic Forecast of the European Commission.[25] Simple 5-means clustering analysis, based on current and projected GDP growth, shows that Greece (BB+) belongs in the same cluster as Croatia (BBB), Cyprus (BBB), Portugal (BBB+), Slovenia (A), Spain (A-) and Poland (A-). In contrast, Italy (BBB) belongs in a cluster with Austria (AA+), Belgium (AA-), Latvia (A-), Netherlands (AAA), Bulgaria (BBB), Denmark (AAA), and Hungary (BBB). The reader will ascertain that the cluster that contains Greece, has no countries rated by Fitch as A and above, in contrast to the one that contains Italy (please refer to Appendix B for a brief explanation of Cluster Analysis). Also, based on Principal Component Analysis (PCA) of the numbers from the European Commission, the component with the highest eigenvalue, explaining 86% of the total variation in country growth, shows GDP growth as consistently down among the years of 2022, 2023 and 2024 for Greece, Portugal, Croatia, Cyprus, Romania, Spain, Slovenia and Poland. Based on Fitch projections, this cluster appears to be converging.

The Solow Growth Model

Explanation of the above must start with the well-known economic fact that rapid GDP growth is often associated with countries that start from a very low capital-labor ratio (k), as opposed to economies that have high ratios and are closer to an equilibrium growth rate. The countries in the cluster that contain Greece, exhibit this characteristic, as is shown below. This section discusses Prof. Robert Solow and his "Contribution to the Theory of Economic Growth" published in 1957.[26] Briefly, the framework of the model rests on capital and labor, specifically, the ratio of capital per labor (the number of robots each worker uses, for example). In Greece the ratio is low and thus, any increase will make the rate of growth in Gross Domestic Product (GDP) jump. To the dismay of critics of Papadopoulos's letter, high growth rates do not betray an economy with higher levels of per-capita- GDP. And even to a communist, that should make sense. Capital as a resource, like all resources, has diminishing returns. Additional capital generates smaller and smaller additions to output as the capital-labor ratio increases. Having started from the very bottom of the pack, as Greece has, should hardly be a reason to celebrate. Formally, in the neoclassical model, capital (K) and labor (L) are combined to produce output (Q), in a production function that is linearly homogeneous (has constant returns to scale), has positive marginal products and has diminishing returns to inputs. Output per Labor depends on the capital-labor ratio (*k*):[27]

$$Q = f(K,L)$$

$$f_K = MPP_K > 0 \text{ and } f_L = MPP_L > 0$$

$$f_{KK} < 0 \text{ and } f_{LL} < 0$$

$$\frac{Q}{L} = f\left(\frac{K}{L}\right) \textit{ stated as } q = \varphi(k)$$

To the extent that a country's population is not distinguished from the labor resource, the last equation states per-capita income (*Q/L*) as a function of the capital-labor ratio (*K/L*). Increasing the capital/labor ratio *k* raises per capita income, but at a decreasing rate. Thus, there are diminishing returns to *k*, the capital/labor ratio. As a result, average physical product of labor (per-capita income) increases at a decreasing rate with *k*. Solow assumes that a constant proportion (*s*) of output Q is invested, net of depreciation and that the labor force grows exponentially. The Solow growth model is thus derived.

$$MPP_K \equiv \frac{\partial Q}{\partial K} = L\varphi'(k)\frac{1}{L} = \varphi'(k) > 0$$

$$f_{KK} = \frac{\partial^2 Q}{\partial K^2} = \frac{\partial}{\partial K}\left[\varphi'(k)\right] = \varphi'' < 0$$

$$\dot{K} = sQ = sL\varphi(k) \textit{ and } \dot{L} = \lambda L$$

$$k \equiv \frac{K}{L} \Rightarrow K = kL \Rightarrow \dot{K} = L\dot{k} + k\lambda L$$

Solow Growth Model: $\dot{k} = s\varphi(k) - \lambda k$

The Method of K-Means Clustering (K = 5)

The Solow Growth Model implies that an economy is in equilibrium when the level of investment into productive (and financial) capital *sf*(*k*) is equal to the growth rate in Labor (or population) times (*k*). Moreover, at low levels of the capital/labor ratio *k*, growth in per capital income (and thus GDP, holding population constant) is much higher, due to the fact that countries (such as Greece and others in the cluster discussed) start from a very low point in that ratio. High GDP growth rates characterize countries that are relatively underdeveloped. In the case of the European Union, the upper echelon of countries has the lowest growth rates in GDP. Theoretically then, this first cluster is closer to their steady state.

Thus, for the purpose of this analysis, the growth rates in GDP for 28 countries were collected from the spring 2023 Economic Forecast of the European Commission, for 2022, 2023 and 2024 as projected. This data was analyzed through the method of k-means clustering, where the number of clusters was set to k=5, arbitrarily (k here is not the same as the capital/labor ratio *k*, in the Solow Growth model). The five clusters, with their average growth rates in each year, are shown below. These clusters are not listed in any particular order. The reader will notice that cluster 1 has the lowest average growth rates in all three years, and it also contains the 'heavy lifters' of productive capacity, i.e., France, Germany, etc. All these lowest growth rates mean is that these economies are closer to an equilibrium or 'steady state' growth rate in the capital/labor ratio. They are growing just as fast as they can, or as fast as their growth in population allows. This point appears to confuse many of the critics of Papadopoulos' letter, which in turn critiques the practices of the Nea Demokratia regime. Such critics of Papadopoulos' letter (who, for obvious reasons are not quoted here) state there is nothing wrong with the Greek economy, look how fast it is growing (see cluster 5, in the next page below). Some, even contend that it was the COVID pandemic that slowed down economic growth in the underdeveloped cluster of the Eurozone (not true).

The truth is that Greece's cluster had made no relative progress in GDP growth, among all nations of the Eurozone. Below I rank the arbitrary five clusters by their average growth rate in each year, relying on the simplifying assumption that the production function that links the capital/labor ratio *k* to per capita output and income is one and the same, across all economies of the Eurozone. It is obvious that Greece fell in the middle of the pack in 2022 and is projected to do the same in 2023 and 2024. Thus, claims that Greece or its cluster in general has done so much better than the rest of the Eurozone are, again, off the mark. Italy's cluster four, on the other hand, has moved 'up' to replace that of Germany, as one that is closest to its equilibrium steady state, based on Fitch projections. Equating Greece to Italy (critics of Papadopoulos say, Greece's having surpassed Italy) is not only dreaming, but economic hubris. Tables 2 and 3 below show that the 'Greece' cluster (the one that contains Greece) ranked third among clusters of all countries in the union. Table 4 shows that, while Greece remains in the third, the 'Italy' cluster is projected to surpass that of 'Germany.' Figure 2 provides a combined picture of tables 2, 3 and 4. It is obvious that the 'Italy' cluster is projected to have the lowest per capita GDP growth, which means (and that is the confusing part) that the cluster is closer to its long-run equilibrium growth in GDP according to its population growth. The 'Greece' and other clusters are not at a capital/labor ratio that will bring them close to their own long-run equilibrium. They grow fast, because they start from a very low point. All that holds given that per Fitch, government debt and public debt are lower. Had Fitch accounted for the repo of retiree funds, Greece may have fallen to the lower ranking 'Romania' cluster and growth.

The method of k-means clustering relies (among other methods) on the Euclidean distance in n-space, which in this case is three-dimensional since the years of 2022, 2023 and 2024 are used in conjunction (please refer to Appendix A). The method is referred to as 'unsupervised' and it is often used at the same time as Principal Component Analysis (PCA) to the degree possible (below). PCA here verifies the results of clustering: Greece is like Portugal, Croatia, Cyprus, Spain, Slovenia and Poland; not like Italy.

Table 1. Growth rates in GDP by 5-means cluster, european union

Country	2022	2023	2024	Cluster
Estonia	-1.3	-0.4	3.1	1
Finland	2.1	0.2	1.4	1
France	2.6	0.7	1.4	1
Germany	1.8	0.2	1.4	1
Lithuania	1.9	0.5	2.7	1
Luxembourg	1.5	1.6	2.4	1
Slovakia	1.7	1.7	2.1	1
Czech Republic	2.5	0.2	2.6	1
Sweden	2.6	-0.5	1.1	1
	1.71	0.47	2.02	
Malta	6.9	3.9	4.1	2
Romania	4.7	3.2	3.5	2
	5.80	3.55	3.80	
Ireland	12	5.5	5	3
	12.00	5.50	5.00	
Austria	5	0.4	1.6	4
Belgium	3.2	1.2	1.4	4
Italy	3.7	1.2	1.1	4
Latvia	2.8	1.4	2.8	4
Netherlands	4.5	1.8	1.2	4
Bulgaria	3.4	1.5	2.4	4
Denmark	3.8	0.3	1.5	4
Hungary	4.6	0.5	2.8	4
	3.80	1.04	1.81	
Croatia	6.2	1.6	2.3	5
Cyprus	5.6	2.3	2.7	5
Greece	5.9	2.4	1.9	5
Portugal	6.7	2.4	1.8	5
Slovenia	5.4	1.2	2.2	5
Spain	5.5	1.9	2	5
Poland	5.1	0.7	2.7	5
	5.77	1.79	2.23	

Table 2. Ranked growth in per capita income (starting at 1.000) for year 2022

Rank	Cluster	2022	Growth
0	0		1.0000
1	3	12%	1.1200
2	2	6%	1.1850
3	5	6%	1.2533
4	4	4%	1.3010
5	1	2%	1.3232

Table 3. Ranked growth in per capita income (starting at 1.000) for year 2022

Rank	Cluster	2023	Growth
0	0		1.0000
1	3	6%	1.0550
2	2	4%	1.0925
3	5	2%	1.1120
4	4	1%	1.1235
5	1	0%	1.1288

Table 4. Ranked growth in per capita income (starting at 1.000) for year 2022

Rank	Cluster	2024	Growth
0	0		1.0000
1	3	5%	1.0500
2	2	4%	1.0899
3	5	2%	1.1142
4	1	2%	1.1367
5	4	2%	1.1573

Figure 2. Ranked growth in per capita income for years 2022, 2023, and 2024

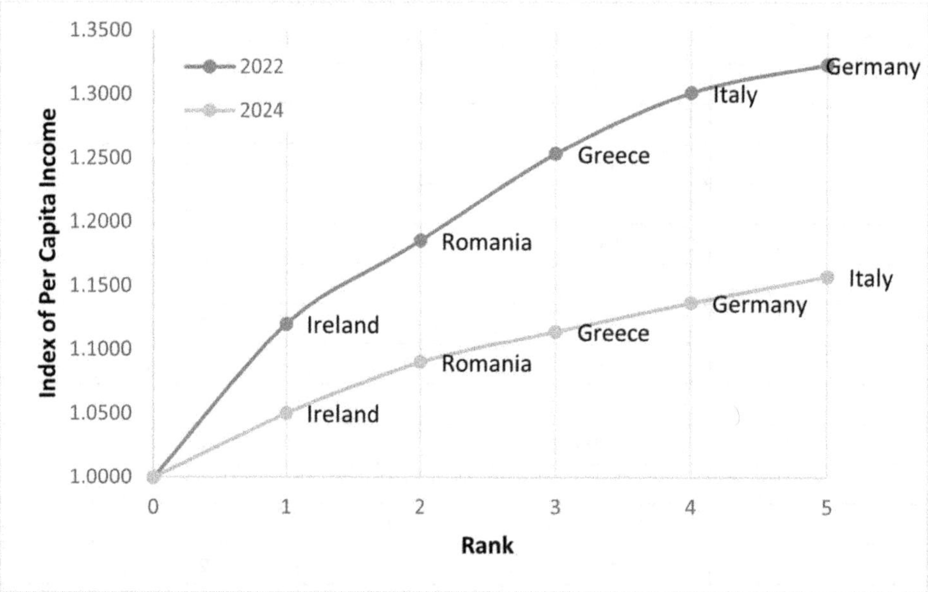

Principal Components of Growth Rates in GDP

This other 'unsupervised' method of examining growth rate data in Europe directs attention to the ways in which years of growth across all countries are correlated. The method finds dimensions of variability that have more meaning than the original variables. A full mathematical treatment is beyond scope. The principal components are linear combinations of the original three variables (growth rates for 2022, those of 2023, and those for 2024). Finding these dimensions requires an optimization algorithm. If the original variables are a matrix $\boldsymbol{X}$, and the square matrix with which they are multiplied in order to be changed into principal components is $\boldsymbol{P}$, the components themselves are $\boldsymbol{X}$ times $\boldsymbol{P}$. Matrix $\boldsymbol{P}$ is called the matrix of eigenvectors, while $\boldsymbol{\Lambda}$ is the matrix of eigenvalues. We denote the covariance matrix of the original variables as $\boldsymbol{\Omega}$. The covariance matrix of the principal components is $\boldsymbol{P}^{T}\boldsymbol{\Omega}\,\boldsymbol{P}$, where superscript 'T' denotes 'transposed.' The PCA method seeks to find vector $\boldsymbol{P}$ that makes the new covariance $\boldsymbol{P}^{T}\boldsymbol{\Omega}$ $\boldsymbol{P}$ equal to matrix, $\boldsymbol{\Lambda}$. In $\boldsymbol{\Lambda}$, elements off the diagonal capture covariance between components, while elements on the diagonal show the variance of components. The former are zero, while the latter are the largest possible in descending order. Components capture the largest uncorrelated variation in data.

Given a variable matrix $\boldsymbol{X}$ and its covariance matrix $\boldsymbol{\Omega}$, the PCA method finds a matrix of eigenvectors $\boldsymbol{P}$ so that $\boldsymbol{P}^{T}\boldsymbol{\Omega}\,\boldsymbol{P} = \boldsymbol{\Lambda}$, where $\boldsymbol{\Lambda}$ is a diagonal matrix of eigenvalues. The eigenvalues are, in essence, just the variances of each of the principal components. The covariance between components (the off-diagonal elements in $\boldsymbol{\Lambda}$), are zero, because components are uncorrelated. The algorithm to derive $\boldsymbol{P}$ is as follows:

1. Maximize the total variance of $\boldsymbol{X}$ with respect to the first vector in $\boldsymbol{P}$, subject to the constraint that the length of that first (eigen)vector is equal to one.
2. Maximize the total variance of $\boldsymbol{X}$ with respect to the second vector in $\boldsymbol{P}$, subject to constraints that its length is also equal to one, and that its dot-product with the first (eigen)vector is zero.
3. Maximize total variance in $\boldsymbol{X}$ with respect to the third vector in $\boldsymbol{P}$, subject to the constraints that its length is one, and its dot-product with both the first and the second (eigen)vectors are zero.

To reiterate, the goal of this analysis is to find patterns among European countries, given their current and projected growth rates in GDP. The latest warning letter by Papadopoulos has caused all kinds of responses that grouped Greece with other countries in the Union based on simple arithmetic; and after having betrayed significant lack of understanding of basic economics. Data analysis, such as is presented here, is the scientific method for detecting patterns that otherwise, would only be expressed as opinion.

Table 5 below shows the way that the three original values (i) growth across all countries in 2022, (ii) growth across all countries in 2023, and (iii) growth across all countries in 2024, are multiplied by, what are 'weights' to arrive at principal components of the three original variables. The process of naming these components is always controversial. But based on the numbers in the table, I have named the three components as 'Down' (growth rates are less and less positive across the three years), 'DnUp' (growth rates were negative in 2022 but are projected as positive later), and 'Butterfly' (positive in 2022, projected negative in 2023, but projected positive in 2024). These patterns are 'hidden' in the data. And based on the eigenvalues of the data, the first component of 'Down' explains 86% of the total variation. That means that the phenomenon of growth rates being positive but going down over time (thus, the respective economies' approaching long-run equilibrium growth) is most prevalent in the data. Second most prevalent is the pattern of growth rates being negative in the past but projected to be positive. The third pattern is that of rates projected as negative in 2023, but positive in 2024. That is dangerous.

Table 5. Eigenvectors of principal components of growth rates in Europe

	PC1	PC2	PC3
2022	-0.8866	-0.4121	0.2100
2023	-0.4208	0.5304	-0.7360
2024	-0.1919	0.7409	0.6436
	Down	**DnUp**	**Butterfly**
Variance Explained:	86%	10%	4%

When growth is ranked based on the value of component 'Down' European countries split again into groups whose component value is less than -5, those between -3 and -5, and those less than -3 (see table in next page). This component captures the phenomenon of fast-lifting out of communist-style low capital/labor ratios and convergence toward long-run equilibrium. Greece is in the first third of countries that still appear to have a long way to go, even if Fitch projections which, as discussed to not take into account everything, come true. Estonia is the only country with the lowest 'Down' in growth rates value. Estonia appears to have reached its equilibrium growth rate in capital/labor, ahead of everyone else. To the sustained dismay of critics of the Papadopoulos letter Italy is in a cluster other than that of Greece.[28] Had Table 6 been ranked by the second component 'DnUp' (growth rate was down but projected as up), Greece would indeed appear as similar to Portugal, Italy, Netherlands, Croatia, Slovenia, Spain, Poland. But that component only 'happens' 10% of the time, as opposed to the first one (86% of the time). Not enough to sustain that Papadopoulos' fears were off, and that Greece was like Italy. Interestingly the third component (growth was up, then down, but is projected up) clusters Greece and Poland together. One might be better off forecasting growth when looking for patterns of similarity between these two economies. It is noted that third components often capture non-linear events, such as bubble-bursting.

The reader can re-sort the above table with respect to columns DnUp and Butterfly, to help establish the claim that Greece would be similar to Italy only 10% of the time, and that the most damaging, non-linear or regime-switching risk to the Eurozone is that Greece most likely aligns with Poland. Further research may go deeper into the similarities of Greece, with Poland. At the present time and for the record, this author fully expects that news about the repurchase agreement of retiree funds into the public debt of Greece, in place of open markets, will be revealed and Greece's rating will drop. The Greek repo was not the same as the U.S. Social Security funds being invested in U.S. Treasury bonds. Market performance of Greek bonds has been supported by the European Union, whom Greece effectively fools by repo-ing out retiree funds, using as collateral the same bonds that are supported by the Union. This is more like mad cow disease, or a pyramid scheme. Nobody knows the fully unsupported value of Greek bonds. In 2010, when Greece defaulted, yields reached a twenty-handle percent and bond values plummeted.

Table 6. Ranking of european growth rates based on first component (down)

Category	2022	2023	2024	Down	DnUp	Butterfly
Ireland	12	5.5	5	-13.91	1.68	1.69
Malta	6.9	3.9	4.1	-8.55	2.26	1.22
Portugal	6.7	2.4	1.8	-7.30	-0.15	0.80
Croatia	6.2	1.6	2.3	-6.61	0.00	1.60
Greece	5.9	2.4	1.9	-6.61	0.25	0.70
Cyprus	5.6	2.3	2.7	-6.45	0.91	1.22
Romania	4.7	3.2	3.5	-6.19	2.35	0.88
Spain	5.5	1.9	2	-6.06	0.22	1.04
Slovenia	5.4	1.2	2.2	-5.71	0.04	1.67
Poland	5.1	0.7	2.7	-5.33	0.27	2.29
Netherlands	4.5	1.8	1.2	-4.98	-0.01	0.39
Austria	5	0.4	1.6	-4.91	-0.66	1.79
Hungary	4.6	0.5	2.8	-4.83	0.44	2.40
Bulgaria	3.4	1.5	2.4	-4.11	1.17	1.15
Italy	3.7	1.2	1.1	-4.00	-0.07	0.60
Denmark	3.8	0.3	1.5	-3.78	-0.30	1.54
Belgium	3.2	1.2	1.4	-3.61	0.36	0.69
Latvia	2.8	1.4	2.8	-3.61	1.66	1.36
France	2.6	0.7	1.4	-2.87	0.34	0.93
Czech Republic	2.5	0.2	2.6	-2.80	1.00	2.05
Slovakia	1.7	1.7	2.1	-2.63	1.76	0.46
Luxembourg	1.5	1.6	2.4	-2.46	2.01	0.68
Lithuania	1.9	0.5	2.7	-2.41	1.48	1.77
Sweden	2.6	-0.5	1.1	-2.31	-0.52	1.62
Finland	2.1	0.2	1.4	-2.21	0.28	1.19
Germany	1.8	0.2	1.4	-1.95	0.40	1.13
Estonia	-1.3	-0.4	3.1	0.73	2.62	2.02

6. SUMMARY AND CONCLUSION

The U.S. retirement system comprises Social Security, DB, and DC plans. Social Security provides resources to retirees of all income groups with higher replacement rates for lower-earning households. Employer-sponsored retirement plans (private-sector and government employer plans, as well as DB and DC plans) and IRAs provide retirement to 80 percent of near-retiree households. The U.S. system generally is successful at allowing most households to maintain their standard of living in retirement. The Greek retirement system, on the other hand, has pillars that are not succinctly identified, have been permeated by disastrous government intervention and may be near a state of unofficial, but impending bankruptcy. An element of commonality between these two otherwise dissimilar systems is the transfer of responsibility for the management of funds and the optimization of performance that comprises the basis for benefits received by retirees. In both systems at start, responsibility for management and optimization rested within the relation between the employer and the employee. In both systems, as the government became gradually involved in ratifying agreements between two groups, responsibility was transferred to separate entities that developed their own set of initiatives and priorities. In the case of Greece, management (as well as custody) of retiree funds fell under the control of the Central Bank, with the pressures exerted by new governments, of which Greece's is not the best known for its ability to balance budgets. In the case of the U. S., regulation with ERISA in the 1970's pushed responsibility toward consultants and advisors, who function as unregulated gatekeepers. Given the current market environment, these entities can negatively affect retiree funds. The combination of no succinct fiduciary responsibility for consultants with QE-induced tail-risk taking may entice large-scale liquidation of assets backing the market performance of retirement accounts. But funds of the U.S. Social Security system, as well as private retirement funds, have always run into the safety of investing into U.S. Treasury bonds.

In contrast to the United States, where the financial market performance of fund assets determines plan benefits, funds intended for retirees in Greece are primarily used for the purpose of manipulating public opinion, regarding the soundness of practices engaged in by the current government. An accounting of fiascos engaged in by Greek government since its inception after 1821, let alone since its inclusion into the Eurozone, was beyond the scope of this analysis. But the perceptions of ownership and the use of resources in a free economy (land, labor, capital, and entrepreneurial activity) have been obfuscated in the mind of the average Greek, one with a legitimate democratic right to vote, by unending sideswiping of accepted economic theory by failed communist propaganda. Compared to the system in the United States, the result is that everyone and no one, has a regulatory responsibility for lapses of fiduciary duty of the funds allotted to the retirement of the Greek public. To the extent that this is only an internal, Greek problem, the reader should not care. But private retirement funds offered to the U.S. investor engage into trading of frontier-market, and sub-emerging market bonds, (even after the obvious miss-rating of Greece's government bonds as "Investment Grade"). Fitch rated Greek government debt as almost as that of countries with better fiscal discipline. Prior to elections, Nea Demokratia entered into repurchase agreements of 46 billion of funds of Greek retirees. Debt-to-GDP of 200% dropped to 175% overnight, without a single official fired? Quantitative analysis of growth rates in GDP for countries of the Eurozone shows that Greece belongs in the group of lowest capital/labor ratios. As a result, any and all increases in capital, even the kind backed by hidden repo agreements, will correspond to growth that is in the highest cluster among Eurozone countries (critics of Papadopoulos got that part backwards). Greece is in the same spot in the Eurozone, as Portugal, Croatia, Cyprus, Spain, Slovenia and Poland.

7. REFERENCES

Alexander, J. (2022). *Prosperity Post-Pandemic*. Australian Strategic Policy Institute.

Amaglobeli, D., Gaspar, V., & Dabla-Norris, E. (2020). *Getting Older by Not Poorer*. International Monetary Fund.

Baily, M. N., Klein, A., & Schardin, J. (2017) *The Impact of the Dodd-Frank Act on Financial Stability and Economic Growth*. Russell Sage Foundation. Bank of Greece. https://www.bankofgreece.gr/enimerosi/grafeio-typoy/

Beveridge, R. A. (2017). *Mortality Differences Between Traditional Medicare and Medicare Advantage*. Sage Publications.

Blakey, R. G. (1926) *The Revenue Act of 1926*. The American Economic Review.

Brady, P., Burham, K., & Holden, S. (2012). *The Success of the U.S. Retirement System*. Investment Company Institute.

Burke, J., & Hung, A. (2015). *Do Financial Advisers Influence Savings Behavior?* Rand Corporation.

Clark, R. L., Craig, L. A., & Wilson, J. W. (2003). *A History of Public Sector Pensions in the United States*. Pension Research Council, Wharton School of the University of Pennsylvania.

Congressional Research Service. (2013) *Individual Retirement Accounts (IRAs): Issues and Proposed Expansion*. CRS Report for Congress RL30255. www.crs.gov

Cook, W. W. (1923). The Mysterious Massachusetts Trusts. *American Bar Association Journal. American Bar Association.*

Costa, D. L. (1998). Evolution of Retirement: An American [University of Chicago Press.]. *Economy and History*, 1880–1990.

Davidson, L. (2016) *The History of Retirement Benefits*. Work Force. https://workforce.com

Department of Treasury. (2021). *Contributions to Individual Retirement Arrangements (IRAs)*. Internal Revenue Service.

Dimiourgia, E. (2023). Liberal Patriots Reformers. *Ethnik Dimiourgia*. https://www.ethnikidimiourgia.gr/

Economy and Finance. (2023) *Spring 2023 Economic Forecast: an improved outlook amid persistent challenges*. European Commission https://economy-finance.ec.europa.eu/economic-forecast-and-surveys/economic-forecasts/spring-2023-economic-forecast-improved-outlook-amid-persistent-challenges_en#documents

Fabozzi, F. J. (2007). *Fixed Income Analysis*. John Wiley & Sons.

Frank, D., & Spencer, B. G. (2008). *What is Retirement? A Review and Assessment of Alternative Concepts and Measures*. McMaster University.

Glasson, W. (1918). *Federal Military Pensions in the United States*. Oxford University Press.

Graebner, W. (1980) *A History of Retirement: The Meaning and Function of an American Institution*. Yale University Press. Greek Law. https://www.elinyae.gr/ethniki-nomothesia/n-28681922-fek-119a-2071922 and https://www.elinyae.gr/ethniki-nomothesia/n-57331932-fek-364a-11101932

Guidolin, M., & Timmermann, A. (2008) *International Asset Allocation Under Regime Switching, Skew and Kurtosis Preferences*. International Labour Organization. https://www.ilo.org/dyn/natlex

Holzman, R., Hinz, R. P., & Dorfman, M. (2008). *Pension Systems and Reform Conceptual Framework*. World Bank.

Jagadeesh, G., & Smellets, K. (2006). *Measuring Social Security's Financial Outlook within an Aging Society*. MIT Press.

James, G., Witten, D., Hastie, T., & Tibshirani, R. (2013). *An Introduction to Statistical Learning with Applications*. Springer, Hellenic Institute of Occupational Health and Safety. https://www.elinyae.gr/ethniki-nomothesia

McGrattan, E. R. (2001). *Taxes, Regulations, and Asset Prices*. Federal Reserve Bank of Minneapolis. doi:10.3386/w8623

Meagher, G., Stebbing, A., & Perche, D. (Eds.). (2022). *Designing Social Service Markets: Risk Regulation and Rent-Seeking*. ANU Press. doi:10.22459/DSSM.2022

Moumtzaki, A. (2018). The Former Minister Who Tried to Warn Greece About the Crisis. *Vice*. https://www.vice.com/sv/article/dp57na/greek-ex-finance-minister-alekos-papadopoulos-interview-876

Nektarios, M., Tinios, P., & Simeonidis, G. (2018) *Pensions for the Young: A Social Insurance System Focused on Growth*. LSE. http://eprints.lse.ac.uk/79268/1/blogs.lse.ac.uk

Olshansky, S. J., Goldman, D. P., & Rowe, J. W. (2015). *Resetting Social Security*. MIT Press. doi:10.1162/DAED_a_00331

Papadopoulos, A. (2023) *The Risks of Embellishing the Fiscal Situation*. Fantomas. https://fantomas.gr/55536-2/

Parsons, J. R. (1962). *The Origins of the Income-and-Resources Amendment to the Social Security Act*. University of Chicago Press. doi:10.1086/641183

Pension Research Council. (2022). Wharton School of Business.

Romig, K., Broaddus, M., & Aron-Dine, A. (2019). *Financial Challenges Facing Social Security and Medicare Largely Unchanged from Last Year, Except for Improvement in Disability Insurance*. Center for Budget and Policy Priorities.

Seburn, P. W. (1991). Evolution of Employer-Provided Defined Benefit Pensions. *Monthly Labor Review*.

Shifflett, C. (1998). *Selected Virginia Statues Relating to Slavery*. Virtual Jamestown.

Sirotaki, A. (2016). *The Insurance System in Greece*. Semantic Scholar.

Solow, R. M. (1957). A Contribution to the Theory of Economic Growth. *The Quarterly Journal of Economics*, 70.

Van Vliet, B., & Xanthopoulos, A. (2016). Iso-Risk: An Analysis of Risk-Taking in Fixed Income Markets. *Applied Economics*, 60.

Whistman, J. (2022) *How Long Does the Average Person Stay at a Job (and How to Increase it)*. Perception Prediction AI. https://www.perceptionpredict.ai

Wire, F. (2023). Greek Stability Programme Underscores Improving. *Public Finance*.

Xanthopoulos, A. (2010). Market Value Signal Extraction and the Misapplication of SFAS 133 in the U.S. GSE's. *Journal of Economic Asymmetries*, 7.

Xanthopoulos, A. (2012) The Entrenched Kurtosis in Current Portfolio Returns. *The Journal of Economic Asymmetries*, Elsevier.

Xanthopoulos, A. (2019). Investment Advising: Pay-to-Play, or Capture? *SPOUDAI Journal of Economics and Business*, *69*, 75–110.

Xydakis, N. (2023) Greeks Suffering from Stockholm Syndrome. *Hellas*. https://hellas.postsen.com/local/359085/Nikos-Xydakis-does-not-take-back-the-Stockholm-syndrome-for-ND-voters.html

ENDNOTES

1 Pension Research Council (2022), The Wharton School of Business

2 Whistman, J. (2022) *How Long Does the Average Person Stay at a Job (and How to Increase it)*, https://www.perceptionpredict.ai

3 Naval Retirement Fund (N.A.T.) - https://www.nat.gr/

4 Greek Law, *Elliniki Nomothesia* https://www.elinyae.gr/ethniki-nomothesia/n-28681922-fek-119a-2071922.

5 Greek Law, *Elliniki Nomothesia* https://www.elinyae.gr/ethniki-nomothesia/n-57331932-fek-364a-11101932

6 This phenomenon is similar to 'responsibility transfer' that has been documented in research regarding the U.S. employees 'insured' i.e., covered by pension, and the fiduciaries of their funds, that is, consultants and managers.

7 Sirotaki A. 2016, *The Insurance System in Greece*, Semantic Scholar

8 Greek Law *Bank of Greece Eminerosi* 1611/1950 - https://www.bankofgreece.gr/enimerosi/grafeio-typoy/

9 The reader may notice the analogy to 'responsibility-transfer' that appears as the root for the risk of demise.

10 Greek Law 4826/2021 - https://www.bankofgreece.gr/enimerosi/grafeio-typoy

11 Nektarios, M., P. Tinios, and G. Simeonidis, 2018, *Pensions for the Young: A Social Insurance System Focused on Growth* - http://eprints.lse.ac.uk/79268/1/blogs.lse.ac.uk.

12 Greece underwent its first round of elections for a new government on May 21, 2023. In those elections, this author has run as Parliamentary Candidate with the political group of Ethniki Dimiourgia (Εθνικη Δημιουργια) let by Thanos Tzimeros. This political group generally advocates for lower taxes and a deflated governmental sector.

13 Webster's Encyclopedic Dictionary of the English Language (1990) p. 349.

14 Fabozzi, F. J. (ed.) 2005 *The Handbook of Fixed Income Securities*, Mc-Graw-Hill.

15 Xanthopoulos, A. 2012 *The Entrenched Kurtosis in Current Portfolio Returns,* The Journal of Economic Asymmetries, Elsevier.

16 Xanthopoulos, A. (2019) *Investment Advising: Pay-to-Play, or Capture?* SPOUDAI Journal of Economics and Business, 69, 75-110.

17 For reasons related to classified documents, President Donald Trump has been indicted on seven criminal charges as of the time of this writing, on June 10, 2023. https://www.msn.com/en-us/news/politics/donald-trump-indicted-how-much-time-in-prison-could-former-president-serve/ar-AA1cnNnx.

18 Van Vliet, B. and A. Xanthopoulos, *Iso-Risk: An Analysis of Risk-Taking in Fixed Income Markets*, Applied Economics, 60.

19 Xanthopoulos, A. (2010) *Market Value Signal Extraction and the Misapplication of SFAS 133 in the U.S. GSE's,* The Journal of Economic Asymmetries 7.

20 Xydakis, N. (2023) *Greeks Suffering from Stockholm Syndrome*, https://hellas.postsen.com/local/359085/Nikos-Xydakis-does-not-take-back-the-Stockholm-syndrome-for-ND-voters.html

21 Moumtzaki, A. (2018) *The Former Minister Who Tried to Warn Greece About the Crisis*, Stuff https://www.vice.com/sv/article/dp57na/greek-ex-finance-minister-alekos-papadopoulos-interview-876

22 Papadopoulos, A. (2023) *The Risks of Embellishing the Fiscal Situation,* https://fantomas.gr/55536-2/

23 International Labour Organization, *Greece*, https://www.ilo.org/dyn/natlex

24 Fitch Wire (2023) *Greek Stability Programme Underscores Improving Public Finance*

25 Economy and Finance (2023) *Spring 2023 Economic Forecast: an improved outlook amid persistent challenges, European Commission* https://economy-finance.ec.europa.eu/economic-forecast-and-surveys/economic-forecasts/spring-2023-economic-forecast-improved-outlook-amid-persistent-challenges_en#documents.

26 Solow, R. M. (1957) *A Contribution to the Theory of Economic Growth*, Quarterly Journal of Economics, 70.

27 It is the one that communist theory is insanely trying to minimize, by attacking a nebulous notion of 'capitalism'.

28 Interestingly, Estonia was the 'model-country' of the Ethniki Dimiourgia party that ran for elections on May 21, 2023, and disbanded afterward. It was Mr. Thanos Tzimeros' favorite example of what Greece could have been.

29 James, G., Witten, D., Hastie, T. and Tibshirani R., (2013) *An Introduction to Statistical Learning with Applications in R*, Springer.

8. APPENDIX: ALGORITHM FOR K-MEANS CLUSTERING

K-means clustering has been used in this work, to counter arguments against Mr. Papadopoulos' claims. In essence he stated that beautifying Greek fiscal numbers before the May 21 2023 election was akin to applying lipstick on a pig. Greece is not like Italy, and growth rates cannot be used as simple argument to claim as such. The methodology is partitioning a data set into k distinct, non-overlapping clusters. I have arbitrarily specified the number of clusters to be k = 4, after ascertaining that countries like Ireland would appear in a cluster all by themselves. The mathematics of the methodology starts by assigning each three-dimensional observation (because there are three years of growth for each country) to exactly one of the 5 clusters, at random. Then, the Euclidean distance between each observation and the means of each of the five resulting clusters is found. Observations are reassigned to the cluster of the shortest distance to its mean. The means are then recalculated, and observations are reassigned. The algorithm ends, when iteration causes no changes or reassigning of observations into new clusters.
Let $C_1, C_2, \ldots, C_k$ denote sets that have in them, the indices of the observations of each cluster. These sets have two properties: (i) each observation belongs to at least one of the clusters, and (ii) the clusters are non-overlapping, that is, no observation belongs to more than one cluster. The within-cluster variation for a cluster, C_k, measures the amount by which the observations within a cluster differ from each other, denoted initially as $W(C_k)$.[29] The problem is to minimize the sum of all such differences/distances:

$$minimize\left\{\sum_{k=1}^{K} W\left(C_k\right)\right\}$$

There are many ways to define "difference." The one used most often, is that of Euclidean distance:

$$W\left(C_k\right)=\frac{1}{\left|C_k\right|}\sum_{i,i'\in C_k}\sum_{j=1}^{p}\left(x_{ij}-x_{i'j}\right)^2$$

In the above, $|C_k|$ denotes the number of observations in the *k*th cluster. Thus, the within-cluster variation of the *k*th cluster is determined through all of the pairwise squared Euclidean distances between the observations of the cluster, divided by the total number of observations in the cluster.
The computational algorithm for determining the k=5 clusters in the analysis above, entail:

1. Randomly assign a number, from 1 to 5, to each of the observations. These assignments of a cluster serve as initial cluster assignments for the observations (this process has been performed by the author in the programming language 'R').
2. Iterate until the cluster assignments stop changing:
   (a) For each of the K clusters, compute the cluster *centroid*. The *k*th cluster centroid is the vector of the p-feature means for the observations in the *k*th cluster.
   (b) Assign each observation to the cluster whose centroid is closest (where *closest* is defined using Euclidean distance).

Chapter 12
Lightweight Deep Learning:
Introduction, Advancements, and Applications

Hari Kishan Kondaveeti
https://orcid.org/0000-0002-3379-720X
Vellore Institute of Technology, India

Valli Kumari Vatsavayi
https://orcid.org/0000-0002-7252-8301
Andhra University, India

Srileakhana Mangapathi
Vellore Institute of Technology, India

Reddy M. Yasaswini
Vellore Institute of Technology, India

ABSTRACT

Lightweight deep learning is a subfield of artificial intelligence and machine learning that prioritises efficiency and compactness while developing deep learning models. It is ideal for low-powered mobile phones, embedded systems, and internet-of-things devices due to their speed and low latency. To make lightweight deep learning models, pruning and quantization are used to remove unnecessary parameters and reduce model weight accuracy. Transfer learning is used to fine-tune a pre-trained deep learning model on a smaller dataset. This chapter introduces the fundamentals of lightweight deep learning, including various lightweight models and their applications across different industries.

DOI: 10.4018/978-1-6684-8386-2.ch012

INTRODUCTION

Lightweight Deep Learning is a branch of Deep Learning that strives to construct neural network models that can perform well even on low-powered platforms such as smartphones, Internet of Things (IoT) devices, and embedded systems. Due to the restricted memory, processing power, and battery life of such devices, it is impossible to install complex deep learning models that need vast computing resources. Lightweight Deep Learning is essential as a result of the growing interest in deploying deep learning models on edge devices. Edge devices often have limited capabilities in terms of their capacity to do sophisticated calculations, hence this limitation necessitates the need for lightweight deep learning. Smart homes, fitness monitors, and smartphone applications that can distinguish faces and voices are just a few examples of emerging technologies.

The Model compression, parameter pruning, quantization, and knowledge distillation are some of the approaches that are employed in Lightweight Deep Learning. These techniques are utilised in order to optimise both the size of the model and its performance. These methods make it possible to minimise the overall size of the model, get rid of any superfluous parameters, and make the necessary computations during inference much easier to do. Reduced model size is one of the many advantages of Lightweight Deep Learning, along with decreased costs, expanded accessibility, and enhanced levels of privacy. However, there are also constraints, such as lower precision, restricted flexibility, complexity, and trade-offs between model size, accuracy, and speed. Additionally, there is a reduction in the overall speed of the model.

ADVANTAGES OF LIGHTWEIGHT DEEP LEARNING

Lightweight deep learning has several advantages over traditional deep learning techniques. In this section, we will discuss some of the significant benefits of lightweight deep learning.

Faster Inference Times

Lightweight deep learning models are significantly smaller than their full-scale counterparts, resulting in faster inference times. This makes them ideal for use cases where real-time processing is critical, such as image or video analysis, natural language processing, and other applications that require quick decision-making.

Lower Memory Usage

Smaller models also require less memory to operate, making them more efficient in resource-constrained environments. This is particularly beneficial for mobile and embedded devices, which have limited resources.

Better Power Efficiency

With lower memory usage and faster inference times, lightweight deep learning models are more power-efficient than traditional deep learning models. This is important for battery-powered devices, such as smartphones, wearables, and IoT devices.

Reduced Hardware Requirements

By creating smaller models, lightweight deep learning reduces hardware requirements for inference. This results in lower hardware costs, making it possible to deploy deep learning models in resource-constrained environments or in applications where cost is a significant factor.

Improved Privacy and Security

Lightweight deep learning reduces the amount of data transferred between devices and servers, protecting user privacy and reducing the risk of sensitive data being exposed. This is particularly important for applications that deal with personal or confidential data.

Flexibility and Adaptability

Lightweight deep learning models are highly adaptable and can be tailored to specific use cases, making them more flexible than traditional deep learning models. This means that they can be optimized for specific hardware or software platforms, making them easier to deploy and maintain.

Broad Range of Applications

lightweight deep learning makes it possible to deploy models in a broader range of applications, including those in developing countries or remote areas with limited access to high-end hardware. This can have a significant impact on industries such as healthcare, agriculture, and education, where access to technology is limited.

LIGHTWEIGHT DEEP LEARNING MODELS

MobileNet

MobileNet is a popular lightweight neural network model that was designed for mobile devices. It is based on a series of depth wise separable convolutions that reduce the number of parameters and computational complexity while maintaining high accuracy. With a small footprint, it can be easily integrated into mobile applications for various purposes, including COVID-19 infection detection, forest fire identification, face recognition, plant disease detection, and medical diagnosis of breast cancer scans.

Kaya et al. (2023) utilized MobileNet for COVID-19 infection detection with high precision, making it a promising tool for screening individuals in remote areas. (Namburu et al.,2023) leveraged MobileNet for identifying forest fires, where the model performed exceptionally well with minimal processing time.

Shukla et al. (2023) developed a face recognition system using MobileNet, achieving a high accuracy rate. Liu et al. (2023) used the model for plant disease detection, contributing to the development of precision agriculture. Moreover, MobileNet has shown promise in medical applications. Ogundokun et al. (2023) employed MobileNet for diagnosing breast cancer scans, and the model demonstrated high accuracy in detecting abnormal cells. The results of their study indicate that MobileNet has the potential to be used as an effective tool in medical diagnosis.

ShuffleNet

ShuffleNet is another popular lightweight neural network model that was designed for mobile devices. It is based on group convolutions and channel shuffling, which significantly reduces the number of parameters and computational complexity while maintaining high accuracy. Applications of ShuffleNet include breast cancer classification, image segmentation, and face detection in video surveillance. Chattopadhyay et al. (2022) utilized ShuffleNet for breast cancer classification, achieving a high accuracy rate in detecting malignant tissues. Gomes et al. (2021) employed the architecture for image segmentation, where the model demonstrated efficient performance while minimizing computational costs. Wang et al. (2021) developed a face detection system in video surveillance using ShuffleNet, demonstrating accurate and efficient processing of data.

SqueezeNet

SqueezeNet is a lightweight neural network model that was designed for image classification tasks. It uses a combination of 1x1 and 3x3 convolutions to reduce the number of parameters while maintaining high accuracy. SqueezeNet has found applications in various domains, including COVID-19 detection, digital image forgery detection, brain tumor classification, face recognition, energy demand forecasting, plant disease detection, facial expression detection, root disease detection, and script recognition. Zhang et al. (2023) employed SqueezeNet for COVID-19 detection using chest X-ray images, achieving high accuracy in detecting the positive cases.

Nirmalapriya et al. (2023) utilized the architecture for digital image forgery detection, where the model demonstrated excellent performance in detecting manipulated images. Rasool et al. (2023) used SqueezeNet for brain tumor classification, achieving high accuracy rates in detecting various types of tumors. Sangamesh et al. (2023) employed SqueezeNet for face recognition, where the model demonstrated efficient processing while achieving high accuracy rates. Other applications of SqueezeNet include energy demand forecasting (Ghadimi & N,2023), plant disease detection (Setiawan et al.,2023), facial expression detection (Sharmili et al.,2023), root disease detection (Jayapalan et al.,2023), and script recognition (br Tarigan et al.,2023). In summary, SqueezeNet is a promising architecture for various deep learning tasks, especially for resource-limited devices, due to its efficiency and low memory usage.

MobileNetV2

MobileNetV2 is an improved version of MobileNet that uses a combination of depth wise and pointwise convolutions to reduce the computational complexity while maintaining high accuracy. This architecture is widely used for various computer vision tasks, including object detection, face recognition, and medical diagnosis. In tomato disease recognition, MobileNetV2 was used to classify the tomato plant's health status accurately, thereby preventing significant crop losses. In facemask detection, MobileNetV2 was utilized to identify people who were not wearing a mask correctly or not wearing it at all. In skin cancer detection, MobileNetV2 was employed to classify images of skin lesions as either benign or malignant with high accuracy.

EfficientNet

EfficientNet is a family of neural network models that were designed to achieve state-of-the-art performance with fewer parameters and lower computational complexity. It uses a combination of compound scaling, efficient block design, and neural architecture search to achieve high accuracy with fewer resources. EfficientNet has shown promising results in various applications in lightweight deep learning including body condition scoring for dairy cows (Zhao et al.,2023), facial emotion recognition (Punuri et al.,2023), skin disease classification (Rafay & Hussain,2023), lung disease detection (Ravi et al.,2023), and plant disease detection (Rajeena et al.,2023). These applications have the potential to revolutionize the industries of agriculture, healthcare, and more by enabling accurate and efficient diagnoses and decision-making.

Tiny-YOLO

Tiny-YOLO is a lightweight neural network model that was designed for object detection tasks. It uses a combination of convolutional layers and a fully connected layer to detect objects with high accuracy while using fewer resources. Tiny-YOLO has shown great promise in various applications, including object detection in real-time video surveillance (Khokhlov et al., 2020), human detection (Sumit et al., 2022), hotspot detection on CCTV videos (Lestari et al., 2019), and face mask detection (Kumar et al., 2021). Its ability to achieve high accuracy in object detection tasks with limited computational resources makes it an attractive option for edge computing applications.

ESPNet

ESPNet is a lightweight neural network model that was designed for semantic segmentation tasks. It uses a combination of dilated convolutions and depth wise separable convolutions to reduce the number of parameters and computational complexity while maintaining high accuracy. It has shown promising results in various applications including speech enhancement and separation toolkit, advancing spoken language, brain tumor image segmentation, and end-to-end automatic speech recognition (ASR) systems. The architecture of ESPNet is designed to efficiently utilize computational resources and reduce memory consumption. It is particularly useful for scenarios where computational resources are limited, such as on edge devices or in mobile applications. The network architecture of ESPNet is based on the spatial pyramid pooling technique, which allows it to extract features from images with varying resolutions. This makes ESPNet suitable for tasks such as object detection and image segmentation, where varying object sizes are present.

LIGHTWEIGHT NEURAL NETWORK MODEL OPTIMIZATION

Lightweight Deep Learning models are designed to be smaller and more efficient than traditional deep learning models, while still maintaining reasonable levels of accuracy. There are several techniques used to optimize the architecture of Lightweight Deep Learning models, including model compression, parameter pruning, quantization, and knowledge distillation.

Model Compression

Model compression is a technique used to reduce the file size of deep learning models. It involves removing redundant information from the model architecture, such as eliminating superfluous layers, reducing the number of filters in each layer, and simplifying the layer connections. By doing so, the compressed model requires less storage space and can be loaded and executed faster, making it suitable for deployment in resource-constrained environments like mobile and edge devices. Additionally, model compression can help improve model efficiency, reduce energy consumption, and increase inference speed. However, the process of compressing a model involves a trade-off between model size, accuracy, and computational complexity, and finding the optimal balance between these factors is an ongoing research challenge.

Parameter Pruning

Parameter pruning is a technique used to reduce the number of parameters in a deep learning model. The goal is to remove individual parameters that do not significantly contribute to the model output, thereby reducing the model size and computational complexity. This can be achieved by setting small or zero values for those parameters, effectively removing them from the model. Pruning can be performed during or after training, and it can result in significant reductions in model size, making it more suitable for deployment on resource-constrained devices. Parameter pruning may also result in a decrease in model accuracy, which can be mitigated by retraining the pruned model or using other techniques like quantization and knowledge distillation.

Quantization

Quantization is a technique used to reduce the storage and memory requirements of deep learning models. It involves reducing the precision of a model's parameters by converting floating-point values to fixed-point values, thereby decreasing the number of bits required to represent each value. This technique can significantly reduce the model's size and improve its speed and efficiency, making it more suitable for deployment on resource-constrained devices. Quantization can also result in a loss of accuracy, particularly if the bit-width of the parameters is reduced too much. Different types of quantization, such as dynamic and static quantization, can be used to balance the trade-off between model size and accuracy.

Knowledge Distillation

Knowledge distillation is a technique used to train a smaller and more efficient model to replicate the behaviour of a larger and more complex model. The method involves using the larger model to generate training data or provide a training objective for the smaller model. During training, the smaller model is trained to match the outputs of the larger model, thereby learning from the knowledge and expertise contained in the larger model. Knowledge distillation can result in significant reductions in model size and computational complexity while retaining a high level of accuracy. The technique is widely used for deployment on resource-constrained devices such as mobile phones and IoT devices.

Pruning and Quantization

Combining pruning and quantization can further optimize a model's size and efficiency by reducing the number of parameters while also decreasing the precision of the remaining parameters, resulting in a highly compressed model suitable for deployment on resource-constrained devices.

APPLICATIONS OF LIGHTWEIGHT DEEP LEARNING

Lightweight deep learning is being increasingly used in various domains such as healthcare, precision agriculture, face recognition, emotion recognition, and object detection. These applications include plant disease detection, COVID-19 detection, facial expression detection, object and human detection, and more, making it a promising technology for solving real-world problems efficiently. Detailed description of various applications is described in the following sub sections.

Healthcare

Lightweight deep learning models have gained popularity in healthcare due to their ability to provide accurate and efficient predictions, even on low-power devices. Researchers have developed various applications of these models in healthcare, such as breast cancer classification, skin disease classification, lung disease detection, skin cancer detection, COVID-19 infection detection, COVID-19 detection, and brain tumor classification.

Chattopadhyay et al. (2022) proposed a lightweight deep learning model for accurate classification of breast cancer using mammograms. Rafay & Hussain (2023) developed a lightweight deep learning model for accurate classification of various skin diseases using dermoscopic images. Ravi et al. (2023) proposed a lightweight deep learning model for detecting lung diseases from chest X-rays. Toğaçar et al. (2021) developed a lightweight deep learning model for accurate detection of skin cancer using dermoscopic images. Kaya et al. (2023) proposed a lightweight deep learning model for detecting COVID-19 infection from chest X-rays. Zhang et al. (2023) developed a lightweight deep learning model for accurate detection of COVID-19 using CT scans. Rasool et al. (2023) proposed a lightweight deep learning model for accurate classification of brain tumors using MRI scans. Ogundokun et al. (2023) proposed a lightweight deep learning model for medical diagnosis of breast cancer from scans. The model can help doctors identify cancerous tissues and improve their diagnosis and treatment practices.

These applications demonstrate the potential of lightweight deep learning models in healthcare for accurate diagnosis and treatment of diseases. Additionally, the ability to deploy these models on low-power devices makes them highly accessible, potentially leading to widespread use in the future.

Precision Agriculture

In precision agriculture, technologies are utilized to optimize crop yield and reduce waste. One such technology that has shown promise in this field is lightweight deep learning models. These models have been applied in various precision agriculture applications, including plant disease detection. Researchers have developed several lightweight deep learning models for accurate detection of plant diseases, such as Rajeena et al. (2023) who used hyperspectral imaging for plant disease detection, Liu et al. (2020) who proposed a model for tomato disease recognition using images, Liu et al. (2023) who developed a model for detecting plant diseases using visible and near-infrared images, Setiawan et al. (2023) who proposed a model for plant disease detection using smartphone images, and Jayapalan et al. (2023) who developed a model for early detection of root diseases in plants using images.

The use of lightweight deep learning models in precision agriculture has several benefits, such as the early detection of plant diseases and the optimization of crop production. By identifying plant diseases early, farmers can take appropriate measures to prevent their spread and reduce crop losses. Additionally, optimizing crop production can lead to better crop yields and more sustainable farming practices.

Face Recognition

Face recognition is a rapidly growing field that has numerous practical applications, particularly in the area of security and surveillance.

Wang et al. (2021) proposed a lightweight deep learning model for face detection in video surveillance, which can detect and track faces in real-time. Sanjaya et al. (2020) developed a lightweight deep learning model for accurate detection of facemasks, which can be useful in monitoring compliance with mask mandates. Kumar et al. (2021) proposed a lightweight deep learning model for face mask detection, which can be deployed on edge devices with limited computational power.

In addition to detection, lightweight deep learning models have also been used in face recognition. Shukla et al. (2023) developed a lightweight deep learning model for accurate face recognition, which can be useful in various applications such as access control and surveillance. Sangamesh et al. (2023) proposed a lightweight deep learning model for face recognition in low-light environments, which can be useful in surveillance applications where lighting conditions may not be optimal.

These applications demonstrate the potential of lightweight deep learning models in face recognition for accurate and efficient detection and recognition of faces, leading to improved security and surveillance practices. Additionally, the ability to deploy these models on low-power devices makes them highly accessible, potentially leading to widespread use in the future.

Emotion Recognition

Emotion recognition is an important research area that has numerous practical applications in various fields, such as mental health, education, and human-computer interaction.

Punuri et al. (2023) proposed a lightweight deep learning model for facial emotion recognition, which can recognize emotions such as happiness, sadness, anger, and surprise from facial expressions. The model is capable of processing images in real-time, making it highly practical for applications such as mental health diagnosis and treatment. Sharmili et al. (2023) developed a lightweight deep learning model for facial expression detection, which can detect and classify facial expressions. The model is capable of processing images with low resolution and has the potential to be deployed on edge devices with limited computational power.

These applications demonstrate the potential of lightweight deep learning models in emotion recognition for accurate and efficient detection of emotions from facial expressions, leading to improved mental health diagnosis and treatment practices, and enhanced human-computer interaction.

Object Detection

Object detection is an important research area that has numerous practical applications in various fields, such as robotics, autonomous vehicles, and surveillance.

Khokhlov et al. (2020) proposed a lightweight deep learning model for object detection, which can detect and classify multiple objects in images in real-time. The model is designed to be highly efficient and can run on low-power devices, making it practical for applications such as robotics and autonomous vehicles. This application demonstrates the potential of lightweight deep learning models in object detection for accurate and efficient detection of multiple objects in images, leading to improved object recognition and tracking practices in various fields. With the growing demand for practical and accessible object detection technology, the use of lightweight deep learning models in this field is likely to increase in the future.

Other Applications

Lightweight deep learning models also have other numerous practical applications across various fields, including image segmentation, speech enhancement, human detection, energy forecasting, and medical diagnosis.

Gomes et al. (2021) proposed a lightweight deep learning model for image segmentation, which can identify and classify different objects in images. The model can process images in real-time, making it practical for applications such as autonomous vehicles and robotics. Zhao et al. (2023) developed a lightweight deep learning model for body condition scoring of dairy cows, which can help farmers identify cows with health issues and improve their management practices. The model is designed to be highly efficient and can run on low-power devices. Watanabe et al. (2018) proposed a speech enhancement and separation toolkit based on lightweight deep learning models. The toolkit can remove background noise and enhance the quality of speech signals, improving the accuracy of speech recognition and natural language processing systems. Arora et al. (2022) developed a lightweight deep learning model for advancing spoken language, which can improve the accuracy of speech recognition and language translation systems.

Boyer et al. (2021) studied the use of transducer-based end-to-end automatic speech recognition (ASR) systems, which can improve the accuracy of ASR models by reducing the number of components and simplifying the model architecture. Sumit et al. (2022) proposed a lightweight deep learning model for human detection, which can identify and track human movements in real-time. The model can be used in various applications, such as security and surveillance. Lestari et al. (2019) developed a hotspots detection system based on lightweight deep learning models for CCTV videos. The system can detect and alert authorities about potential fire hotspots, improving fire prevention and management practices. Namburu et al. (2023) proposed a lightweight deep learning model for forest fire identification, which can detect and classify different types of fire in real-time. The model can be used in various applications, such as firefighting and forest management. Ghadimi & N (2023) developed a lightweight deep learning model for energy demand forecasting, which can help utilities and energy companies predict energy demand and plan their operations accordingly. Tarigan et al. (2023) developed a lightweight deep learning model for script recognition.

POTENTIAL BENEFITS AND LIMITATIONS OF LIGHTWEIGHT DEEP LEARNING

Potential Benefits

1. More Efficiency: Lightweight deep learning models use fewer parameters, training and inference durations are reduced. They become more effective in terms of energy usage and computing capacity as a result.
2. Reduced Memory Footprint: Lightweight deep learning models are better suited for deployment on systems with low memory requirements, such as mobile and IoT devices and use less memory to store the model parameters.
3. Reduced Latency: Deep learning models that are lightweight have faster inference times, which reduces the latency for real-time applications.
4. Enhanced Accessibility: As lightweight deep learning models may be used on low-end devices, a larger audience can use them.
5. Restricted Model Capacity: Lightweight deep learning models contain fewer parameters than bigger models, which may restrict their modelling capacity and result in reduced accuracy and performance. Striking the ideal balance between model size and performance can be difficult since lowering the size of the model might result in a loss of accuracy.
6. Limited Training Data: In order to obtain an acceptable level of accuracy, lightweight deep learning models may need a significant quantity of training data, which may not be accessible in all applications.

Limitations

While lightweight deep learning offers several advantages, it also has some significant limitations that need to be considered. These include reduced model complexity, limited model capacity, hardware limitations, optimization challenges, limited research, and compatibility issues. Understanding these limitations is critical to making informed decisions about when and where to use lightweight deep learning techniques

1. The accuracy and performance of lightweight deep learning models are often lower than those of bigger models due to the trade-off between model size and accuracy.
2. Reduced Model Capacity: Lightweight deep learning models may have a limited modelling capacity due to the fewer parameters they use, which might result in decreased accuracy and performance.
3. Limited Training Data: In order to obtain an acceptable level of accuracy, lightweight deep learning models may need a significant quantity of training data, which may not be accessible in all applications.
4. Striking the ideal balance between model size and performance can be difficult since lowering the size of the model might result in a loss of accuracy.

5. Lack of Standardization: Because lightweight deep learning models are not yet standardised, it may be difficult for developers to compare them and choose the best one for their application.
6. Computing Overhead: Although lightweight deep learning models have fewer parameters, they may still need a lot of computing power to train and use them, which can be problematic for devices with little processing power.
7. Hardware Limitations: While lightweight deep learning models can reduce hardware requirements, they still require some level of hardware support. This can limit the range of devices on which they can be deployed and may require specific hardware configurations.
8. Optimization Challenges: Optimizing lightweight deep learning models for specific hardware or software platforms can be challenging. This requires specialized knowledge and expertise in both deep learning and hardware optimization.

FUTURE DIRECTIONS AND RESEARCH OPPORTUNITIES

In recent years, as the demand for efficient, low-power AI systems has increased, lightweight deep learning has become an increasingly vital area of study. Here are some possible directions for future research in this field. Compressing or quantizing models is one of the most common techniques for creating lightweight models. This entails minimising the quantity of model parameters or, correspondingly, the precision of the parameters. Future research could concentrate on enhancing the efficacy and efficiency of these methods. AutoML (automated machine learning) has shown great promise in optimizing deep learning models, but most of the existing methods are designed for large-scale models. Future research could focus on developing AutoML methods that are specifically designed for lightweight models.

Efficient hardware for lightweight models are developing hardware specifically designed for running lightweight models could greatly improve their efficiency. Future research could focus on developing specialized processors or hardware accelerators that can run these models efficiently. Domain-specific models are another approach to creating lightweight models is to develop models that are specifically designed for a particular domain or task. For example, a model designed for image classification in the medical field might have different requirements than a model designed for image classification in the automotive industry. Future research could focus on developing domain-specific models that are highly optimized for their specific use cases. Transfer learning has been highly effective in reducing the amount of data needed to train deep learning models. Future research could focus on developing transfer learning techniques that are specifically designed for lightweight models, making it possible to train these models with even less data. Hybrid models that combine deep learning with other machine learning techniques, such as decision trees or random forests, could be an effective way to create lightweight models that still have strong predictive power. Future research could focus on developing and optimizing these hybrid models.

CONCLUSION

In conclusion, lightweight deep learning models have the potential to provide better accessibility, decreased latency, decreased memory footprint, and improved efficiency. They do, however, have drawbacks and difficulties, including a trade-off between model size and accuracy, a restricted model capacity, a lack of standardisation, and computational overhead. They also have constraints in terms of training data and model size. It's crucial to carefully analyse the advantages and disadvantages of using lightweight deep learning models as well as the particular application's needs. While selecting a lightweight deep learning model, developers should also promote critical thinking and careful thought and take into account the trade-offs between model size, accuracy, and computing needs.

Also, it is crucial to keep researching and developing in the area of lightweight deep learning since this might result in better models and methods that meet the present issues and obstacles. Lightweight deep learning has the ability to significantly improve and progress a wide range of applications with careful analysis and continuing research.

REFERENCES

Arora, S., Dalmia, S., Denisov, P., Chang, X., Ueda, Y., Peng, Y., & Watanabe, S. (2022, May). Espnet-slu: Advancing spoken language understanding through espnet. In *ICASSP 2022-2022 IEEE International Conference on Acoustics, Speech and Signal Processing (ICASSP)* (pp. 7167-7171). IEEE.

Boyer, F., Shinohara, Y., Ishii, T., Inaguma, H., & Watanabe, S. (2021, December). A study of transducer based end-to-end ASR with ESPnet: Architecture, auxiliary loss and decoding strategies. In *2021 IEEE Automatic Speech Recognition and Understanding Workshop (ASRU)* (pp. 16-23). IEEE.

Tarigan, Y. F., Gunawan, T. S., & Hayadi, B. H. (2023, March). Combination Of SqueezeNet And Multilayer Backpropagation Algorithm In Hanacaraka Script Recognition. In International Conference on Information Science and Technology Innovation (ICoSTEC) (Vol. 2, pp. 163-170). IEEE.

Chattopadhyay, S., Dey, A., Singh, P. K., & Sarkar, R. (2022). DRDA-Net: Dense residual dual-shuffle attention network for breast cancer classification using histopathological images. *Computers in Biology and Medicine*, *145*, 105437. doi:10.1016/j.compbiomed.2022.105437 PMID:35339096

GhadimiN. Squeezenet for the Forecasting of the Energy Demand Using a Combined Version of Sewing Training-Based Optimization Algorithm. SSRN 4360713. doi:10.1016/j.heliyon.2023.e16827

Gomes, R., Rozario, P., & Adhikari, N. (2021, May). Deep learning optimization in remote sensing image segmentation using dilated convolutions and ShuffleNet. In *2021 IEEE International Conference on Electro Information Technology (EIT)* (pp. 244-249). IEEE. 10.1109/EIT51626.2021.9491910

Jayapalan, D. F. S., & Ananth, J. P. (2023). Root disease classification with hybrid optimization models in IoT. *Expert Systems with Applications*, *226*, 120150. doi:10.1016/j.eswa.2023.120150

Kaya, Y., & Gürsoy, E. (2023). A MobileNet-based CNN model with a novel fine-tuning mechanism for COVID-19 infection detection. *Soft Computing*, *27*(9), 1–15. doi:10.100700500-022-07798-y PMID:36618761

Khokhlov, I., Davydenko, E., Osokin, I., Ryakin, I., Babaev, A., Litvinenko, V., & Gorbachev, R. (2020, May). Tiny-YOLO object detection supplemented with geometrical data. In *2020 IEEE 91st Vehicular Technology Conference (VTC2020-Spring)* (pp. 1-5). IEEE. 10.1109/VTC2020-Spring48590.2020.9128749

Kumar, A., Kalia, A., Sharma, A., & Kaushal, M. (2021). A hybrid tiny YOLO v4-SPP module based improved face mask detection vision system. *Journal of Ambient Intelligence and Humanized Computing*, 1–14. PMID:34691278

Lestari, D. P., Kosasih, R., Handhika, T., Sari, I., & Fahrurozi, A. (2019, September). Fire hotspots detection system on CCTV videos using you only look once (YOLO) method and tiny YOLO model for high buildings evacuation. In *2019 2nd International Conference of Computer and Informatics Engineering (IC2IE)* (pp. 87-92). IEEE.

Liu, J., & Wang, X. (2020). Early recognition of tomato gray leaf spot disease based on MobileNetv2-YOLOv3 model. *Plant Methods*, *16*(1), 1–16. doi:10.118613007-020-00624-2 PMID:32523613

Namburu, A., Selvaraj, P., Mohan, S., Ragavanantham, S., & Eldin, E. T. (2023). Forest Fire Identification in UAV Imagery Using X-MobileNet. *Electronics (Basel)*, *12*(3), 733. doi:10.3390/electronics12030733

Nirmalapriya, G., Maram, B., Lakshmanan, R., & Navaneethakrishnan, M. (2023). ASCA-squeeze net: Aquila sine cosine algorithm enabled hybrid deep learning networks for digital image forgery detection. *Computers & Security*, *128*, 103155. doi:10.1016/j.cose.2023.103155

Nuechterlein, N., & Mehta, S. (2019). 3D-ESPNet with pyramidal refinement for volumetric brain tumor image segmentation. In *Brainlesion: Glioma, Multiple Sclerosis, Stroke and Traumatic Brain Injuries: 4th International Workshop*. Springer International Publishing.

Ogundokun, R. O., Misra, S., Akinrotimi, A. O., & Ogul, H. (2023). MobileNet-SVM: A Lightweight Deep Transfer Learning Model to Diagnose BCH Scans for IoMT-Based Imaging Sensors. *Sensors (Basel)*, *23*(2), 656. doi:10.339023020656 PMID:36679455

Punuri, S. B., Kuanar, S. K., Kolhar, M., Mishra, T. K., Alameen, A., Mohapatra, H., & Mishra, S. R. (2023). Efficient Net-XGBoost: An Implementation for Facial Emotion Recognition Using Transfer Learning. *Mathematics*, *11*(3), 776. doi:10.3390/math11030776

Rafay, A., & Hussain, W. (2023). EfficientSkinDis: An EfficientNet-based classification model for a large manually curated dataset of 31 skin diseases. *Biomedical Signal Processing and Control*, *85*, 104869. doi:10.1016/j.bspc.2023.104869

Rajeena, P. P. (1938). F., SU, A., Moustafa, M. A., & Ali, M. A. (2023). Detecting Plant Disease in Corn Leaf Using EfficientNet Architecture—An Analytical Approach. *Electronics (Basel)*, *12*(8). Advance online publication. doi:10.3390/electronics12081938

Rasool, M., Ismail, N. A., Al-Dhaqm, A., Yafooz, W., & Alsaeedi, A. (2023). A Novel Approach for Classifying Brain Tumours Combining a SqueezeNet Model with SVM and Fine-Tuning. *Electronics (Basel)*, *12*(1), 149. doi:10.3390/electronics12010149

Ravi, V., Acharya, V., & Alazab, M. (2023). A multichannel EfficientNet deep learning-based stacking ensemble approach for lung disease detection using chest X-ray images. *Cluster Computing*, *26*(2), 1181–1203. doi:10.100710586-022-03664-6 PMID:35874187

Sangamesh, H., Viswanatha, V. M., Petli, V., & Patil, N. B. (2023, February). A Novel Approach for Recognition of Face by Using Squeezenet Pre-Trained Network. In *2023 IEEE International Conference on Integrated Circuits and Communication Systems (ICICACS)* (pp. 1-5). IEEE.

Sanjaya, S. A., & Rakhmawan, S. A. (2020, October). Face mask detection using MobileNetV2 in the era of COVID-19 pandemic. In *2020 International Conference on Data Analytics for Business and Industry: Way Towards a Sustainable Economy (ICDABI)* (pp. 1-5). IEEE. 10.1109/ICDABI51230.2020.9325631

Setiawan, W., & Rulaningtyas, R. (2023, January). Visual explanation of maize leaf diaseases classification using squeezenet and gradient-weighted class activation map. In AIP Conference Proceedings (Vol. 2679, No. 1, p. 020002). AIP Publishing LLC. doi:10.1063/5.0111276

Sharmili, N., Yonbawi, S., Alahmari, S., Lydia, E. L., Ishak, M. K., Alkahtani, H. K., & Mostafa, S. M. (2022). *Earthworm Optimization with Improved SqueezeNet Enabled Facial Expression Recognition Model.* Tech Science Press.

Toğaçar, M., Cömert, Z., & Ergen, B. (2021). Intelligent skin cancer detection applying autoencoder, MobileNetV2 and spiking neural networks. *Chaos, Solitons, and Fractals*, *144*, 110714. doi:10.1016/j.chaos.2021.110714

Wang, P., Zhang, J., & Zhu, H. (2021). Fire detection in video surveillance using superpixel-based region proposal and ESE-ShuffleNet. *Multimedia Tools and Applications*, 1–28.

WatanabeS.HoriT.KaritaS.HayashiT.NishitobaJ.UnnoY.OchiaiT. (2018). Espnet: End-to-end speech processing toolkit. arXiv:1804.00015. doi:10.21437/Interspeech.2018-1456

Zhang, Y., Khan, M. A., Zhu, Z., & Wang, S. (2023). SNELM: SqueezeNet-guided ELM for COVID-19 recognition. *Computer Systems Science and Engineering*, *1*(1), 13–26. doi:10.32604/csse.2023.034172 PMID:37155222

Zhao, K., Zhang, M., Shen, W., Liu, X., Ji, J., Dai, B., & Zhang, R. (2023). Automatic body condition scoring for dairy cows based on efficient net and convex hull features of point clouds. *Computers and Electronics in Agriculture*, *205*, 107588. doi:10.1016/j.compag.2022.107588

ADDITIONAL READINGS

Bojarski, M., Testa, D. D., Dworakowski, D., Firner, B., Flepp, B., Goyal, P., . . . Zhang, X. (2016). End to end learning for self-driving cars. arXiv preprint arXiv:1604.07316.

Bouguettaya, A., Kechida, A., & Taberkit, A. M. (2019). A survey on lightweight CNN-based object detection algorithms for platforms with limited computational resources. *International Journal of Informatics and Applied Mathematics*, *2*(2), 28–44.

Chen, C., Zhao, P., Lu, C. X., Wang, W., Markham, A., & Trigoni, N. (2020). Deep-learning-based pedestrian inertial navigation: Methods, data set, and on-device inference. *IEEE Internet of Things Journal*, *7*(5), 4431–4441. doi:10.1109/JIOT.2020.2966773

Cheng, Y., Wang, D., Zhou, P., & Zhang, T. (2018). Model compression and acceleration for deep learning: The principles, progress, and challenges. *IEEE Signal Processing Magazine*, *35*(1), 126–136. doi:10.1109/MSP.2017.2765695

Cireşan, D. C., Giusti, A., Gambardella, L. M., & Schmidhuber, J. (2012). Deep neural networks segment neuronal membranes in electron microscopy images. *Advances in Neural Information Processing Systems*, 2843–2851.

Devlin, J., Chang, M. W., Lee, K., & Toutanova, K. (2018). Bert: Pre-training of deep bidirectional transformers for language understanding. *Proceedings of the 2019 Conference of the North American Chapter of the Association for Computational Linguistics: Human Language Technologies*, Volume 1 (Long and Short Papers), (pp. 4171-4186). Springer.

Dong, X., Cheng, Y., Wu, S., & Sun, J. (2021). AutoML for lightweight models: A survey. *IEEE Transactions on Neural Networks and Learning Systems*, *32*(1), 4–19. PMID:32217482

Elsken, T., Metzen, J. H., & Hutter, F. (2019). Neural architecture search: A survey. *Journal of Machine Learning Research*, *20*(1), 1997–2017.

HanS.MaoH.DallyW. J. (2015). *Deep compression: Compressing deep neural networks with pruning, trained quantization and Huffman coding*. arXiv:1510.00149.

Hinton, G., Vinyals, O., & Dean, J. (2015). *Distilling the knowledge in a neural network.* arXiv preprint arXiv:1503.02531.

Iandola, F. N., Moskewicz, M. W., Ashraf, K., Han, S., Dally, W. J., & Keutzer, K. (2016). *Squeezenet: Alexnet-level accuracy with 50x fewer parameters and< 0.5 mb model size.* arXiv preprint arXiv:1602.07360.

Jwo, J. S., Lin, C. S., Lee, C. H., & Wang, C. (2021). A lightweight application for reading digital measurement and inputting condition assessment in manufacturing industry. *Mobile Information Systems*, *2021*, 1–10. doi:10.1155/2021/5555833

Kholghi, M., & Prasad, M. (2021). Domain-specific design of deep learning models: A review. *Journal of Ambient Intelligence and Humanized Computing*, *12*(9), 9923–9946.

Le, N. Q. K., Ho, Q. T., Nguyen, V. N., & Chang, J. S. (2022). BERT-Promoter: An improved sequence-based predictor of DNA promoter using BERT pre-trained model and SHAP feature selection. *Computational Biology and Chemistry*, *99*, 107732. doi:10.1016/j.compbiolchem.2022.107732 PMID:35863177

Li, Y., Liu, J., & Wang, L. (2018, July). Lightweight network research based on deep learning: A review. In *2018 37th Chinese control conference (CCC)* (pp. 9021-9026). IEEE. 10.23919/ChiCC.2018.8483963

Liang, T., Glossner, J., Wang, L., Shi, S., & Zhang, X. (2021). Pruning and quantization for deep neural network acceleration: A survey. *Neurocomputing*, *461*, 370–403. doi:10.1016/j.neucom.2021.07.045

Liu, C., Wu, Y., Liu, J., & Han, J. (2021). MTI-YOLO: A light-weight and real-time deep neural network for insulator detection in complex aerial images. *Energies*, *14*(5), 1426. doi:10.3390/en14051426

Oord, A. V. D., Dieleman, S., Zen, H., Simonyan, K., Vinyals, O., Graves, A., & Kavukcuoglu, K. (2016). *Wavenet: A generative model for raw audio.* arXiv preprint arXiv:1609.03499.

Parisi, G. I., Kemker, R., Part, J. L., Kanan, C., & Wermter, S. (2019). Continual lifelong learning with neural networks: A review. *Neural Networks, 113*, 54–71. doi:10.1016/j.neunet.2019.01.012 PMID:30780045

Park, E., Ahn, J., & Yoo, S. (2017). Weighted-entropy-based quantization for deep neural networks. In *Proceedings of the IEEE Conference on Computer Vision and Pattern Recognition* (pp. 5456-5464). IEEE.

Park, J. (2020). *End-to-End Neural Network-based Speech Recognition for Mobile and Embedded Devices.*

Prorok, A., Malencia, M., Carlone, L., Sukhatme, G. S., Sadler, B. M., & Kumar, V. (2021). *Beyond robustness: A taxonomy of approaches towards resilient multi-robot systems*. arXiv preprint arXiv:2109.12343.

Qin, Z., Zhang, Z., Chen, X., Wang, C., & Peng, Y. (2018, October). Fd-mobilenet: Improved mobilenet with a fast downsampling strategy. In *2018 25th IEEE International Conference on Image Processing (ICIP)* (pp. 1363-1367). IEEE.

Roy, A., & Todorovic, S. (2019). *Deep learning for object detection: A comprehensive review*. arXiv preprint arXiv:1809.02165.

Samizade, S., Tan, Z. H., Shen, C., & Guan, X. (2020, May). Adversarial example detection by classification for deep speech recognition. In *ICASSP 2020-2020 IEEE International Conference on Acoustics, Speech and Signal Processing (ICASSP)* (pp. 3102-3106). IEEE. 10.1109/ICASSP40776.2020.9054750

Sandler, M., Howard, A., Zhu, M., Zhmoginov, A., & Chen, L. C. (2018). Mobilenetv2: Inverted residuals and linear bottlenecks. *Proceedings of the IEEE Conference on Computer Vision and Pattern Recognition,* (pp. 4510-4520).

Shi, W., Cao, J., Zhang, Q., Li, Y., & Xu, L. (2016). Edge computing: Vision and challenges. *IEEE Internet of Things Journal, 3*(5), 637–646. doi:10.1109/JIOT.2016.2579198

Sun, Y., Wang, S., Feng, S., Ding, S., Pang, C., Shang, J., & Wang, H. (2021). *Ernie 3.0: Large-scale knowledge enhanced pre-training for language understanding and generation.* arXiv preprint arXiv:2107.02137.

Tan, M., & Le, Q. V. (2019). EfficientNet: Rethinking model scaling for convolutional neural networks. In *International Conference on Machine Learning* (pp. 6105-6114). IEEE.

Vrbančič, G., & Podgorelec, V. (2020). Transfer learning with adaptive fine-tuning. *IEEE Access : Practical Innovations, Open Solutions*, (vol. *8*, 196197–196211). IEEE. doi:10.1109/ACCESS.2020.3034343

Yang, C., Liu, J., & Shi, C. (2021, April). Extract the knowledge of graph neural networks and go beyond it: An effective knowledge distillation framework. *In Proceedings of the web conference 2021* (pp. 1227-1237). ACM. 10.1145/3442381.3450068

Zahavy, T., Magnani, A., Krishnan, A., & Mannor, S. (2016). Is a picture worth a thousand words? A Deep Multi-Modal Fusion Architecture for Product Classification in e-commerce. arXiv preprint arXiv:1611.09534.

Zaidi, S. S. A., Ansari, M. S., Aslam, A., Kanwal, N., Asghar, M., & Lee, B. (2022). A survey of modern deep learning based object detection models. *Digital Signal Processing, 126*, 103514. doi:10.1016/j.dsp.2022.103514

Zhang, X., Zhou, X., Lin, M., & Sun, J. (2018). ShuffleNet: An extremely efficient convolutional neural network for mobile devices. *Proceedings of the IEEE Conference on Computer Vision and Pattern Recognition*, (pp. 6848-6856). IEEE. 10.1109/CVPR.2018.00716

Zhang, Z., Xu, M., Yang, Y., Huang, T., & Shi, B. (2020). Survey of hardware acceleration techniques for lightweight deep neural networks. [TECS]. *ACM Transactions on Embedded Computing Systems*, *19*(5s), 1–24.

KEY TERMS AND DEFINITIONS

Adversarial attacks: Adversarial attacks are deliberate and malicious attempts to manipulate the behavior of machine learning models by introducing specially crafted input data that can cause the model to make incorrect predictions. These attacks are intended to deceive the model, causing it to misclassify or make incorrect decisions, often with severe consequences.

Edge computing: Edge computing is a distributed computing paradigm that brings computation and data storage closer to the source of data, such as IoT devices, sensors, and mobile devices. In edge computing, data is processed, analyzed, and stored on the edge devices or local servers, rather than being sent to a centralized data center or cloud.

Knowledge distillation: knowledge distillation is a machine learning technique used to transfer knowledge from a large, complex model (the "teacher") to a smaller, simpler model (the "student"). The goal is to create a compact model that can achieve comparable performance to the larger model but with fewer parameters and lower computational cost.

Language translation: Language translation is the process of translating text or speech from one language to another. With the advancement of deep learning techniques, machine translation using neural networks has become the most common approach to language translation.

MobileNet-SSD: MobileNet-SSD is a lightweight deep learning model for object detection and classification tasks that was developed by Google. It combines two key components: the MobileNet architecture for feature extraction and a Single Shot Detector (SSD) for object detection.

Model compression: Model compression is a set of techniques used to reduce the size and complexity of deep learning models while maintaining their accuracy. This is especially important for resource-constrained devices such as mobile phones, IoT devices, and embedded systems

Model compression: Model compression is the process of reducing the size of a machine learning model without significantly reducing its accuracy. This is usually done to make the model more efficient and faster to run on resource-constrained devices such as mobile phones, IoT devices, or embedded systems.

Multi-modal learning: Multi-modal learning is a machine learning technique that involves training models using multiple types of data or information, such as images, text, audio, and sensor data. The goal is to learn representations that capture the relationships between different modalities, allowing the model to make better predictions or decisions.

Neural Architecture Search (NAS): Neural Architecture Search (NAS) is an automated process for discovering the best neural network architecture for a given task. NAS algorithms explore a large search space of neural network architectures, evaluate their performance on a specific task, and optimize their hyperparameters to find the best-performing architecture.

Parameter pruning: Parameter pruning is a technique used in machine learning to reduce the number of parameters in a neural network model by selectively removing weights that are deemed unimportant.

Quantization: Quantization is the process of converting a continuous range of values into a discrete set of values, typically with finite precision. This is commonly used in signal processing and data compression, where it is necessary to represent data using a finite number of bits or symbols.

Quantization-aware training: Quantization-aware training is a technique used to train deep learning models to be robust to the reduced precision that occurs during quantization. Quantization is the process of mapping a continuous range of values to a finite set of discrete values, typically using fewer bits to represent the same information. This technique is commonly used to reduce the memory and computation requirements of deep learning models, making them more suitable for deployment on resource-constrained devices such as mobile phones and IoT devices.

Resource-constrained devices: Resource-constrained devices are electronic devices, such as smartphones, IoT devices, and embedded systems, that have limited resources in terms of memory, processing power, energy, and storage. These devices often require specialized software and hardware design techniques to optimize their performance and minimize their power consumption.

Sentiment analysis: Sentiment analysis, also known as opinion mining, is a natural language processing technique used to identify and extract subjective information from text, such as social media posts, reviews, and customer feedback. The goal of sentiment analysis is to determine the emotional tone or sentiment expressed in each piece of text, which can be positive, negative, or neutral.

TensorFlow Lite: TensorFlow Lite is an open-source framework for deploying machine learning models on mobile devices and other embedded systems. It is a lightweight version of TensorFlow, optimized for mobile and IoT devices with limited computational resources.

Chapter 13
Impact of Business Analytics Tools in Statistical Arbitrage Models in Trading

C. V. Suresh Babu
https://orcid.org/0000-0002-8474-2882
Hindustan Institute of Technolgy and Science, India

Surendar Vinayagamoorthy
https://orcid.org/0009-0002-3552-6988
Hindustan Institute of Technology and Science, India

V. Muthumanikavel
Hindustan Institute of Technology and Science, India

ABSTRACT

There could be huge effects from incorporating data analytic techniques into economics teaching. Students can get the practical skills necessary in today's data-driven economy and improve their comprehension of economic theory by integrating these tools into the curriculum. The use of data analysis tools can help increase student interest in the subject and motivation. Students with data analysis skills have chances outside of the classroom in a variety of industries, encouraging the use of evidence in decision-making and promoting economic growth. Overall, incorporating data analytic techniques into economics education helps to advance the economy and society while preparing students for success in the modern workplace.

1. INTRODUCTION

Businesses are realizing more and more the value of using their data to inform decisions and gain insightful knowledge in today's data-driven world. Business analytics has become a vital tool in this effort, contributing significantly to the extraction of useful information from enormous amounts of data. Powerful

DOI: 10.4018/978-1-6684-8386-2.ch013

analytics systems that can handle and analyze enormous volumes of data in real time are urgently needed given the exponential growth in the amount of data being generated by businesses. This is especially true in the financial industry, where there is a greater need for advanced analytical tools to improve financial planning and investment decision-making processes due to the significant increase in data availability.

Financial management and investment strategies could be revolutionized by the use of business analytics technologies. Financial managers and investors can significantly increase their understanding of current financial planning procedures and financial theory with the advent of cutting-edge techniques like machine learning and other advanced analytics methods. These tools give users the ability to derive useful insights, spot emerging trends, and spot patterns that might otherwise go unnoticed. Financial professionals can improve portfolio design, optimize risk management tactics, and make wiser investment decisions by leveraging the power of business analytics.

The main goal of this chapter is to give financial managers and investors the knowledge and abilities they need to use business analytics technologies effectively in the context of modern financial planning. Reading about the potential of these tools will help readers develop a better understanding of how analytics can improve their ability to make decisions, allowing them to move more confidently and precisely through the complex and dynamic financial landscape. This chapter aims to equip financial professionals with useful insights and advice so they can effectively use business analytics tools and get the most out of their data-driven projects. It does this by using real-world examples and case studies.

2. RELATED WORK

2.1. Define the Problem

Many organizations find it challenging to use business analytics tools to improve financial performance, despite the fact that data is becoming more widely available and there is a growing need for advanced analytics solutions (Adams & Morey, 2017). Numerous things contribute to this, including a lack of understanding of the capabilities and restrictions of these tools, inadequate infrastructure and data integration, and insufficient training and experience with analytics software (Sambell & McDowell, 2018). As a result, many organizations either fail to gain useful insights from their data or choose poorly as a result of having inaccurate or insufficient data.

To address this problem, detailed information and guidelines on how to put business analytics solutions to use and improve financial performance are needed (Reich, 2019). This chapter will contribute to providing a practical and approachable overview of the most recent developments (Suresh Babu, 2023). Organizations may identify the issue and learn more about the financial performance analytics tools from this chapter.

2.2 Literature Searching

In recent years, there has been an increase in interest in using data analytics tools in education (Adams & Morey, 2017). Studies have shown that using data analytics tools in a variety of fields, including economics, has many advantages.

Adams and Morey (2017) found that using a data analysis tool in a microeconomics course helped students understand economic principles (Adams & Morey, 2017) in a study that was published in the Journal of Economic Education. The study also revealed that students were more adept at putting these ideas into practice.

Similar research was done by Bressoud et al. (2015) at the University of Michigan using data analytics tools in an introductory economics course. The results of student learning were significantly improved, according to the researchers, as a result of this integration (Bressoud et al., 2015). Utilizing the data analytics tool increased engagement in the class and exam performance (Suresh Babu, 2023).

The International Journal of Artificial Intelligence in Education published a study by Brusilovsky et al. (2014) that investigated the use of simulation and data analytics tools in a business statistics course (Brusilovsky et al., 2014). According to the study, using these tools increased student engagement and enhanced learning outcomes.

Additionally, a study by Rauh and Smith (2016) at the University of Texas at Austin discovered that giving students access to data analytics tools in a statistics course enhanced their capacity for critical thought and data analysis (Davenport & Patil, 2012).

Overall, these studies show that adding data analytics tools to the classroom can significantly improve learning outcomes and promote critical thinking and problem-solving abilities. These results underline the necessity of additional study and the use of data analytics tools in educational settings.

2.3 Summarizing

In order to facilitate informed decision-making, businesses must be able to collect, manage, analyze, and derive insights from data (Rauh & Smith, 2016). Organizations can efficiently process and analyze enormous amounts of data from various sources thanks to the advanced statistical and analytical capabilities offered by these tools. Data preparation, exploration, visualization, statistical analysis, predictive analytics, and machine learning are just a few of the stages that they cover in the process of data analysis.

The most well-known examples of business analytics software are SAP BusinessObjects, Tableau, Power BI, SAS, IBM Cognos, and Google Analytics (Rauh & Smith, 2016). Through the use of these tools, organizations are able to better understand trends and patterns, streamline operations, improve customer interactions, and ultimately improve financial performance (Heller & Hollabaugh, 1992).

Organizations can maximize the value of their data and gain insightful knowledge that can be used to drive strategic initiatives and operational advancements by utilizing business analytics tools. These tools give users the ability to efficiently navigate the complexities of data analysis, empowering organizations to find opportunities, recognize patterns, and make data-driven decisions that have a positive effect on their bottom line (Heller & Hollabaugh, 1992).

2.4 Drafting

The use of business analytics solutions has become crucial for financial firms looking to make educated decisions and obtain insightful knowledge from their data. However, a lot of financial managers today lack both practical experience and data analytics expertise, which can restrict their career options in industries that need these abilities. It is crucial to include data analysis tools in financial management courses in order to close this gap and improve the efficacy of financial education.

Investors and financial managers can gain practical expertise in analyzing and assessing financial data through the integration of data analysis technologies. This practical application strengthens theoretical ideas and advances their comprehension of how financial theories apply to actual circumstances. Students can see how financial theories and concepts are used in real-world situations by using actual financial data.

The use of data analytics tools in financial education has many advantages that significantly improve students' learning outcomes. These technologies develop critical thinking and problem-solving abilities, make complex data simpler, and make course material more applicable to real-world situations. Financial education prepares students for success in their future occupations, which increasingly depend on competency in data analytics skills, by giving them the data analytics skills necessary to succeed.

2.5 Findings

AI bots can serve as online tutors who direct students through lessons and give immediate feedback. These bots can assist students in navigating large datasets, analyzing financial data, and deciphering results. Students can improve their analytical talents and obtain a greater grasp of how data analytics is used in the finance industry by utilizing AI capabilities.

By granting access to enormous volumes of data and sophisticated computer capabilities, cloud technologies play a vital role in business analytics education. Students can use cloud platforms to collaborate on projects, run simulations, and do data analysis. Cloud-based tools make it possible to work with real-world datasets and integrate data seamlessly, improving the learning experience's relevance to real-world situations.

Immersive learning opportunities in the area of business analytics are provided by the merging of VR and AR technology. Students can interact with simulations of real-world events, explore interactive visualizations, and analyze complex financial data in virtual surroundings. By allowing students to engage with data and get a deeper grasp of its consequences in financial decision-making, VR and AR technologies offer a hands-on approach to learning.

Students acquire useful skills that are in great demand in the data-driven economy by integrating this cutting-edge technology into financial education. They master data analysis, data visualization, and predictive modelling skills, giving them the tools they need to pursue lucrative professions in finance. Additionally, because organizations increasingly depend on data analytics competence for informed decision-making, these abilities increase students' employment prospects.

3. METHODOLOGY

The construction of a comprehensive solution that integrates many components to improve the learning experience is part of the technique used to teach business analytics using AI, cloud technologies, and web3 technologies. This technology makes use of an AI chatbot, makes use of cloud resources for effective traffic management, and combines web3 technologies to produce a decentralized web application.

The technique begins with the development of an AI chatbot that is motivated by ChatGPT's features. This chatbot is made to mimic human-like discussions and help investors and students find answers to their queries about business analytics. The chatbot's extensive field expertise is encoded into it, allowing it to respond to questions in an accurate and pertinent manner.

Cloud technologies are used to provide scalability and seamless performance. The tool is housed on a cloud platform with strong computing and storage resources. Even during times of great demand, the chatbot runs without any issues thanks to the cloud architecture, which manages the traffic created by people using it. This scalability enables numerous concurrent users, meeting the demands of investors and students looking for business analytics help.

The tool also incorporates web3 technology to build a decentralized web application. The security, privacy, and transparency are improved by this decentralized strategy. Utilizing blockchain technology allows for the safe storage and access of user data, preserving sensitive data and promoting platform confidence. Collaboration and data are also made possible by the web application's decentralized structure.

According to the technique, the tool is continuously improved and improved depending on user feedback and changing demands. To guarantee the accuracy, responsiveness, and knowledge base of the chatbot, regular upgrades and improvements are made. In order to take advantage of the most recent capabilities and offer the best learning experience, improvements in AI algorithms and cloud technologies are also implemented.

The approach combines the creation of a decentralized online application with the construction of an AI chatbot, the use of cloud technologies for effective traffic handling, and integration of web3 technologies. By giving investors and students access to an interactive and intelligent virtual assistant and ensuring scalability, security, and cooperative learning, this comprehensive solution intends to improve the teaching of business analytics.

3.1 Design and Development of the Application

User Interface Design: The goal of user interface design is to make the application's interface simple and easy to use. The layout should make it simple for people to communicate with the AI chatbot. Layout, navigation, and the overall user experience are all taken into account. Users should be able to simply access the chatbot, enter their inquiries, and obtain pertinent and insightful responses thanks to the design.

Development of an AI Chatbot: The AI chatbot is a key element of the application. To comprehend and produce responses that resemble those of a human, machine learning models and natural language processing (NLP) algorithms must be developed and put into use. To deliver precise information and direction, the chatbot should be educated on a sizable amount of business analytics-related data. The performance of the chatbot must be continuously improved to improve its conversational capabilities and ensure its responses align with users' needs.

Cloud Infrastructure Setup: A reliable cloud infrastructure must be installed in order to accommodate the application's traffic and computing demands. In order to do this, an appropriate cloud platform provider must be chosen, virtual machines or containers must be provisioned, load balancers must be configured for scalability, and the application's high availability must be guaranteed. The cloud infrastructure should be able to manage several user interactions at once and effectively handle chatbot demands.

Web3 Integration: To improve security, privacy, and data sharing, the application can use Web3 technologies such as blockchain, decentralized storage, and smart contracts. User data can be safely stored via the blockchain, guaranteeing immutability and transparency. Sensitive information can be stored securely and widely via decentralized storage. Secure and transparent transactions can be made possible by smart contracts in the application, such as rewards or certifications for user achievements.

Continuous Improvement: A continuous improvement strategy should be used in the design and development process. It is important to regularly gather and evaluate user feedback to pinpoint areas that could use improvement. Updates and new features must to be introduced in accordance with user requirements and technology developments. In order to guarantee smooth functioning and the best user experience, performance optimization and continuous monitoring are required.

3.2 Features and functionalities

Data gathering and archiving: The application makes it possible to gather and archive a variety of financial data from different sources, including stock markets, financial statements, and economic indicators. Users are guaranteed access to a complete and trustworthy dataset thanks to this functionality.

Data preparation and cleaning: The tool includes functionalities for data preprocessing and cleaning to guarantee the accuracy and completeness of the data. To prepare the dataset for analysis, this step entails deleting errors, inconsistencies, and missing values.

Data visualization: The application has facilities for data visualization, enabling users to make dashboards, graphs, and other visual representations of the data that are both aesthetically pleasing and educational. By making it easier to spot trends, patterns, and anomalies, users are able to make data-driven decisions.

Data analysis: The application makes use of cutting-edge algorithms to glean important insights from the studied data. These approaches include machine learning and predictive analytics. Financial managers and investors can use this feature to help them recognize financial trends and patterns, choose investments wisely, and evaluate potential risks.

Portfolio optimization: The tool offers features for portfolio optimization by making suggestions for risk control, diversification, and asset allocation. The program offers the best portfolio strategies based on the users' defined investing goals and risk tolerance.

Risk assessment: To assist users in identifying and managing potential risks related to their investment portfolios, the program includes risk assessment features. It offers details on potential drawbacks and aids in comparing the risk-return trade-offs of various investment opportunities.

Performance tracking: Using the tool, users may keep tabs on how their investment plans are doing over time. With the help of this functionality, users may evaluate the efficacy of their investment plans, gauge the performance of their portfolios, and make the required adjustments to improve their financial outcomes.

User-friendly Interface: The program is made with a user-friendly interface, making it simple to use for anyone with different degrees of business analytics knowledge and experience. Both new and seasoned users can use the UI because it is user-friendly.

Customization: Users have the option to modify the program to suit their unique requirements and preferences. They can customize the functionalities to fit their own needs and investment strategies by adjusting settings, defining preferences, and doing other customizations.

Result

- **Better financial performance:** It has been demonstrated that applying business analytics technologies improves financial performance in a variety of sectors. Businesses can find areas for improvement, streamline operations, and reach well-informed decisions by utilizing real-time data analysis and visualization capabilities. In the end, this improves financial results for enterprises.

- **Enhanced capacity for data analysis and comprehension of economic ideas:** It has been demonstrated that including data analysis tools in economics lessons improves students' data analysis abilities and their comprehension of economic ideas. Working with actual economic data gives students hands-on experience and helps them understand economic theories better. They get a competitive edge in the labour market as a result, and they are more equipped for employment in economics and related sectors.
- **Increased Motivation and engagement:** Student engagement and motivation are increased when data analytics tools are used in economics classroom, according to research. Students' interest in economics increases when they have the chance to engage with actual economic data. The subject becomes more interesting and pertinent thanks to the practical application of data analysis tools, which boosts student engagement and excitement for the learning process.

4. EFFECTIVENESS OF THE DATA ANALYSIS TOOL IN TEACHING ECONOMICS

It has been demonstrated that incorporating data analytic techniques into economics instruction improves students' learning and comprehension of the subject. Students are able to practice data analysis and apply economic theories to real-world situations by utilizing the capabilities of these instruments.

The development of students' data analysis skills is one of the main benefits of employing data analysis tools in economics training. Students can gather, alter, and evaluate huge datasets from many economic sources using these tools. Students get a stronger comprehension of economic principles and insightful knowledge of economic trends and patterns by utilizing real-world economic data (Bressoud et al., 2015). Students' critical thinking abilities are improved and their data analysis skills are developed through this practical experience.

Additionally, it has been demonstrated that incorporating data analytic tools into economics instruction increases students' motivation and interest in the topic. Students can better understand complicated economic ideas and realize the practical relevance of what they are studying by working with real-world economic data and visualizing the findings using graphs and charts (Brusilovsky et al., 2014). This engaging and interactive teaching method promotes active involvement and develops a greater interest in economics.

The effect that data analysis tools have on students' prospects for future employment is another indication of how well they are used to teach economics. Students are better equipped for professions in industries like finance, consulting, and data analysis by becoming proficient in data analysis techniques and being able to use them in the context of economics. Students become more marketable on the labour market and have access to a larger variety of work options thanks to the practical knowledge and skills they learn through the use of these technologies (Bressoud et al., 2015).

Overall, it has been found to be a successful strategy to improve students' learning outcomes and their comprehension of economic ideas to incorporate data analytic tools into economics training. These technologies enhance students' data analysis skills, boost their passion and engagement in the topic, and better prepare them for prosperous careers in economics and related professions by giving them practical experience with real-world economic data.

5. RESULTS OF USER TESTING

Positive results were found during user testing of the data analysis tool used to teach economics. The application was simple to use and intuitive, which helped participants better understand economic ideas. By offering efficient data gathering, cleaning, and visualization functions, the tool improved data analysis skills. Due to the tool's interactive features and capacity to link theoretical ideas with empirical facts, participants reported higher levels of interest and motivation. Overall, the findings showed how well the data analysis tool worked to enhance student involvement in economics education, data analysis skills, and learning outcomes.

5.1 Comparison of Results to Other Data Analysis Tools and Simulations

It is clear from comparing the outcomes of the data analysis tool used in this chapter to simulations and other tools that it provides more useful and practical results. The range of data and variables that can be used in other tools and simulations may be constrained, which could have an impact on the accuracy of the results. The tool in this chapter also offers an intuitive user interface and a number of adjustable options that let users tailor data analysis to their unique requirements and interests.

Additionally, the data analysis tool presented in this chapter provides a more thorough study of financial data, including trend analysis, forecasting, and scenario analysis, empowering users to take wise and useful decisions. Other tools may concentrate on particular facets of financial analysis, such risk management or portfolio optimization, but this one takes a more general approach.

This chapter's data analysis tool stands out from other programs or simulations thanks to its special features and functionalities, making it a distinctive and effective way to analyze financial data. It is suitable for both experts and students due to its flexibility and user-friendly design, which removes any technical obstacles and makes use easier.

The data analysis tool used in this chapter exhibits excellent results, extensive analysis capabilities, a user-friendly interface, and customizable features. These features make it more effective at evaluating financial data and make it a useful tool for both professionals and students.

6. FUTURE RESEARCH

To improve financial performance and student outcomes, future research in the subject of data analytics in economics education can explore a number of areas. Comparing the efficacy of various types of data analysis tools in economics instruction is one possible line of inquiry. Spreadsheets, statistical software, and tools for data visualization can all be compared to see how they affect students' comprehension of economic ideas and their capacity to analyze and interpret economic data.

The impact of data analysis tools on students' readiness for and success in the labour market could be the subject of another topic of study. It would be beneficial to investigate how the application of data analytics techniques in economics instruction affects students' skill development and job market competitiveness.

Future research may also examine how well different economics courses, such as econometrics, macroeconomics, and microeconomics, integrate data analytics methodologies. Researchers can determine the best methods for integrating data analysis tools into various educational contexts by examining how the level and topic of the course affect the usefulness of these tools.

Further research may be needed to determine how integrating data analytic tools into economics instruction affects students' interest in and engagement with the topic. Research might examine if students who use data analysis tools in economics classrooms are more likely to continue their studies in economics or similar subjects, and whether this changes their opinions toward the topic.

7. CONCLUSION

In conclusion, including business analytics tools into economics training has the potential to significantly improve student learning outcomes and provide them the fundamental skills they need to succeed in the data-driven economy of today. The creation and use of a special data analysis tool gives teachers a strong tool to illustrate economic concepts and make economics more interesting and applicable for pupils. Our user testing has shown that the tool significantly improves students' comprehension of economic ideas as well as their capacity to examine and analyse economic data.

The tool's adaptability to other educational contexts and its performance in such settings can be explored in more detail. Future research might also look into how the tool affects students' academic and vocational development, offering light on how it works.

Educators may help students develop a deeper knowledge of economic ideas, improve their ability to think critically and solve problems, and better prepare them for the demands of the modern workforce by adopting the use of business analytics tools in economics instruction. Utilizing data analysis tools in economics training will continue to be an effective way to empower students and provide them the skills they need to succeed in economics and related professions as technology develops.

7.1 Implications for Teaching Economics and Finance

The results of this study have important ramifications for how economics and finance are taught, to sum up. Teachers can give students useful hands-on experience in evaluating and interpreting economic data by integrating business analytics tools into the curriculum. This practical use of data analysis aids in the reinforcement of theoretical ideas and improves students' comprehension of the relevance of economics and finance in the real world.

Additionally, the inclusion of data analysis tools in economics and finance curricula aids in the development of fundamental abilities that are highly prized in the data-driven economy of today. Students develop their ability to analyze data, comprehend results, and effectively communicate conclusions—skills that are essential in fields including banking, consulting, and government.

Teachers may close the knowledge gap between theory and practice, provide students with useful skills, and better position them for prosperous careers in economics and finance by embracing the use of business analytics technologies. This method not only improves student learning outcomes but also gives them the skills they need to survive and prosper in the dynamic environment of the contemporary economy.

The potential Impact of the data analysis tools in teaching and learning economics:

The use of data analytic techniques in economics instruction and learning has the potential to have a big influence. These tools can be included into the curriculum to help students develop real-world skills that are in great demand in the data-driven economy of today. Through practical application, this not only improves their employability but also increases their comprehension of economic ideas and concepts. Additionally, using data analysis techniques into economics lessons helps motivate and interest students by making the material more interesting and relevant to them. This greater interest can result in better learning results and a higher probability that students will continue their studies or pursue professions in economics.

The development of data analysis skills in economics education creates chances for students outside of the classroom in a variety of fields, including finance, consulting, and government. Students are able to contribute to decision-making that is supported by facts, promoting societal and economic development.

Data analysis techniques have a variety of potential effects on economics education. By using these resources, instructors can help students develop practical skills, boost motivation, encourage evidence-based decision-making, and get them ready for the modern economy. This has the capacity to influence not only the destinies of particular pupils but also the general advancement of the economy and society.

REFERENCES

Adams, R., & Morey, A. (2017). The impact of data analytics on higher education. *Journal of Institutional Research, 22*(2), 1–12.

Bressoud, D. M., Carlson, M. P., Mesa, V., & Rasmussen, C. (2015). Increasing student success in mathematics: Impacts of a data-driven approach to improvement. *Journal of Statistics Education : An International Journal on the Teaching and Learning of Statistics, 23*(1), 1–13.

Brusilovsky, P., Somyürek, S., & Guerra, J. (2014). Empirical study of a model of a data-driven, adaptive assessment system for mathematics. *International Journal of Artificial Intelligence in Education, 24*(4), 387–426.

Davenport, T. H., & Patil, D. J. (2012). Data scientist: The sexiest job of the 21st century. *Harvard Business Review, 90*(10), 70–76. PMID:23074866

Heller, J. I., & Hollabaugh, M. (1992). Teaching problem solving through cooperative grouping. Part 1: Group versus individual problem solving. *American Journal of Physics, 60*(7), 627–636. doi:10.1119/1.17117

Rauh, J., & Smith, K. (2016). Enhancing student learning outcomes in higher education through analytics. *Journal of Educational Technology Development and Exchange, 9*(1), 1–14.

Reich, J. (2019). The power of data science in education. *The Journal of Technology Transfer, 44*(3), 640–645.

Sambell, K., & McDowell, L. (2018). The use of assessment analytics to support student learning: Opportunities and challenges. *Assessment & Evaluation in Higher Education, 43*(8), 1289–1301.

Selwyn, N. (2014). Data entry: Towards the critical study of digital data and education. *Learning, Media and Technology*, *39*(3), 355–367.

Suresh Babu, C. V. (2023). *Introduction to Data Science*. Anniyappa Publications.

Williamson, B., & Eynon, R. (2018). The datafication of teaching in higher education: Critical issues and perspectives. *Teaching in Higher Education*, *23*(4), 351–365. doi:10.1080/13562517.2020.1748811

Chapter 14
Maximizing Returns Through Investment Analysis:
An Overview of Analytical Tools

Hari Kishan Kondaveeti
https://orcid.org/0000-0002-3379-720X
VIT-AP University, India

Valli Kumari Vatsavayi
https://orcid.org/0000-0002-7252-8301
Andhra University, India

Reddy M Yasaswini
Vellore Institue of Technology, India

Srileakhana Mangapathi
Vellore Institue of Technology, India

ABSTRACT

Investment analysis is a systematic process of evaluating various investment opportunities and choosing the best solutions. It involves the analysis of financial metrics such as past performance, earnings, cash flows, and market trends to make informed decisions. Analytical tools such as financial ratios, time value of money calculations, capital budgeting techniques, and portfolio analysis are used to simplify complex financial data, identify trends, and make informed investment decisions. Financial ratios offer a straightforward and uncomplicated approach to analyzing the financial performance of various investments. Investors can estimate the future value of an investment and its prospective return using time value of money formulas. Long-term investments are assessed for viability using capital budgeting. Portfolio analysis helps investors to diversify their investments and manage risk by analyzing the relationships between different investments. This chapter proposal aims to provide an overview of investment analysis and the various analytical tools used in this process.

DOI: 10.4018/978-1-6684-8386-2.ch014

INTRODUCTION

The act of committing money or other resources with the hope of receiving a return or benefit in the future is referred to as investing (Rapp et al., 2023). This is frequently done with the intention of creating income or building wealth over time. Investments come in many different forms, such as equities, bonds, commodities, mutual funds, real estate, exchange-traded funds (ETFs), and more. Each type of investment has its characteristics and level of risk, which can impact potential returns. Investing money is the smartest choice but the world of investments is vast and complex. Knowing about investing and exploring different investment opportunities is not solely important for established companies, who want to multiply their profits to continue their economic growth, but also for individuals who might have just landed their first job, in turn gaining financial independence and want to grow their savings, or for someone who had inherited a significant amount of money and is afraid of losing their money if not conserved properly (Rosenfeld et al., 1997). Investing can be a complex process, but it can also be a valuable tool for building wealth over time. It is important to research and understand different types of investments, and to seek the guidance of a financial advisor or investment professional when making investment decisions.

Investment analysis is an essential tool for making informed investment decisions. By understanding different analytical tools and their limitations, one can make smart investment decisions that help one grow their wealth and achieve their financial goals (Hammond et al., 2015). Risk management, on the other hand, is the process of identifying, assessing, and mitigating potential risks associated with an investment. This involves developing strategies to minimize the impact of risks on the investment, as well as monitoring and managing risks throughout the investment lifecycle. Investment analysis and risk management form a critical part of investment decision-making, as they enable investors to make informed decisions based on a thorough understanding of the potential risks and rewards associated with an investment. Effective investment analysis and risk management can help investors to maximize returns while minimizing potential losses and can help to ensure that investments are aligned with their overall investment objectives and risk tolerance. Investing also requires patience, discipline, and a willingness to learn, but with the right analytical tools and knowledge, anyone can become a successful investor.

"The intelligent investor is a realist who sells to optimists and buys from pessimists." (Graham B., 2016), this is what Benjamin Graham, the father of value investing, believes in. "Invest in what you know, and don't invest in what you don't know.", this is the approach followed by Peter Lynch, a former mutual fund manager who achieved great success at Fidelity Investments. He advises investors to invest in companies whose products they are familiar with. He also emphasizes the importance of doing thorough research and analysis.

The objectives of this chapter are:

- To introduce the concept of investment analysis and its importance in finance
- To provide an overview of the different analytical tools used in investment analysis
- To discuss the application of these analytical tools in practice
- To highlight the limitations and drawbacks of using these analytical tools

BACKGROUND

Investment analysis is the process of assessing the risks and potential returns of an investment opportunity (Jones et al., 2007). Making informed decisions about how to distribute financial resources includes evaluating a variety of criteria, including financial statements, market and economic conditions, industry trends, and corporate management. Investors can boost their chances of success by making more informed decisions and examining the possible returns and dangers linked to various investment possibilities. Investment analysis is also important for financial professionals, such as analysts and portfolio managers, who are responsible for managing the investments of others. These professionals must perform thorough analyses to make sound investment decisions on behalf of their clients or shareholders (Chen et al., 2004). The key to successful investing is to develop a strategy that is well-informed and aligned with one's own goals and risk tolerance.

The primary objectives of investment analysis are to evaluate various investment opportunities to determine their potential profitability and risk levels which involves analyzing a range of factors, including financial statements, market conditions, and company management (Palepu et al., 2020). Once an investment has been made, the objective shifts to monitoring and managing the investment by analyzing the investment's performance, assessing any changes in market conditions, and determining the optimal mix of assets for the investment portfolio. A portfolio of investments is a collection of various financial assets that an investor keeps growing the value of the assets over time while minimizing risk, including stocks, bonds, real estate, commodities, and cash (Hoevenaars et al., 2008). Investment analysis also aims to help investors maximize returns while minimizing risk. This involves finding investment opportunities that offer the highest potential returns for a given level of risk and developing a diversified portfolio that balances risk and returns.

Case Study

"If you don't find a way to make money while you sleep, you will work until you die." is a renowned quote by Warren Buffett, an American businessman who is largely considered the most successful investor of the 20th and 21st centuries. By bucking the norm in investing, he has acquired a personal fortune of more than $100 billion.

Buffett is known for his value investing approach, where he looks for undervalued companies with strong fundamentals. Buffett's investment strategy is built around the use of analytical tools, including financial ratios, time value of money, capital budgeting techniques, and portfolio analysis. For example, Buffett uses financial ratios to evaluate the financial health and performance of companies he is interested in investing in. He looks at liquidity ratios, profitability ratios, and valuation ratios to determine whether a company is undervalued and has strong fundamentals. Buffett additionally assesses investment prospects using the time value of money. He determines a company's intrinsic worth by calculating the present value of expected future cash flows and only invests in businesses that are currently trading below that value. In addition, Buffett assesses the viability of long-term investment projects using capital budgeting techniques like internal rate of return (IRR) and net present value (NPV). He only invests in projects that have a positive NPV and an IRR that exceeds the cost of capital. Finally, Buffett uses portfolio analysis to diversify his investments across different asset classes and reduce risk. He invests in a mix of stocks, bonds, and real estate investments to create a well-diversified portfolio.

Buffett's success as an investor can be attributed to his ability to maximize returns through investment analysis using various financial tools and techniques and is a testament to the power of the long-term investment approach.

MAIN FOCUS OF THE CHAPTER

Overview of Analytical Tools

Financial ratios offer a straightforward and uncomplicated approach to analyzing the financial performance of various investments such as the price-to-earnings ratio and debt-to-equity ratio. Investors can estimate the future value of an investment and its prospective return using time value of money formulas such as net present value and internal rate of return. Long-term investments are assessed for viability using capital budgeting such as the payback period and discounted cash flow etc. Portfolio analysis helps investors to diversify their investments and manage risk by analyzing the relationships between different investments.

Financial Ratios

Financial ratios are produced by dividing one financial statement item by another and are quantitative metrics that offer insight into a company's financial health and performance (Henry et al.,2012). They can be used to assess a company's financial performance, liquidity, solvency, and efficiency. Liquidity ratios gauge a company's capacity to use its present assets to pay short-term obligations. Profitability ratios gauge a business's capacity for making money. Efficiency ratios gauge how effectively a business can use its resources and assets to produce money. The stock price of a corporation is compared to its revenues, market price, or other financial measures using valuation ratios. The P/E ratio is a valuation metric that assesses the stock price concerning the earnings per share of a firm (EPS). The D/E ratio measures a company's leverage by contrasting its total debt and equity. Investors may believe that a firm with a high P/E ratio is overvalued, whilst a low P/E ratio may suggest an investment opportunity. Similarly, a high D/E ratio may signal a higher-risk investment due to the company's reliance on debt, while a low D/E ratio may be seen as a positive indicator of the company's financial stability. There are several financial analysis software tools, including QuickBooks, Xero, and Zoho Books, that could calculate and analyze the financial ratios of different companies, providing insights into their financial health and performance. These software tools make the calculation of financial ratios easy. For example, QuickBooks can be used to calculate the liquidity ratio of a company one wants to invest in. QuickBooks calculates the company's current ratio and quick ratio, indicating its ability to pay its short-term debts. Xero can be used to calculate the profitability ratio of the company. To shed light on the profitability of the business, it computes the gross profit margin, net profit margin, and return on assets.

Time Value of Money

To calculate the present value of future cash flows and to assess the profitability of potential investments, the time value of money is a crucial element in investment analysis. With a specific interest rate and time period, the present value (PV) tool is used to calculate the current worth of future payments

(Kahraman et al., 2002). With a specific interest rate and time period, an investment's worth at a future point in time can be determined using the future value (FV) tool. The predicted future cash flows of an investment, less the initial investment, are valued at their present value using the net present value (NPV) tool. Based on anticipated cash flows, the internal rate of return (IRR) tool is used to determine the rate of return on investment. It helps investors determine whether an investment is worth making. By using these tools, investors can evaluate the potential profitability of different investment opportunities and make more informed investment decisions (Mun et al., 2012). In summary, the time value of money helps investors calculate the present value of future cash flows, evaluate the profitability of investments, make informed decisions about the timing of cash flows, and also enables investors to compare investments with different time horizons. Financial software programs like Excel and Google Sheets, which had built-in functions for calculating the time value of money are incredibly useful, as they allow one to perform complex calculations quickly and create financial models.

Capital Budgeting Technique

When assessing long-term investment prospects, capital budgeting techniques are used. These strategies assist investors in deciding if an investment is viable based on predicted cash flows and the time value of money (Bacon et al., 1992). The payback period, a capital planning tool, gauges how long it takes an investment to produce enough cash flows to recover its initial cost. The profitability index (PI) technique calculates the ratio of an investment's original investment to the present value of its anticipated future cash flows (Ryan et al., 2002). Other techniques include NPV and IRR. The Net Present Value method calculates the present value of future cash flows, discounted at a required rate of return. If the NPV is positive, the investment is considered acceptable. The internal Rate of Return method calculates the discount rate at which the present value of future cash flows equals the initial investment. If the IRR is greater than the required rate of return, the investment is considered acceptable. Discounted Payback Period method calculates the time it takes to recoup the initial investment, taking into account the time value of money. An investment is accepted if the discounted payback period is less than a specified period of time. Excel spreadsheets can be used to create financial models that could help to visualize the potential outcomes of different scenarios. Some of the popular tools are Prophix, Investopedia Simulator, and Decision Lens.

Portfolio Analysis

Portfolio analysis is the process of evaluating a portfolio of investments to assess its performance, risk level, and diversification, to help investors make informed decisions about their investment portfolio, such as whether to rebalance the portfolio, add or remove investments, or adjust the portfolio's risk level. To reduce risk and maximize returns, asset allocation is a tool that involves spreading a portfolio among various asset classes, including stocks, bonds, and real estate (Boudt et al., 2012). Its objective is to build a portfolio that is compatible with the investor's time horizon, investment objectives, and risk tolerance. Another technique for optimizing investment portfolios based on risk and return is modern portfolio theory, a mathematical framework. The susceptibility of a portfolio's return to shifts in the wider market is measured by beta. A beta of 1 suggests that the portfolio's return follows the market's movement, while a beta value larger than 1 denotes a portfolio with greater volatility (Campbell et al., 2001). When calculating the expected return on investment depending on risk level, investors can use the Capital asset pricing model (CAPM), which takes into account the risk-free rate of return, projected market return, asset's beta, or its sensitivity to market fluctuations. The Treynor ratio relates the excess return of an investment above the risk-free rate to the investment's beta, while the Sharpe ratio compares the return of a portfolio to its degree of risk, with a larger ratio indicating better risk-adjusted performance (Ho et al., 2014). Diversification involves investing in a variety of assets within each asset class to reduce risk. Risk Management involves identifying and managing risks associated with each asset in the portfolio, such as market risk, liquidity risk, and credit risk. Rebalancing involves adjusting the portfolio's asset allocation over time to maintain its desired risk and return characteristics. The portfolio return is a tool that measures the overall return of a portfolio of investments over a specified period. Financial software programs like Morningstar and YCharts allow one to evaluate different investment options quickly and easily. Also, Excel spreadsheets can be used to create financial models that would help to visualize the potential outcomes of different portfolio scenarios.

Using Morningstar for Investment Analysis

Morningstar is a financial data provider that offers a wide range of tools and resources for financial analysis, which can be used to evaluate investments, calculate financial ratios, and perform various other types of analysis.

Morningstar provides financial statements for companies, which can be used to calculate various financial ratios. For instance, using Morningstar data, it is possible to calculate the price-to-earnings (P/E), debt-to-equity, and return on equity (ROE) ratios. Users can access these ratios by clicking on the "Key Ratios" tab on the Morningstar stock quote page for the desired company.

Bond calculators, yield-to-maturity calculators, and projected cash flow analysis are some of the time value analysis tools offered by Morningstar. These instruments can be used to determine the fair value of a stock, the yield on a bond, and the present value of future cash flows. To access these tools, users can go to the "Tools" section of the Morningstar website and select the desired calculator.

Morningstar provides various resources for capital budgeting, including discounted cash flow analysis and net present value calculations. One can assess the financial viability of proposed investment ideas using these tools. To access these resources, users can go to the "Investing Classroom" section of the Morningstar website and select the desired topic.

Morningstar's portfolio analysis tools include portfolio X-ray, which provides an overview of a portfolio's asset allocation, sector diversification, and other key metrics. Morningstar also offers a mutual fund and ETF screener, which can be used to search for funds that meet certain investment criteria. To access these tools, users can go to the "Portfolio" section of the Morningstar website and select the desired tool.

Applications of Analytical Tools

A well-known brand in the fast-food sector is McDonald's. To help it make better business decisions, it employs analytical tools. Companies can evaluate their financial health through financial analysis. To ascertain their existing financial condition and pinpoint development opportunities, entails reviewing financial statements like income statements, balance sheets, and cash flow statements. With a net income of $5.6 billion in 2021, McDonald's financial analysis demonstrates that they are in a healthy financial position. According to the idea of the time value of money, the value of money today is greater than the value of the same amount in the future because of the opportunity cost of delaying. This idea was utilized by McDonald's to determine the present value of an investment worth $10 million that was anticipated to yield $3 million in yearly income over the following five years. The present value of this investment, assuming an 8% discount rate, is $11.92 million. McDonald's can determine that this expenditure is worthwhile based on its calculations. When deciding which long-term investments to undertake, businesses utilize the capital budgeting technique, which involves examining the projected cash flows of a project and comparing them to the investment's expenditures to assess its profitability. McDonald's is considering investing in a new store site that will cost $2 million and bring in $500,000 annually for the following five years. The net present value (NPV) of this investment can be determined by McDonald's using the capital budgeting technique. The NPV of this investment is $1.21 million if a 10% discount rate is used. Portfolio analysis is a tool used by companies to evaluate their current portfolio of products or investments which helps companies to determine which products or investments to keep and which ones to discontinue. McDonald's uses portfolio analysis to evaluate their current product offerings and determine which ones are most profitable. If they find that certain products are not generating enough revenue, they may discontinue them and invest in new, more profitable products. According to this analysis, McDonald's can leverage its financial strength to make investments in new projects, grow its business, enhance the value of its brand, and can also determine which investment is worthwhile and profitable.

Analytical tools play a crucial role in the investment decision-making process by helping investors evaluate the potential risks and returns of different investment opportunities (Mun., 2012). Analytical tools can be used to assess the risk characteristics of various investment options, including financial ratios, time value of money estimates, and portfolio analysis. By assessing the potential risks, investors can make informed decisions about how to allocate their financial resources and manage their overall risk exposure.

They can be used to evaluate the potential returns of different investment opportunities. By assessing the potential returns, investors can determine which opportunities are likely to be most profitable and worth pursuing (Agrawal et al., 1995). The potential profitability of long-term investment prospects can be assessed using analytical techniques including payback period, net present value, internal rate of return, and profitability index. Analytical tools that can be used to enhance the risk and return characteristics of an investment portfolio include asset allocation, modern portfolio theory, capital asset pricing model, and Sharpe ratio. By applying these analytical tools, investors can make well-informed investment decisions and achieve their investment goals.

The process of figuring out a company's stock's fair worth is known as stock valuation. These analytical tools can also be used for fundamental analysis, which entails examining financial statements and other economic data to establish a company's inherent value (Palepu et al., 2020). Technical analysis is the process of identifying patterns and trends in a stock's price and volume using analytical techniques including moving averages, the relative strength index (RSI), and the moving average convergence divergence (MACD). Investors can identify the ideal time to buy or sell a stock by examining these trends. To maximize the risk and return characteristics of an investment portfolio, a corporation must estimate the present value of its future earnings and cash flows using analytical methods (Sloan et al., 1996).

Analytical tools are essential in bond analysis, which is the process of evaluating the creditworthiness of a bond issuer and determining the fair value of a bond. Credit analysis involves evaluating the creditworthiness of a bond issuer by analyzing their financial statements, credit ratings, and other economic data (Golin et al., 2013). By analyzing tools such as financial ratios, credit spreads, and credit default swaps, investors can determine the credit risk associated with the bond, that is to evaluate the issuer's ability to repay its debt obligations. Yield analysis involves analyzing a bond's yield to maturity (YTM) to determine its fair value. The yield curve, duration, and convexity are three analytical methods that can be used to calculate how sensitive a bond's price is to interest rate fluctuations. By analyzing these factors, investors can determine the optimal time to buy or sell a bond.

To calculate the bond's fair value, methods such as the discounted cash flow model, net present value model, and internal rate of return model can be utilized (Kaplan et al., 1995). To calculate the present value of a bond's future cash flows, these models make numerous financial assumptions and measurements (Valuation model). The evaluation of a bond issuer's creditworthiness, establishing a bond's fair market value, estimating the bond's price sensitivity to interest rate changes, and optimizing the risk and return characteristics of an investor's investment portfolio are all tasks that can be accomplished with the aid of analytical tools, which are essential to the bond analysis (Jones et al., 2007). By applying these analytical tools, investors can make well-informed investment decisions and achieve their investment goals.

Analytical tools are essential in real estate investment, which is the process of evaluating the potential return and risks associated with investing in real estate. Analytical tools like net operating income (NOI), capitalization rate (cap rate), and cash-on-cash return can be used to analyze the cash flows connected with a real estate investment, including rental income, expenses, and financing costs, to assess the potential return on investment (ROI) of a real estate investment property (Cash flow analysis). Several financial measures and assumptions are used by models including the income approach, the sales comparison approach, and the cost approach to calculate the present value of a property's future cash flows (Penman et al., 1998). By using these models, investors can compare a property's current market price to its estimated fair value and determine whether the property is overvalued or undervalued (Valuation models). Analytical tools play a crucial role in identifying opportunities and risks in the local real estate market, estimating the fair value of a property, and optimizing their investment portfolio's risk and return characteristics. By applying these analytical tools, investors can make well-informed investment decisions and achieve their investment goals.

Limitations and Drawbacks of Analytical Tools

While analytical tools can be valuable in informing investment decisions and are critical to maximizing returns through investment analysis, overreliance on these tools can lead to several issues as they have their fair share of limitations and drawbacks. Financial measures like the debt-to-equity ratio and price-to-earnings ratio, for instance, helped assess a company's financial health but they might be deceptive if used alone without taking other aspects like industry trends and economic conditions into account (Musallam et al., 2018). Time value of money calculations is important for evaluating the potential profitability of an investment over time, but they rely on assumptions about future cash flows, which are subjected to uncertainty and volatility (Dixit et al., 2009). Similarly, financial ratios assume that companies have consistent accounting policies, which may not be the case for all companies. Because relying on assumptions about variables like interest rates and inflation could be challenging to anticipate with accuracy, capital budgeting approaches like Net Present Value and Internal Rate of Return estimates could be difficult and time-consuming (Ramanujam et al., 1984).

Another limitation is that analytical tools may be biased based on the individual or group who developed them (Purcell et al., 2007). For example, some valuation models may be biased towards a particular industry or type of investment, which may result in incorrect valuations for other industries or investments.

Investment analysis and decision-making rely on accurate and reliable data to make informed decisions and if the data used in the analysis is incomplete or inaccurate, the results may be misleading

(Eddy et al., 2012). However, it can be challenging to obtain high-quality data, especially in emerging markets or industries where data is scarce or unreliable. For example, financial ratios rely on accurate and consistent financial statements. However, if the financial statements are incomplete or inaccurate, the ratios will not accurately reflect the company's financial health.

In addition, some data may not be readily available, which can limit the scope of analysis. For example, private companies may not disclose their financial information, making it difficult to analyze their performance and prospects. Furthermore, some data may be subjective or difficult to quantify. For example, customer satisfaction, employee morale, and brand reputation are all important factors in a company's performance, but they can be challenging to measure objectively.

Another limitation and drawback of analytical tools is model complexity. Some analytical tools can be intricate and challenging to use, necessitating a high level of knowledge and training (Anderson et al., 2001). As a result, there is a risk that the user may misinterpret or misuse the tool, leading to incorrect results. Also, complex models can be time-consuming and expensive to develop and maintain and this can be a significant barrier for small businesses or individual investors who may not have the resources to develop or purchase sophisticated analytical tools (Rizos et al., 2016).

A big drawback of analytical tools is the overreliance on the tools themselves. Even though analytical tools rely on algorithms and mathematical models to analyze data, they may not take into account qualitative factors or subjective judgments that can also have an impact on investment decisions (Adler et al., 2009). As a result, while analytical tools can offer insightful information and help guide investment decisions, they should not be the only basis for making decisions.

It is crucial to combine analytical techniques with other types of analysis, such as qualitative analysis and expert judgment, to get around the aforementioned constraints. Human judgment and experience can provide valuable insights that may not be captured by analytical tools alone (Landauer et al.,1998). Using data from multiple sources can help verify and cross-check the accuracy and reliability of the data. Validating the data can help ensure that it is accurate and complete. Using standard models that are widely accepted and understood in the industry can help ensure that the results of the analysis are easily understood by stakeholders (De Bruin et al., 2005). Mainly, clear communication of the results of the analysis is essential in ensuring that the decision-makers and investors understand the implications of the analysis and can make informed decisions based on the results.

FUTURE RESEARCH DIRECTIONS

There are several potential future research directions related to investment analysis. The growth of Machine Learning has been exponential over the last few decades and with the increasing availability of big data and advancements in machine learning and artificial intelligence, there is potential for these technologies to be used in investment analysis. Future research could explore the potential benefits and limitations of using these technologies in investment analysis. Behavioral finance is an emerging field that studies the impact of psychological biases on investment decision-making. Future research could explore how to integrate behavioral finance concepts into investment analysis to improve decision-making. With the growing interest in sustainable investing, future research could explore the use of analytical tools to evaluate the environmental, social, and governance factors that impact investment decisions. As cryptocurrencies and blockchain technology continue to gain popularity, future research could explore the use of analytical tools to analyze and evaluate these types of investments. Real-time data analysis has the potential to provide more timely and accurate insights for investment decision-making. Future research could explore the use of real-time data analysis in investment analysis and how it compares to more traditional approaches. Overall, there are many potential future research directions related to investment analysis, and advances in technology, behavioral finance, and sustainable investing are likely to be important areas of focus.

CONCLUSION

Investing requires more than just luck and speculation, but a deep understanding of the fundamentals and analytical tools. Investment analysis is an essential process for making informed investment decisions. It involves a range of analytical tools, including financial ratios, time value of money, capital budgeting techniques, portfolio analysis, and others. One of the main objectives of investment analysis is to evaluate investment opportunities and determine the best allocation of resources. Analyzing stocks, bonds, and real estate investments using analytical tools can help investors make informed decisions and achieve their investment goals. However, there are several limitations and drawbacks to using analytical tools, including assumptions and biases, data quality and availability, and model complexity. Overreliance on analytical tools can also lead to issues such as a lack of human judgment, blind spots and biases, and inaccurate data. To overcome these limitations and drawbacks, it is essential to use tools in conjunction with human judgment, identify and mitigate biases, validate data, and use multiple tools to provide a more comprehensive analysis. Overall, investment analysis is a critical process for making informed investment decisions, and using a range of analytical tools can help investors achieve their investment goals. However, decision-makers should be aware of the limitations and drawbacks of these tools and use them thoughtfully and deliberately. The chapter proposal concludes by giving a general review of investment analysis and the numerous analytical techniques employed in this process. The objectives and tentative topics of the chapter are designed to provide a comprehensive understanding of the subject matter, from the basics of investment analysis to the practical application of analytical tools and their limitations. The proposed chapter is aimed at students and professionals in finance, accounting, and economics, and will provide a valuable resource for anyone interested in investment analysis and financial decision-making.

REFERENCES

Abreu, M., & Mendes, V. (2010). Financial literacy and portfolio diversification. *Quantitative Finance*, *10*(5), 515–528. doi:10.1080/14697680902878105

Adler, R., Ewing, J., & Taylor, P. (2009). Citation statistics: A report from the International Mathematical Union (IMU) in cooperation with the International Council of Industrial and Applied Mathematics (ICIAM) and the Institute of Mathematical Statistics (IMS). *Statistical Science*, *24*(1), 1–14. doi:10.1214/09-STS285

Agrawal, J., & Kamakura, W. A. (1995). The economic worth of celebrity endorsers: An event study analysis. *Journal of Marketing*, *59*(3), 56–62. doi:10.1177/002224299505900305

Anderson, T., Liam, R., Garrison, D. R., & Archer, W. (2001). *Assessing teaching presence in a computer conferencing context.*

Bacon, C. J. (1992). The use of decision criteria in selecting information systems/technology investments. *Management Information Systems Quarterly*, *16*(3), 335–353. doi:10.2307/249532

Berk, J., & DeMarzo, P. (2017). *Corporate finance*. Pearson Education.

Boudt, K., Carl, P., & Peterson, B. G. (2012). Asset allocation with conditional value-at-risk budgets. *The Journal of Risk*, *15*(3), 39–68. doi:10.21314/JOR.2013.258

Brealey, R. A., Myers, S. C., & Marcus, A. J. (2017). *Fundamentals of corporate finance*. McGraw-Hill Education.

Brigham, E. F., & Houston, J. F. (2019). *Fundamentals of financial management*. Cengage Learning.

Buffet, W. E. (1984). The superinvestors of Graham-and-Doddsville. Hermes, Columbia Business School.

Campbell, J. Y., Lettau, M., Malkiel, B. G., & Xu, Y. (2001). Have individual stocks become more volatile? An empirical exploration of idiosyncratic risk. *The Journal of Finance*, *56*(1), 1–43. doi:10.1111/0022-1082.00318

Chen, J., Zhu, Z., & Xie, H. Y. (2004). Measuring intellectual capital: A new model and empirical study. *Journal of Intellectual Capital*, *5*(1), 195–212. doi:10.1108/14691930410513003

De Bruin, T., Rosemann, M., Freeze, R., & Kaulkarni, U. (2005). Understanding the main phases of developing a maturity assessment model. In *Australasian Conference on Information Systems (ACIS)* (pp. 8-19). Australasian Chapter of the Association for Information Systems.

Dincer, H., Hacioglu, U., Tatoglu, E., & Delen, D. (2016). A fuzzy-hybrid analytic model to assess investors' perceptions for industry selection. *Decision Support Systems*, *86*, 24–34. doi:10.1016/j.dss.2016.03.005

Dixit, A. K., & Pindyck, R. S. (2009). The options approach to capital investment. In *The economic impact of knowledge* (pp. 325–340). Routledge.

Eddy, D. M., Hollingworth, W., Caro, J. J., Tsevat, J., McDonald, K. M., & Wong, J. B. (2012). Model transparency and validation: A report of the ISPOR-SMDM Modeling Good Research Practices Task Force–7. *Medical Decision Making*, *32*(5), 733–743. doi:10.1177/0272989X12454579 PMID:22990088

John Edwards (2021) *The Top 10 Investment Tools for 2021*. U.S. News & World Report.

Fabozzi, F. J., & Markowitz, H. (2011). *The theory and practice of investment management*. John Wiley & Sons. doi:10.1002/9781118267028

Gitman, L. J., & Zutter, C. J. (2019). *Principles of managerial finance*. Pearson Education.

Golin, J., & Delhaise, P. (2013). *The bank credit analysis handbook: a guide for analysts, bankers and investors*. John Wiley & Sons.

Graham, B. (2016). *The Intelligent Investor*. Harper Business.

Graham, B., & Dodd, D. L. (2009). *Security analysis: Principles and technique*. McGraw-Hill Education.

Hagstrom, R. G. (2005). *The Warren Buffett way*. John Wiley & Sons.

Hammond, J. S., Keeney, R. L., & Raiffa, H. (2015). *Smart choices: A practical guide to making better decisions*. Harvard Business Review Press.

Hawawini, G., & Viallet, C. (2010). *Finance for executives: Managing for value creation*. Cengage Learning.

Henry, E., Robinson, T. R., & Van Greuning, J. H. (2012). Financial analysis techniques. *Financial reporting & analysis*, 327-385.

Ho, C. S. F., Abd Rahman, N. A., Yusuf, N. H. M., & Zamzamin, Z. (2014). Performance of global Islamic versus conventional share indices: International evidence. *Pacific-Basin Finance Journal, 28*, 110–121. doi:10.1016/j.pacfin.2013.09.002

Hoevenaars, R. P., Molenaar, R. D., Schotman, P. C., & Steenkamp, T. B. (2008). Strategic asset allocation with liabilities: Beyond stocks and bonds. *Journal of Economic Dynamics & Control, 32*(9), 2939–2970. doi:10.1016/j.jedc.2007.11.003

Jensen, M. (2001). Value maximization, stakeholder theory, and the corporate objective function. *European Financial Management*, *7*(3), 297–317. doi:10.1111/1468-036X.00158

Johnson, N. (2021). *The Best Investment Research Websites*. Investopedia.

Jones, C. P. (2007). *Investments: analysis and management*. John Wiley & Sons.

Kahraman, C., Ruan, D., & Tolga, E. (2002). Capital budgeting techniques using discounted fuzzy versus probabilistic cash flows. *Information Sciences*, *142*(1-4), 57–76. doi:10.1016/S0020-0255(02)00157-3

Kaplan, S. N., & Ruback, R. S. (1995). The valuation of cash flow forecasts: An empirical analysis. *The Journal of Finance*, *50*(4), 1059–1093. doi:10.1111/j.1540-6261.1995.tb04050.x

Kogut, B., & Kulatilaka, N. (1994). Options thinking and platform investments: Investing in opportunity. *California Management Review*, *36*(2), 52–71. doi:10.2307/41165744

Landauer, T. K., Foltz, P. W., & Laham, D. (1998). An introduction to latent semantic analysis. *Discourse Processes*, *25*(2-3), 259–284. doi:10.1080/01638539809545028

Leonard, T. (2021). *The Best Investment Software of 2021*. Benzinga.

Mercer, C. D. (2021). *The Best Stock Analysis Software for 2021*. Investopedia.

Mun, J. (2012). *Real options analysis: Tools and techniques for valuing strategic investments and decisions* (Vol. 320). John Wiley & Sons. doi:10.1002/9781119201618

Musallam, S. R. (2018). Exploring the relationship between financial ratios and market stock returns. *Eurasian Journal of Business and Economics*, *11*(21), 101–116. doi:10.17015/ejbe.2018.021.06

Palepu, K. G., Healy, P. M., & Peek, E. (2013). *Business analysis and valuation: Using financial statements*. Cengage Learning.

Penman, S. H., & Sougiannis, T. (1998). A comparison of dividend, cash flow, and earnings approaches to equity valuation. *Contemporary Accounting Research, 15*(3), 343–383. doi:10.1111/j.1911-3846.1998.tb00564.x

Purcell, S., Neale, B., Todd-Brown, K., Thomas, L., Ferreira, M. A., Bender, D., Maller, J., Sklar, P., de Bakker, P. I. W., Daly, M. J., & Sham, P. C. (2007). PLINK: A tool set for whole-genome association and population-based linkage analyses. *American Journal of Human Genetics, 81*(3), 559–575. doi:10.1086/519795 PMID:17701901

Rapp, D. J., Rapp, A., & Daher, T. (2023). Opportunity discovery or judgment? Value investing's incompatibility with Austrian economics revisited. *The Review of Austrian Economics*, 1–25. doi:10.100711138-023-00616-0

Rashid, C. A. (2018). The efficiency of financial ratios analysis for evaluating companies' liquidity. *International Journal of Social Sciences & Educational Studies, 4*(4), 110.

Rizos, V., Behrens, A., Van der Gaast, W., Hofman, E., Ioannou, A., Kafyeke, T., Flamos, A., Rinaldi, R., Papadelis, S., Hirschnitz-Garbers, M., & Topi, C. (2016). Implementation of circular economy business models by small and medium-sized enterprises (SMEs): Barriers and enablers. *Sustainability (Basel), 8*(11), 1212. doi:10.3390u8111212

Rosenfeld, S. A. (1997). Bringing business clusters into the mainstream of economic development. *European Planning Studies, 5*(1), 3–23. doi:10.1080/09654319708720381

Ross, S. A., Westerfield, R. W., & Jaffe, J. F. (2018). *Corporate finance*. McGraw-Hill Education.

Ryan, P. A., & Ryan, G. P. (2002). Capital budgeting practices of the Fortune 1000: How have things changed? *Journal of Business and Management, 8*(4), 355–364.

Sloan, R. G. (1996). Do stock prices fully reflect information in accruals and cash flows about future earnings? *The Accounting Review*, 289–315.

ADDITIONAL READING

Bodie, Z., Kane, A., & Marcus, A. J. (2014). *Investments* (10th ed.). McGraw-Hill Education.

Brealey, R. A., Myers, S. C., & Allen, F. (2017). *Principles of corporate finance*. McGraw-Hill Education.

Brigham, E. F., & Houston, J. F. (2016). *Fundamentals of financial management* (14th ed.). Cengage Learning.

Brueggeman, W. B., & Fisher, J. D. (2013). *Real estate finance and investments* (14th ed.). McGraw-Hill Education.

Fabozzi, F. J., & Choudhry, M. (2015). *The handbook of European fixed income securities*. John Wiley & Sons.

Fries, T. (2021). The Top 6 Best Investment Software in 2021. *Forbes*.

Markowitz, H. M. (1952). Portfolio selection. *The Journal of Finance*, *7*(1), 77–91.

McDonald's Corporation. (2021). *Annual Report 2021*. McDonald's. https://www.sec.gov/ix?doc=/Archives/edgar/data/63908/000006390821000023/mcd-20211231.htm

Mercer, C. D. (2021). *The Best Financial Analysis Software for 2021*. Investopedia.

Morningstar. (n.d.). *Key Ratios*. Morningstar. https://www.morningstar.com/stocks

Morningstar. (n.d.). *Bond Calculator*. Morningstar. https://www.morningstar.com/bondcalculator

Morningstar. (n.d.). *Understanding Capital Budgeting*. Morningstar. https://www.morningstar.com/education/understanding-capital-budgeting

Morningstar. (n.d.). *Portfolio X-Ray*. Morningstar. https://www.morningstar.com/portfolio/portfolio-x-ray

Palepu, K. G., Healy, P. M., Wright, S., Bradbury, M., & Coulton, J. (2020). *Business analysis and valuation: Using financial statements*. Cengage AU.

Peterson Drake, P., & Fabozzi, F. J. (2012). *Analysis of Investments and Management of Portfolios* (10th ed.). John Wiley & Sons.

Ross, S. A., Westerfield, R. W., & Jordan, B. D. (2018). *Essentials of corporate finance*. McGraw-Hill Education.

KEY TERMS AND DEFINITIONS

Analysis: Analysis is the process of breaking down complex or abstract concepts or phenomena into simpler, more manageable components to better understand or evaluate them. It involves examining and interpreting data or information to identify patterns, relationships, or trends, and to draw meaningful conclusions or make informed decisions.

Bond Analysis: Bond analysis is the process of evaluating the creditworthiness of a bond issuer and the potential risks and returns of investing in a bond. It involves analyzing factors such as the bond's credit rating, yield to maturity, duration, and call provisions to make informed investment decisions.

Capital Budgeting Techniques: Capital budgeting techniques refer to a set of analytical tools used to evaluate investment opportunities in long-term assets. These techniques help in assessing the feasibility of an investment project and its potential to generate cash flows.

Debt-to-equity (D/E) ratio: The D/E ratio is a leverage ratio that compares a company's total debt to its total equity. It is calculated by dividing the total debt by the total equity of the company.

Financial ratios are tools used to analyze a company's financial performance by comparing different financial figures. They provide a quick and easy way to assess a company's financial health and performance by analyzing its financial statements.:

Investment Analysis: Investment analysis involves evaluating an investment opportunity's potential risks and returns. It is the process of examining and evaluating financial and economic information to make informed investment decisions.

Investment decision-making: Investment decision-making involves assessing the potential risks and returns of an investment opportunity and making a decision to invest or not to invest. It involves considering factors such as investment objectives, risk tolerance, and financial resources to make informed investment decisions.

Investment: Investment refers to the allocation of resources, typically money, intending to generate future income or profit. It involves making a conscious decision to purchase an asset or securities with the expectation of earning a return on the investment over some time.

Portfolio Analysis: Portfolio analysis is a process of evaluating the performance of a portfolio of investments. It involves examining the portfolio's risk and return characteristics, diversification, and asset allocation to determine its overall performance.

Portfolio: A portfolio is a collection of financial assets such as stocks, bonds, and cash equivalents held by an individual, a company, or an institution. It is designed to achieve a specific investment objective, which could be capital appreciation, income generation, or a combination of both.

Price-to-earnings (P/E) ratio: The P/E ratio is a valuation ratio that measures the price of a company's stock relative to its earnings per share (EPS). It is calculated by dividing the current market price per share by the EPS of the company.

Real Estate Investment: Real estate investment refers to the purchase, ownership, and management of properties to generate income or profit. It involves buying properties such as commercial or residential real estate, land, or buildings with the expectation of earning rental income, capital appreciation, or a combination of both.

Stock Valuation: Stock valuation is the process of determining the intrinsic value of a stock based on its expected future cash flows. It involves analyzing a company's financial statements and industry trends to estimate its growth potential and determine its fair value.

Time Value of Money: Financial ratios are tools used to analyze a company's financial performance by comparing different financial figures. They provide a quick and easy way to assess a company's financial health and performance by analyzing its financial statements.

Compilation of References

Abreu, M., & Mendes, V. (2010). Financial literacy and portfolio diversification. *Quantitative Finance*, *10*(5), 515–528. doi:10.1080/14697680902878105

Adams, R., & Morey, A. (2017). The impact of data analytics on higher education. *Journal of Institutional Research*, *22*(2), 1–12.

Adams, W. P., & Sherali, H. D. (1993). Mixed-integer bilinear programming problems. *Mathematical Programming*, *59*(1-3), 279–305. doi:10.1007/BF01581249

Adler, R., Ewing, J., & Taylor, P. (2009). Citation statistics: A report from the International Mathematical Union (IMU) in cooperation with the International Council of Industrial and Applied Mathematics (ICIAM) and the Institute of Mathematical Statistics (IMS). *Statistical Science*, *24*(1), 1–14. doi:10.1214/09-STS285

Afrizal, S. H., Hidayanto, A. N., Handayani, P. W., Budiharsana, M., & Eryando, T. (2019). Narrative review for exploring barriers to readiness of electronic health record implementation in primary health care. *Healthcare Informatics Research*, *25*(3), 141–152. doi:10.4258/hir.2019.25.3.141 PMID:31406606

Agˇralı, S., & Geunes, J. (2009). Solving knapsack problems with s-curve return functions. *European Journal of Operational Research*, *193*(2), 605–615. doi:10.1016/j.ejor.2007.10.060

Agostinelli, A., Denk, T. I., Borsos, Z., Engel, J., Verzetti, M., Caillon, A., Huang, Q., Jansen, A., Roberts, A., Tagliasacchi, M., Sharifi, M., Zeghidour, N., & Frank, C. (2023). MusicLM: generating music from text. arXiv. https://arxiv.org/abs/2301.11325

Agrawal, J., & Kamakura, W. A. (1995). The economic worth of celebrity endorsers: An event study analysis. *Journal of Marketing*, *59*(3), 56–62. doi:10.1177/002224299505900305

Alexander, J. (2022). *Prosperity Post-Pandemic*. Australian Strategic Policy Institute.

Ali, A. K. (2011). Inventory management in pharmacy practice: A review of the literature. *Archives of Pharmacy Practice (Mumbai)*, *2*(4), 151.

AlshaterM. (2022). Exploring the Role of Artificial Intelligence in Enhancing Academic Performance: A Case Study of ChatGPT. SSRN. doi:10.2139/ssrn.4312358

Altman, S. (2022). *Tweet by Sam Altman* [WWW Document]. Twitter. https://twitter.com/sama/status/1601731295792414720

Amaglobeli, D., Gaspar, V., & Dabla-Norris, E. (2020). *Getting Older by Not Poorer*. International Monetary Fund.

Anagnostopoulos, K. P., & Mamanis, G. (2011). Multiobjective evolutionary algorithms for complex portfolio optimization problems. *Computational Management Science*, *8*(3), 259–279. doi:10.100710287-009-0113-8

Anderson, T., Liam, R., Garrison, D. R., & Archer, W. (2001). *Assessing teaching presence in a computer conferencing context.*

Androulakis, I. P., Maranas, C. D., & Floudas, C. A. (1995). αbb: A global optimization method for general constrained nonconvex problems. *Journal of Global Optimization*, *7*(4), 337–363. doi:10.1007/BF01099647

Ante, L., & Fiedler, I. (2020). Cheap Signals in Security Token Offerings (STOs). *Quantitative Finance and Economics*, *4*(4), 608–639. doi:10.3934/QFE.2020028

Arancibia-Ibarra, C., Flores, J. I. R., & Van Heijster, P. (2022). Stability Analysis of a Modified Leslie–Gower Predation Model With Weak Allee Effect in the Prey. *Frontiers in Applied Mathematics and Statistics*, *7*, 731038. doi:10.3389/fams.2021.731038

Ariza Ramirez, W., Leong, Z. Q., Nguyen, H. D., & Jayasinghe, S. G. (2020). Exploration of the applicability of probabilistic inference for learning control in underactuated autonomous underwater vehicles. *Autonomous Robots*, *44*(6), 1121–1134. doi:10.100710514-020-09922-z

Aroomoogan, K. (2020). How Artificial Intelligence Can Enable Ethically Driven Investments. *Forbes*. https://www.forbes.com/sites/forbesfinancecouncil/2020/09/23/how-artificial-intelligence-can-enable-ethically-driven-investments/?sh=168099eb6fc1

Arora, S., Dalmia, S., Denisov, P., Chang, X., Ueda, Y., Peng, Y., & Watanabe, S. (2022, May). Espnet-slu: Advancing spoken language understanding through espnet. In *ICASSP 2022-2022 IEEE International Conference on Acoustics, Speech and Signal Processing (ICASSP)* (pp. 7167-7171). IEEE.

Arulkumaran, K., Deisenroth, M. P., Brundage, M., & Bharath, A. A. (2017). Deep reinforcement learning: A brief survey. *IEEE Signal Processing Magazine*, *34*(6), 26–38. doi:10.1109/MSP.2017.2743240

Ascani, I., Ciccola, R., & Chiucchi, M. S. (2021). A Structured Literature Review about the Role of Management Accountants in Sustainability Accounting and Reporting. In Sustainability, 13(4). MDPI AG. doi:10.3390u13042357

Atamtürk, A., Berenguer, G., & Shen, Z.-J. (2012). A conic integer programming approach to stochastic joint location-inventory problems. *Operations Research*, *60*(2), 366–381. doi:10.1287/opre.1110.1037

Axiomatic Basics of e-Economics Munich Personal RePEc Archive. (n.d.). MPRA. https://mpra.ub.uni-muenchen.de/24331/

Azaria, A. (2022). *ChatGPT Usage and limitations*. HAL. https://hal.science/hal-03913837

Bacon, C. J. (1992). The use of decision criteria in selecting information systems/technology investments. *Management Information Systems Quarterly*, *16*(3), 335–353. doi:10.2307/249532

Baily, M. N., Klein, A., & Schardin, J. (2017) *The Impact of the Dodd-Frank Act on Financial Stability and Economic Growth*. Russell Sage Foundation. Bank of Greece. https://www.bankofgreece.gr/enimerosi/grafeio-typoy/

Balakrishnan, A., & Graves, S. C. (1989). A composite algorithm for a concave-cost network flow problem. *Networks*, *19*(2), 175–202. doi:10.1002/net.3230190202

Baldvinsdottir, G., Burns, J., Nørreklit, H., & Scapens, R. W. (2009). The image of accountants: From bean counters to extreme accountants. *Accounting, Auditing & Accountability Journal*, *22*(6), 858–882. doi:10.1108/09513570910980445

Barboza, F., Kimura, H., & Altman, E. (2017). Machine learning models and bankruptcy prediction. *Expert Systems with Applications*, *83*, 405–417. doi:10.1016/j.eswa.2017.04.006

Barnes, M., Oner, N., Ray, M. N., & Zengul, F. D. (2018). Exploring the association between quality and financial performance in US hospitals: a systematic review. *Journal of Health Care Finance, 44*(2). CDC.gov. https://www.cdc.gov/nchs/hus/topics/health-care-expenditures.htm#featured-charts

Bashir, I. (2018). *Mastering blockchain: Distributed ledger technology, decentralization, and smart contracts explained* (2nd ed.). Packt Publishing.

Bassett, C. (n.d.). *The Benefits of Insurance to Individuals, Organizations and Society.* LinkedIn. https://www.linkedin.com/pulse/benefits-insurance-individuals-organizations-society-chase-bassett/

BassoJ.FarhiE.MarwahaK.VillalongaB.ZhouL. (2021). The Quantum Approximate Optimization Algorithm at high depth for MaxCut on large-girth regular graphs and the Sherrington-Kirkpatrick model. ArXiv. https://arxiv.org/abs/2110.14206

Bell, E., Harley, B., & Bryman, A. (2022). *Business Research Methods* (6th ed.). Oxford University Press.

Belotti, P., Lee, J., Liberti, L., Margot, F., & Wächter, A. (2009). Branching and bounds tighteningtechniques for non-convex minlp. *Optimization Methods & Software, 24*(4-5), 597–634. doi:10.1080/10556780903087124

Belzunce, F., Martínez-Riquelme, C., & Mulero, J. (2016). Univariate stochastic orders. In Elsevier eBooks (pp. 27–113). doi:10.1016/B978-0-12-803768-3.00002-8

Bengio, Y., Lodi, A., & Prouvost, A. (2021). Machine learning for combinatorial optimization: A methodological tour d'horizon. *European Journal of Operational Research, 290*(2), 405–421. doi:10.1016/j.ejor.2020.07.063

Benhamou, E., Saltiel, D., Ohana, J.-J., & Atif, J. (2021, January 10). *Detecting and adapting to crisis pattern with context based Deep Reinforcement Learning.* Presented at the 2020 25th International Conference on Pattern Recognition (ICPR), Milan, Italy. 10.1109/ICPR48806.2021.9412958

Benson, H. P. (1985). A finite algorithm for concave minimization over a polyhedron. *Naval Research Logistics Quarterly, 32*(1), 165–177. doi:10.1002/nav.3800320119

Benson, H. P. (1990). Separable concave minimization via partial outer approximation and branch and bound. *Operations Research Letters, 9*(6), 389–394. doi:10.1016/0167-6377(90)90059-E

Benson, H. P., & Erenguc, S. S. (1990). An algorithm for concave integer minimization over a polyhedron. [NRL]. *Naval Research Logistics, 37*(4), 515–525. doi:10.1002/1520-6750(199008)37:4<515::AID-NAV3220370406>3.0.CO;2-X

Benson, H. P., & Horst, R. (1991). A branch and bound-outer approximation algorithm for concave minimization over a convex set. *Computers & Mathematics with Applications (Oxford, England), 21*(6-7), 67–76. doi:10.1016/0898-1221(91)90161-V

Berk, J., & DeMarzo, P. (2017). *Corporate finance.* Pearson Education.

Beveridge, R. A. (2017). *Mortality Differences Between Traditional Medicare and Medicare Advantage.* Sage Publications.

Bhatt, H., Mehta, S., & D'mello, L. R. (2015). Use of ID3 decision tree algorithm for placement prediction. *International Journal of Computer Science and Information Technologies, 6*(5), 4785–4789.

Bittencourt, H. R., & Clarke, R. T. (2003, July). Use of classification and regression trees (CART) to classify remotely-sensed digital images. In *IGARSS 2003. 2003 IEEE International Geoscience and Remote Sensing Symposium. Proceedings (IEEE Cat. No. 03CH37477)* (*Vol. 6*, pp. 3751-3753). IEEE. 10.1109/IGARSS.2003.1295258

Blakey, R. G. (1926) *The Revenue Act of 1926.* The American Economic Review.

Bluhm, D. J., Harman, W., Lee, T. W., & Mitchell, T. R. (2010). Qualitative Research in Management: A Decade of Progress. In Journal of Management Studies, 48 (8), 1866–1891. Wiley. doi:10.1111/j.1467-6486.2010.00972.x

Bohner, M., Dannan, F. M., & Streipert, S. (2018). A nonautonomous Beverton–Holt equation of higher order. *Journal of Mathematical Analysis and Applications*, *457*(1), 114–133. doi:10.1016/j.jmaa.2017.07.051

BommaritoI. I. M.KatzD. M. 2022. GPT takes the bar exam. arXiv:2212.14402.

Borogovac, M. (2014). Comparison of the Standard Rating Methods and the New General Rating Formula. *SOA ARCH 2014.1 Proceedings.*

Borogovac, M. (2015). Two applications of Brouwer's fixed point theorem: In insurance and in biology models. *Journal of Difference Equations and Applications*, *22*(6), 727–744. doi:10.1080/10236198.2015.1134519

Bots, J. M., Groenland, E., & Swagerman, D. M. (2009). An empirical test of Birkett's competency model for management accountants: Survey evidence from Dutch practitioners. In Journal of Accounting Education, 27 (1). Elsevier BV. doi:10.1016/j.jaccedu.2009.06.001

Boudt, K., Carl, P., & Peterson, B. G. (2012). Asset allocation with conditional value-at-risk budgets. *The Journal of Risk*, *15*(3), 39–68. doi:10.21314/JOR.2013.258

Boyer, F., Shinohara, Y., Ishii, T., Inaguma, H., & Watanabe, S. (2021, December). A study of transducer based end-to-end ASR with ESPnet: Architecture, auxiliary loss and decoding strategies. In *2021 IEEE Automatic Speech Recognition and Understanding Workshop (ASRU)* (pp. 16-23). IEEE.

Brady, P., Burham, K., & Holden, S. (2012). *The Success of the U.S. Retirement System.* Investment Company Institute.

Brealey, R. A., Myers, S. C., & Marcus, A. J. (2017). *Fundamentals of corporate finance.* McGraw-Hill Education.

Breiman, L., Friedman, J., Olshen, R., & Stone, C. (1984). *Cart.* Classification and regression trees. . doi:10.1201/9781315139470

Breiman, L. (1996). Bagging predictors. *Machine Learning*, *24*(2), 123–140. doi:10.1007/BF00058655

Bressoud, D. M., Carlson, M. P., Mesa, V., & Rasmussen, C. (2015). Increasing student success in mathematics: Impacts of a data-driven approach to improvement. *Journal of Statistics Education : An International Journal on the Teaching and Learning of Statistics*, *23*(1), 1–13.

Bretthauer, K. M., & Cabot, A. V. (1994). A composite branch and bound, cutting plane algorithm for concave minimization over a polyhedron. *Computers & Operations Research*, *21*(7), 777–785. doi:10.1016/0305-0548(94)90007-8

Bretthauer, K. M., Victor Cabot, A., & Venkataramanan, M. (1994). An algorithm and new penalties for concave integer minimization over a polyhedron. [NRL]. *Naval Research Logistics*, *41*(3), 435–454. doi:10.1002/1520-6750(199404)41:3<435::AID-NAV3220410309>3.0.CO;2-6

Breusch, T. (1978). Testing for Autocorrelation in Dynamic Linear Models. *Australian Economic Papers*, *17*(31), 334–355. doi:10.1111/j.1467-8454.1978.tb00635.x

Brigham, E. F., & Houston, J. F. (2019). *Fundamentals of financial management.* Cengage Learning.

Brown, A. (2022). *Why ChatGPT will change digital transformation* [WWW Document]. BCS.

Brown, T. (2020). Language models are few-shot learners. arXiv preprint arXiv:2005.14165.

Brown, R. L., & Gottlieb, L. R. (2001). *Introduction to Ratemaking and Loss Reserving for Property and Casualty Insurance* (2nd ed.). ACTEX Publications.

Brown, T., Mann, B., Ryder, N., Subbiah, M., Kaplan, J. D., Dhariwal, P., Neelakantan, A., Shyam, P., Sastry, G., & Askell, A. (2020). Language models are few-shot learners. *Advances in Neural Information Processing Systems*, *33*, 1877–1901.

Brusilovsky, P., Somyürek, S., & Guerra, J. (2014). Empirical study of a model of a data-driven, adaptive assessment system for mathematics. *International Journal of Artificial Intelligence in Education*, *24*(4), 387–426.

Budding, T., de Jong, G., & Smit, M. (2022). New development: Bridging the gap—analysis of required competencies for management accountants in the public sector. In Public Money & Management, 42 (7), 565–568). Informa UK Limited. doi:10.1080/09540962.2022.2068862

Buffet, W. E. (1984). The superinvestors of Graham-and-Doddsville. Hermes, Columbia Business School.

Buhmann, H. (1970). *Mathematics Methods in Risk Theory*. Springer-Verlag.

Burke, J., & Hung, A. (2015). *Do Financial Advisers Influence Savings Behavior?* Rand Corporation.

Burns, J., & Baldvinsdottir, G. (2005). An institutional perspective of accountants' new roles—The interplay of contradictions and praxis. *European Accounting Review*, *14*(4), 725–757. doi:10.1080/09638180500194171

Butler, J., Jia, J., & Dyer, J. (1997). Simulation techniques for the sensitivity analysis of multi-criteria decision models. *European Journal of Operational Research*, *103*(3), 531–546. doi:10.1016/S0377-2217(96)00307-4

Byrne, S., & Pierce, B. (2007). Towards a more comprehensive understanding of the roles of management accountants. *European Accounting Review*, *16*(3), 469–498. doi:10.1080/09638180701507114

Cabot, A. V. (1974). Variations on a cutting plane method for solving concave minimization problems with linear constraints. *Naval Research Logistics Quarterly*, *21*(2), 265–274. doi:10.1002/nav.3800210206

Campbell, J. Y., Lettau, M., Malkiel, B. G., & Xu, Y. (2001). Have individual stocks become more volatile? An empirical exploration of idiosyncratic risk. *The Journal of Finance*, *56*(1), 1–43. doi:10.1111/0022-1082.00318

Cannon, A. R. (2008). Inventory improvement and financial performance. *International Journal of Production Economics*, *115*(2), 581–593. doi:10.1016/j.ijpe.2008.07.006

Caprara, A., Pisinger, D., & Toth, P. (1999). Exact solution of the quadratic knapsack problem. *INFORMS Journal on Computing*, *11*(2), 125–137. doi:10.1287/ijoc.11.2.125

Carl Borg, C. C. (2006). *VMI – A study of benefits with a VMI system*. Jönköping University.

Casino, F., Dasaklis, T. K., & Patsakis, C. (2019). A systematic literature review of blockchain-based applications: Current status, classification and open issues. *Telematics and Informatics*, *36*, 55–81. doi:10.1016/j.tele.2018.11.006

Cesarone, F., S. A. & Tardella, F. (2009). *Efficient algorithms for mean-variance portfolio optimization with hard real-world constraints*. 72:37–56.

Chattopadhyay, S., Dey, A., Singh, P. K., & Sarkar, R. (2022). DRDA-Net: Dense residual dual-shuffle attention network for breast cancer classification using histopathological images. *Computers in Biology and Medicine*, *145*, 105437. doi:10.1016/j.compbiomed.2022.105437 PMID:35339096

Chatzis, S. P., Siakoulis, V., Petropoulos, A., Stavroulakis, E., & Vlachogiannakis, N. (2018). Forecasting stock market crisis events using deep and statistical machine learning techniques. *Expert Systems with Applications*, *112*, 353–371. doi:10.1016/j.eswa.2018.06.032

Chen, M., Tworek, J., Jun, H., Yuan, Q., & Pinto, H. P. O. (2021). Evaluating large language models trained on code. arXiv. https://arxiv.org/abs/2107.03374

Chen, Y., & Eger, S. (2022). Transformers go for the LOLs: Generating (humourous) titles from scientific abstracts end-to-end. http://dx.doi.org/ doi:10.48550/ARXIV

Chenhall, R. H., & Moers, F. (2015). The role of innovation in the evolution of management accounting and its integration into management control. *Accounting, Organizations and Society*, *47*, 1–13. doi:10.1016/j.aos.2015.10.002

Chen, J., Zhu, Z., & Xie, H. Y. (2004). Measuring intellectual capital: A new model and empirical study. *Journal of Intellectual Capital*, *5*(1), 195–212. doi:10.1108/14691930410513003

Chen, L., & Chen, F. (2009). Global stability of a Leslie–Gower predator–prey model with feedback controls. *Applied Mathematics Letters*, *22*(9), 1330–1334. doi:10.1016/j.aml.2009.03.005

ChenY.AndiappanM.JenkinT.OvchinnikovA. (2023). A Manager and an AI Walk into a Bar: Does ChatGPT Make Biased Decisions Like We Do? doi:10.2139/ssrn.4380365

Chimmula, V. K. R., Zhang, L., Malik, H., & Kumar Yadav, A. (2021). Deep learning and statistical-based daily stock price forecasting and monitoring. In Studies in Big Data (pp. 203–216). doi:10.1007/978-981-33-4412-9_13

Chua, A.Y.K., Pal, A., and Banerjee, S. (2023). AI-enabled investment advice: Will users buy it? *Computers is human behaviors*, 138. doi:10.1016/j.chb.2022.107481

Clark, R. L., Craig, L. A., & Wilson, J. W. (2003). *A History of Public Sector Pensions in the United States*. Pension Research Council, Wharton School of the University of Pennsylvania.

Coad, A. (1996). Smart work and hard work: Explicating a learning orientation in strategic management accounting. *Management Accounting Research*, *7*(4), 387–408. doi:10.1006/mare.1996.0022

Congressional Research Service. (2013) *Individual Retirement Accounts (IRAs): Issues and Proposed Expansion.* CRS Report for Congress RL30255. www.crs.gov

Cook, W. W. (1923). The Mysterious Massachusetts Trusts. *American Bar Association Journal. American Bar Association.*

Corporate Finance Institute. (2023a). Cash Equivalents. *Corporate Finance Institute*. https://corporatefinanceinstitute.com/resources/accounting/cash-equivalents/

Corporate Finance Institute. (2023b). Reinsurance Companies. *Corporate Finance Institute*. https://corporatefinanceinstitute.com/resources/wealth-management/reinsurance-companies/

Costa, D. L. (1998). Evolution of Retirement: An American [University of Chicago Press.]. *Economy and History*, 1880–1990.

Coyle, J. J., Langley, C. J., Novack, R. A., & Gibson, B. (2016). *Supply chain management: A logistics perspective.* Nelson Education.

Damali, U., Fredendall, L. D., Miller, J. L., Moore, D., & Dye, C. J. (2022). Enhancing patient participation in healthcare operations through patient training and education using the theoretical lens of media synchronicity. *Decision Sciences*, *53*(4), 750–770. doi:10.1111/deci.12514

Damali, U., Miller, J. L., Fredendall, L. D., Moore, D., & Dye, C. J. (2016). Co-creating value using customer training and education in a healthcare service design. *Journal of Operations Management, 47*(1), 80–97. doi:10.1016/j.jom.2016.10.001

Daskin, M. S., Coullard, C. R., & Shen, Z.-J. M. (2002). An inventory-location model: Formulation, solution algorithm and computational results. *Annals of Operations Research, 110*(1-4), 83–106. doi:10.1023/A:1020763400324

Dasu, T., & Johnson, T. (2003). *Exploratory Data Mining and Data Cleaning.* Wiley. doi:10.1002/0471448354

Davenport, T. H., & Patil, D. J. (2012). Data scientist: The sexiest job of the 21st century. *Harvard Business Review, 90*(10), 70–76. PMID:23074866

Davidson, L. (2016) *The History of Retirement Benefits.* Work Force. https://workforce.com

De Bruin, T., Rosemann, M., Freeze, R., & Kaulkarni, U. (2005). Understanding the main phases of developing a maturity assessment model. In *Australasian Conference on Information Systems (ACIS)* (pp. 8-19). Australasian Chapter of the Association for Information Systems.

Deconinck, E., Hancock, T., Coomans, D., Massart, D. L., & Vander Heyden, Y. (2005). Classification of drugs in absorption classes using the classification and regression trees (CART) methodology. *Journal of Pharmaceutical and Biomedical Analysis, 39*(1-2), 91–103. doi:10.1016/j.jpba.2005.03.008 PMID:15946819

Deming, W. E. (2018). *Out of the Crisis, reissue.* MIT press. doi:10.7551/mitpress/11457.001.0001

den Boer, A. V. (2015). Dynamic pricing and learning: Historical origins, current research, and new directions. *Surveys in Operations Research and Management Science, 20*(1), 1–18. doi:10.1016/j.sorms.2015.03.001

Department of Treasury. (2021). *Contributions to Individual Retirement Arrangements (IRAs).* Internal Revenue Service.

Dhyani Bhatt, S., Jayaswal, S., Sinha, A., & Vidyarthi, N. (2021). Alternate second order conic program reformulations for hub location under stochastic demand and congestion. *Annals of Operations Research, 304*(1), 481–527. doi:10.100710479-021-03993-6

Dijkhuizen, G., & Faigle, U. (1993). A cutting-plane approach to the edge-weighted maximal clique problem. *European Journal of Operational Research, 69*(1), 121–130. doi:10.1016/0377-2217(93)90097-7

Dimiourgia, E. (2023). Liberal Patriots Reformers. *Ethnik Dimiourgia.* https://www.ethnikidimiourgia.gr/

Dincer, H., Hacioglu, U., Tatoglu, E., & Delen, D. (2016). A fuzzy-hybrid analytic model to assess investors' perceptions for industry selection. *Decision Support Systems, 86*, 24–34. doi:10.1016/j.dss.2016.03.005

Dixit, A. K., & Pindyck, R. S. (2009). The options approach to capital investment. In *The economic impact of knowledge* (pp. 325–340). Routledge.

Dolce, V., Emanuel, F., Cisi, M., & Ghislieri, C. (2020). The soft skills of accounting graduates: Perceptions versus expectations. *Accounting Education, 29*(1), 57–76. doi:10.1080/09639284.2019.1697937

Dowling, M., & Lucey, B. (2023). ChatGPT for (Finance) research: The Bananarama Conjecture. *Finance Research Letters, 53*, 103662. doi:10.1016/j.frl.2023.103662

Dr, B. Otto, D. (2023). *Generative Artificial Intelligence (GAI) Ethics Taxonomy- Applying Chat GPT for Robotic Process Automation (GAI-RPA) as Business Case.* SSRN. doi:10.2139/ssrn.4385025

Duverne, D., & Hele, J. (2016). How the Insurance Industry Manages Risk, 55-76. In Oxford University Press eBooks. doi:10.1093/acprof:oso/9780198788812.003.0004

Economy and Finance. (2023) *Spring 2023 Economic Forecast: an improved outlook amid persistent challenges*. European Commission https://economy-finance.ec.europa.eu/economic-forecast-and-surveys/economic-forecasts/spring-2023-economic-forecast-improved-outlook-amid-persistent-challenges_en#documents

Eddy, D. M., Hollingworth, W., Caro, J. J., Tsevat, J., McDonald, K. M., & Wong, J. B. (2012). Model transparency and validation: A report of the ISPOR-SMDM Modeling Good Research Practices Task Force–7. *Medical Decision Making, 32*(5), 733–743. doi:10.1177/0272989X12454579 PMID:22990088

Eisenhardt, K. M., & Graebner, M. E. (2007). Theory Building From Cases: Opportunities And Challenges. In Academy of Management Journal, 50(1). doi:10.5465/amj.2007.24160888

Elhedhli, S., Wang, Y., & Saif, A. (2018). Service system design with immobile servers, stochastic demand and concave-cost capacity selection. *Computers & Operations Research, 94*, 65–75. doi:10.1016/j.cor.2018.01.019

Endenich, C. (2014). Economic crisis as a driver of management accounting change: Comparative evidence from Germany and Spain. *Journal of Applied Accounting Research, 15*(1), 123–149. doi:10.1108/JAAR-11-2012-0075

Espinosa, O., & Zarruk, A. A. (2021). *The importance of actuarial management in insurance business decision-making in the twenty-first century.* British Actuarial Journal., doi:10.1017/S1357321721000155

Fabozzi, F. J. (2007). *Fixed Income Analysis.* John Wiley & Sons.

Fabozzi, F. J., & Markowitz, H. (2011). *The theory and practice of investment management.* John Wiley & Sons. doi:10.1002/9781118267028

Falk, J. E., & Hoffman, K. L. (1986). Concave minimization via collapsing polytopes. *Operations Research, 34*(6), 919–929. doi:10.1287/opre.34.6.919

Falk, J. E., & Hoffman, K. R. (1976). A successive underestimation method for concave minimization problems. *Mathematics of Operations Research, 1*(3), 251–259. doi:10.1287/moor.1.3.251

Falk, J. E., & Soland, R. M. (1969). An algorithm for separable nonconvex programming problems. *Management Science, 15*(9), 550–569. doi:10.1287/mnsc.15.9.550

Fallon, N. (2023). 6 Biggest Business Insurance Risks (and How to Mitigate Them). *Business News Daily.* https://www.businessnewsdaily.com/9024-biggest-business-insurance-risks.html

Fama, E. F. (1970). Efficient Capital Markets: A Review of Theory and Empirical Work. *The Journal of Finance, 25*(2), 383–417. doi:10.2307/2325486

Fama, E. F., & French, K. R. (1993). Common risk factors in the returns on stocks and bonds. *Journal of Financial Economics, 33*(1), 3–56. doi:10.1016/0304-405X(93)90023-5

Farahani, R. Z., Rashidi Bajgan, H., Fahimnia, B., & Kaviani, M. (2015). Location-inventory problem in supply chains: A modelling review. *International Journal of Production Research, 53*(12), 3769–3788. doi:10.1080/00207543.2014.988889

Feldman, E., Lehrer, F., & Ray, T. (1966). Warehouse location under continuous economies of scale. *Management Science, 12*(9), 670–684. doi:10.1287/mnsc.12.9.670

Fontes, D. B., & Gonçalves, J. F. (2007). Heuristic solutions for general concave minimum cost network flow problems. *Networks, 50*(1), 67–76. doi:10.1002/net.20167

Frank, D., & Spencer, B. G. (2008). *What is Retirement? A Review and Assessment of Alternative Concepts and Measures.* McMaster University.

Franke, F., & Hiebl, M. R. W. (2022). Big data and decision quality: the role of management accountants' data analytics skills. In International Journal of Accounting & Information Management, 31(1), 93–127. Emerald. doi:10.1108/IJAIM-12-2021-0246

Freund, Y. (1995). Boosting a weak learning algorithm by majority. *Information and Computation, 121*(2), 256–285. doi:10.1006/inco.1995.1136

Friedman, J., Hastie, T., & Tibshirani, R. (2000). Additive logistic regression: A statistical view of boosting (with discussion and a rejoinder by the authors). *Annals of Statistics, 28*(2), 337–407. doi:10.1214/aos/1016218223

Fu , L., & Wu, C.P. (2005). General Iteration Algorithm for Classification Ratemaking. Casualty Actuarial Society Forum.

Gallo, G., Hammer, P. L., & Simeone, B. (1980). Quadratic knapsack problems. In *Combinatorial Optimization* (pp. 132–149). Springer. doi:10.1007/BFb0120892

Gallo, G., & Ülkücü, A. (1977). Bilinear programming: An exact algorithm. *Mathematical Programming, 12*(1), 173–194. doi:10.1007/BF01593787

Gambella, C., Ghaddar, B., & Naoum-Sawaya, J. (2021). Optimization problems for machine learning: A survey. *European Journal of Operational Research, 290*(3), 807–828. doi:10.1016/j.ejor.2020.08.045

GhadimiN. Squeezenet for the Forecasting of the Energy Demand Using a Combined Version of Sewing Training-Based Optimization Algorithm. SSRN 4360713. doi:10.1016/j.heliyon.2023.e16827

Gheisariha, E., Tavana, M., Jolai, F., & Rabiee, M. (2021). A simulation–optimization model for solving flexible flow shop scheduling problems with rework and transportation. *Mathematics and Computers in Simulation, 180*, 152–178. doi:10.1016/j.matcom.2020.08.019

Giacosa, E., Alam, G. M., Culasso, F., & Crocco, E. (2023). Stress-inducing or performance-enhancing? Safety measure or cause of mistrust? The paradox of digital surveillance in the workplace. In Journal of Innovation & Knowledge, 8(2) 100357. Elsevier BV. doi:10.1016/j.jik.2023.100357

Giacosa, E., Culasso, F., & Crocco, E. (2022). Customer agility in the modern automotive sector: how lead management shapes agile digital companies. In *Technological Forecasting and Social Change* (Vol. 175, p. 121362). Elsevier BV. doi:10.1016/j.techfore.2021.121362

Gitman, L. J., & Zutter, C. J. (2019). *Principles of managerial finance*. Pearson Education.

Glasson, W. (1918). *Federal Military Pensions in the United States*. Oxford University Press.

Goffard, P. (2021). Sequential Monte Carlo samplers to fit and compare insurance loss models. *Scandinavian Actuarial Journal*, 1–23. doi:10.1080/03461238.2022.2145577

Golin, J., & Delhaise, P. (2013). *The bank credit analysis handbook: a guide for analysts, bankers and investors*. John Wiley & Sons.

Golubin, A., & Gridin, V. N. (2022). Optimal insurance strategy in a risk process under a safety level imposed on the increments of the process. *Scandinavian Actuarial Journal, 2023*(1), 20–37. doi:10.1080/03461238.2022.2075282

Gomes, R., Rozario, P., & Adhikari, N. (2021, May). Deep learning optimization in remote sensing image segmentation using dilated convolutions and ShuffleNet. In *2021 IEEE International Conference on Electro Information Technology (EIT)* (pp. 244-249). IEEE. 10.1109/EIT51626.2021.9491910

González-Olivares, E., Mena-Lorca, J., Rojas-Palma, A., & Flores, J. I. R. (2011). Dynamical complexities in the Leslie–Gower predator–prey model as consequences of the Allee effect on prey. *Applied Mathematical Modelling*, *35*(1), 366–381. doi:10.1016/j.apm.2010.07.001

Goovaerts, M. J., De Vylder, F., & Haezendonck, J. (1984). *Insurance Premiums: Theory and Application*. North-Holland.

Goretzki, L., Lukka, K., & Messner, M. (2018). Controllers' use of informational tactics. *Accounting and Business Research*, *48*(6), 700–726. doi:10.1080/00014788.2017.1407627

Goretzki, L., Strauss, E., & Weber, J. (2013). An institutional perspective on the changes in management accountants' professional role. *Management Accounting Research*, *24*(1), 41–63. doi:10.1016/j.mar.2012.11.002

Graebner, M. E., Martin, J. A., & Roundy, P. T. (2012). Qualitative data: Cooking without a recipe. In Strategic Organization, 10(3). SAGE Publications. doi:10.1177/1476127012452821

Graebner, W. (1980) *A History of Retirement: The Meaning and Function of an American Institution*. Yale University Press. Greek Law. https://www.elinyae.gr/ethniki-nomothesia/n-28681922-fek-119a-2071922 and https://www.elinyae.gr/ethniki-nomothesia/n-57331932-fek-364a-11101932

Graham, B. (2016). *The Intelligent Investor*. Harper Business.

Graham, A., Davey-Evans, S., & Toon, I. (2012). The developing role of the financial controller: Evidence from the UK. *Journal of Applied Accounting Research*, *13*(1), 71–88. doi:10.1108/09675421211231934

Graham, B., & Dodd, D. L. (2009). *Security analysis: Principles and technique*. McGraw-Hill Education.

Grant, N., & Metz, C. (2022). A new chat bot is a 'Code Red' for Google's search business. *New York Times*.

Gray, K. E. Jr, & Dewar, R. (1971). Axiomatic Characterization of the Time-Weighted Rate of Return. *Management Science*, *18*(2), B-35. doi:10.1287/mnsc.18.2.B32

Griffith, E., & Metz, C. (2023, January). *A new area of A.I. booms, even amid the tech gloom.*

Griggs, K. N., Ossipova, O., Kohlios, C. P., Baccarini, A. N., Howson, E. A., & Hayajneh, T. (2018). Healthcare blockchain system using smart contracts for secure automated remote patient monitoring. *Journal of Medical Systems*, *42*(7), 1–7. doi:10.100710916-018-0982-x PMID:29876661

Grimm, T. W., & Gregoriou, G. N. (2017). *The Handbook of UCITS: Fundamentals, Application, and Law*. Wiley.

Guidolin, M., & Timmermann, A. (2008) *International Asset Allocation Under Regime Switching, Skew and Kurtosis Preferences*. International Labour Organization. https://www.ilo.org/dyn/natlex

Guisewite, G. M., & Pardalos, P. M. (1990). Minimum concave-cost network flow problems: Applications, com- plexity, and algorithms. *Annals of Operations Research*, *25*(1), 75–99. doi:10.1007/BF02283688

Guisewite, G. M., & Pardalos, P. M. (1993). A polynomial time solvable concave network flow problem. *Networks*, *23*(2), 143–147. doi:10.1002/net.3230230208

Hagstrom, R. G. (2005). *The Warren Buffett way*. John Wiley & Sons.

Hajiaghayi, M. T., Mahdian, M., & Mirrokni, V. S. (2003). The facility location problem with general cost func- tions. *Networks*, *42*(1), 42–47. doi:10.1002/net.10080

Hajian, A., & Chang, H.-C. (2022). *A Blockchain-Based Smart Grid to Build Resilience Through Zero-Trust Cybersecurity.*

Hajian, A., Prybutok, V. R., & Chang, H. C. (2023). An empirical study for blockchain-based information sharing systems in electronic health records: A mediation perspective. *Computers in Human Behavior*, *138*, 107471. doi:10.1016/j.chb.2022.107471

Halbouni, S. S., & Nour, M. A. (2013). An empirical investigation of the impact of globalisation and information technology on the role of the management accountant: Evidence from the United Arab Emirates. International Journal of Accounting. *Auditing and Performance Evaluation*, *9*(3), 286–306. doi:10.1504/IJAAPE.2013.055898

Halton, C. (2022). Inflationary Risk Definition, Ways to Counteract It. *Investopedia*. https://www.investopedia.com/terms/i/inflationrisk.asp

Hammond, J. S., Keeney, R. L., & Raiffa, H. (2015). *Smart choices: A practical guide to making better decisions*. Harvard Business Review Press.

Hamza, A., Alqahtani, M., Elkamchouchi, H., Alshahrani, D. H., Alzahrani, H., Maray, J. S., & Aziz, M. (2022). Hyperparameter Tuned Deep Autoencoder Model for Road Classification Model in Intelligent Transportation Systems. *Applied Sciences (Basel, Switzerland)*, *12*(20).

Harrington, L. (2021). Quality Measurement. In A. Giardino, L. Riesenberg, & P. Varkey (Eds.), *Medical Quality Management* (pp. 41–61). Springer., doi:10.1007/978-3-030-48080-6_3

Harvey, J. (2015). *Complex service delivery processes: Strategy to operations*. Quality Press.

Hawawini, G., & Viallet, C. (2010). *Finance for executives: Managing for value creation*. Cengage Learning.

Hayes, T., Usami, S., Jacobucci, R., & McArdle, J. J. (2015). Using Classification and Regression Trees (CART) and random forests to analyze attrition: Results from two simulations. *Psychology and Aging*, *30*(4), 911–929. doi:10.1037/pag0000046 PMID:26389526

Heilpern, S. (2002). Using Choquet integral in economics. *Statistical Papers (Berlin, Germany)*, *43*(1), 53–73. doi:10.100700362-001-0086-3

Heineke, J. (1995). Strategic operations management decisions and professional performance in US HMOs. *Journal of Operations Management*, *13*(4), 255–272. doi:10.1016/0272-6963(95)00035-6

Heller, J. I., & Hollabaugh, M. (1992). Teaching problem solving through cooperative grouping. Part 1: Group versus individual problem solving. *American Journal of Physics*, *60*(7), 627–636. doi:10.1119/1.17117

Henry, E., Robinson, T. R., & Van Greuning, J. H. (2012). Financial analysis techniques. *Financial reporting & analysis*, 327-385.

He, W., Zhang, J., & Li, W. (2020). Information Technology Solutions, Challenges, and Suggestions for Tackling the COVID-19 Pandemic. *International Journal of Information Management*, *102287*. doi:10.1016/j.ijinfomgt.2020.1022 PMID:33318721

Hidayattullah, S., Surjandari, I., & Laoh, E. (2020, October 17). *Financial statement fraud detection in Indonesia listed companies using machine learning based on meta-heuristic optimization*. Presented at the 2020 International Workshop on Big Data and Information Security (IWBIS), Depok, Indonesia. 10.1109/IWBIS50925.2020.9255563

Hilal, M., Elkamchouchi, A., Alotaibi, D. H., Maray, S. S., Othman, M., Abdelmageed, M., & Eldesouki, A. S. (2022). Manta Ray Foraging Optimization with Transfer Learning Driven Facial Emotion Recognition. *Sustainability*, *14*(21).

Hiller, K., Mahlendorf, M. D., & Weber, J. (2014). Management accountants' occupational prestige within the company: A social identity theory perspective. *European Accounting Review, 23*(4), 671–691. doi:10.1080/09638180.2013.849204

Hirchoua, B., Ouhbi, B., & Frikh, B. (2021). Deep reinforcement learning based trading agents: Risk curiosity driven learning for financial rules-based policy. *Expert Systems with Applications, 170*(114553), 114553. doi:10.1016/j.eswa.2020.114553

Ho, C. S. F., Abd Rahman, N. A., Yusuf, N. H. M., & Zamzamin, Z. (2014). Performance of global Islamic versus conventional share indices: International evidence. *Pacific-Basin Finance Journal, 28*, 110–121. doi:10.1016/j.pacfin.2013.09.002

Hoevenaars, R. P., Molenaar, R. D., Schotman, P. C., & Steenkamp, T. B. (2008). Strategic asset allocation with liabilities: Beyond stocks and bonds. *Journal of Economic Dynamics & Control, 32*(9), 2939–2970. doi:10.1016/j.jedc.2007.11.003

Hoffman, K. L. (1981). A method for globally minimizing concave functions over convex sets. *Mathematical Programming, 20*(1), 22–32. doi:10.1007/BF01589330

Holmberg, K., & Tuy, H. (1999). A production-transportation problem with stochastic demand and concave pro- duction costs. *Mathematical Programming, 85*(1), 157–179. doi:10.1007101070050050

Holzman, R., Hinz, R. P., & Dorfman, M. (2008). *Pension Systems and Reform Conceptual Framework.* World Bank.

Horst, R. (1976). An algorithm for nonconvex programming problems. *Mathematical Programming, 10*(1), 312–321. doi:10.1007/BF01580678

Horst, R., & Thoai, N. V. (1998). An integer concave minimization approach for the minimum concave cost capacitated flow problem on networks. *OR-Spektrum, 20*(1), 47–53. doi:10.1007/BF01545530

Horst, R., Thoai, N. V., & Benson, H. P. (1991). Concave minimization via conical partitions and polyhedral outer approximation. *Mathematical Programming, 50*(1-3), 259–274. doi:10.1007/BF01594938

Huang, S., & Grady, P. (2022, September). *Generative AI: A creative new world.* Sequoia Capital. https://www.sequoiacap.com/article/generative-ai-a-creative-new-world/

Huff, P. L. (2014). The GoalProject: A Group Assignment to Encourage Creative Thinking, Leadership Abilities and Communication Skills. In Accounting Education, 23(6). Informa UK Limited. doi:10.1080/09639284.2014.974198

Hurlimann, W. (1997). On Quasi-Mean Value Principles. *Blatter der Deutschen Gesellschaft fur Versicherungsmathematik, XXIII*, 1–16.

Hurlimann, W. (1998). On Stop-Loss Order and the Distortions Pricing Principles. *ASTIN Bulletin, 28*(2), 119–134. doi:10.2143/AST.28.1.519082

Hyvönen, T., Jarvinen, J., & Pellinen, J. (2015). Dynamics of creating a new role for business controllers. *Finnish Journal of Business Economics, 64*(1), 21–39.

Istratescu, V. I. (1981). *Fixed Point Theory.* Reidel Publishing Company. doi:10.1007/978-94-009-8177-5

Jabbari, M., Sheikh, S., Rabiee, M., & Oztekin, A. (2022). A collaborative decision support system for multi-criteria automatic clustering. *Decision Support Systems, 153*, 113671. doi:10.1016/j.dss.2021.113671

Jagadeesh, G., & Smellets, K. (2006). *Measuring Social Security's Financial Outlook within an Aging Society.* MIT Press.

James, G., Witten, D., Hastie, T., & Tibshirani, R. (2013). *An Introduction to Statistical Learning with Applications.* Springer, Hellenic Institute of Occupational Health and Safety. https://www.elinyae.gr/ethniki-nomothesia

Jayapalan, D. F. S., & Ananth, J. P. (2023). Root disease classification with hybrid optimization models in IoT. *Expert Systems with Applications*, *226*, 120150. doi:10.1016/j.eswa.2023.120150

Jeet, V., Kutanoglu, E., & Partani, A. (2009). Logistics network design with inventory stocking for low-demand parts: Modeling and optimization. *IIE Transactions*, *41*(5), 389–407. doi:10.1080/07408170802512602

Jensen, M. (2001). Value maximization, stakeholder theory, and the corporate objective function. *European Financial Management*, *7*(3), 297–317. doi:10.1111/1468-036X.00158

Jensen, M. C. (1968). The Performance of Mutual Funds in the Period 1945-1964. *The Journal of Finance*, *23*(2), 389–416. doi:10.1111/j.1540-6261.1968.tb00815.x

Jiang, M., & Wang, X. (2021). Research on intelligent prediction method of financial crisis of listed enterprises based on random forest algorithm. *Security and Communication Networks*, *2021*, 1–7. doi:10.1155/2021/3807480

John Edwards (2021) *The Top 10 Investment Tools for 2021*. U.S. News & World Report.

Johnson, E. L., Mehrotra, A., & Nemhauser, G. L. (1993). Min-cut clustering. *Mathematical Programming*, *62*(1-3), 133–151. doi:10.1007/BF01585164

Johnson, N. (2021). *The Best Investment Research Websites*. Investopedia.

Jones, C. P. (2007). *Investments: analysis and management*. John Wiley & Sons.

Jönsson, S. (2009). The study of controller agency. In Accounting, organizations and institutions: Essay in honour of Anthony Hopwood. doi:10.1093/acprof:oso/9780199546350.003.0011

Joudaki, H., Rashidian, A., Minaei-Bidgoli, B., Mahmoodi, M., Geraili, B., Nasiri, M., & Arab, M. (2014). Using data mining to detect health care fraud and abuse: A review of literature. *Global Journal of Health Science*, *7*(1), 194–202. doi:10.5539/gjhs.v7n1p194 PMID:25560347

Kagan, J. (2021a). Substandard Insurance. *Investopedia*. https://www.investopedia.com/terms/s/substandard-insurance.asp

Kagan, J. (2021b). Insurance Risk Class Definition and Associated Premium Costs. *Investopedia*. https://www.investopedia.com/terms/i/insurance-risk-class.asp

Kahraman, C., Ruan, D., & Tolga, E. (2002). Capital budgeting techniques using discounted fuzzy versus probabilistic cash flows. *Information Sciences*, *142*(1-4), 57–76. doi:10.1016/S0020-0255(02)00157-3

Kaplan, S. N., & Ruback, R. S. (1995). The valuation of cash flow forecasts: An empirical analysis. *The Journal of Finance*, *50*(4), 1059–1093. doi:10.1111/j.1540-6261.1995.tb04050.x

Karimi-Mamaghan, M., Mohammadi, M., Meyer, P., Karimi-Mamaghan, A. M., & Talbi, E.-G. (2022). A state-of-the-art machine learning at the service of meta-heuristics for solving combinatorial optimization problems. *European Journal of Operational Research*, *296*(2), 393–422. doi:10.1016/j.ejor.2021.04.032

Karlsson, B., Hersinger, A., & Kurkkio, M. (2019). Hybrid accountants in the age of the business partner: Exploring institutional drivers in a mining company. *Journal of Management Control*, *30*(2), 185–211. doi:10.100700187-019-00280-1

Kaya, Y., & Gürsoy, E. (2023). A MobileNet-based CNN model with a novel fine-tuning mechanism for COVID-19 infection detection. *Soft Computing*, *27*(9), 1–15. doi:10.100700500-022-07798-y PMID:36618761

Keha, A. B., de Farias, I. R. Jr, & Nemhauser, G. L. (2006). A branch-and-cut algorithm without binary variables for nonconvex piecewise linear optimization. *Operations Research*, *54*(5), 847–858. doi:10.1287/opre.1060.0277

Kelleher, J. D., Tierney, B., & Tierney, B. (2018). *Data Science An Introduction.* CRC Press.

Kesavan, P., Allgor, R. J., Gatzke, E. P., & Barton, P. I. (2004). Outer approximation algorithms for separable nonconvex mixed-integer nonlinear programs. *Mathematical Programming, 100*(3), 517–535. doi:10.100710107-004-0503-1

Khalehoghli, S., Rahimi, H., & Gordji, M. E. (2020). Fixed Point Theorem in R-Metric Spaces with Applications. *AIMS Mathematics, 5*(4), 312–315. doi:10.3934/math.2020201

Khan, A. T., Cao, X., Brajevic, I., Stanimirovic, P. S., Katsikis, V. N., & Li, S. (2022). Non-linear activated beetle antennae search: A novel technique for non-convex tax-aware portfolio optimization problem. *Expert Systems with Applications, 197*, 116631. doi:10.1016/j.eswa.2022.116631

Khokhlov, I., Davydenko, E., Osokin, I., Ryakin, I., Babaev, A., Litvinenko, V., & Gorbachev, R. (2020, May). Tiny-YOLO object detection supplemented with geometrical data. In *2020 IEEE 91st Vehicular Technology Conference (VTC2020-Spring)* (pp. 1-5). IEEE. 10.1109/VTC2020-Spring48590.2020.9128749

Kian, R., & Kargar, K. (2016). Comparison of the formulations for a hub-and-spoke network design problem under congestion. *Computers & Industrial Engineering, 101*, 504–512. doi:10.1016/j.cie.2016.09.019

Kim, Y., Kang, D., Jeon, M., & Lee, C. (2019). Gan-mp hybrid heuristic algorithm for non-convex portfolio optimization problem. *The Engineering Economist, 64*(3), 196–226. doi:10.1080/0013791X.2019.1620391

Kocher, R., Emanuel, E. J., & DeParle, N. A. M. (2010). The Affordable Care Act and the future of clinical medicine: The opportunities and challenges. *Annals of Internal Medicine, 153*(8), 536–539. doi:10.7326/0003-4819-153-8-201010190-00274 PMID:20733178

Kogut, B., & Kulatilaka, N. (1994). Options thinking and platform investments: Investing in opportunity. *California Management Review, 36*(2), 52–71. doi:10.2307/41165744

KoH.LeeJ. (2023). Can Chatgpt Improve Investment Decision? From a Portfolio Management Perspective. doi:10.2139/ssrn.4390529

Koh, H. C., & Tan, G. (2005). Data mining applications in healthcare. Journal of healthcare information management. *Journal of Healthcare Information Management, 19*(2), 64–72. PMID:15869215

Kolm, P. N., & Ritter, G. (2019). Modern perspectives on reinforcement learning in finance. *SSRN, 1*(1). doi:10.2139srn.3449401

Konno, H. (1976). A cutting plane algorithm for solving bilinear programs. *Mathematical Programming, 11*(1), 14–27. doi:10.1007/BF01580367

Krugman, P. (2022, December 6). Does ChatGPT Mean Robots Are Coming For the Skilled Jobs? *The New York Times*. https://www.nytimes.com/2022/12/06/opinion/chatgpt-ai-skilled-jobs-automation.html

Kubat, M., & Kubat, J. A. (2017). *An introduction to machine learning* (Vol. 2). Springer International Publishing. doi:10.1007/978-3-319-63913-0

Kumar, A., Kalia, A., Sharma, A., & Kaushal, M. (2021). A hybrid tiny YOLO v4-SPP module based improved face mask detection vision system. *Journal of Ambient Intelligence and Humanized Computing*, 1–14. PMID:34691278

Kuno, T., & Utsunomiya, T. (2000). A lagrangian based branch-and-bound algorithm for production-transportation problems. *Journal of Global Optimization, 18*(1), 59–73. doi:10.1023/A:1008373329033

Lambert, C., & Sponem, S. (2012). Roles, authority and involvement of the management accounting function: A multiple case-study perspective. *European Accounting Review, 21*(3), 565–589.

Landauer, T. K., Foltz, P. W., & Laham, D. (1998). An introduction to latent semantic analysis. *Discourse Processes, 25*(2-3), 259–284. doi:10.1080/01638539809545028

Lantz, B. (2019). *Machine Learning with R: Expert techniques for predictive modeling* (3rd ed.). Packt.

Lee, E. K., Atallah, H. Y., Wright, M. D., Thomas, C., IV, Post, E. T., Wu, D. T., & Haley, L. L., Jr. (2016). *Systems analytics: modeling and optimizing clinic workflow and patient care. Healthcare Analytics: From Data to Knowledge to Healthcare Improvement*, 263-299. Mayo Clinic. https://www.mayoclinic.org/medical-professionals/trauma/news/how-mayo-clinic-has-addressed-hospital-capacity-challenges/mac-20527287

Lee, S., & Grossmann, I. E. (2001). A global optimization algorithm for nonconvex generalized disjunctive pro- gramming and applications to process systems. *Computers & Chemical Engineering, 25*(11-12), 1675–1697. doi:10.1016/S0098-1354(01)00732-3

Leonard, T. (2021). *The Best Investment Software of 2021*. Benzinga.

Lepistö, L., & Ihantola, E. M. (2018). Understanding the recruitment and selection processes of management accountants: An explorative study. *Qualitative Research in Accounting & Management, 15*(1), 104–123. doi:10.1108/QRAM-11-2016-0080

Lestari, D. P., Kosasih, R., Handhika, T., Sari, I., & Fahrurozi, A. (2019, September). Fire hotspots detection system on CCTV videos using you only look once (YOLO) method and tiny YOLO model for high buildings evacuation. In *2019 2nd International Conference of Computer and Informatics Engineering (IC2IE)* (pp. 87-92). IEEE.

Liang, D., Lu, C. C., Tsai, C. F., & Shih, G. A. (2016). Financial ratios and corporate governance indicators in bankruptcy prediction: A comprehensive study. *European Journal of Operational Research, 252*(2), 561–572. doi:10.1016/j.ejor.2016.01.012

Li, D., Sun, X., & Wang, F. (2006). Convergent lagrangian and contour cut method for nonlinear integer program- ming with a quadratic objective function. *SIAM Journal on Optimization, 17*(2), 372–400. doi:10.1137/040606193

Ling, T., & Cai, Y. (2022). Financial crisis prediction based on long-term and short-term memory neural network. *Wireless Communications and Mobile Computing, 2022*, 1–8. doi:10.1155/2022/5728470

Linsley, P., & Linsley, A. (2014). Cultural theory of risk and the notion of "management accountants as strategists". In *Management control and uncertainty* (pp. 224–238). Palgrave Macmillan. doi:10.1057/9781137392121_15

Lintner, J. (1965). The valuation of risk assets and the selection of risky investments in stock portfolios and capital budgets. *The Review of Economics and Statistics, 47*(1), 13–37. doi:10.2307/1924119

Liu, J., & Wang, X. (2020). Early recognition of tomato gray leaf spot disease based on MobileNetv2-YOLOv3 model. *Plant Methods, 16*(1), 1–16. doi:10.118613007-020-00624-2 PMID:32523613

Li, Y., Lin, Y., & Shu, J. (2021). Location and two-echelon inventory network design with economies and disec- onomies of scale in facility operating costs. *Computers & Operations Research, 133*, 105347. doi:10.1016/j.cor.2021.105347

Lo, A. W. (2004). The Adaptive Markets Hypothesis. *Journal of Portfolio Management, 30*(5), 15–29. doi:10.3905/jpm.2004.442611

Locatelli, M., & Thoai, N. V. (2000). Finite exact branch-and-bound algorithms for concave minimization over polytopes. *Journal of Global Optimization*, *18*(2), 107–128. doi:10.1023/A:1008324430471

Locke, S. (2022, December 6). What is AI chatbot phenomenon ChatGPT and could it replace humans? *The Guardian*. https://www.theguardian.com/technology/2022/dec/05/what-is-ai-chatbot-phenomenon-chatgpt-and-could-it-replace-humans

Lu, D., Gzara, F., & Elhedhli, S. (2014). Facility location with economies and diseconomies of scale: Models and column generation heuristics. *IIE Transactions*, *46*(6), 585–600. doi:10.1080/0740817X.2013.860508

Lusardi, A., & Mitchell, O. S. (2014). The Economic Importance of Financial Literacy: Theory and Evidence. *Journal of Economic Literature*, *52*(1), 34. doi:10.1257/jel.52.1.5 PMID:28579637

Mahdoudi, H., & Boussetta, M. (2017). UCITS in Morocco: Evolution, challenges and perspectives. *International Journal of Economics, Commerce and Management.*

Mahesh, B. (2020). Machine learning algorithms-a review. *International Journal of Science and Research (IJSR).[Internet]*, *9*, 381–386.

Mahmoudi, M., & Gharehchopogh, F. S. (2018). An improvement of shuffled frog leaping algorithm with a decision tree for feature selection in text document classification. *CSI Journal on Computer Science and Engineering*, *16*(1), 60–72.

Maisel, L., & Cokins, G. (2013). *Predictive business analytics: Forward looking capabilities to improve business performance*. John Wiley & Sons.

Maiti, M. (2022, December 16). How An Actuary Decides Your Insurance Policy Premiums—Know Criteria, Factors Involved. *Outlook India*. https://www.outlookindia.com/. https://www.outlookindia.com/business/how-an-actuary-decides-your-insurance-policy-premiums-know-criteria-factors-involved--news-245409

Majthay, A., & Whinston, A. (1974). Quasi-concave minimization subject to linear constraints. *Discrete Mathematics*, *9*(1), 35–59. doi:10.1016/0012-365X(74)90070-3

Mallappa, M., & Talawar, A. S. (2020). Premium Calculation for Different Loss Discrete Analogues of Continuous Distributions Utility Theory. *International Journal of Agricultural and Statistics Sciences*, *16*(1), 61–72.

Marche, S. (2022, December 6). The College Essay Is Dead. *The Atlantic*. https://www.theatlantic.com/technology/archive/2022/12/chatgpt-ai-writing-college-student-essays/672371/

Markovitz, H. M. (1952). Portfolio selection. *The Journal of Finance*, *7*(1), 77–91.

Markowitz H. (1959). *Portfolio Selection: Efficient Diversification of Investments*. Yale University.

Markowitz, H. (1999). The early history of portfolio theory: 1600–1960. *Financial Analysts Journal.*

MartiG. 2022. From data to trade: A machine learning approach to quantitative trading. SSRN:4315362. doi:10.2139/ssrn.4315362

McCormick, G. P. (1976). Computability of global solutions to factorable nonconvex programs: Part i—convex underestimating problems. *Mathematical Programming*, *10*(1), 147–175. doi:10.1007/BF01580665

McGrattan, E. R. (2001). *Taxes, Regulations, and Asset Prices*. Federal Reserve Bank of Minneapolis. doi:10.3386/w8623

McKee, F., & Noever, D. (2022). Chatbots in a botnet world. arXiv. https://arxiv.org/abs/2212.11126

Meagher, G., Stebbing, A., & Perche, D. (Eds.). (2022). *Designing Social Service Markets: Risk Regulation and Rent-Seeking*. ANU Press. doi:10.22459/DSSM.2022

Megahed, F. M., Chen, Y. J., Ferris, J. A., Knoth, S., & Jones-Farmer, L. A. (2023). How Generative AI models such as ChatGPT can be (Mis)Used in SPC Practice, Education, and Research? An Exploratory Study. https://doi.org/doi:10.48550/arXiv.2302.10916

Mercer, C. D. (2021). *The Best Stock Analysis Software for 2021*. Investopedia.

Metawa, N., Nguyen, P. T., Le Hoang Thuy To Nguyen, Q., Elhoseny, M., & Shankar, K. (2021). Internet of things enabled financial crisis prediction in enterprises using optimal feature subset selection-based classification model. *Big Data*, *9*(5), 331–342. doi:10.1089/big.2020.0192 PMID:34030465

Mhlanga, D. (2020). Industry 4.0 in finance: The impact of artificial intelligence (AI) on digital financial inclusion. *International Journal of Financial Studies*, *8*(3), 45. doi:10.3390/ijfs8030045

Mishkin, F. S. (1991). *Asymmetric Information and Financial Crises: A Historical Perspective.* NBER Working Paper No. w3400.

Mitra, S., & Padman, R. (2016). Understanding the Role of Social Media in Healthcare via Analytics: a Health Plan Perspective. *Healthcare Analytics: From Data to Knowledge to Healthcare Improvement*, 593–625. doi:10.1002/9781118919408.ch20

Mittal, B. (1999). The advertising of services: Meeting the challenge of intangibility. *Journal of Service Research*, *2*(1), 98–116. doi:10.1177/109467059921008

Mohammed, M. A., Lakhan, A., Abdulkareem, K. H., & Garcia-Zapirain, B. (2023). A hybrid cancer prediction based on multi-omics data and reinforcement learning state action reward state action (SARSA). *Computers in Biology and Medicine*, *154*, 106617. doi:10.1016/j.compbiomed.2023.106617 PMID:36753981

Mortazavi, A., Toğan, V., & Nuhoğlu, A. (2018). Interactive search algorithm: A new hybrid metaheuristic optimization algorithm. *Engineering Applications of Artificial Intelligence*, *71*, 275–292. doi:10.1016/j.engappai.2018.03.003

Moumtzaki, A. (2018). The Former Minister Who Tried to Warn Greece About the Crisis. *Vice.* https://www.vice.com/sv/article/dp57na/greek-ex-finance-minister-alekos-papadopoulos-interview-876

Mousavi, S. M., Sadeghi R, K., & Lee, L. S. (2023). An interactive analytics approach for sustainable and resilient case studies: A machine learning perspective. *Journal of Business Analytics*, 1–18.

Mun, J. (2012). *Real options analysis: Tools and techniques for valuing strategic investments and decisions* (Vol. 320). John Wiley & Sons. doi:10.1002/9781119201618

Musallam, S. R. (2018). Exploring the relationship between financial ratios and market stock returns. *Eurasian Journal of Business and Economics*, *11*(21), 101–116. doi:10.17015/ejbe.2018.021.06

Mu, Y., Liu, X., Yang, Z., & Liu, X. (2017). A parallel C4. 5 decision tree algorithms based on MapReduce. *Concurrency and Computation*, *29*(8), e4015. doi:10.1002/cpe.4015

Namburu, A., Selvaraj, P., Mohan, S., Ragavanantham, S., & Eldin, E. T. (2023). Forest Fire Identification in UAV Imagery Using X-MobileNet. *Electronics (Basel)*, *12*(3), 733. doi:10.3390/electronics12030733

Nash, J. (1951). Non Cooperative Games. *Annals of Mathematics*, *54*(2), 286–295. doi:10.2307/1969529

National Academies Press (US). (1993). *Risk Selection, Risk Sharing, and Policy.* Employment and Health Benefits - NCBI Bookshelf. https://www.ncbi.nlm.nih.gov/books/NBK235988/

Nektarios, M., Tinios, P., & Simeonidis, G. (2018) *Pensions for the Young: A Social Insurance System Focused on Growth.* LSE. http://eprints.lse.ac.uk/79268/1/blogs.lse.ac.uk

Nelson, E. C., Mohr, J. J., Batalden, P. B., & Plume, S. K. (1996). Improving Health Care, Part 1: The Clinical Value Compass. *The Joint Commission Journal on Quality Improvement*, *22*(4), 243–258. doi:10.1016/S1070-3241(16)30228-0 PMID:8743061

Nguyen, A., Lamouri, S., Pellerin, R., Tamayo, S., & Lekens, B. (2022). Data analytics in pharmaceutical supply chains: State of the art, opportunities, and challenges. *International Journal of Production Research*, *60*(22), 6888–6907. doi:10.1080/00207543.2021.1950937

Nieto, J. J., & Guez-Lo'pez, R. R. (2005). Contractive Mapping Theorems in Partially Ordered Sets and Application to Ordinary Differential Equations. *Order*, *22*(3), 223–239. doi:10.100711083-005-9018-5

Nirmalapriya, G., Maram, B., Lakshmanan, R., & Navaneethakrishnan, M. (2023). ASCA-squeeze net: Aquila sine cosine algorithm enabled hybrid deep learning networks for digital image forgery detection. *Computers & Security*, *128*, 103155. doi:10.1016/j.cose.2023.103155

Niszczota, P., & Abbas, S. (2023). GPT as a Financial Advisor. http://dx.doi.org/doi:10.2139/ssrn.4384861

Ni, W., Shu, J., Song, M., Xu, D., & Zhang, K. (2021). A branch-and-price algorithm for facility location with general facility cost functions. *INFORMS Journal on Computing*, *33*(1), 86–104. doi:10.1287/ijoc.2019.0921

Nnorom, S. U., & Olagbaju, O. O. (2020). Principals' quality management skills as determinants of goal attainment in secondary schools in Ahiazu Mbaise local government area, Imo state. *International Journal on Integrated Education*, *3*(10), 87–91. doi:10.31149/ijie.v3i10.692

Nuechterlein, N., & Mehta, S. (2019). 3D-ESPNet with pyramidal refinement for volumetric brain tumor image segmentation. In *Brainlesion: Glioma, Multiple Sclerosis, Stroke and Traumatic Brain Injuries: 4th International Workshop*. Springer International Publishing.

O'Kelly, M. E., & Bryan, D. (1998). Hub location with flow economies of scale. *Transportation Research Part B: Methodological*, *32*(8), 605–616. doi:10.1016/S0191-2615(98)00021-6

Oesterreich, T. D., & Teuteberg, F. (2019). The role of business analytics in the controllers and management accountants' competence profiles: An exploratory study on individual-level data. *Journal of Accounting & Organizational Change*.

Ogundokun, R. O., Misra, S., Akinrotimi, A. O., & Ogul, H. (2023). MobileNet-SVM: A Lightweight Deep Transfer Learning Model to Diagnose BCH Scans for IoMT-Based Imaging Sensors. *Sensors (Basel)*, *23*(2), 656. doi:10.339023020656 PMID:36679455

Olshansky, S. J., Goldman, D. P., & Rowe, J. W. (2015). *Resetting Social Security*. MIT Press. doi:10.1162/DAED_a_00331

Open A. I. (2015, December 11). *About OpenAI*. OpenAI. https://openai.com/about/

Open A. I. (2022a, November). *ChatGPT: Optimizing language models for dialogue*. OpenAI. https://openai.com/

Open A. I. (2022c, April). *DALL.E 2*. Open AI. https://openai.com/dall-e-2/.

Ozsen, L., Coullard, C. R., & Daskin, M. S. (2008). Capacitated warehouse location model with risk pooling. [NRL]. *Naval Research Logistics*, *55*(4), 295–312. doi:10.1002/nav.20282

Palepu, K. G., Healy, P. M., & Peek, E. (2013). *Business analysis and valuation: Using financial statements*. Cengage Learning.

Papadopoulos, A. (2023) *The Risks of Embellishing the Fiscal Situation*. Fantomas. https://fantomas.gr/55536-2/

Park, K., Lee, K., & Park, S. (1996). An extended formulation approach to the edge-weighted maximal clique problem. *European Journal of Operational Research, 95*(3), 671–682. doi:10.1016/0377-2217(95)00299-5

Parmas, P., Rasmussen, C. E., Peters, J., & Doya, K. (2018). PIPPS: Flexible model-based policy search robust to the curse of chaos. *International Conference on Machine Learning*, (pp. 4065–4074).

Parsons, J. R. (1962). *The Origins of the Income-and-Resources Amendment to the Social Security Act.* University of Chicago Press. doi:10.1086/641183

Paulsson, G. (2012). The Role of Management Accountants in New Public Management. In Financial Accountability & Management, 28 (4), 378–394. Wiley. doi:10.1111/j.1468-0408.2012.00552.x

Penman, S. H., & Sougiannis, T. (1998). A comparison of dividend, cash flow, and earnings approaches to equity valuation. *Contemporary Accounting Research, 15*(3), 343–383. doi:10.1111/j.1911-3846.1998.tb00564.x

Pension Research Council. (2022). Wharton School of Business.

Pentico, D. W., & Drake, M. J. (2011). A survey of deterministic models for the EOQ and EPQ with partial backordering. *European Journal of Operational Research, 214*(2), 179–198. doi:10.1016/j.ejor.2011.01.048

Perboli, G., & Arabnezhad, E. (2021). A Machine Learning-based DSS for mid and long-term company crisis prediction. *Expert Systems with Applications, 174*(114758), 114758. doi:10.1016/j.eswa.2021.114758

Pfleeger, S. L., & Caputo, D. D. (2012). Leveraging behavioral science to mitigate cyber security risk. *Computers & Security, 31*(4), 597–611. doi:10.1016/j.cose.2011.12.010

Pisinger, D. (2007). The quadratic knapsack problem—A survey. *Discrete Applied Mathematics*, 155(5):623–648. Quesada, I. and Grossmann, I. E. (1995). A global optimization algorithm for linear fractional and bilinear programs. *Journal of Global Optimization, 6*(1), 39–76.

Punuri, S. B., Kuanar, S. K., Kolhar, M., Mishra, T. K., Alameen, A., Mohapatra, H., & Mishra, S. R. (2023). Efficient Net-XGBoost: An Implementation for Facial Emotion Recognition Using Transfer Learning. *Mathematics, 11*(3), 776. doi:10.3390/math11030776

Purcell, S., Neale, B., Todd-Brown, K., Thomas, L., Ferreira, M. A., Bender, D., Maller, J., Sklar, P., de Bakker, P. I. W., Daly, M. J., & Sham, P. C. (2007). PLINK: A tool set for whole-genome association and population-based linkage analyses. *American Journal of Human Genetics, 81*(3), 559–575. doi:10.1086/519795 PMID:17701901

Quinlan, J. R. (1996). Improved use of continuous attributes in C4. 5. *Journal of Artificial Intelligence Research, 4*, 77–90. doi:10.1613/jair.279

Quinlan, J. R. (2014). *C4. 5: programs for machine learning*. Elsevier. doi:10.1016/j.procs.2016.04.224

Radford, A., Narasimhan, K., Salimans, T., & Sutskever, I. (2018). *Improving language understanding by generative pre-training*. OpenAI. https://cdn.openai.com/research-covers/language-unsupervised/language_understanding_paper.pdf

Rafay, A., & Hussain, W. (2023). EfficientSkinDis: An EfficientNet-based classification model for a large manually curated dataset of 31 skin diseases. *Biomedical Signal Processing and Control, 85*, 104869. doi:10.1016/j.bspc.2023.104869

Raffel, C. (2019). Exploring the limits of transfer learning with a unified text-to-text transformer. arXiv preprint arXiv:1910.10683.

Rajeena, P. P. (1938). F., SU, A., Moustafa, M. A., & Ali, M. A. (2023). Detecting Plant Disease in Corn Leaf Using EfficientNet Architecture—An Analytical Approach. *Electronics (Basel), 12*(8). Advance online publication. doi:10.3390/electronics12081938

Rajic, V., Azdejkovic, D., & Loncar, D. (2014). Fixed Point Theory and Possibilities of Application in Different Fields of an Economy. *UDK:330.42:515.126.4.*. https://www.researchgate.net/publication/283393893 doi:10.5937/ekopre1408382R

Rajpurkar, P., Chen, E., Banerjee, O., & Topol, E. J. (2022). AI in health and medicine. *Nature Medicine*, *28*(1), 31–38. doi:10.103841591-021-01614-0 PMID:35058619

Ramezankhani, A., Pournik, O., Shahrabi, J., Azizi, F., & Hadaegh, F. (2015). An application of association rule mining to extract risk pattern for type 2 diabetes using tehran lipid and glucose study database. *International Journal of Endocrinology and Metabolism*, *13*(2), e25389. doi:10.5812/ijem.25389 PMID:25926855

Rapp, D. J., Rapp, A., & Daher, T. (2023). Opportunity discovery or judgment? Value investing's incompatibility with Austrian economics revisited. *The Review of Austrian Economics*, 1–25. doi:10.100711138-023-00616-0

Rashid, C. A. (2018). The efficiency of financial ratios analysis for evaluating companies' liquidity. *International Journal of Social Sciences & Educational Studies*, *4*(4), 110.

Rasool, M., Ismail, N. A., Al-Dhaqm, A., Yafooz, W., & Alsaeedi, A. (2023). A Novel Approach for Classifying Brain Tumours Combining a SqueezeNet Model with SVM and Fine-Tuning. *Electronics (Basel)*, *12*(1), 149. doi:10.3390/electronics12010149

Rauh, J., & Smith, K. (2016). Enhancing student learning outcomes in higher education through analytics. *Journal of Educational Technology Development and Exchange*, *9*(1), 1–14.

Ravi, V., Acharya, V., & Alazab, M. (2023). A multichannel EfficientNet deep learning-based stacking ensemble approach for lung disease detection using chest X-ray images. *Cluster Computing*, *26*(2), 1181–1203. doi:10.100710586-022-03664-6 PMID:35874187

Real-Miranda, R., & López-Barrientos, J. D. (2022). A Geologic-Actuarial Approach for Insuring the Extraction Tasks of Non-Renewable Resources by One and Two Agents. *Mathematics*, *10*(13), 2242. doi:10.3390/math10132242

Recchia, D. R., Cramer, H., Wardle, J., Lee, D. J., Ostermann, T., & Lauche, R. (2022). Profiles and predictors of healthcare utilization: Using a cluster-analytic approach to identify typical users across conventional, allied and complementary medicine, and self-care. *BMC Health Services Research*, *22*(1), 29. doi:10.118612913-021-07426-9 PMID:34986866

Reich, J. (2019). The power of data science in education. *The Journal of Technology Transfer*, *44*(3), 640–645.

Reiter, K. L., & Song, P. H. (2021). *Gapenski's Healthcare Finance: An Introduction to Accounting and Financial Management* (7th ed.). Health Administration Press.

Rikhardsson, P., & Yigitbasioglu, O. (2018). Business intelligence & analytics in management accounting research: Status and future focus. *International Journal of Accounting Information Systems*, *29*, 37–58. doi:10.1016/j.accinf.2018.03.001

Rizos, V., Behrens, A., Van der Gaast, W., Hofman, E., Ioannou, A., Kafyeke, T., Flamos, A., Rinaldi, R., Papadelis, S., Hirschnitz-Garbers, M., & Topi, C. (2016). Implementation of circular economy business models by small and medium-sized enterprises (SMEs): Barriers and enablers. *Sustainability (Basel)*, *8*(11), 1212. doi:10.3390u8111212

Robinson, R., & Hudali, T. (2017). The HOSPITAL score and LACE index as predictors of 30 day readmission in a retrospective study at a university-affiliated community hospital. *PeerJ*, *5*, e3137. doi:10.7717/peerj.3137 PMID:28367375

Rolf, B., Jackson, I., Müller, M., Lang, S., Reggelin, T., & Ivanov, D. (2022). A review on reinforcement learning algorithms and applications in supply chain management. *International Journal of Production Research*, 1–29. doi:10.1080/00207543.2022.2140221

Romig, K., Broaddus, M., & Aron-Dine, A. (2019). *Financial Challenges Facing Social Security and Medicare Largely Unchanged from Last Year, Except for Improvement in Disability Insurance*. Center for Budget and Policy Priorities.

Ronald, D., Trevin, L., & Swinkels. (2019). Historical returns of the market portfolio. *Review of Asset Pricing Studies.*

Rosenfeld, S. A. (1997). Bringing business clusters into the mainstream of economic development. *European Planning Studies*, *5*(1), 3–23. doi:10.1080/09654319708720381

Ross, S. (2021). How Do Insurance Companies Make Money? Business Model Explained. *Investopedia*. https://www.investopedia.com/ask/answers/052015/what-main-business-model-insurance-companies.asp

Roth, A. V., & Menor, L. J. (2003). Insights into service operations management: A research agenda. *Production and Operations Management*, *12*(2), 145–164. doi:10.1111/j.1937-5956.2003.tb00498.x

Ruan, N., & Sun, X. (2006). An exact algorithm for cost minimization in series reliability systems with multiple component choices. *Applied Mathematics and Computation*, *181*(1), 732–741. doi:10.1016/j.amc.2006.02.001

Ryan, P. A., & Ryan, G. P. (2002). Capital budgeting practices of the Fortune 1000: How have things changed? *Journal of Business and Management*, *8*(4), 355–364.

Ryoo, H. S., & Sahinidis, N. V. (1995). Global optimization of nonconvex nlps and minlps with applications in process design. *Computers & Chemical Engineering*, *19*(5), 551–566. doi:10.1016/0098-1354(94)00097-2

Ryoo, H. S., & Sahinidis, N. V. (1996). A branch-and-reduce approach to global optimization. *Journal of Global Optimization*, *8*(2), 107–138. doi:10.1007/BF00138689

Sadeghi, J., Mousavi, S. M., Niaki, S. T. A., & Sadeghi, S. (2013). Optimizing a multi-vendor multi-retailer vendor managed inventory problem: Two tuned meta-heuristic algorithms. *Knowledge-Based Systems*, *50*, 159–170. doi:10.1016/j.knosys.2013.06.006

Sadeghi, J., & Niaki, S. T. A. (2015). Two parameter tuned multi-objective evolutionary algorithms for a bi-objective vendor managed inventory model with trapezoidal fuzzy demand. *Applied Soft Computing*, *30*, 567–576. doi:10.1016/j.asoc.2015.02.013

Sadeghi, R. J. K., Prybutok, V. R., & Sauser, B. (2022). Theoretical and practical applications of blockchain in healthcare information management. *Information & Management*, *59*(6), 103649. doi:10.1016/j.im.2022.103649

Saha, E., & Ray, P. K. (2019). Modelling and analysis of inventory management systems in healthcare: A review and reflections. *Computers & Industrial Engineering*, *137*, 106051. doi:10.1016/j.cie.2019.106051

Saif, A. (2016). *Supply chain network design with concave costs: Theory and applications.*

Saif, A., & Elhedhli, S. (2016a). Cold supply chain design with environmental considerations: A simulation- optimization approach. *European Journal of Operational Research*, *251*(1), 274–287. doi:10.1016/j.ejor.2015.10.056

Saif, A., & Elhedhli, S. (2016b). A lagrangian heuristic for concave cost facility location problems: The plant location and technology acquisition problem. *Optimization Letters*, *10*(5), 1087–1100. doi:10.100711590-016-0998-4

Sambell, K., & McDowell, L. (2018). The use of assessment analytics to support student learning: Opportunities and challenges. *Assessment & Evaluation in Higher Education*, *43*(8), 1289–1301.

Samuel, A. L. (1959). Some studies in machine learning using the game of checkers. *IBM Journal of Research and Development*, *3*(3), 210–229. doi:10.1147/rd.33.0210

Sangamesh, H., Viswanatha, V. M., Petli, V., & Patil, N. B. (2023, February). A Novel Approach for Recognition of Face by Using Squeezenet Pre-Trained Network. In *2023 IEEE International Conference on Integrated Circuits and Communication Systems (ICICACS)* (pp. 1-5). IEEE.

Sanjaya, S. A., & Rakhmawan, S. A. (2020, October). Face mask detection using MobileNetV2 in the era of COVID-19 pandemic. In *2020 International Conference on Data Analytics for Business and Industry: Way Towards a Sustainable Economy (ICDABI)* (pp. 1-5). IEEE. 10.1109/ICDABI51230.2020.9325631

Santhi, G., & Karthikeyan, K. (2016). Recent review article on pharmaceutical inventory models. *International Journal of Pharm Tech Research*, *9*(5), 435–443.

Schapire, R. E. (1990). The strength of weak learnability. *Machine Learning*, *5*(2), 197–227. doi:10.1007/BF00116037

Seburn, P. W. (1991). Evolution of Employer-Provided Defined Benefit Pensions. *Monthly Labor Review*.

Securities and Exchange Commission. (1987). *Regulation D Revisions; Exemption for Certain Employee Benefit Plans*. Release No. 33-6683. January 16. [52 FR 3015].

Selwyn, N. (2014). Data entry: Towards the critical study of digital data and education. *Learning, Media and Technology*, *39*(3), 355–367.

Setiawan, W., & Rulaningtyas, R. (2023, January). Visual explanation of maize leaf diaseases classification using squeezenet and gradient-weighted class activation map. In AIP Conference Proceedings (Vol. 2679, No. 1, p. 020002). AIP Publishing LLC. doi:10.1063/5.0111276

Shankland, S. (2022). *Why Everyone's Obsessed with ChatGPT, the Mind-Blowing AI Chatbot* [WWW Document]. CNET. https://www.cnet.com/tech/computing/why-everyones-obsessed-withchatgpt-the-mind-blowing-ai-chatbot/

Shanmuganathan, M. (2020). Behavioural finance in an era of artificial intelligence: Longitudinal case study of robo-advisors in investment decisions. *Journal of Behavioral and Experimental Finance, 27*, doi:10.1016/j.jbef.2020.100297

Sharmili, N., Yonbawi, S., Alahmari, S., Lydia, E. L., Ishak, M. K., Alkahtani, H. K., & Mostafa, S. M. (2022). *Earthworm Optimization with Improved SqueezeNet Enabled Facial Expression Recognition Model*. Tech Science Press.

Sharpe & William, F. (1964). Capital Asset Prices – A Theory of Market Equilibrium Under Conditions of Risk. Research Gate.

Sharpe & William, F. (1994). The Sharpe Ratio. *The Journal of Portfolio Management*.

Shectman, J. P., & Sahinidis, N. V. (1998). A finite algorithm for global minimization of separable concave pro- grams. *Journal of Global Optimization*, *12*(1), 1–36. doi:10.1023/A:1008241411395

Shen, Z.-J. M., Coullard, C., & Daskin, M. S. (2003). A joint location-inventory model. *Transportation Science*, *37*(1), 40–55. doi:10.1287/trsc.37.1.40.12823

Shen, Z.-J. M., & Qi, L. (2007). Incorporating inventory and routing costs in strategic location models. *European Journal of Operational Research*, *179*(2), 372–389. doi:10.1016/j.ejor.2006.03.032

Shifflett, C. (1998). *Selected Virginia Statues Relating to Slavery*. Virtual Jamestown.

Shi, Z., Zhu, J., & Wei, H. (2022). SARSA-based delay-aware route selection for SDN-enabled wireless-PLC power distribution IoT. *Alexandria Engineering Journal*, *61*(8), 5795–5803. doi:10.1016/j.aej.2021.11.029

Shmueli, G., Bruce, P. C., Yahav, I., Patel, N. R., & Lichtendahl, K. C. Jr. (2018). *Data Mining for Business Analytics: Concepts, Techniques, and Applications in R* (1st ed.). Wiley.

Shrestha, A., & Shrestha, S. (2019). Financial Market Prediction Using Deep Learning: A Review and Taxonomy of Recent Research. *Journal of Financial Markets*, *46*, 1–24.

Shu, J., Teo, C.-P., & Shen, Z.-J. M. (2005). Stochastic transportation-inventory network design problem. *Operations Research*, *53*(1), 48–60. doi:10.1287/opre.1040.0140

Shyalika, C., Silva, T., & Karunananda, A. (2020). Reinforcement learning in dynamic task scheduling: A review. *SN Computer Science*, *1*(6), 1–17. doi:10.100742979-020-00326-5

SingerU.PolyakA.HayesT.YinX.AnJ.ZhangS.HuQ.YangH.AshualO.GafniO.ParikhD.GuptaS.TaigmanY. (2022). Make-A-Video: text-to-video generation without text-video data. arXiv article available at: https://arxiv.org/abs/2209.14792

Singh, S., & Gupta, P. (2014). Comparative study ID3, cart, and C4. 5 decision tree algorithm: A survey. [IJAIST]. *International Journal of Advanced Information Science and Technology*, *27*(27), 97–103.

Singh, V., Chen, S.-S., Singhania, M., Nanavati, B., Kar, A. K., & Gupta, A. (2022). How are reinforcement learning and deep learning algorithms used for big data based decision making in financial industries–A review and research agenda. *International Journal of Information Management Data Insights*, *2*(2), 100094. doi:10.1016/j.jjimei.2022.100094

Sinha, A., Das, A., Anand, G., & Jayaswal, S. (2023). A general purpose exact solution method for mixed integer concave minimization problems. *European Journal of Operational Research*, *309*(3), 977–992. doi:10.1016/j.ejor.2023.02.005

Sirotaki, A. (2016). *The Insurance System in Greece*. Semantic Scholar.

Sloan, R. G. (1996). Do stock prices fully reflect information in accruals and cash flows about future earnings? *The Accounting Review*, 289–315.

Smith, E. M., & Pantelides, C. C. (1997). Global optimisation of nonconvex minlps. *Computers & Chemical Engineering*, *21*(1-2), S791–S796. doi:10.1016/S0098-1354(97)00146-4

Soland, R. M. (1971). An algorithm for separable nonconvex programming problems ii: Nonconvex constraints. *Management Science*, *17*(11), 759–773. doi:10.1287/mnsc.17.11.759

Soland, R. M. (1974). Optimal facility location with concave costs. *Operations Research*, *22*(2), 373–382. doi:10.1287/opre.22.2.373

Solow, R. M. (1957). A Contribution to the Theory of Economic Growth. *The Quarterly Journal of Economics*, 70.

Soteriou, A. C., & Chase, R. B. (1998). Linking the customer contact model to service quality. *Journal of Operations Management*, *16*(4), 495–508. doi:10.1016/S0272-6963(98)00026-6

Sphicas, G. P. (2006). EOQ and EPQ with linear and fixed backorder costs: Two cases identified and models analyzed without calculus. *International Journal of Production Economics*, *100*(1), 59–64. doi:10.1016/j.ijpe.2004.10.013

Spieske, A., Gebhardt, M., Kopyto, M., & Birkel, H. (2022). Improving resilience of the healthcare supply chain in a pandemic: Evidence from Europe during the COVID-19 crisis. *Journal of Purchasing and Supply Management*, *28*(5), 100748. doi:10.1016/j.pursup.2022.100748

State Bank of Pakistan. (n.d.). State Bank of Pakistan. https://www.sbp.org.pk/m_policy/mp-learn-3.asp

Strome, T. L. (2013). *Healthcare Analytics*. Wiley.

Suresh Babu, C. V. (2023). *Introduction to Data Science*. Anniyappa Publications.

Taha, H. A. (1973). Concave minimization over a convex polyhedron. *Naval Research Logistics Quarterly*, *20*(3), 533–548. doi:10.1002/nav.3800200313

Tarigan, Y. F., Gunawan, T. S., & Hayadi, B. H. (2023, March). Combination Of SqueezeNet And Multilayer Backpropagation Algorithm In Hanacaraka Script Recognition. In International Conference on Information Science and Technology Innovation (ICoSTEC) (Vol. 2, pp. 163-170). IEEE.

Tawarmalani, M., & Sahinidis, N. V. (2004). Global optimization of mixed-integer nonlinear programs: A theoret- ical and computational study. *Mathematical Programming, 99*(3), 563–591. doi:10.100710107-003-0467-6

Tawarmalani, M., & Sahinidis, N. V. (2005). A polyhedral branch-and-cut approach to global optimization. *Mathematical Programming, 103*(2), 225–249. doi:10.100710107-005-0581-8

Taylor, M. J., McNicholas, C., Nicolay, C., Darzi, A., Bell, D., & Reed, J. E. (2014). Systematic review of the application of the plan–do–study–act method to improve quality in healthcare. *BMJ Quality & Safety, 23*(4), 290–298. doi:10.1136/bmjqs-2013-001862 PMID:24025320

ten Rouwelaar, H., Schaepkens, F., & Widener, S. K. (2020). Skills, Influence, and Effectiveness of Management Accountants. In Journal of Management Accounting Research, 33(2) 211–235. American Accounting Association. doi:10.2308/jmar-18-048

Tersine, R. J. (1993). *Principles of inventory and materials management* (4th ed.). Prentice Hall.

Thakur, L. S. (1991). Domain contraction in nonlinear programming: Minimizing a quadratic concave objective over a polyhedron. *Mathematics of Operations Research, 16*(2), 390–407. doi:10.1287/moor.16.2.390

Toğaçar, M., Cömert, Z., & Ergen, B. (2021). Intelligent skin cancer detection applying autoencoder, MobileNetV2 and spiking neural networks. *Chaos, Solitons, and Fractals, 144*, 110714. doi:10.1016/j.chaos.2021.110714

Treynor, J. L. (1965). How to rate management of investment funds. *Harvard Business Review*, 63–75.

Tuckson, R. V., Edmunds, M., & Hodgkins, M. L. (2017). Telehealth. *The New England Journal of Medicine, 377*(16), 1585–1592. doi:10.1056/NEJMsr1503323 PMID:29045204

Tuomela, T. S. (2005). The interplay of different levers of control: A case study of introducing a new performance measurement system. *Management Accounting Research, 16*(3), 293–320. doi:10.1016/j.mar.2005.06.003

Ture, M., Tokatli, F., & Kurt, I. (2009). Using Kaplan–Meier analysis together with decision tree methods (C&RT, CHAID, QUEST, C4. 5 and ID3) in determining recurrence-free survival of breast cancer patients. *Expert Systems with Applications, 36*(2), 2017–2026. doi:10.1016/j.eswa.2007.12.002

Tuy, H. (1964). Concave programming under linear constraints. *Soviet Mathematics, 5*, 1437–1440.

Tuy, H. (1992). On nonconvex optimization problems with separated nonconvex variables. *Journal of Global Optimization, 2*(2), 133–144. doi:10.1007/BF00122050

Tuy, H., Dan, N. D., & Ghannadan, S. (1993). Strongly polynomial time algorithms for certain concave minimiza- tion problems on networks. *Operations Research Letters, 14*(2), 99–109. doi:10.1016/0167-6377(93)90102-M

Tuy, H., Thieu, T., & Thai, N. Q. (1985). A conical algorithm for globally minimizing a concave function over a closed convex set. *Mathematics of Operations Research, 10*(3), 498–514. doi:10.1287/moor.10.3.498

Two Applications of Brouwer's Fixed Point Theorem: in Insurance and in Biology Models. (2015, December 22). Papers with Code. https://math.paperswithcode.com/paper/two-applications-of-brouwer-s-fixed-point

Tyrrell, J. (2022). *ChatGPT versus Google – the future of search* [WWW Document]. TechHQ.

Uthayakumar, R., & Priyan, S. (2013). Pharmaceutical supply chain and inventory management strategies: Optimization for a pharmaceutical company and a hospital. *Operations Research for Health Care*, *2*(3), 52–64. doi:10.1016/j.orhc.2013.08.001

Van Vliet, B., & Xanthopoulos, A. (2016). Iso-Risk: An Analysis of Risk-Taking in Fixed Income Markets. *Applied Economics*, 60.

Vanian, J. (2022). *Why tech insiders are so excited about ChatGPT, a chatbot that answers questions and writes essays* [WWW Document]. CNBC. https://www.cnbc.com/2022/12/13/chatgpt-is-anew-ai-chatbot-that-can-answer-questions-and-write-essays.html

Venkateswarlu, Y., Baskar, K., Wongchai, A., Gauri Shankar, V., Paolo Martel Carranza, C., Gonzáles, J. L. A., & Murali Dharan, A. R. (2022). An efficient outlier detection with deep learning-based financial crisis prediction model in Big Data environment. *Computational Intelligence and Neuroscience*, *4948947*, 1–10. doi:10.1155/2022/4948947 PMID:36017455

Von Luxburg, U. (2007). A tutorial on spectral clustering. *Statistics and Computing*, *17*(4), 395–416. doi:10.100711222-007-9033-z

Von-Neumann, J. (1928). On the Theory of Games of Strategy. *Mathematische Annalen*, *100*, 295–320.

Voss, C., Roth, A. V., & Chase, R. B. (2008). Experience, service operations strategy, and services as destinations: Foundations and exploratory investigation. *Production and Operations Management*, *17*(3), 247–266. doi:10.3401/poms.1080.0030

Vuik, S. I., Mayer, E. K., & Darz, A. (2016). Patient Segmentation Analysis Offers Significant Benefits for Integrated Care and Support. *Health Affairs*, *35*(5), 769–775. doi:10.1377/hlthaff.2015.1311 PMID:27140981

Wang, F. (2019). A new exact algorithm for concave knapsack problems with integer variables. *International Journal of Computer Mathematics*, *96*(1), 126–134. doi:10.1080/00207160.2017.1418505

Wang, P., Zhang, J., & Zhu, H. (2021). Fire detection in video surveillance using superpixel-based region proposal and ESE-ShuffleNet. *Multimedia Tools and Applications*, 1–28.

Wang, S., & Young, V. R. (1998). Ordering of Risks: Utility Theory Verse Yaari's Dual Theory of Risk. *Insurance, Mathematics & Economics*, *23*(2), 1–14. doi:10.1016/S0167-6687(97)00036-X

Wang, S., Young, V. R., & Panjer, H. H. (1997). Axiomatic Characterisation of Insurance Prices. *Insurance, Mathematics & Economics*, *21*(2), 173–183. doi:10.1016/S0167-6687(97)00031-0

Wang, X., Zhou, C., & Xu, X. (2019). Application of C4. 5 decision tree for scholarship evaluations. *Procedia Computer Science*, *151*, 179–184. doi:10.1016/j.procs.2019.04.027

WatanabeS.HoriT.KaritaS.HayashiT.NishitobaJ.UnnoY.OchiaiT. (2018). Espnet: End-to-end speech processing toolkit. arXiv:1804.00015. doi:10.21437/Interspeech.2018-1456

Watkins, C. J., & Dayan, P. (1992). Q-learning. *Machine Learning*, *8*(3-4), 279–292. doi:10.1007/BF00992698

Weber, J. (2011). The development of controller tasks: Explaining the nature of controllership and its changes. *Journal of Management Control*, *22*(1), 25–46. doi:10.100700187-011-0123-x

WenzlaffK.SpaethS. 2022. Smarter than humans? Validating how OpenAI's ChatGPT model explains crowdfunding, alternative finance and community finance. SSRN:4302443. doi:10.2139/ssrn.4302443

What to do with your cash now. (2022, August 1). https://www.fidelity.com/learning-center/trading-investing/managing-cash

Whistman, J. (2022) *How Long Does the Average Person Stay at a Job (and How to Increase it)*. Perception Prediction AI. https://www.perceptionpredict.ai

White, H. (1980). A heteroskedasticity-consistent covariance matrix estimator and a direct test for heteroskedasticity. *Econometrica, 48*(4), 817. doi:10.2307/1912934

Why go into Insurance Law ? (n.d.). University of Law. https://www.law.ac.uk/employability/legal-practice-areas/insurance-law/

Wikipedia contributors. (2023). Fixed-point theorem. *Wikipedia*. https://en.wikipedia.org/wiki/Fixed-point_theorem

Williamson, B., & Eynon, R. (2018). The datafication of teaching in higher education: Critical issues and perspectives. *Teaching in Higher Education, 23*(4), 351–365. doi:10.1080/13562517.2020.1748811

Windeck, D., Weber, J., & Strauss, E. (2015). Enrolling managers to accept the business partner: The role of boundary objects. *The Journal of Management and Governance, 19*(3), 617–653. doi:10.100710997-013-9277-2

Wire, F. (2023). Greek Stability Programme Underscores Improving. *Public Finance*.

Witzgall, C. (1975). Mathematical methods of site selection for electronic message systems (ems). *STIN, 76*, 18321. doi:10.6028/NBS.IR.75-737

Wu, C.-C., & Chen, W.-P. (2022). What's an AI name worth? The impact of AI ETFs on their underlying stocks. *Finance Research Letters, 46*, 102474. doi:10.1016/j.frl.2021.102474

Wu, T., & Zhang, K. (2014). A computational study for common network design in multi-commodity supply chains. *Computers & Operations Research, 44*, 206–213. doi:10.1016/j.cor.2013.11.009

Xanthopoulos, A. (2012) The Entrenched Kurtosis in Current Portfolio Returns. *The Journal of Economic Asymmetries*, Elsevier.

Xanthopoulos, A. (2010). Market Value Signal Extraction and the Misapplication of SFAS 133 in the U.S. GSE's. *Journal of Economic Asymmetries*, 7.

Xanthopoulos, A. (2019). Investment Advising: Pay-to-Play, or Capture? *SPOUDAI Journal of Economics and Business, 69*, 75–110.

Xiong, L., Sun, T., & Green, R. (2022). Predictive analytics for 30-day hospital readmissions. *Mathematical Foundations of Computing, 5*(2), 93–111. doi:10.3934/mfc.2021035

Xydakis, N. (2023) Greeks Suffering from Stockholm Syndrome. *Hellas*. https://hellas.postsen.com/local/359085/Nikos-Xydakis-does-not-take-back-the-Stockholm-syndrome-for-ND-voters.html

Yazdifar, H., & Tsamenyi, M. (2005). Management accounting change and the changing roles of management accountants: A comparative analysis between dependent and independent organizations. *Journal of Accounting & Organizational Change, 1*(2), 180–198. doi:10.1108/18325910510635353

Yue, Q. (2016). Dynamics of a modified Leslie–Gower predator–prey model with Holling-type II schemes and a prey refuge. *SpringerPlus, 5*(1), 461. doi:10.118640064-016-2087-7 PMID:27119065

YueT.AuC. C. (2023). GPTQuant's Conversational AI: Simplifying Investment Research for All. *SSRN*. doi:10.2139/ssrn.4380516

Yue, T., Au, D., Au, C. C., & Iu, K. Y. (2023). *Democratizing Financial Knowledge with ChatGPT by OpenAI: Unleashing the Power of Technology*. SSRN., doi:10.2139srn.4346152

Yu, Y., & Liu, J. (2022). Optimizing film companies' marketing strategy using blockchain and Recurrent Neural Network model. *Computational Intelligence and Neuroscience, 4139074*, 1–13. Advance online publication. doi:10.1155/2022/4139074 PMID:36120666

Zacharis, N. Z. (2018). Classification and regression trees (CART) for predictive modeling in blended learning. *International Journal of Intelligent Systems and Applications, 3*(3), 1–9. doi:10.5815/ijisa.2018.03.01

Zaremba, A., & Demir, E. (2023). *ChatGPT: Unlocking the Future of NLP in Finance.* SSRN., doi:10.2139srn.4323643

Zarifhonarvar, A. (2023). *Economics of ChatGPT: A Labor Market View on the Occupational Impact of Artificial Intelligence.* SSRN., doi:10.2139srn.4350925

Zhang, R., & Sheng, J. (2022). Optimization of Virtual Network Mapping Based on Improved Ant Colony Algorithm in Complex Network Environments. *Scientific Programming, 2022*, 1–8. doi:10.1155/2022/7343493

Zhang, Y., Khan, M. A., Zhu, Z., & Wang, S. (2023). SNELM: SqueezeNet-guided ELM for COVID-19 recognition. *Computer Systems Science and Engineering, 1*(1), 13–26. doi:10.32604/csse.2023.034172 PMID:37155222

Zhao, K., Zhang, M., Shen, W., Liu, X., Ji, J., Dai, B., & Zhang, R. (2023). Automatic body condition scoring for dairy cows based on efficient net and convex hull features of point clouds. *Computers and Electronics in Agriculture, 205*, 107588. doi:10.1016/j.compag.2022.107588

Zhong, Q., Ding, L., Liu, J., Du, B., & Tao, D. (2023). Can ChatGPT Understand Too? A Comparative Study on ChatGPT and Fine-tuned BERT. https://doi.org/ doi:10.48550/arXiv.2302.10198

Zhong, X., Williams, M., Li, J., Kraft, S. A., & Sleeth, J. S. (2016). Discrete-Event Simulation for Primary Care Redesign: Review and a Case Study. *Healthcare Analytics: From Data to Knowledge to Healthcare Improvement,* 399–426. doi:10.1002/9781118919408.ch13

About the Contributors

Reza Gharoie Ahangar is an Assistant Professor of Business Analytics at Lewis University in Romeoville, Chicago area. He holds: a B.Sc. in Business Management, an MBA in Finance, an MSc in Finance, an MSc in Business Analytics, and a Ph.D. in Management Science with a minor in Economics. Dr. Ahangar is a member of Production and Operations Management Society (POMS), Institute for Operations Research and the Management Sciences (INFORMS), Decision Sciences Institute (DSI), and Association of Scientists, Developers, and Faculties (ASDF). He has been a teaching assistant and instructor at The University of North Texas for seven years and has authored nine books and book chapters as well as several journals and conference publications with more than fifty technical publications and over 650 google scholar citations. His research works are cited by the top 0.1% of most-read authors in academia. He serves as an editorial board member & reviewer for several scientific journals.

* * *

C.V. Suresh Babu, is a pioneer in content development. A true entrepreneur, he founded Anniyappa Publications, a company that is highly active in publishing books related to Computer Science and Management. Dr. C.V. Suresh Babu has also ventured into SB Institute, a center for knowledge transfer. He holds a Ph.D. in Engineering Education from the National Institute of Technical Teachers Training & Research in Chennai, along with seven master's degrees in various disciplines such as Engineering, Computer Applications, Management, Commerce, Economics, Psychology, Law, and Education. Additionally, he has UGC-NET/SET qualifications in the fields of Computer Science, Management, Commerce, and Education. Currently, Dr. C.V. Suresh Babu is a Professor in the Department of Information Technology at the School of Computing Science, Hindustan Institute of Technology and Science (Hindustan University) in Padur, Chennai, Tamil Nadu, India. For more information, you can visit his personal blog at .

Zineb Bellache, financial manager in the Moroccan social security fund. In charge of the management of the treasury and the investment, of the gross surplus of the receipts, and doctoral student in third year at the university HASSAN II, laboratory of Modelling Applied to Economy and Management (MAEGE). After obtaining my baccalaureate in physics in 2014, I did a bachelor's degree in applied mathematics in social science, then I got a master's degree in actuarial and market finance in 2019. During this course, I had the opportunity to develop a lot of skills, during internships in different fields and as well as professional experiences.

Uzay Damali is an associate professor of Operations Management at the University of Wisconsin La Crosse. He is the director of the Healthcare Analytics Management Program, and teaches courses in operations management, healthcare management and healthcare analytics management. He holds a doctorate in supply chain and operations management from Clemson University, and published in Journal of Operations Management and Decision Sciences. His current research interests include improving healthcare service quality.

Arka Das is working as Senior Operations Research Engineer at Micron Technology, Inc. Arka is responsible for supply chain optimization for the global supply chain at Micron Technology. Arka is pursuing his Ph.D. (Thesis Submitted) in Operations Research with a specialization in Machine Learning from the Indian Institute of Management, Ahmedabad (IIMA). His thesis, "Exact Solution Methods for Solving Non-convex Optimization Problems," focuses on designing new algorithms for solving non-convex problems arising in operations management. In the thesis, he solved various problems, including facility location problems, hub location problems, production transportation problems, and concave knapsack problems. He has been an avid researcher, contributing to various international conferences. He has also published a paper on European Journal of Operational Research with the title, "A general purpose exact solution method for mixed integer concave minimization problems".

Agata Fietko is a Business Analytics major at Lewis University. She holds an Associate Degree in Science from the College of DuPage.

Daniele Giordino is a PhD Student from the University of Turin. Currently holds a BA(Hons) and MSc in Accounting and Finance from the University of Winchester, UK.

Ava Hajian is a Ph.D. candidate (ABD) in Data Science in Information Science at University of North Texas with interests in blockchain, cyber-security, and machine learning in information sharing systems. Ava currently teaches Data Modeling, SQL, and Visualization. She has published articles in several reputable academic journals, including Computer in Human Behavior and Journal of Marketing Communications as well as book chapters and conference papers. Her work has also been presented at various conferences. Ava's research focuses on the application of blockchain technology in information sharing systems, as well as exploring the role of machine learning in business applications.

Hulya Kocyigit is a postdoctoral fellow at the Icahn School of Medicine at Mount Sinai. She earned her Ph.D. in Biostatistics at the University of Georgia and her MS in Statistics at Georgia State University. Prior to graduate school, She received her Bachelor's degree in Statistics and Economics from Selcuk University. She was a lecturer at the Karamanoglu Mehmetbey University from 2021 to 2023. Her research focuses on the intersection of causal inference, machine learning, and biomarker methods in medicine, in particular cancer data analysis and simulation studies.

Hari Kishan Kondaveeti is working as an Associate Professor in the School of Computer Science Engineering (SCOPE), acting as Deputy Director of Engineering Clinics at VIT-AP University, Andhra Pradesh, India. He served as a Core Member of Innovation and Incubation Center (IIC). He is an IBM Certified Data Science Professional and NASSCOM Associate Analyst certified faculty and handling multiple Data Analytics courses. He worked as Research Associate in the Naval Science & Technological

Laboratory, Andhra Pradesh, India. He is interested in teaching, scientific article writing, developing IoT solutions. He has filed several patents, and authored technical articles, conference papers, journals, and book chapters. He is acting as a reviewer in SCIE journals IEEE Sensors Journal, IET Image Processing, IET Electronics Letters, Frontiers of Computer Science, Journal of Super Computing, International Journal of Medical Informatics, IEEE Access and ESCI Journals International Journal of Information Technology Research (JITR), Journal of Information Retrieval Research (IJIRR). He acted as Convener for ICCIDE-2022 and served in the committees of several conferences such as AISP-2021, ICCIDE-2021, ICECCME 2021, ISCDA-2020, AISP-2020, ICCIDE-2020, RACSPA-2019, ICACCI-2017, ICCSA-2017, etc. Dr. Kishan attended, organized, and acted as a resource person in several FDPs, workshops, refresher courses, international guest lectures, and technical talks in his domain and expertise. He received the Best Guru Male Award 2020 by GISR Foundation, and Best Research with a patent award (2021), Beyond and Above Award (2019) by VIT-AP University, Amaravati, and Top 50 Tech-savvy Academicians in Higher Education Across India for the year 2019. He is a Life member in international professional bodies such as ISTE, SCRS, CSI, IUPRAI, ISSIP, IRED, ISRS, ISSE, SSI, CEGR, ISRD. Member in EAI, CSTA, IPRG, IAENG, SDIWC, ICST, ICTA, IEI, INFORMS, DSA, SCIEI, ICSES, IAASSE, IETE, ACM and IEEE. Fellow Member, International Scientific Research Organization for Science, Engineering, and Technology (ISROSET), India. Associate Member, Universal Association of Computer and Electronics Engineers (UACEE), USA. He is acting as Honorary Member of Asian Council of Science Editors.

Valli Kumari Vatsavayi is a professor of computer science and systems engineering, Andhra University. She is an active consultant to several government/public sector/private organisations. She successfully completed six consultant projects for Naval Science and Technological Laboratories and two projects of DST, Govt of India. She has successfully managed the computerisation of Integrated Common Entrance Test (ICET) for MCA/ MBA in AP State, on behalf of Convener and APSCHE from 2009 to 2011 and Education Common Entrance Test(EdCET) from 2012 to 2014. She is a member of IEEE, ACM, CRSI and CSI. She is the founder Vice-Chair of IEEE Vizag Bay Subsection. She is also the Executive Member of Andhra Pradesh State Knowledge Mission and state nodal officer for Digital India Week, 2015.

Eunjung Lee is an Assistant Professor in Business Analytics in the College of Business at Lewis University. She earned her Ph.D. in Information Technology Management from the Lubar School of Business, University of Wisconsin-Milwaukee. Her research interests focus on analyzing online data from different perspectives such as customers and business owners. Prior to joining Lewis University, she was an Assistant Professor at Indiana State University and taught data analysis courses. She also worked as a system engineer at Samsung and worked for the strategic planning team at LG.

Ahmet S. Ozkul is an Associate Professor in the Department of Economics and Business Analytics at the University of New Haven, Connecticut. He holds a doctorate degree in operations management from Clemson University. Dr. Ozkul teaches courses in operations, information systems, and business analytics. His current research interests include coordination in the supply chain, improving service quality and business analytics applications. His work has been published in operations, information systems, business analytics and educational technology journals.

Meysam Rabiee is an Assistant Professor of Business Analytics at the University of Colorado Denver. He received his Ph.D. in Operations & Business Analytics from the Lundquist College of Business at the University of Oregon. Meysam's research focuses on developing decision support systems and applying analytics tools for social good, with a primary interest in healthcare analytics, sustainable supply chain, machine learning, evolutionary algorithms, and group decision-making. He has published several articles in reputable academic journals and received multiple awards, including the Robin & Roger Best Teaching Award and the Robin & Roger Best Research Award from the University of Oregon.

Yasaswini Reddy M. is a Student at VIT-AP university, currently pursuing her B.Tech in the branch of Computer Science and Engineering with Specilization in Artificial Intelligence. She is an AI and Data Science enthusiast.

Baranidharan Subburayan working as assistant Professor at School of Commerce and Management, Christ University, Bangalore. He has 6 years teaching experience and 5 years of research experience. He has published 41 research articles in international and national journal which are indexed in Scopus, WoS, Proquest, ABDC, etc., 6 patents, 20 blogs and 3 ISBN edited books. He is expertise in financial econometrics, stock market technical analysis, commodity market, derivatives and mutual fund analysis.

Russell Sadeghi is a recent graduate with a Bachelor of Science in Industrial Engineering from the University of Science and Technology of Mazandaran in Iran. He achieved a GPA of 3.77 out of 4.00. His capstone project analyzes pharmaceutical distribution centers and the role of machine learning algorithms. Russell has received academic honors for achieving the highest one-year cumulative GPA along with his TA and RA performance among undergraduate students. Russell has published papers, all focused on topics such as inventory problems, supply chain disruptions, and machine learning. His research interests include data science, optimization, business analytics, machine learning, statistics, simulation, and modeling. Russell has industry experience working as a Stock Analyst.

S M Nazmuz Sakib was born in Bangladesh on the 16th of April in 2001. He achieved his Primary School Certificate (PSC) from Cotton Research Station School, Sreepur, Gazipur and after several months of studying Class 6 in Alhaz Dhanai Bepari Memorial High School, Sreepur, Gazipur, he relocated to Jashore. He accomplished his Junior School Certificate (JSC) from Jagodishpur Mirzapur Ismail Secondary School, Jagodishour, Chaowgacha, Jashore and his Secondary School Certificate (SSC) from A. K. High School And College, Dhania, Dhaka-1236. He obtained his Higher Secondary Certificate (HSC) from Chowgacha Government College, Chowgacha, Jashore. He received a BSc in Business Studies, earning a CGPA of 4 out of 4 (1st class 1st) with 97.06% marks from School of Business and Trade, an online business school situated in Switzerland. He completed an MBA in Human Resources from International MBA Institute, an online business institute in Switzerland. He studied Bachelor of Laws (Hon's) or LLB(Hon's) at Dhaka International University, Dhaka, Bangladesh and obtained 1st class. He has accomplished CPD verified advanced diploma and diploma programs i.e. Advanced Diploma in Tissue Engineering, Advanced Diploma in Genetic Engineering - Theory and Application, Diploma in Fashion Design, Diploma in Nutrition, Therapeutics and Health, Diploma in Biology, Diploma in Pharmacy Technician, Software Test Engineer Diploma (Advanced), Advanced Diploma in Soil Science and Technology, Diploma in Energy Economics, Energy Systems and Environmental Impact, Advanced Diploma in Political Ideologies, Diploma in Community Psychology, Diploma in Training of Trainers, Advance

Diploma in Principles of Industrial Engineering, Advanced Diploma in Production & Operation Management, Advanced Diploma in Modelling and Analytics for Supply Chain Management, Business Administration Diploma (Foundation), Diploma in Effective Human Resource Administration, Diploma in Audio System Engineering, Diploma in ISO Standards - Integrated Management System (IMS), Diploma in Lean Manufacturing - Productive Management with Fundamental Tools, Advanced Diploma in Tourism and Hospitality Management, Diploma in Web Design, Diploma in Human Resources, and Diploma in Basic English Grammar, Diploma in River Engineering and has obtained certifications such as TESOL from Arizona State University, TEFL from Teacher Record, Scrum Master Professional Certificate (SMPC®), EF SET Certificate (C2 Level), Google IT Support Professional Certificate, Google Data Analytics Professional Certificate, Google Project Management Professional Certificate, Google Business Intelligence Professional Certificate, Google Digital Marketing & E-commerce Professional Certificate and IBM New Collar: Customer Engagement Specialist credential etc. As a multidisciplinary researcher, he has published several articles in the Asian Pacific Journal of Environment and Cancer, Simulacra, Journal of Innovation Information Technology and Application (JINITA), Waste Technology, and The IUP Journal of Electrical and Electronics Engineering. Several of his articles are published by Cambridge Open Engage, a publication of Cambridge University Press. Some of the titles of his published research works include “The Impact of Oil and Gas Development on the Landscape and Surface in Nigeria,” “Assessing the Impact of Arctic Melting in the Predominantly Multilateral World System,” “LiDAR Technology - An Overview,” “Exploring the Intersection of Software Engineering and Mobile Technology from 2010 to 2021: A Review of Recent Research”, This paper presents a comprehensive review of recent research on the intersection of software engineering and mobile technology. The review method involves a systematic literature search and analysis of relevant research articles. The study identifies key trends and challenges in the field, including the need for better testing and debugging tools, and the emergence of new technologies such as mobile cloud computing. Innovative solutions are proposed to address these challenges. The research focuses on topics such as mobile application development, mobile databases, and mobile security. The paper provides a concise summary of the major findings and proposed solutions. The study concludes that the field of software engineering and mobile technology is rapidly evolving, and further research is needed to effectively address the challenges and keep pace with the dynamic nature of the field; “Comparing the sociology of culture in Bangladesh and India: Similarities and differences in Bangladeshi and Indian cultures”, The sociology of culture is an important field that examines how societies create, maintain, and transform their cultural practices and beliefs. In the context of Bangladesh and India, this field is particularly relevant due to their rich and diverse cultural heritage. This paper explores the sociology of culture in these countries, focusing on cultural similarities and differences. Through a literature review of research from anthropology, sociology, history, and related fields, we will examine the historical background of cultural development in both countries, considering the impact of colonialism, nationalism, globalization, language, ethnicity, and religion. We will then present a comparative analysis of cultural practices, beliefs, and values, drawing on empirical data and case studies. This paper aims to contribute to our understanding of the sociology of culture in Bangladesh and India by shedding light on their diverse cultural heritage and exploring the ways in which cultural practices and values are shaped by historical, social, and political factors. By comparing the cultural similarities and differences between these nations, we hope to deepen our understanding of how culture is influenced by the broader social and political context; “Electrochemical Waste Water Treatment.”. Published chapters i.e. “Chapter 3: Artificial Intelligence Model for Analyzing the Buying Patterns of Customers” and “Chapter 11: Restaurant Sales Prediction

Using Machine Learning" of the book titled "Handbook of Research on AI and Machine Learning Applications in Customer Support and Analytics", "Chapter 15: The Role of Innovation in Driving the Bioeconomy: The Challenges and Opportunities (pages 288-311)" of the book, "Handbook of Research on Bioeconomy and Economic Ecosystems"; The bioeconomy presents a promising opportunity for sustainable economic growth, but it also poses several challenges that require innovative solutions. This chapter provides an overview of the bioeconomy and its key components, including biotechnology, agriculture, and forestry. It then explores some of the challenges associated with the bio economy, such as the need to balance economic growth with environmental sustainability, the potential risks of genetically modified organisms, and the need to ensure that the benefits are shared equitably across society. Finally, it discusses the potential for new bio-based products and services, the creation of new jobs and economic opportunities, and the potential to contribute to global sustainability goals.. He developed a sociological concept "Sakibphobia" which has impact on several fields including Psychology, Sociology, Health Science etc. 82 scientists, researchers, students and others contributed in the research titled, "S M Nazmuz Sakibs Toxic Comparative Theory, Sakibphobia with Structural Functionalism, Symbolic Interactionism, and Conflict Perspective, A Sociological Analysis" which is published in the International Journal of Nursing Care and Research, a publication of CME Live publishes. Sakibphobia is a relatively new concept that describes the fear or hatred of individuals towards those who they perceive as more successful or accomplished than themselves. In this research article, we conduct a comparative analysis of Sakibphobia with three major sociological perspectives: Structural Functionalism, Symbolic Interactionism, and Conflict Perspective. Our study utilizes a literature review approach to analyze the theoretical frameworks, assumptions, and implications of these perspectives on Sakibphobia. The result of our analysis suggests that while each perspective provides unique insights and explanations, none of them can fully capture the complexity and dynamics of Sakibphobia. However, a synthesis of these perspectives can help to develop a more comprehensive understanding of Sakibphobia and its implications for individuals and society."

Apostolos Xanthopoulos holds an MBA degree with concentration in finance, a second master's in economics, from the University of Texas at Arlington, and a Ph.D. in Management Science with concentration in Finance, from the Illinois Institute of Technology. In academic roles, the author has taught in various institutions in Chicago and published several articles. As an industry professional the author has worked at Bank of America, KPMG, Deutsche Bank and Mercer Investment Consulting among other, in risk management/quantitative analysis/research. The author is Professor of Practice in Data Analytics at Lewis University.

Index

G

H

I

K

L

M

N

P

Q

R

S

Premier Reference Source
Tax Audit and Taxation in the Paradigm of Sustainable Development
TAX

Premier Reference Source
Controlling Epidemics With Mathematical and Machine Learning Models

Premier Reference Source
School-Museum Relationships and Teaching Social Sciences in Formal Education

Premier Reference Source
Sociological Perspectives on Sustainable Development and Poverty Reduction in Rural Populations

www.ingramcontent.com/pod-product-compliance
Lightning Source LLC
LaVergne TN
LVHW062142300926
849161LV00010B/2604